THE POLITICS OF THEORY

Proceedings of the Essex conference
on the Sociology of Literature
July 1982

edited by

Francis Barker
Peter Hulme
Margaret Iversen
Diana Loxley

University of Essex
Colchester
1983

Essex Conference on the Sociology of
    Literature (1982: Colchester)
    The politics of theory.
    1. Literature-Philosophy-Congresses
    I. Title   II. Barker, Francis
    801   PN45

    ISBN 0-901726-21-4

PREFACE

At the Essex Sociology of Literature conference in 1976 it was decided to hold a series of conferences that would focus successively on a number of critical historical moments. The ambition was that such a series of conferences and their resultant proceedings would bring together historical and literary theory and research with the effect of making a concentrated and significant impact on the areas they addressed. Four conferences followed in this historical series and details of them can be found inside the back cover.

The 1982 conference, whose proceedings are collected in this volume, set out to assess the developments in literary theory over the years since the initial conference, with special attention to their political implications.

For their help with organizing and running the conference we would like to thank Jennifer Stone, Noreen Proudman, Celia Hirst, and Jean Poynter.

The editors
University of Essex
April 1983

CONTENTS

SEXUAL/TEXTUAL POLITICS Toril Moi	1
WRITING LIKE A WOMAN: A QUESTION OF POLITICS Terry Lovell	15
NOTES ON "POST-FEMINISM" Mary Russo	27
THE HORRORS OF POWER: A CRITIQUE OF 'KRISTEVA' Jennifer Stone	38
THE MOTHER TONGUE Jane Gallop	49
KLEINIAN PSYCHOANALYSIS AND THE THEORY OF CULTURE Michael Rustin	57
A REPLY TO MICHAEL RUSTIN: KLEINIAN PSYCHOANALYSIS AND THE THEORY OF CULTURE Graham Seymour	71
POLITICS, PEDAGOGY, WORK: REFLECTIONS ON THE 'PROJECT' OF THE LAST SIX YEARS David Punter	79
THE FREEDOM OF THE CRITIC AND THE HISTORY OF THE TEXT L.A. Jackson	94
IN DEFENCE OF REDUCTIONISM Ian H. Birchall	107
THE TRAJECTORY OF *SCREEN*, 1971-79 Antony Easthope	121
NATIONAL LANGUAGE, EDUCATION, LITERATURE Renée Balibar	134
THE BOUNDARIES OF HEGEMONY John Oakley, Roger Bromley and Sue Harper	148
ORIENTALISM AND ITS PROBLEMS Dennis Porter	179
DIFFERENCE, DISCRIMINATION AND THE DISCOURSE OF COLONIALISM Homi K. Bhabha	194
THE NEW ART HISTORY Margaret Iversen	212
ANNUS MIRABILIS: SYNCHRONY AND DIACHRONY John Frow	220
BAKHTIN, MARXISM, AND POST-STRUCTURALISM Graham Pechey	234
CAPITALISING HISTORY: NOTES ON *THE POLITICAL UNCONSCIOUS* Samuel Weber	248

SEXUAL/TEXTUAL POLITICS

Toril Moi

The title of this paper: 'Sexual/Textual Politics' indicates the major conflict within the field of feminist literary criticism today: the conflict between the desire to give a politically committed reading of the literary text, and the desire to work on textual problems, to ponder the problems of the text as a signifying practice. This conflict might be rephrased as a disagreement over whether to stress the word 'feminist' or the word 'literary' in 'feminist literary criticism', at least if we take 'literary' to mean 'textual'. Most feminist critics usually claim that they have given equal attention to both aspects in their work. In order to discover the real state of affairs we must therefore practise what Paul Ricoeur has called *l'herméneutique du soupçon'* a hermeneutics of suspicion - on the text of the feminist critic. In this paper I will try to uncover the underlying theoretical assumptions in much Anglo-American feminist criticism, and oppose this to some of the theoretical work done by French feminists, particularly by Julia Kristeva. The first part of the paper is called 'Sexual Politics' and deals with the Anglo-American approach to feminist criticism, whereas part II is called 'Textual Politics' and deals with the French approach. Part III, 'Perspectives', may be read as a tentative conclusion.

1. Sexual Politics. The Anglo-American Approach

Anglo-American feminist criticism has in general been strongly politically committed. It has vigorously challenged the patriarchal literary canon in many different ways: through a focusing on the social and literary situation of the woman as writer, the woman as reader and the woman as critic and teacher. The Anglo-American tradition has highlighted the patriarchal mechanisms at work within the literary institution, mechanisms which have prevented women from writing, or if writing, from being published, from being recognized, from being integrated into the literary canon and from being accepted as part of the syllabus in educational institutions. In a general way we can say that Anglo-American feminist criticism has been very strong on challenging the literary institution and its strategies for constituting what at any given time is recognized as the existing literary canon. But when it comes to the actual reading of the literary text, feminist critics in this tradition have on the whole shown very little originality, except in the choice of themes to be emphasized, when compared to the male critics who have actively collaborated in establishing the present literary canon. The textual views of Anglo-American feminist critics are often indistinguishable from their male, humanist counterparts, and I will later argue that this in itself is incompatible with the radical challenge feminists otherwise present to the literary canon.

The main thrust of Anglo-American criticism has been (and remains) the study of works written by women, mostly inspired by the explicit or implicit desire to find out what makes women's texts different from men's. (1) The quest for a feminine tradition in literature has inspired numerous feminist studies of individual women writers, and some larger historical overviews of women writers in a given period. Much feminist scholarship has also been devoted to the search for forgotten or neglected women writers, and the recent publication and popularity of writers like Olive Schreiner, Charlotte Perkins Gilman and Kate Chopin are due to these feminist efforts.

The most influential works in this branch of feminist criticism have been the more ambitious attempts to rewrite literary history from a feminist perspective. At least three remarkable works should be mentioned in this context: Elaine Showalter's *A Literature of Their Own* (1977), Ellen Moer's *Literary Women* (1977) and Sandra Gilbert and Susan Guber's *The Madwoman in the Attic* (1979). Though the latter is marked by the influence of psychoanalysis, and in general signifies a new departure for feminist criticism in America, these books have in common the fact that they all deal exclusively with women writers and try to establish a specifically feminine tradition in literary history.

The scholarship and style of the feminist research within the Anglo-American tradition is largely indistinguishable from that of similar male research, except in the relatively few cases where the feminist critic feels obliged to plunge into 'personal' anecdotes and confessions in order to make the point that the personal is political. The feminism of all these forms of research resides in the political perspective which is brought to bear on the literary material. This political perspective is of course a feminist perspective, but within this category, we can find everything from radical separatist feminism to bourgeois liberal feminism and marxist feminism. Feminism also seems to accommodate empiricism and humanism as easily as theoreticism and structuralism, at least at the moment. For a feminist critic the discovery of all these conflicting tendencies within her chosen field often leads to a new recognition of the need for theory. Recently we have therefore seen the appearance of quite a few articles dealing or purporting to deal with the theory of feminist criticism in the Anglo-American tradition. (2)

It is evidently impossible here to give a thorough survey of existing Anglo-American feminist theory. I therefore now propose to examine two articles by Elaine Showalter, who is generally acknowledged as a representative exponent for the best kind of Anglo-American feminist criticism. The aim of this exploration is to expose the kind of theoretical assumptions feminist critics within this tradition invariably rely on, and the sort of difficulties they are likely to run into, and not to detract from the very valuable contribution Showalter's empirical work has made to feminist literary studies. The first article is called 'Towards a Feminist Poetics' (hereafter: 'Poetics') and was published in 1979. The second, published two years later, is entitled 'Feminist Criticism in the Wilderness' (hereafter: 'Wilderness').

In the first article ('Poetics'), Showalter distinguishes between two forms of feminist criticism. The first type is concerned with woman as reader, and Showalter labels this 'feminist critique'. The second type deals with woman as writer, and Showalter calls this 'gynocritics'. 'Feminist critique' deals with works by male authors, and Showalter tells us that this form of criticism is a 'historically grounded inquiry which probes the ideological assumptions of literary phenomena' ('Poetics' 25). It is noticeable that this sort of suspicious approach to the literary text is largely absent in Showalter's second category, since among the primary concerns of 'gynocritics' we find 'the history, themes, genres and structures of literature by women' as well as the 'psychodynamics of female creativity' and 'studies of particular writers and works'('Poetics' 25). There is no indication here that the feminist critic concerned with women as writers should bring other than sympathetic, identity-seeking notions to bear on works written by women. The *herméneutique du soupçon*, which assumes that the text is not, or not only, what it pretends to be, and therefore looks for underlying contradictions and conflicts as well as absences and silences in the text, seems to be reserved for texts written by men. The feminist critic must in other words realize that the woman-produced text will occupy a totally different status from the 'male'text. Showalter writes that the feminist critique is too male-oriented, since the study of male literature prevents the feminist critic from 'learning what women have felt and experienced' ('Poetics' 27).

The implication is not only that the feminist critic should turn to 'gynocritics', the study of women's writings, precisely in order to learn 'what women have felt and experienced', but also that this experience is directly available in the texts written by women. The text has disappeared or become the transparent medium through which 'experience' can be seized. This is one of the main tenets of Anglo-American feminist criticism: the belief that texts express experience, and that the more 'authentic' the experience is felt to be by the critic, the better and more valuable the text will be. (3)

This way of seeing the text as the transmitter of authentic, 'human' experience is normally known as 'humanism' rather than as feminism, and is of course a particular variant of bourgeois ideology. In Showalter's case, her humanist position is also tinged by a good portion of empiricism. She rejects theory as something invented by men, and which apparently only can be used on men's texts ('Poetics' 27-28). 'Gynocritics' on the other hand, frees itself from this sort of pandering to male values and seeks to 'focus ... on the newly visible world of female culture' ('Poetics' 28). The search for the 'muted' female culture can best be carried out by applying anthropological theories to the situation and the writings of the woman writer. Showalter states: 'Gynocritics is related to feminist research in history, anthropology, psychology and sociology, all of which have developed hypotheses of a female subculture ...' ('Poetics' 28). The feminist critic should in other words attend to historical, anthropological, psychological and sociological themes and factors in relation to the female author she is working on: in fact, to everything but the text as a signifying process. The only influences Showalter seems to recognize as constitutive of the text are of an empirical and extra-literary sort. This attitude, coupled with her fear of male theory and general appeal to human experience, draws her dangerously close to the male, critical hierarchy she seeks to oppose for its patriarchal values.

In her second article, written two years later, Showalter basically repeats the same themes, and the article's main function seems to be to underline the fact that Showalter has come to see the necessity of theory as even more pressing than two years earlier. But in spite of this insight, she blithely characterises interpretation as an 'eclectic and wide-ranging' thing ('Wilderness'182) and thus escapes awkward 'male' questions like What is interpretation? What does it mean to read? What is a text? Showalter again rejects all meddling with 'male critical theory' since it 'keeps us dependent upon it and retards our progress in solving our own theoretical problems' ('Wilderness' 183). The naive dichotomy between 'male critical theory' and 'our own theoretical problems' can of course easily be deconstructed. The interesting thing is that as Showalter denounces the 'white fathers' of Lacan, Macherey and Engels ('Wilderness' 183-184), she ends up extolling the virtues of the cultural theory developed by Edwin Ardener and Clifford Geertz as particularly suitable for 'gynocritical' activity. Despite a feeble excuse for this glaring inconsistency on the last page of her article ('Wilderness' 205), she nevertheless manages thoroughly to confuse the reader who has followed her so far: should the aspiring 'gynocritic' use 'male' theory or should she not? Showalter's final answer to this question is that: 'No theory, however suggestive, can be a substitute for the close and extensive knowledge of women's texts which constitutes our essential subject ' ('Wilderness' 205). And so we are back where we started: the lack of a suitable theory of feminist criticism has become a virtuous necessity, since too much dabbling in theory would prevent us from gaining 'the close and extensive knowledge of women's texts' which Showalter herself has displayed so brilliantly in *A Literature of Their Own*. Her device seems to be that if we stick to cultural theory, we are at least safe from textual theory. And her fear of the text and its problems is well justified, since any real engagement with this field of enquiry would lead to the exposure of the fundamental complicity between this empiricist and humanist variety of feminist criticism and the male literary and academic hierarchy it denounces.

I will briefly try to show how this complicity works. The Anglo-American feminist critic has waged war against the self-sufficient canonization of male bourgeois values as the basis for the selection of the literary canon. But they have not challenged the very notion of such a canon. Showalter's aim is to create a separate canon of women's writing, not to abolish all canons. And this new canon will, if Showalter's theoretical writings are anything to go by, function in just as authoritarian and hierarchical a way as the old canon. The role of the feminist critic is still to sit quietly and listen to her mistress' voice, as it expresses authentic female experience, in the same way as the humanist listens reverentially to the expression of universal human experience in the male text. The feminist reader is not given leave to get up and challenge this female voice - and the Female Text rules as despotically as the old male text.

To ask theoretical questions about the nature of the text and the process of reading becomes sacrilegious since such enquiries in the end would destroy the hierarchical relationship between author and reader. If texts are seen as signifying processes and both writing and reading become textual production, it is quite likely that even texts written by women will be subjected to irreverent and respectless scrutiny by feminist critics. And if this were to happen, it is clear that the showalterian 'gynocritic' would have to seek support and refuge in the arms of the few male, humanist empiricists still left on the American campus.

The limitations of the Anglo-American approach to feminist criticism become clear when this criticism is confronted with a woman's text which does not conform to the humanist's expectations of authentic and realistic expression of human or female experience. It is not a coincidence that Anglo-American feminist criticism has dealt overwhelmingly with Victorian literature. Monique Wittig's *Les guérillères* from 1969 is an example of a different sort of text. This utopian text consists of a series of fragments depicting life in an amazonian society which is involved in a war against men. Finally the war is won by the women and peace is celebrated by them and the young men who have been won over to their cause. This fragmented text is interrupted at regular intervals by a different text: a series of women's names printed in capital letters in the middle of a blank page. In addition to the hundreds of names contained in this series, the text also contains a couple of poems and three large circles which are presented as symbols of the vulva, a symbolism

which is rejected as a form of inverted sexism at a later stage in the
book. Wittig's text offers no individual characters, no psychology and
no recognizable 'experience' to be deeply felt by the reader. But it is
evident that the text is a strong feminist text, and as such even Anglo-
American feminist critics often feel they have to deal with it. Nina
Auerbach, an established American feminist critic, has in her book
Communities of Women made an effort to cope with *Les guérillères*. The
outcome of her efforts is dubious, as when she comments on the women's
names intervening in the text:

> The women's names that are ritualistically chanted seem
> a human joke, since they are attached to no characters
> we come to know ... Though these names take on their own
> incantatory life, the empty resonance of their sound is
> also the death of the real people we used to read novels
> to meet. (190-91)

When the text no longer offers an individual which is seen as the transcendental origin of experience and language, humanist feminism must lay
down its arms. Auerbach therefore wistfully hopes for better days in a
humanist-feminist future: 'Perhaps once women have proved their strength
to themselves, it will be possible to return to the individuality of
Meg, Jo, Beth, and Amy, or to the humanly interdependent courtesy of
Cranford' (191).

The reactionary aspects of Anglo-American feminist criticism are here
clearly exposed. These are obviously not the only aspects of this
sort of feminist criticism: as I have said before I appreciate and ad-
mire much of the truly iconoclastic and revolutionary work done by Anglo-
American feminist critics, but it seems to me that the only way of avoiding the sort of conclusions Nina Auerbach arrives at, is to turn to the
problems of the text. And here we can find invaluable inspiration in
the work of French feminist theoreticians.

2. Textual Politics: The French Approach

The theoretical work done in France is varied, extensive and complex. In the space I have at my disposal, it is impossible to do
justice to the multiplicity of ideas which have come from French feminists. I will therefore first state what I take to be some of the limitations of much French theory, and then briefly present some aspects of
the work of Julia Kristeva, whom I consider the most important of the
French feminist theoreticians.

All French feminist theory is influenced by what Showalter undoubtedly would call the 'white fathers' of Jacques Lacan and Jacques
Derrida. Many French feminists are also well acquainted with the European philosophical tradition, including marxism, and they tend to take
for granted that their readers share this background. Their work will
therefore often seem difficult and abstract to a reader not steeped in
the same intellectual tradition.

It may also seem disconcerting to discover that there exists very
little feminist literary criticism in France. French feminists have preferred to produce creative texts or to write on textual, linguistic,
semiotic or psychoanalytic theory. Julia Kristeva is a notable exception in that she has brought psychoanalytic and semiotic theory to bear
on modernist texts - though the resulting 'literary criticism' is wholly
concerned with structural (linguistic and psychic) aspects of the text,
and offers little consolation to the reader looking for human judgments
and evaluations of authenticity in literary criticism. The relative
lack of a specific literary criticism is accompanied by a total lack of
interest in challenging the academic literary canon. Most French

feminist work is published as part of a general intellectual debate
and not as efforts to get jobs or promotion in the academic hierarchy.
In spite of this relative freedom from academic constraints, they seem
happy to accept the established canon, at least the canon of French
modernism which contains almost exclusively male writers. There can
be no doubt that the Anglo-American feminist tradition has been incom-
parably stronger when it comes to challenging the social and political
strategies of the literary institution. The French feminists on the
other hand have given much valuable thought to the problem of the text,
and of the relations between women and textual production, but sometimes this attention to the text has been at the expense of a wider,
socio-political analysis. Particularly in the works of Hélène Cixous
and Luce Irigaray it is easy to find a scandalous lack of interest in
the social and political aspects of women's oppression. Their tendencies to fall into biologism and essentialism have also received due
criticism both in France and abroad. (4)

For French feminist theoreticians the concept of difference is
central. In order to show how the feminine subject is constituted as
different from the masculine subject, both Irigaray and Kristeva draw
heavily on psychoanalytic theory. The advantage of bringing in psychoanalysis in connection with women and writing is that, particularly in
Lacanian theory, the subject is constituted as an effect of the acquisition of language. If there is difference between masculine and feminine subjects, there will therefore also be a theoretically significant difference in the relationship of the subject to language.

In *La révolution du langage poétique*, published in Paris in 1974,
Kristeva bases her own theory of language on Lacan's distinction between the imaginary and the symbolic order, a distinction which participants at this conference probably will be well acquainted with. Let
me therefore just remind you very briefly of one or two general points
concerning this theory. For Lacan, to enter into the symbolic order
from the imaginary means to accept the phallus as the representation of
the Law of the Father. All human culture and all life in society is
dominated by the symbolic order, and thus by the phallus as the sign of
lack - the lack in question being the absence of the imaginary unity
with the mother. The subject may or may not like this order of things,
but it has no choice: to refuse to accept the separation from the mother,
to remain in the imaginary, is equivalent to becoming psychotic and to
become incapable of living in human society.

According to Lacan this process is common to all human subjects.
But feminists have objected that the Lacanian 'subject' in fact corresponds to a masculine subject. The importance accorded to the oedipal
crisis and the oedipal threat of castration as a reason for giving up
the imaginary unity with the mother, the feminists argue, fits in quite
neatly with Freudian theory on the psychosexual development of boys, but
not so well with what we know of girls' development, and particularly
not with the relative lack of importance of the threat of castration for
girls. Lacan pays little attention to this aspect of sexual differentiation, but both Kristeva and Irigaray have tried to develop Lacan's
theories in order to account for sexual difference.

Philip E. Lewis has pointed out that all of Kristeva's work up to
1974, the year in which the *Révolution du langage poétique* was published, constitutes an extensive attempt to define or apprehend what
Kristeva calls the *procès de signifiance* or the signifying process
(Lewis 30). (5) In order to approach this problem, she displaces
Lacan's distinction between the imaginary and the symbolic into a distinction between the semiotic and the symbolic. The interaction between

these two terms then constitute the signifying process.

The semiotic is linked to the pre-oedipal primary processes, the basic pulsions which Kristeva sees as basically anal and oral (life vs. death, expulsion vs. introjection) and as simultaneously dichotomous and heterogeneous. The endless flow of pulsions is gathered up in the *chora*, which Plato in the *Timaeus* defines as 'an invisible and formless being which receives all things and in some mysterious way partakes of the intelligible, and is most incomprehensible'(*Roudiez* 6). Kristeva appropriates and redefines Plato's concept and concludes that the *chora* is neither a sign nor a position, but 'a wholly provisional articulation which is essentially mobile and constituted of movements and their ephemeral stases ... Neither model nor copy, it is anterior to and underlies figuration and therefore also specularisation, and only admits analogy with vocal or kinetic rhythm' (*Révolution* 24). (6)

For Kristeva, *signifiance* is a question of positioning. The semiotic continuum must be cut or split if signification is to be produced. This splitting (*coupure*) of the semiotic *chora* is the *thetic* phase (from *thesis*), and it enables the subject to attribute differences and therefore signification to what was the ceaseless heterogeneity of the *chora*. Kristeva follows Lacan in positing the mirror-phase as the first step which 'opens the way for the constitution of all objects which from now on will be detached from the semiotic *chora*' (*Révolution* 44), and the oedipal phase with its threat of castration as the moment in which the process of separation or splitting is fully achieved.

Summing up her views on the acquisition of language, Kristeva states that 'the acquisition of language may now be considered a sharp and dramatic confrontation between this position - separation - identification and the motility of the semiotic *chora*' (*Révolution* 44). In this process, the thetic as the positioning instance becomes the threshold between the semiotic and the symbolic, assuring the positioning of the imago, of castration and of the semiotic motility which is the condition of signification and without which language cannot exist (see *Révolution* 46).

Once the subject has entered into the symbolic order, the *chora* will be more or less successfully repressed. If not totally repressed, it can be perceived as a pulsional pressure on symbolic language: as contradictions, meaninglessness, disruption, silences and absences in the symbolic language. The *chora* is a rhythmic pulsion and not a new language. So far, it is important to bear in mind that Kristeva's presentation of the constitution of the subject and the signifying process is mostly concerned with developments in the pre-oedipal phase where sexual difference does not exist. The question of difference only becomes relevant at the point of entry into the symbolic order, and Kristeva discusses the situation for little girls at this point in her book *Des chinoises*, translated as *About Chinese Women*, published in France in the same year as the *Révolution*. Here Kristeva points out that since the semiotic *chora* is pre-oedipal, it is linked to the mother, whereas the symbolic, as we know, is dominated by the Law of the Father. Faced with this situation, the little girl has to make a choice: 'either she identifies with her mother, or she raises herself to the symbolic stature of her father. In the first case, the pre-Oedipal phases (oral and anal eroticism) are intensified' (*Chinese* 28). If, on the other hand, the little girl identifies with her father, 'the access she gains to the symbolic dominance [will] censor the pre-Oedipal phase and wipe out the last traces of dependence on the body of the mother ' (*Chinese* 29).

Kristeva thus delineates two different options for women: mother-identification which will intensify the pre-oedipal components of the woman's psyche and make her marginal to the symbolic order, or father-identification which will create a woman who will derive her identity from the same symbolic order. From these passages it should be clear that Kristeva does not define feminity as a pre-oedipal and revolutionary essence. Far from it, femininity for Kristeva comes about as the result of a series of options which are also presented to the little boy. This is surely why she states quite flatly at the beginning of *About Chinese Women* that 'woman as such does not exist" (16).

Kristeva's position leads her, in an article entitled 'Woman's Time', to argue that the feminist struggle must be seen as historically and politically a three-tiered struggle:

1) Women demand equal access to the symbolic order. Liberal feminism. Equality.

2) Women reject the male symbolic order in the name of difference. Radical feminism. Femininity extolled.

3) (and this is Kristeva's own position). Women reject the dichotomy masculine vs. feminine as metaphysical.

Kristeva is equally critical towards women who believe that women will be free as soon as we get enough women prime ministers as towards women who emphasise the inherent difference of women. She explicitly rejects the attitude of female writers whose pen is 'devoted to phantasmatic attacks against Language and Sign as the ultimate support of phallocratic power, in the name of a semi-aphonic corporality whose truth can only be found in that which is "gestural" and "tonal"' ('Women's Time' 32).

The claim put forward by the Marxist-Feminist Literature Collective (30) and by Beverly Brown and Parveen Adams that Kristeva associates the semiotic with the feminine is based on a misreading. The fluid motility of the semiotic is indeed associated with the pre-oedipal phase and therefore with the pre-oedipal mother, but Kristeva makes it quite clear that she, as Freud and Klein, sees the pre-oedipal mother as a phallic mother - as a figure which encompasses both masculinity and femininity. This fantasmatic figure which looms as large for baby boys as for baby girls, cannot, as Brown and Adams are well aware of (40), be reduced to an example of 'femininity' for the simple reason that the opposition between feminine and masculine does not exist in pre-oedipality. And Kristeva knows this as well as anybody. Any strengthening of the semiotic, which does not know sexual difference, must therefore lead to a weakening of traditional gender-divisions, and not at all to a reinforcement of traditional notions of 'femininity'. This is why Kristeva can state her own position in the following terms:

> In the third attitude, which I strongly advocate - which I imagine? - the very dichotomy man/woman as an opposition between two rival entities may be understood as belonging to metaphysics. What can 'identity', even 'sexual identity', mean in a new theoretical and scientific space where the very notion of identity is challenged? ('Women's Time' 33-34)

On this background it is difficult to maintain that Kristeva should hold an essentialist or even biologistic notion of femininity. (7) It is certainly true that Kristeva, with Freud, believes that the body forms the material basis for the constitution of the subject. But this in no way entails a simplistic equation of desire with physical needs, as Jean Laplanche has shown. What it does entail is that for instance oral and anal drives are considered to be oral and anal precisely because they only come into existence as an anaclitic spin-off of the satisfaction of those purely physical needs.

For Kristeva, then, women are no more a potentially revolutionary force than men, at least not from a purely psychological point of view. Men can also take up a marginal position in the symbolic order, as Kristeva's analyses of male avant-garde artists have shown. In the *Révolution*, she points out that Artaud, among others, strongly stresses the fluidity of sexual identification for the artist when he stated that 'the "author" becomes at once his "father", "mother" and "himself"' (606).

The revolutionary subject, whether masculine or feminine, is a subject which is able to let the *jouissance* of the semiotic motility disrupt the strict symbolic order. The example par excellence of this kind of revolutionary activity is to be found in the writings of late 19th century avant-garde poets like Lautrémont and Mallarmé. Since the semiotic never can take over the symbolic, one may ask how it can make itself felt at all. Kristeva's answer to this point is that the only possible way of releasing some of the semiotic pulsions into the symbolic is through the predominantly anal (but also oral) activity of expulsion or rejection. In textual terms this translates itself as negativity, a negativity which masks the death-drive, which Kristeva sees as perhaps the most fundamental semiotic pulsion. The poet's negativity is then analysable as a series of ruptures, absences and breaks in the symbolic language, as well as in his thematic preoccupations. But this stress on negativity and disruption, rather than for example on organisation and solidarity, leads Kristeva to an anarchist political position. And on this point I agree with the Marxist-Feminist Literature Collective who qualify her poetics as 'politically unsatisfactory' (30). Allon White also accuses Kristeva of political impotence, stating that her politics 'remain purified anarchism in a perpetual state of self-dispersal' (16-17). On the other hand, I can't see that Kristeva's theories necessarily must end in anarchism, since she throughout her works also emphasises the necessity of the symbolic as the scene where social action takes place. That she herself draws certain conclusions from her work, should not prevent us from drawing others. Her critique of symbolic language could and should be a valuable dimension of any Marxist analysis of the conditions for revolutionary activity.

For a Marxist, the major problem in Kristeva's writing is the fact that she is unable in the end to account for the relations between the subject and society. Though she in an exemplary fashion discusses the social and political background to the poets she studies in the *Révolution*, it still is not clear why it is so important that certain literary practices should break up language when they seem to do very little to break up anything else. She essentially seems to argue that the disruption of the subject, the *sujet en procès* displayed in these texts prefigures or parallels revolutionary disruptions of society. But her only argument in support of this relationship seems to be one of comparison or homology. And it is not only in the *Révolution* that Kristeva takes this position. In her latest book, *Pouvoirs de l'horreur*, she again raises the question, and her answer is just as disappointing (see 82). However fruitful this position may be for the analysis of texts, politically it is a dead end. Again I do not believe that this *impasse* invalidates her work, but rather that it reduces the scope of the claims one may reasonably make for her theories.

Her later works, of great relevance for feminists, are deeply concerned with the question of motherhood. Already in the *Révolution* she claimed that it is not woman as such which is repressed in patriarchal society, but motherhood (453). The problem is not women's *jouissance* alone, as Lacan has it in *Encore*, but the necessary relationship between reproduction and *jouissance*:

If the position of women in the social code is a problem
today, it does not at all rest in a mysterious question
of feminine *jouissance* ... but deeply, socially and symbolically in the question of reproduction and the *jouissance*
which is articulated therein (462).

This perspective opens an extraordinarily fruitful field of investigation for feminists, and Kristeva has herself contributed several fasci-
nating analyses of the representation of motherhood in Western culture,
particularly as embodied in the figure of the Madonna ('Hérétique de
l'amour'), and in Western pictorial art ('Motherhood according to
Giovanni Bellini'). Her preoccupation with the figure of the Madonna
constitutes a significant development of her work in the *Révolution*
in that it questions the role of women in society and in the symbolic
order through an ideological and psychoanalytic analysis of the material
basis for women's oppression: motherhood.

For if women occupy or can come to occupy a marginal position within the symbolic order, it becomes possible to construe them as the limit
or the border-line of that order. From a phallocentric point of view
women will then come to represent the necessary frontier between man and
chaos, but because of their very marginality they will also always seem
to recede into and merge with the chaos of the outside. Women seen as
the limit of the symbolic order will in other words share in the disconcerting properties of all frontiers: they will neither be inside nor
outside, neither known or unknown. It is this position which has enabled male culture sometimes to vilify women as representing darkness
and chaos, to view them as Lilith or the Whore of Babylon, and sometimes
to elevate them as the representatives of a higher and purer nature, to
venerate them as Virgins and Mothers of God. In the first instance the
borderline is seen as part of the chaotic wilderness outside, and in the
second it is seen as an inherent part of the inside: the part which pro-
tects and shields the symbolic order from the imaginary chaos.

3. Perspectives

From this short account of feminist theory, one can draw one important conclusion: there is no specific feminist literary criticism if
by this one understands some sort of method or approach which should be
inherently and exclusively feminist. There is no method or theoretical
approach used in feminist criticism which is not also used or usable by
non-feminist critics. The problem for feminist critics is to find out
which theories and methods are compatible with a feminist stance and
which are not, and as we have seen I believe that for instance the humanist empiricism examined in the first part of this paper is an example
of such incompatibility.

The aims of feminist criticism are or should be revolutionary. It
is politics, the opposition to patriarchy and sexism in all its forms,
which gives feminist criticism its specificity. This feminist commitment
necessarily also entails the opposition to the exploitative, hierarchical
and authoritarian structures of capitalism, and this is why feminist
criticism is and must be a revolutionary form of criticism. It is because Kristeva tries to theorize the revolutionary potential of women
and not because she is a semiotician that she can be considered a feminist critic. The problem for the Anglo-American feminist critic resides
in the contradiction between their strong political position and the inherently reactionary literary theory they also practise and defend.

A further example of the reactionary consequences of the identity-
seeking humanist reading is to be found in the absence of any challenge
to the concept of literature in the Anglo-American tradition. Where the

French have substituted texts or 'writing' for literature and are sceptical about the ideological implications of the word 'literature', the Anglo-American feminists do not seem to perceive this as a problem. This is all the more grievous since the general conventions for deciding what is literary have always excluded women's writings as best they could - as they have excluded working class writers. Nursery rhymes, fairy tales, children's books, popular romantic literature - the majority of such texts have been written by women and none has been found worthy of full 'literary' status.

Feminist theory and practice have, as we have seen, deconstructed the opposition between literature and non-literature, between canon and non-canon, but even this is not enough. It is also necessary to deconstruct the hierarchical opposition between author and reader and between text and reader. This has long been seen as an important practical task in the women's movement. Though feminist criticism has its background and its main source of inspiration in the women's movement, it has not always followed up the lead given by the movement on this point. The women's movement has always seen cultural oppression as an important part of patriarchal oppression as a whole, and through many practical activities it has challenged established notions of what culture is and how it is produced: writers' workshops, street theatre, collective art-work and exhibitions have questioned the whole established dichotomy between active producer and passive consumer of texts and other cultural products. Anglo-American feminist criticism has on the whole decided not to notice this development and has therefore lost out on the possibility of participating in and influencing feminist cultural practice. The French feminists have not only encouraged feminist creative practices (through for instance the magazine *des femmes en mouvements* published by *des femmes*), but they have also taken advantage of existing textual theory to deconstruct the opposition between producer and consumer of texts and other cultural practices. They have extended the notion of text to cover all signifying practices from political theatre to the representation of women in advertisements and the language of fashion. Literature is only one category in this spectrum, and as we have seen, not even necessarily the best defined and the most privileged one.

In textual terms both Kristeva, Cixous and others (like for instance Roland Barthes) have stressed the importance of the concept of *jouissance*. For Kristeva and Cixous *jouissance* is what happens when writing becomes pulsional pleasure linked to the presence of the *chora* (Kristeva) or the mother's body (Cixous). And for Barthes, *jouissance* is what the reader experiences when producing or possibly re-producing precisely the kind of text which suspends the bland certainties of the ego dominated by the symbolic order. And so in the last instance it is impossible to distinguish between the productive *jouissance* of the writer, the *jouissance* of the text and the productive *jouissance* of the reader: the hierarchy between these terms has been broken down.

The situation, then, is this: On the one hand we have in France an active and energetic development of feminist theory concerned with female creativity and textual production. On the other hand we have the strong, politically committed institutional critique developed in the Anglo-American tradition. The French often seem to forget about the historical and social aspects of women's oppression, whereas the Anglo-Americans cling in the main to a reactionary humanist empiricism and refuse to see problems of textual theory as relevant for feminist criticism. The French have done very little work in the field of literary criticism and cultural studies, while the Anglo-Americans have flooded the academic market with empirical and empiricist literary studies. It is our task now to take feminist criticism one step further and transform it into the politically

committed and the theoretically highly developed criticism it clearly
has the potential to become.

NOTES

1. Early works by American feminist critics like Millett and Ellmann did discuss works by male writers and critics in an attempt to locate misrepresentation (stereotyping) of women in the male text.
2. For other theoretical articles within the Anglo-American tradition, see for instance Jehlen, Kolodny, 'Notes' and Kolodny, 'Dancing'.
3. In 'Notes' (85) Kolodny also extolls the virtues of a literature which will 'reveal to us what it **feels like** to be trapped in ... different settings'.
4. For an English language introduction to French feminist theory see Marks and Courtivron, editors. As a first encounter with Cixous' and Irigaray's ideas, see Kuhn, Cixous, Wenzel and Irigaray. Jones and Burke also give useful introductions to French theory and to Irigaray respectively. For a critique of Irigaray see Plaza, and for a general critique of the circle around *des femmes*, of which Cixous is a prominent member, see *Questions féministes*.
5. For other English language introductions to Kristeva, see Coward and Ellis and Féral.
6. All quotations from the *Révolution* are translated by me.
7. For a discussion of this question from a somewhat different angle, see Pajaczkowska.

WORKS CITED

Auerbach, Nina. *Communities of Women: An Idea in Fiction*. Cambridge, Mass.: Harvard University Press, 1978.

Brown, Beverly and Adams, Parveen. 'The Feminine Body and Feminist Politics', *m/f*, no.3, 1979, 35-50.

Burke, Carolyn. 'Irigaray through the Looking Glass', *Feminist Studies*, vol.7, no.2 (1981), 288-306.

Cixous, Hélène. 'Castration or Decapitation?' tr. by Annette Kuhn, *Signs*, vol.7, no.1 (1981) 41-55.

Coward, Rosalind and Ellis, John. *Language and Materialism*, London: RKP, 1977.

Ellmann, Mary. *Thinking About Women*. New York: Harcourt, 1968.

Féral, Josette. 'Antigone or the Irony of the Tribe', *Diacritics*, Fall 1978, 2-14.

Gilbert, S.M. and Gubar, S. *The Madwoman in the Attic*, New Haven: Yale University Press, 1979.

Irigaray, Luce. 'And the One Doesn't Stir Without the Other', tr. by Hélène Vivienne Wenzel, *Signs*, vol.7, no.1 (1981),60-67.

Jehlen, Myra. 'Archimedes and the Paradox of Feminist Criticism', *Signs*, vol.6, no.4 (1981), 575-601.

Jones, Ann Rosalind. 'Writing the Body: Toward an Understanding of L'Ecriture Feminine', *Feminist Studies*, vol.7, no.2 (1981), 247-263.

Kolodny, Annette. 'Some Notes on Defining a "Feminist Literary Criticism"', *Critical Inquiry*, vol.2, no.1 (1975), 75-92.

―――――― 'Dancing Through the Minefield: Some Observations on the Theory, Practice and Politics of a Feminist Literary Criticism', *Feminist Studies*, vol.6, no.1, (1980), 1-25.

Kristeva, Julia. *La révolution du langage poétique*. Paris: Le Seuil, 1974.

―――――― *About Chinese Women*, tr. by Anita Barrows, London: Marion Boyars, 1977.

―――――― 'Motherhood according to Giovanni Bellini', in *Desire in Language*, 237-270. The first part of this essay is also translated under the title 'The Maternal Body' by Claire Pajaczkowska in *m/f* no. 5 & 6, 1981, 158-163.

―――――― 'Hérétique de l'amour', *Tel Quel*, no.74, automne 1977, 30-49.

―――――― 'Women's Time', tr. by Alice Jardine and Harry Blake, *Signs*, vol.7, no.1 (1981), 13-35.

―――――― *Desire in Language: A Semiotic Approach to Literature and Art*. Edited by Léon S. Roudiez, tr. by Alice Jardine, Thomas Gore and Léon Roudiez, New York: Columbia University Press, 1980.

―――――― *Pouvoirs de l'horreur*, Paris: Le Seuil, 1980.

Kuhn, Annette. 'Introduction to Hélène Cixous's "Castration or Decapitation?"', *Signs*, vol.7, no.1 (1981), 36-40.

Lacan, Jacques. *Encore. Le séminaire livre XX*. Paris: Le Seuil, 1975.

Laplanche, Jean. *Life and Death in Psychoanalysis*. Tr. by Jeffrey Mehlman, Baltimore: Johns Hopkins University Press, 1976.

Lewis, Philip E. 'Revolutionary Semiotics', *Diacritics*, vol.4, no.3 (Fall 1974), 28-32.

Marks, Elaine and Courtivron, Isabelle de, editors. *New French Feminisms*, Amherst, Mass.: Univ. of Massachusetts Press, 1979.

Marxist-Feminist Literature Collective. 'Women's Writing: *Jane Eyre, Shirley, Villette, Aurora Leigh*', *Ideology & Consciousness*, vol.1, no.3 (Spring 1978), 27-48.

Millett, Kate. *Sexual Politics* (1970), London: Virago, 1977.

Moers, Ellen. *Literary Women* (1977), London: The Women's Press, 1978.

Pajaczkowska, Claire. 'Introduction to Kristeva', *m/f*, no. 5 & 6, 1981, 149-157.

Plaza, Monique. '"Phallomorphic Power" and the Psychology of "Woman"', *Ideology & Consciousness*, no.4, Autumn 1978, 4-36.

Questions féministes (collective). 'Variations on Common Themes', in Marks and Courtivron (eds.), 212-230.

Roudiez, Léon S. 'Introduction' to Julia Kristeva, *Desire in Language*, 1-20.

Showalter, Elaine. *A Literature of Their Own. British Women Novelists from Brontë to Lessing*, Princeton, N.J.: Princeton University Press, 1977.

Showalter, Elaine. 'Towards a Feminist Poetics', in Mary Jacobus (ed.) *Women Writing and Writing About Women*, London: Croom Helm, 1979, 22-41.

——————————— 'Feminist Criticism in the Wilderness', *Critical Inquiry*, vol.8, no.2 (Winter 1981), 179-205.

Wenzel, Hélène Vivienne. 'Introduction to Luce Irigaray's "And the One Doesn't Stir Without the Other"', *Signs*, vol.7, no.1 (Autumn 1981), 56-59.

White, Allon, *'L'éclatement du sujet', The Theoretical Work of Julia Kristeva*, University of Birmingham Centre for Contemporary Studies, Stencilled Occasional Paper no.49, Birmingham, 1977.

Wittig, Monique. *Les Guérillères*. Paris: Minuit, 1969. Translated as *Les Guerillères* by David Le Vay, London: Peter Owen, 1971.

WRITING LIKE A WOMAN: A QUESTION OF POLITICS

Terry Lovell

The problem of determining what is and ought to be the relationship between feminist politics and literary theory and practice will be the subject of this paper. It will take us into similar debates to those which structured marxist cultural politics over more than a hundred years. But gender cuts across class, and marxist categories have sometimes proved problematic when applied to the analysis of women in capitalist society. Feminist cultural politics does not occupy exactly the same terrain as that mapped out in terms of class relations.

The history of feminism has always been closely linked with literature and literary criticism, from Mary Wollstonecraft to Kate Millett and contemporary radical feminism. Classical marxism by contrast, placed the problem of the relationship between working class politics and literature/art fairly low on the agenda. Classical marxist historiography was primarily informed by economic and political theory. Perry Anderson argues that Western marxism has suffered from the obverse problem: '... a studied silence ... in those areas most central to the classical traditions of historical materialism ...' (Anderson, 1976) combined with a shift towards philosophy. This shift facilitated the breaching of questions traditionally seen as pertaining to 'the superstructure', and it is from Western marxism that marxist cultural studies emanate. But the effect has been that the two have developed relatively separately. Marxist economic history and marxist cultural studies make little reference to one another. (The Essex Conference on Sociology of Literature regularly clashes with the CSE summer conference.) Analysis of class relationships, for marxists, typically begins, then, with economic production; with public political struggles around the workplace, political organisations and the state, while analysis of gender relations, for feminists, tends to centre around the 'private sphere' of family and personal life about which marxism has little to say, and to move very easily on to a consideration of literature and art.

Public and Private Spheres

The idea that the capitalist mode of production is characterised by a process of differentiation into two separate, gender-related spheres, is associated with the work of Eli Zaretsky (Zaretsky, 1976). The public sphere is the sphere of waged work and of politics; the private encompasses family and personal life. It has been argued, by Zaretsky and others, that in the early 19th century, with the separation of home from workplace, women were withdrawn from the public sphere, confined in the private. As a result, qualities held appropriate to work and to political struggle came to be seen as masculine, while personal life was feminised. Nineteenth century feminism, from about the 1860s onwards, fought for women's rights in the public sphere; the right to a broader range of occupations, to education, and for political representation and legal status. The social relations of family and personal life were hardly questioned. Twentieth century feminism has perceived that women's oppression in one sphere is fundamentally related to their position of subordination in the other, so that it is necessary to fight for change in both spheres.

'Public' and 'private' spheres are problematic as descriptive categories. While Zaretsky places them within a broadly marxist framework, sociological structural functionalists such as Talcott Parsons used a rather similar schema of specialisation and differentiation which was also gender-based (Parsons, 1956), and Zaretsky's adaptation does not manage to avoid the theoretical and empirical objections to the functionalist version (Beechey, 1978). Women of all classes, it is true, were denied political and legal rights until the legislation of the latter half of the 19th and early 20th centuries. But it was only 'ladies' who were excluded from waged work outside the home, for a period of about a hundred years. Working class women, despite the myth of the male breadwinner earning a family wage, have always undertaken paid work (Barrett and McIntosh, 1980). It is the way in which their labour has been used, the kinds of employment they have found, which marks them off from their brothers and husbands. Secondly, it is misleading to think of social relations within the family as 'personal', while those outside it are impersonal. It is true that the social relations of capitalist production are impersonal, particularly in large-scale factory production. But this is not true to the same extent of all work relations outside the home. Work situations and work relations vary a great deal in this respect, and work relations may spill over into the 'private' sphere of leisure, entertainment, friendship. This division also neglects the extent to which the home is a place of work. The domestic labour debate raised important questions about the value of the contribution of domestic labour in the home to the family's real income, and to the workings of the capitalist economy (Malos, 1980). Finally, it takes at least two people to make a personal relationship, and the notion that it is women and not men who are 'specialists' in personal life is rather peculiar. It is true that women are traditionally held responsible for the success or failure of such relationships, but what this means is that men and women enter into personal relationships in different ways: both with each other, and with others of the same sex.

If the notion of separate, gender-related spheres is misleading as a description of the organisation of social life under capitalism, it is far more compelling as a description of social norms, and of the way in which people experience their lives. It is certainly true that at the level of ideology, work has been 'masculinised', personal life 'feminised'. What interests me here is the manner in which this gender construction has affected the self-identity and the public image of the literary producer, particularly the novel writer.

Literary Production and Gender

The penetration of capital, and the transformation of literature into a commodity, has been limited to the stages of printing and publishing, and distribution. The first stage of literary production has been untouched either by technological transformation or by the division of labour. Unlike other forms of intellectual work, novel writing has not become institutionalised within the University. In terms of masculine/feminine poles of ideology, novel-writing is deeply ambivalent, like all categories of so-called 'creative writing'. It is paid work, work for breadwinners; and despite recurrent male complaints of female competition, it is dominated by men. Richard Altick estimates that the proportion of female to male novelists remained at about 20%, from 1800-1935 (Altick, 1957). Yet novel-writing is frequently seen as 'feminine' rather than 'masculine'. Even male writers can be found who make this association. John Fowles links all kinds of creativity with femininity. However, this does not mean that he considers it fit work for women. 'There are', he tells us, 'Adam-women and Eve-men; singularly few of the world's great progressive artists and thinkers, have not belonged to the latter category ' (Fowles, 1981, p.157).

John Fowles' views are of course his own. But I believe he articulates the gender ambiguity of literary production in our culture. However, a recent massive contribution to feminist literary theory has argued the opposite case. Sandra Gilbert and Susan Gubar claim that

> In patriarchal Western culture ... the text's author is a father, a progenitor, an aesthetic patriarch whose pen is an instrument of generative power like his penis. (Gilbert and Gubar, 1979, p.6)

They back up their claim with quotations from literary men and women:

> The artist's most essential quality is masterly execution, which is a kind of male gift, and especially marks off men from women ... (Gerald Manley Hopkins, 1886)

> Literature is not the business of a woman's life, and it cannot be ... (Robert Southey, 1837)

> Jane Austen's novels fail because her writing lacks a strong male thrust. (Anthony Burgess)

> Literary women lack that blood congested genital drive which energises every great style. (William Gass)

These quotations fail to establish Gilbert and Gubar's claim - in fact they cast doubt upon it. Where femininity and masculinity are strongly marked in culture and ideology, they do not have to be stridently claimed. The writers she quotes protest too much. Their over-insistence paradoxically confirms the gender-ambiguity of 'creative writing' in Western culture, rather than establishing its masculine credentials.

Perhaps this is a further reason for the greater interest which feminism as opposed to socialism has displayed for literature. Literary production has been a contested area vis-à-vis gender in a way in which it has not been for class. I want to argue that this gender ambiguity has made it easier for women and for feminists to breach literary production, but that this has created particular problems for feminist literary theory.

First, though, it is necessary to substantiate my claim that literary production *is* gender ambiguous.

    i. I would hazard a guess that there is no strong association among the population at large, of creative writing with 'manliness' - quite the opposite in fact.

    ii. The study of literature and languages, through the school system and at university, is heavily dominated by female students.

    iii. Women gained access to novel-writing and to other forms of literary work at a time when they were excluded from virtually all other (middle-class) professions except governessing. It was, moreover, the only paid occupation in which they could hope to achieve independence and financial parity with men (Showalter, 1979a).

    iv. Novel writing is a form of domestic production. Here, home and workplace have never been separated. It is an individual and personalised form of production.

    v. Fictional worlds have been largely restricted to the sphere which is conventionally and ideologically assigned to women, or for which women are assumed to have a special responsibility - that of personal relations.

> ... the development of the novel has been closely bound up with the social and political position of women ... there is a fundamental continuity which firmly places them in a private domestic world where emotions and personal relationships

are at once the focus of moral value and the core of women's experience. In the novel women are 'prisoners' of feeling and of private life. (Stubbs, 1979, p.x)

Naturally, male writers have struggled against this taint of feminine identification. Hence the sentiments quoted above. They have often done so by denigrating their female colleagues. Women, urged to write, if they must, like ladies, were despised as inferior when they did, attacked as 'unfeminine' when, like Charlotte Brontë, they did not (Showalter, 1979a). Certain genres have been marked off as 'lesser' forms, and ceded to women (e.g. romantic fiction). Others have been developed and colonised as vehicles of strident masculinity (the Hemingway-Miller-Mailer school attacked by Kate Millett (Millett, 1977). More recently, structuralist theory applied to literature has offered a new offensive in the field of literary criticism. Showalter argues that 'The new sciences of the text ... have offered literary critics the opportunity to demonstrate that the work they do is as manly and aggressive as nuclear physics - not intuitive, expressive, feminine ' (Showalter, 1979b). Where structuralism is allied to Lacanian psychoanalytic theory, the bid to masculinise is strongest. Variants of this approach have consigned the feminine *per se* to absence, silence, incoherence, even madness. Several feminists have attempted to construct theories of feminine identity and a feminist aesthetic upon this marginal territory ceded by a phallocentric theory of language. I believe this to be a mistaken strategy, for it abandons territory which can and ought to be defended against masculine imperialism; coherence, rationality, articulateness.

Meanwhile marxist economic history and politics have preferred less introspective terrain, such as the analysis and attempted annexation of 'the commanding heights' of the economy. Needless to say, literary production is not found there - not even the Frankfurt School's 'culture industry'. I am not denying that there is a long tradition of marxist literary theory and practice - but it has never coexisted very comfortably with marxist economics, history, and politics.

Marxist literary theory has been organised around the problem of the relationship between the working class, working class politics, and literature. It has posed a series of questions similar to those now being broached by feminism.

i. Can literature expose class oppression and the contradictions of the capitalist mode of production? Or does it necessarily and inevitably provide ideological cover for that oppression?

ii. If literature produces bourgeois ideology, is this a function of the class identity of its producers, or is the production of ideological effects a function of the forms in which literature has developed?

iii. Can certain literary forms produce 'positive images' of the working class? Or mobilise the working class politically? Which forms lend themselves best to this? Does revolutionary politics require revolution in literary form - the radical subversion of existing forms?

In other words, can literary production be captured by and for the working class, and if so, what kind of literary production?

Working Class Culture

Such questions cannot of course be answered through the analysis of literature alone. It is also necessary to look at the reading habits, education, culture, of the working class. Political and aesthetic strategies have varied according to the assessment made of 'working class culture'.

Pessimistic assessments (the Frankfurt School) see it as hopelessly contaminated by bourgeois ideology, capitalist social relations, the desire for easy escapism. Such views generate aesthetic strategies organised around 'demystification' on the one hand, and deconstructionist avant garde interventions on the other. Optimists tend to prefer Gramsci's account of the incoherent, *ad hoc* nature of working class culture, comprising both accumulations of ideology and of experience. They stress the positive underbelly, those radical elements which must be worked on and developed so that they feed and fuel radical politics.

But the concept of working class culture has not been neutral as regards gender. Whether we are invited to examine working class attitudes, work practices, leisure habits, etc., we are usually shown a predominantly male culture. This is particularly obvious in the so-called 'proletarian novels' of the sixties, and is equally evident in more recent work on 'youth culture'.

'Women's Culture'

If the grass roots level of socialist politics and aesthetics is the working class and working class culture, then, by analogy, the grass roots for feminists would seem to be women and women's culture. But there are difficulties in speaking of 'women's culture' because of the way that women are divided by class. Insofar as the attempt is made to identify specifically 'female' ways of behaving, relating, working, speaking, writing, it tends to focus on those areas of life which women share rather than those experiences which divide them. But it is in the so-called 'public sphere' that women's experience has the greatest diversity, because it is here that class and education are primarily determining. What women share is their experience in the private sphere - home, family, personal relations. I remember Juliet Mitchell in the early days of the Women's Liberation Movement in Britain remarking, in a talk, on the ease with which women of very different class and educational backgrounds, thrown together in a hospital ward, can communicate across these differences around common experiences of childbirth, housework, husbands, children, etc. Later she wrote:

> What is women's concrete situation in contemporary capitalist society? What is the universal or general area which defines her oppression? The family and the psychology of femininity are clearly crucial here. However inegalitarian her situation at work ... it is within the development of her feminine psyche and her ideological and socio-economic role as mother and housekeeper that woman finds the oppression that is hers alone. (Mitchell, 1971, p.21)

There is a danger, however, that if feminists look for 'women's culture' and find it in the realm of the personal and private, they will reinforce the ideological gender stereotype of two separate spheres. The public world of work and politics is part of women's experience even if they are typically placed within it in a different way from men. There are certain areas of experience and self-identity which women share across class, with other women, and others which they share across sex, with men and women of their own class.

It is in the triple context, then, of (i) a dominant culture which identifies women with the private and personal, so that their role in the 'public sphere' becomes invisible; (ii) a feminist movement which, wanting to unite women around their common oppression, focuses on those areas of experience which they share; and (iii) the development of the novel as conventionally and predominantly narratives of personal relations, that the role of women in fiction and its relation to feminism must be placed.

Writing Like a Woman

Just as working class novelists have been assessed by socialists in terms of their support or betrayal of working class culture and politics, so women writers have been arraigned retrospectively against the bar of contemporary feminism. Much of the re-writing of the history of literature by feminists has been concerned to identify incipient, covert or overt feminism in novels written by women. It has searched for evidence of a specifically feminine sensibility or style which distinguishes them from their male colleagues. In this genre, one of the most damning things that can be said of a woman is that she writes like a man:

> ... for the first time in the 19th century women proved that they could write novels like men ... It was left to the 20th century women writers to show that they could write like women. (Miles, 1974, p.42)

Elaine Showalter utilises the concept of 'female subculture' or literary tradition (Showalter, 1979a). She distinguishes three phases in its development, three ways in which women writers 'wrote like women'. The first, the feminine, lasted from 1840-1880, and was characterised by an imitation of prevailing modes of writing and the internalisation of its standards. The second, designated 'the feminist', saw, from 1880-1920, widespread protest against these standards and the advocacy of women's rights; the third, the female, transcends mere protest and inaugurates a process of self-discovery by women writers.

In identifying a 'female subculture' Showalter warns against the danger of reiterating gender stereotypes in transvalued form, but does not always succeed in avoiding it herself. In general, feminist assessments of women writers tend to shift uncomfortably between two positions, both of which are forcibly stated and left in unresolved conflict in the *locus classicus* of feminist aesthetics, Virginia Woolf's *Room of One's Own*. On the one hand Woolf enjoins women to 'write like women', on the other, to transcend their sex. By 'writing like a woman' she seems to mean two things. Firstly, that the privileged woman with 'a room of her own, and £500 a year' plus sufficient education and talent to write fiction, should not betray her sex - the mass of ordinary women who do not have these privileges. They should write about the experience of those women who '... have sat indoors all these millions of years, so that by this time the very walls are so permeated by their creative force ... that it must needs harness itself to pens and brushes ...' (Woolf, 1977, p.83). Secondly, that women writers should find a style 'natural' to them. But this will be very different from the prevailing 'male' style of writing:

> The weight, the pace, the stride of a man's mind are too unlike her own for her to lift anything substantial from him successfully ... The sentence that was current at the beginning of the nineteenth century ran something like this perhaps. 'The grandeur of their works was an argument with them, not to stop short, but to proceed ... etc.' That is a man's sentence; behind it one can see Johnson, Gibbon and the rest. It was a sentence that was unsuited for a woman's use ... (Woolf, 1977, p.73)

Women, then, were to 'write like women'. But Woolf is equally insistent that great writing is androgynous, and that women only enter the ranks of greatness on condition that they leave behind them their grievances as women - the resentment, frustration and anger which she sees as marring the work of Charlotte Brontë.

The claim that women write, or ought to write, like women, is still advanced today, by both misogynists such as those quoted by Gilbert and Gubar (for the other side of the claim that great writing is male, is the inferiority of 'female' writing), and in transvalued form, by feminists. Women as writers are faced with the same dreary paradox in almost every field they enter, from sport to all kinds of intellectual activities, to manual work: if they are good at it, they are 'like men', and their femininity is impugned. If they stick to acceptable 'feminine' forms of these activities, their feminine status is secure, but they are treated with contempt. Feminist resistance to this type of patriarchal double-bind must include the reassessment and revaluation of despised 'feminine' forms. But there is a danger in insisting that women restrict themselves to these forms alone. The old lines between masculine/feminine are reinforced, and women who wish to reappropriate territory colonised as 'masculine' should not have to run the gauntlet of feminist charges that they, treacherously, 'write like men'.

The claim that women 'write like women' has been advanced on a number of grounds:

i. That women use language differently from men

This claim has received a new boost from Lacanian psychoanalytic theory, and especially from feminist Lacanians such as Kristeva (1980) and Irigaray (1974), notwithstanding Lacan's own disavowal of their work. As this approach to language and writing is discussed in other Conference papers, I will not attempt to summarise it here. It is difficult and obscure, in all its variants, and is open to rather different interpretations, so that any given 'Lacanian' theory of women and writing will be contentious and open to challenge from within. But its frequent effect on feminist criticism is a celebration of feminine marginality, and of the exclusion of women from patriarchal language and culture on terms acceptable to them:

Femininity itself ... becomes the repressed term by which discourse is made possible. The feminine takes its place with the absence, silence or incoherence that discourse represses. Women face the choice; entry into culture on condition of submission to phallocentricity; refusal, and a reinscribing of the feminine as marginal madness or nonsense. (Jacobus, 1979, p.12)

Women, of course, have no monopoly on silence, madness, incoherence. We are castigated as gossips; we have always been enthusiastic readers of fiction; and female children generally develop verbal and literary skills earlier than males. But Lacanianism can perhaps claim immunity from empirical evidence about the actual linguistic behaviour of men and women, on the grounds that 'masculine' and 'feminine' are positions which individuals come to occupy through their acquisition of language and culture, rather than traits typical of male and female. Sex and gender are related but do not neatly overlap. This argument has a certain degree of truth. If sex completely determined gender, then there would be no need for the distinction between them. Recognition of the distinction leaves room for a certain lack of fit between biological sex, and traits and behaviour designated 'masculine' or 'feminine' within a given culture. However, unless there is considerable congruence, there would be no room for debate. Biological determinists explain gender in terms of sex, and explain the apparent deviations in a variety of ways. Beatrice Faust redefines biological sex in terms of hormone balance rather than genital difference, and reduces gender differential social behaviour to this base (Faust, 1981). Socio-cultural determinists use examples of deviation from the 'norm' as evidence that gender is not a function of biology, and explain such congruence as does exist between biological sex and gender expectations, by social, psychological and ideological conditioning. Were there no congruence, the ideological nature of the categories 'masculine' and 'feminine' would be absolutely transparent; were there complete congruence, sociological and cultural explanations would begin to look a little thin. In either case it is clear why parties to the debate cannot altogether ignore empirical questions to do with the actual behaviour and characteristics of males and females. There can be no rational grounds for designating character traits, or behaviour 'feminine' unless they are more frequently found among women than men. I remain to be convinced that 'silence, madness, incoherence, nonsense' are 'feminine' in this sense. Moreover, some of the characteristics of 'the poetic' are arguably more often displayed by men than by women in their writing.

The early history of the English novel provides us with an interesting test case. Both Defoe and Richardson wrote novels in the first person, with female narrators/heroines. Defoe's Moll has been characterised as 'Defoe in drag' (Sherbo, 1969). Many critics have argued that Moll is unconvincing - the muscles and the hairy legs are too visible. Richardson, on the other hand, is often judged to have had a 'feminine sensibility', so successfully did he pass off Clarissa's letters as 'feminine writing', and indeed succeeding generations of women writers confirmed that judgement by emulating Richardson's epistolary style. An interesting gloss on this question is offered by Terry Eagleton (Eagleton, 1982). He registers the differences between Clarissa's and Lovelace's letters, but argues, paradoxically, that Clarissa writes like a man, Lovelace like a woman. His grounds for so designating the two styles are theoretical, his theory deriving from Derrida and Kristeva. But I do not believe that grounds for his assertion can be found outside of theory. I would make quite the opposite judgement about the two styles, on the grounds that while the majority of English novel writers, male and female, are closer to Clarissa's 'transparent' style of language use, those who prefer Lovelace's play, his dissolution of boundaries, arguably include more men than women. Game-playing, rule-breaking, are a function of confidence of legitimate status, of knowledge of the game and of its rules. Because women in our society are more likely than men to have a socialised fear of their own inadequacy, they are less, not more,likely to engage in such rule-breaking play.

ii. That women have a distinctive 'sensibility'

Here, too, learnt conventions may be mistaken for innate propensities. In the last quarter of the 18th century there was a certain 'feminisation' of cultural values in Britain associated with changes in the class structure as well as in the family (Stone, 1977; Eagleton, 1982). This period saw the development of the novel of 'sensibility', a genre which subsequently attracted many women writers, but which was initiated by men like Mackenzie and Sterne. Yet it is true that sex is one of the major bases of social differentiation in our society, and that women, and men as a result, have systematically different social experiences. This experience, plus their socialisation into 'feminine' identities generates a 'feminine' sensibility more often in women than in men. Yet experience and 'sensibility', as the 'structuralist' school has insisted to its credit, do not translate directly into linguistic style, novelistic conventions. These are rule-governed and can be learnt. It may of course be the case that certain styles and genres have some kind of affinity with the 'feminine sensibility'. It is true that certain genres are widely recognised as 'women's genres' and that these genres often attract women writers.

iii. That women writers are most numerous in women's genres

I have already mentioned the novel of sensibility. Other genres associated particularly with women include the gothic romance, domestic gothic, Mills & Boon type romance, melodrama. They also attract a large female readership. Feminist cultural politics should take due account of cultural forms which are popular with women. Their popularity requires an explanation, and these genres may well provide space for feminist work in exploring, extending, transforming them.

The conclusion must be, however, that the proposition that women 'write like women' is as problematic as the concept of 'female culture', and as the categories of 'masculine/feminine' when these are taken to denote either properties and qualities intrinsic to either sex, or properties and qualities which are so defined by theoretical fiat independently of their association with males and females. Writing *per se*, is gender ambiguous in our culture, and 'masculine' and 'feminine' labels are even more difficult to apply than is the case with other activities. What counts as 'masculine/feminine' is to some extent a matter of changing conventions, and conventions can be learnt. The sexual and gender identities of authors cannot be inferred from his/her skill in utilising different conventions.

If these points are conceded, then the question for feminists shifts. It is no longer a question of identifying ways of writing peculiar to women, but the political question of 'writing like a feminist'. How can we identify feminist aesthetic strategies? What possibilities do traditions of 'feminine' writing, 'feminine' genres, offer for feminism? What restrictions and limitations do they carry? Can conventionally 'masculine' styles and genres be colonised and appropriated to feminist ends? Are there any forms or genres which are so irretrievably bound up with sexism that they can serve no other ends?

Writing Like a Feminist

For present purposes, if we take a crude division between those genres which use (changing) conventions of realism, and those which are non-realist, including fantasy forms, then 'feminine' forms of each may be identified. Women have specialised in novels of domestic realism, in romantic fiction, and in what Moers calls 'the female gothic' (Moers, 1977). They have also contributed in large numbers to detective fiction.

'Realism' is a notoriously difficult concept, which has its meaning coloured by that with which it is being contrasted in any given usage. Here, we have realism vs. escapist novels (detective and romantic fiction), and realism vs. fantasy. Escapist forms stay within the bounds of possibility, by recognising naturalistic laws of cause and effect, but they deal with the exceptional, the unusual, and with chance. Fantasy is, according to Todorov's definition, a hybrid form, in between 'the marvellous', which recognises no boundaries to cause-effect relations, and realism (Todorov, 1973). We are held in suspense between naturalistic and marvellous explanations of the novel's events. The Gothic novel belongs to the fantastic, and the 'domestic gothic' of Charlotte Brontë remains tenuously linked to it, although her 'strange happenings' are almost always given naturalistic explanations. These are broad categories, and many novels do not belong unambiguously to one or the other. For example, many novels of 'domestic realism', such as those of Jane Austen, have strong elements of wish-fulfilment in their Cinderella motifs. And where realism shifts from social realism to psychological realism, the boundaries between realism and fantasy break down, since fantasy is part of 'inner reality'. In certain examples of the fantastic, we cannot tell whether we are being offered the paranoid fantasies of the narrator, or a chilling tale which, given a 'willing suspension of disbelief', we can accept as a possible world. Examples would be *Mysteries of Udolpho* and *Frankenstein*, and a whole range of persecution novels.

What does all this have to do with politics and aesthetics of feminism? Feminism has two goals; understanding women's oppression and

identifying its causes, and intervening to change it. This involves the
political mobilisation of women who are not feminists, and who may even be
opposed to what they understand by the term.

But if feminism is not to be arbitrary and voluntaristic, it must be
based on the existence, at some level, of a widely diffused consciousness
among women that they are oppressed and that they wish things could be
different. 'If we define interests totally independently of the orientations of those concerned, "religious mania alone speaks here" ' (Mann,
1970). In other words, the goals and strategies of feminism must be
articulated with felt oppression, and with the utopian hopes, fears,
wishes, aspirations of women. Marx dismissed as 'utopian' any form of
socialism which was not based on a scientific analysis of 'the laws of
motion' of the capitalist mode of production. But successful political
struggles always depend on their ability to connect with utopias - with
the belief and hope that things might be better.

These considerations may suggest certain tentative guidelines for
feminist aesthetic strategies.

1. Feminists should always take seriously those forms of writing
which have been traditionally associated with women as producers or
readers. *Pace* Ros Coward (Coward, 1980), while Mills & Boon romances
are not, it is true, feminist by virtue of being written and read by
women, they are of vital interest to feminism for what they reveal of
female fantasies which are not entirely a function of ideological
conditioning against their objective interests;

2. Feminism does not carry imperatives as to form. Feminist intervention is possible and necessary at all levels of cultural production, and in most genres. It is presented with different problems
in different forms and at different levels.

i. Realism

A common *cri de coeur* of the women's movement has been for more
'realistic' or 'positive' images of women. This plea has been
exposed to the critique of realism, representation and narrative as
ideology developed within various structuralist schools. Patricia
Stubbs offers an interesting gloss on the problem of realism. She
considers it necessary for feminism to break outside the mould of
available realist forms, paradoxically because they are at once not
realistic enough, and too realistic; too realistic, because of the
problem ...

> peculiar to realist fiction - that of how to incorporate
> into a form whose essential characteristic is the explora-
> tion of existing realities, experiences and aspirations
> which go well beyond the possibilities afforded by that
> reality. (Stubbs, 1979, p.234)

Realist fiction is limited by its very nature she thinks, and can
only '... diagnose existing contradictions and existing suffering
...' (Stubbs, 1979, p.235). Hence it is 'too realistic'; but at the
same time not realistic enough. For she goes on to assert that
realism is restricted in its ability to perform even this task of
critical analysis for feminism, because of the restriction of its
fictional world to personal relations and the private sphere:

> It has strengthened the dominant assumption about the
> world of private experience being the only really impor-
> tant part of a woman's life. (Stubbs, 1979, p.234)

It follows that feminist strategies would require the breaking of the
boundaries which conventionally restrict the fictional world of

realism in this manner. The problem is whether this can be done without destroying at the same time the pleasure of realist narratives. For it is not only women who are confined in cultural myth and ideology to the private and the personal; so, too, is pleasure. It is not sought, in fiction or in reality, in the 'masculine' world of work and politics.

ii. Non-realist forms

Stubbs argues that non-realist narratives such as those of detective fiction, or fantasy, offer greater potential for feminist writers. I would argue that they simply offer a different set of problems, neither more nor less intractable than those of realism. 'Realism', like 'scientific socialism', connotes 'to be taken seriously'. It is because they wish to be taken seriously that many socialist and feminist writers have looked to this genre. Non-realism, like 'utopian socialism' connotes 'not to be taken seriously'. It licenses escape, fantasy, pleasure. It is because they emphasise the pleasurable that those socialists and feminist who recognise the political importance of pleasure, escape, fantasy, have tried to work within these genres. The problem here is how feminists may work through and on these forms without having their feminism discounted because they work in forms which need not be taken seriously - because they work, as it were, under licence.

iii. Avant garde and 'deconstruction'

The problems faced by socialists and feminists who reject both realism and non-realist popular genres have been well rehearsed elsewhere (Brecht, 1977). They centre around accessibility.

3. The politics of a work will be a function of its context as much of its style or form. It is sometimes possible to alter the context of a work through intervention at the moment of reception rather than production. There are feminist strategies of reading as well as of writing (Kuhn, 1982).

4. What feminism needs in the field of cultural politics is a united front against sexism and oppression; an exploration of what a 'feminist' intervention would or might consist in, across a variety of different genres, rather than a formula for producing feminist fiction. With apologies to Brecht, we may end by asserting that

> Our concept of feminism must be broad, political, and sovereign over all conventions.

BIBLIOGRAPHY

Altick, R., *The English Common Reader* (University of Chicago Press, 1957).

Anderson, P., *Considerations on Western Marxism* (New Left Books, 1976).

Barrett, M. and McIntosh, M., 'The Family Wage' in *Capital and Class* (11, 1980).

Beechey, V., 'Women and Production: a critical analysis of some sociological theories of women's work' in A. Kuhn and A.-M. Wolpe, eds., *Feminism and Materialism* (Routledge & Kegan Paul, 1978).

Coward, R., 'Are Women's Novels Feminist Novels?', *Feminist Review* (5, 1980).

Eagleton, T., *The Rape of Clarissa*, (Oxford, 1982).

Faust, B., *Women, Sex and Pornography* (London, 1981).

Fowles, J., *The Aristos* (Triad Granada, 1981).

Gilbert, S. M. and Gubar, S., *The Madwoman in the Attic* (Yale, 1979).

Irigary, L., *Speculum de l'autre femme* (Paris, 1974).

Jacobus, M. (ed.), *Women Writing and Writing about Women* (Croom Helm, 1979).

Kristeva, J., *Desire in Language: a semiotic approach to art* (Columbia, 1980).

Kuhn, A., *Women's Pictures: Feminism and Cinema* (Routledge & Kegan Paul, 1982).

Malos, E., *The Politics of Housework* (Allison & Busby, 1980).

Mann, M., 'The Social Cohesion of Liberal Democracy', *American Sociological Review*, Vol.35, 3 (1970).

Miles, R., *The Fiction of Sex* (London, 1974).

Millett, K., *Sexual Politics* (Virage, 1977).

Mitchell, J., *Women's Estate* (Penguin, 1971).

Moers, E., *Literary Women* (Women's Press, 1977).

Parsons, T., *The Social System* (Free Press, 1956).

Sherbo, A., 'Defoe as Transvestite' in *Studies in the 18th Century English Novel* (Michigan, 1969).

Showalter, E., *A Literature of Their Own* (Virago, 1979a).

'Towards a Feminist Poetics', in M. Jacobus, *op.cit.* (1979b).

Stone, L., *The Family, Sex and Marriage in England, 1500-1800* (Weidenfeld & Nicolson, 1977).

Stubbs, P., *Women and Fiction: Feminism and the Novel, 1880-1920* (Methuen, 1979).

Todorov, T., *The Fantastic* (Cornell, 1973).

Woolf, V., *A Room of One's Own* (Granada, 1977).

Zaretsky, E., *Capitalism, the Family and Personal Life* (Pluto, 1976).

NOTES ON "POST-FEMINISM"

Mary Russo

It is not my purpose to define "post-feminism". "Post-feminism", as I have understood it, is not an idea whose time has come. Except in its least interesting aspects, it is not an idea at all, although I can imagine that others may be intent on knowing it as such.

Overheard at this conference on "The Politics of Theory" and seen in the writings of the two figures I will discuss - Maria-Antonietta Macciocchi and Julia Kristeva - "post-feminism" is something else. Something like "post-structuralism" but unlike it, since, after all, feminism in its fullest sense includes the most significant movement for social change of the last decade. (1) "Post-feminism" sounds like an insult, a wounding blow to a hard-won identification of common cause and lives already under siege by a New Right; at least it sounds like that to some. Others, feminists and not, are relieved if not reassured by precisely this move away from the logic of Identity and see in it a necessary containment of certain discursive elements characterizing particularly Anglo-American feminism. Anti-feminists, unnamed and legion on the Left, may be especially pleased and welcome "post-feminism" as feminism's younger, more sophisticated, and less rancourous step-sister. For many, the first sense of "post-feminism" works across all these feelings, loyalties, disturbances and hurt.

The term, like theory more generally, comes across other complexities of national origin and destination as it crosses geographical and ideological boundaries, its uses and meaning altered by different social and cultural contexts and times. (2) A major purpose of this paper, written out of an American context, to be received primarily in England, and referring specifically to events of the last decade in France and in Italy, is to address some of these difficulties.

But I would like to begin most simply, moving from first impressions to what we may slowly infer: "Post-feminism" might be approached as a new and consummately social acquaintance, known superficially and in part. With such a strategy (like the old blind men and the elephant) we might touch upon it warily, asking the same sort of interesting questions: What does it look like? Is it long or short? What is its shape? Is it round, how does it curve? How old is it? Where does it come from? Who are its friends?

* * *

Macciocchi: "Le Post-Féminisme" and "Retro" Politics

> Dix ans après 1968: "Mesdames les féministes, la fête est finie. Retournez au lit ... " (3)
>
> Maria-Antonietta Macciocchi, "Le Post-Féminisme"

If it was unpredicted by political theory that Feminism in its latest wave would emerge first, in the United States, from the Civil Rights and New Left movements of the 1960s, it seems inevitable that "Post-Feminism" when it came, and it has, would come out of the France of the late 1970s. Now, is it so remarkable that such an inglorious term (echoing those other afterwords - post-structuralism, post-modernism, post-marxism, etc.) might be coined by a foreign intellectual living in Paris, Maria-Antonietta Macciocchi?

Macciocchi, always a controversial figure, was one of the few women of prominence in the Italian Communist Party. Her career has followed the post-war history of the European Left from the Resistance, through electoral and cultural politics and debates over Eurocommunism and ideology. (4) Her *Letters to Louis Althusser From Within the Communist Party*, written in 1968, were documents of a lively and hopeful political practice of, in the old-fashioned Gramscian term, "an organic intellectual". (5) Over a decade later, she survived in an aftermath which to some is as bitter, if not as dramatic, as the post-revolutionary world of the theorists of Western Marxism, Korsch, Gramsci, and young Lukács. Many European Left intellectuals have been saddened and dismayed by the course of events since 1968; Macciocchi has been consistently and flamboyantly outraged. Bidding farewell in 1977 to the party which has expelled her, she sloganizes insolently *"After Marx, April"*, (6) in exile from even the Autonomous post-political politics to which she, at least temporarily, subscribed. Two years afterward, in a perfectly consonant rhetoric, she proclaims the death of the old "historical feminism" along with the past absolute "historical Left", and calls for "Feminism with a Human Face" (7) - as if feminism were an orthodoxy and as if that "human face" would not be gendered, or if it were gendered would not for the first time since the Humanism of the 15th century be gendered male.

"We are already navigating in the estuary of Post-feminism, sails down", she writes. "Why should we lie (to ourselves)?" (8)

As she goes on to describe it, in a stylistically remarkable preface to *De la France*, a volume of collaborative essays from her seminar at Vincennes, "Post-feminism" is not so much a time as a watery space, inside a crisis (Marxism is now outside, at sea), and this inside is murky with broken signs, symbols, archetypes, and rhetorics of philosophical and political disaster, hyperbolically recalled in her simulacrum of an unnamed cultural catastrophe. (9) The unaccounted for traces of concentration camps, fascism, nazism, racism, terrorism, and female complicity in the above surface as a scattered debris. There are, as well, last taunts directed towards old enemies in the women's movement: the separatists ("apartheid in the gulag"); (10) reproductive rights activists (called "the abortionists" echoing an old argument against the rationalization of reproduction as being in the interest of Capital). (11) In this regard, she points back to the horizon and "the great white whale" of pregnancy, its enormous belly surfacing as "the iceberg (all metaphors are mixed in her discourse) of feminism", (12) hiding desire and deeper questions of sexuality. Discarded in this tidal pool are female idols - goddesses, tragic heroines, saints, especially virgin martyrs - St. Agnes, and St. Lucy plucking out her eyes because she has seen the male genitals, and a certain Mother (whose?) evoked as the hallucination of an infantilized women's movement. (13)

All this horror and hyperbole to say that post-feminism is here, which may or may not be news, and to conclude (in a curiously solicitous direct address to some bewildered reader from her drunken boat) that it isn't after all so bad. If a cheerful outcome is not so easy to see, it may be because what Macciocchi and her Post-feminism offer is less a vision than an incitement, a provocation in the style of Italian semiotic delinquency, shaped in the forms of certain currents of French thought of the 1970s. The emphasis on fluidity, on inner-spatial dimensionality, implosion, rupture, and surfacing of concurrent movement of various substrata (here cultural), disorganization, disunity, disidentification and dissent from orthodoxies of all kinds but especially the hierarchies of the organized Left, are characteristic in different and partial ways of French "new Philosophy", deconstruction, discourse theory, certain modes of sciences, and although Macciocchi fails to mention it, a strong current of Feminism. (14) Though she is an astute reporter of cultural and political drifts, Macciocchi is not herself a theorist. It is left to someone more theoretically disposed to make explicit these connections between science, politics, philosophy, social movement, and the crises of feminism.

Kristeva: Cultural Catastrophism and Feminism of the Third Kind

Julia Kristeva, in an article recently translated in the United States as "Women's Time", very broadly charts these very complex concurrences. Moving within the same political drift and with similar imagery as Macciocchi, she names the new feminism, not a feminism in the old sense of social group or movement but as a new mutation called "the Third Generation". (15) This new generation does not simply follow upon the old second generation which was identified with the concepts, problematics and failures of European nationalism, socialism, existentialism (especially consciousness and identification), but transverses these and various other social and cultural developments. In her plotting, the use of the word "generation" implies "less a chronology than a signifying space, both a corporeal and desiring mental space". (16) This space might be visualized as multi-dimensional and vectored, with arrows pointing backwards as well as forwards, across, up and down; not unlike her earlier use of Chora, this space also implies the maternal function. Here the semiotic model is expanded to deal with many other categories, including history. (In fact, the Nietzschean historiographical categories of cyclical and monumental modes of history are incorporated into this new generational space.) This theoretical model, like the mathematical categories of catastrophe theory (17) from which it is largely drawn, is indeterminate, focussed on surfaces and effects or traces rather than cause, and thrillingly elliptical, if you have the time.

At the level of the subject, the "third generation" suggests a discursive positioning or attitude. To see why this attitude is more congenial to Kristeva than that of the second generation (characterized by an existentialist subject) it may be useful briefly to review and interrogate her earlier positioning of women and feminism within the simpler parameters of writing and the intellectual.

Detour: 1977

The year that Macciocchi involuntarily left the party (PCI) may soon rival 1968 as a watershed of politics and culture with the collapse in France of the Union of the Left and the emergence in Italy of the "movement of 77" which was characterized initially by a cultural presence of the economically and politically marginalized, mostly youth, underemployed or unemployed workers, and unaffiliated radicals, "rejects of the historical compromise", and then by a spiral of repression and violence. In the same year, 1977, Julia Kristeva introduced a special feminist issue of the prestigious journal *Tel Quel* with a redefinition of the intellectual. In contrast to the Gramscian model as the representative of class or bloc, or the existentialist model of the intellectual as representative of consciousness, "the new type of intellectual" is non-representative and defined functionally by position. (18) This emphasis on positionality belongs, of course, to a current analysis of power as being located everywhere, non-totalized except by the claim of State and the counterclaim of the organized Opposition. The position of the new intellectual is characterized by Kristeva as one of <u>dissent</u>: "A specter is haunting Europe: the specter of dissidents." (19) She identifies three types of dissidents: the rebel who is locked into a traditional struggle of opposition and reinforcement; the psychoanalyst who dismantles the totalizing habits of rational consciousness; and the writer. By "writer" she refers to the avant-garde figures like Artaud, Bataille, Sollers, whose work "plays, transgresses and pluralizes". These writer-dissidents are closer, then, to the psychoanalyst than to the rebel, since writing in this sense is a signifying practice in which the effects of the unconscious through the imaginary or semiotic (*semiotique*) appear as ruptures of the symbolic chain. Writing here is subversive, disruptive, polyvalent, polylogical, marginal, dispersive.

And what of women? And what of feminism? Does not our marginality, our Otherness, our exile from the Symbolic, from Law and Culture, not place us, for once at least advantageously? Is feminism not by definition a dissidence?

Well, to begin with writing, if the question is one of the sexual division of women from men, the answer from Kristeva is empirically, no. In fact, from her interviews and from her general disregard of women writers, Kristeva seems to be saying that women aren't avant-garde enough. We are still too realistic, or at best romantic. In any case, literarily homely and out of date. As for feminism:

> I am quite dedicated to the feminist movement but I think feminism or any other movement need not expect unconditional backing on the part of an intellectual woman. (20)

This is puzzling to me only because such theoretical disassociations or misassociations seem to be so sure of the "they" of feminism from which they dissent, while those of us who see ourselves historically within feminism have more and more trouble in discerning our "we" both practically and discursively. This is not to say that it is the essentialist mystifications of "Woman" (which Macciocchi has consistently attacked) or the simpler forms of identification which characterized the earlier stages of consciousness raising between sovereign selves will do anyone. They will not: as much as theory, this is a lesson of recent historical practice. But, as has been argued elsewhere, is an intellectual project which is in the habit of dissolving unities and subverting orthodoxies in danger of seeing unities and orthodoxies where they do not exist?

But perhaps this is a minor point. Kristeva goes beyond (or should I say to the side of) the question of a particular woman's or women's relation to dissent: she speaks of the Mother. In her remarks on the new intellectual, and in her later work, she claims motherhood and the material as a position, a site of the problem of the limits of the human subject on the border of language. Here, there is an interesting parallel with Macciocchi in her work on women and Fascism. Macciocchi also focuses on the Mother but in a mediating ideological role between the family and the State: in her most public aspect as mother, as Roman matron giving consent to the sexual and political domination of the Father-Head of the State. (21) Macciocchi insists that motherhood as an institution is crucially conserving of both the physical and social reproduction of the human and as such (as Kristeva is quick to recognize) at the very antipode of dissent.

Unlike Macciocchi, however, who has in mind a full subject (with a human face) restored to history (along with a burden of guilt for fascist ideology), Kristeva is interested in the functional position of the maternal as the body (material condition) upon which the semiotic is articulated. The rhythms, intonations, gestures, anterior to the infant's first phonemes, morphemes, lexemes, and sentences suggest to Kristeva the same heterogeneity - the same pulsating, glimmering, jocose, dispersive poetics - as the language of the avant-garde and other dissenting irrational, prerational, or "transrational" discourses, including the language of madness. The dissenting subject is placed precariously on the hysterical verge of rationalism and of dissolution.

And again, what of women? Are we not caught just between the devil of totalizing phallologocentric Identity and the deep blue sea of (pulsating?) femininitude?

Again, not exactly, for Kristeva is not speaking specifically to the condition of mothers as women, or women as mothers with any positivity - although she assumes this link. Her assumption of the link between women and mothering has, in fact, been challenged by feminists here and in France who suspect in this move another biologistic retreat. I think this is not the case, or at least I hope not. At any rate, I cannot judge the scientific validity of her theory as it touches upon the linguistic questions of speech and child development or the phantasmatic meaning of giving birth. Contextually, French intellectual life is always in less danger than our own of succumbing to the ideologies of naturalism, biologism, or empiricism. In France, what is more often at stake is a kind of culturalism subsuming the world into the art of language. Kristeva's work is both most susceptible and to me most audacious and brilliant when her theoretical moves are most overtly cultural, as for instance in her essay on Renaissance painting and the art of Giovanni Bellini. (22) Here she reads behind the Christian Humanist image of Mother and Child, usually seen as the embodiment of the Renaissance concept of figurable, representable Man, another uncontainable, unrepresentable, unimagined presence - in spaces, color, and volume, the repressed but luminous Kristevian Madonna. Here, in an important historical moment as the image of Western man is consolidated with cultural and political force, Kristeva's formulation is truly shattering and subversive. As a cultural practice, such criticism is transformative of our understanding.

But again, and for the last time, is it transformative politically and for women? Has she too put women in their place?

If that place is purely negatory, as a living questioning of representation and rationality, yes. This critical negativity too often absent in the early American feminist largely moral discourse, and the problemization of the subject in Kristeva's work has been very instructive. Unlike some French feminists, she does not look toward or foresee a separatist feminine discourse that would speak for, around, or from the body. If my repeated questioning of her theoretical discourse on the intellectual, and on motherhood and culture, suggests that I want her to insist on such a possibility, that is not my intention. It is just that like many discussions of phenomena like hysteria, the anguish of women suffering somatizations and silences is forgotten in the discovering of an alternative way of writing. They are easily forgotten because to be recalled they would be recalled as subjects of history, and as Macciocchi's work demonstrates, both the concept of history and its subject are now a critical problem - if what we mean by history is the rationality of the past that suggests a rational intervention.

Post-Feminism and "*Le temps des femmes*"

It is the problem of history which confronts Kristeva in "Women's Time". The following paragraph brings together most explicitly the positioning of the new third generational feminist in the time and the company he or she keeps:

> The hysteric (either male or female) who suffers from
> reminiscences would (rather) recognise his or herself in
> the anterior temporal modalities: cyclical or monumental.
> This antinomy, one perhaps embedded in psychic structures,
> becomes nonetheless, within a given civilization, an anti-
> nomy among social groups and ideologies in which the radi-
> cal positions of certain feminists would rejoin the discourse
> of marginal groups of spiritual or mystical inspiration and
> strangely enough, rejoin recent scientific preoccupations.
> Is it not true that the problematic of a time indissociable
> from space, and a space time on infinite expansion, or
> rhythmed by accidents or catastrophes, preoccupies both
> space science and genetics. (23) (emphasis mine)

Now, if there are grave intellectual dangers in a separatist view of women and of "feminine" discourse, are there not some cautions to be taken into account in the positioning of a feminism within a most generalized hysteria; there, having left even a limited determinacy behind, having disallowed the idea of an historically determined conjuncture, having characterized the earlier feminists' identity as a "shock" effect - a kind of felicitous accident - it rejoins the other mutations and left-overs of cultural catastrophism?

The first and most general warning comes from René Thom himself, the mathematician who developed catastrophe theory. Simply, he says to watch out for delirium:

> It is an enormous step from noticing the presence of iso-
> morphic morphological accidents on different substrates,
> to establishing some fundamental coupling between these
> substrates to explain these analogies, and it is precisely
> this step that delirious thinking takes. (24)

His point is not to disallow the use of analogy in scientific thinking but rather to privilege and maintain the discretion of formal thought. He prefers, he writes, "magic that has been psychoanalyzed and made conscious of its structures". (25)

On the one hand, one can be grateful to Kristeva for bringing her discussion of the subject to the level of the group and for her enlarged perspective which, as did Macciocchi's introduction, allows us to see some very interesting analogical relations on various levels. On the other hand, her discourse would seem to lack "that fundamental coupling" of explanation that might have been provided, at another critical conjuncture, by history. The absence of history or another sort of formal explanation suggests a magical interconnection. Precisely since her discourse here is not merely a kind of theoretical fine-tuning but names the state of a whole world, it cannot be taken for granted that the delirium-effects which such magical interconnections make are harmless, disinterested, subversive or benign.

Contexts: Dissidence and Dissonance

Which brings us to the question of practice. If practice cannot quickly be deduced from such discussions, one can at least grasp the style.

Elizabeth Hardwick is one American writer who understands this style very well. Her novel, *Sleepless Nights*, is set in "a Woman's city" of insomnia, subways, and the blues; filled with easy ladies who give themselves over to love, to gambling, to a line from Shakespeare, above all, to the weak (as in "the tyranny of the weak") and shame (as in her pivotal quotation from Nietzsche: "Shame is inventive").

... with the weak something is always happening: improvisations, surprise, suspense, injustice, manipulation, hypochondria, secret drinking, crying, hiding in the garden, driving off in the middle of the night. The weak have the purest sense of history. Anything can happen. Each of them is a palmist reading his own hand. (26)

It is not surprising that Nietzsche should be brought out from behind such a passage for in these unexpected moves, in these histrionic manipulations of place and moment, there is the unburdening of history and the promise of a new start, endless new starts. The weak are irrepressible. "Shame is inventive."

This eventfulness is, in a novel, both bewildering and hilarious; it may well be political. But in Hardwick's book, the weak are most often alone. In the cultural politic which informs much irrationalist theory in France and Italy, they have each other. Who are they? There are many lists. This one is drawn from a dialogue between Gilles Deleuze and Michel Foucault on the subject of the intellectuals and power: "Women, prisoners, conscripted soldiers, hospital patients, homosexuals" (27) (and, I would add for the occasion, professors of the humanities). This is not just a question of politics making strange bedfellows. Women have been in worse company. But even if one agrees that there is, in the last analysis, a common enemy of marginalized social groups and that these groups finally enter into an alliance with the proletariat "since power is exercised in the way it is in order to maintain capitalist exploitation", this does not happen as Foucault says in this dialogue, "naturally". (28) How do local and regional struggles connect? What, outside of literary and cultural contexts, is practice? Replies Deleuze:

Practice is a set of relays between theoretical points ... " (29)

I think this is a fine answer. But who will do the leg work?

The connections between radical critiques of society and the feminist project are there to be made, theoretically and historically. But if the relationship between Marxism and feminism is, in Heidi Hartmann's phrase, "an unhappy marriage", why should we assume on such short acquaintance that feminism and neomarxist or unmarxist theories go hand in hand? It is to be questioned not only what such intellectual projects offer us but how the historical specificities of feminism (including barely noted or silenced theoretical work) are, in this powerfully elliptical theory, almost swept away.

It does not detract from their interest and possibility to say that these critical refinements come out of an economically and politically depressed situation. The feminist discourse in France and Italy, whether it comes through the politically or metapolitically contaminated rhetoric of the two figures which I chose to discuss, or through the "purer" feminist writing of others like Cixous or Irigaray, is located (1) within the strong presence of an organized and popular Left and (2) within the history of its failures. Both elements are strong. In the U.S. our situation is quite different. The connections between oppressed groups are drawn over time and with some difficulty. For if power is everywhere, it is not equally or self-evidently everywhere at the same time. Oppression is not democratic and judging these differences is a question not merely of understanding but of struggle. And the concepts of struggle and insurgency, it seems to me, must be distinguished from merely making a scene.

It is Macciocchi and Kristeva in this paper who have suggested the cultural texture of "post-feminism". In each of their writing, it emerges as dissidence.

The rhetoric of dissidence is heard easily in the United States; it echoes out an old romantic individualism. The historical realities which have given rise to such dissident discourses, particularly as they swerve towards intellectual anarchy, are harsher and more difficult to make out. The French questioning of the relationship between intellectuals and power in Italy takes the form of an interrogation with grave consequence. The long-awaited trial of Toni Negri, the Italian philosopher accused of various crimes relating his writing and speech to terrorism, and the trials, arraignments, depositions, legal repentances and disassociations of the estimated 3,000 persons in jail, many of whom are writers, professors and ex-students, as well as the long and growing list of the wounded and dead makes any careless connections between intellectual anarchy and practice, at this juncture, unthinkable. In the moral economy, many ideas, like imported luxury items, are bought more cheaply in New York or New Haven.

I would conclude with an allegory, not so much of good writing as of bad politics in my own context. The heroine of perhaps the most well-read popular novel on the women's movement, *The Women's Room*, having escaped the horrors of a fifties suburban marriage, and graduate education in English, is left at the novel's end with her consciousness raised about as far as it can go, and wandering about a lonely beach (back to Nature) in Maine where she is miserably underemployed. She is wondering whether after all she needs a keeper and what it has all come to:

I have opened all the windows of my head.
I have opened all the pores of my body.
But only the tide rolls in. (30)

She might have learned about the pathetic f(ph)allacy in graduate school or from the French feminists. But never mind that a half-drowned man isn't rolling in - she's where she is and what else isn't rolling in is just as important: money and job offers because she is a late-comer to a devastated profession. Her raised consciousness is not power; neither is her literary culture in a country where the lower classes see it (rightly) as an agency of their oppression and where the ruling class despisingly suspects (rightly) that it may generate critique.

In the United States, feminism has represented the most widespread social critique of culture and everyday life. Feminist literary studies, through which much European philosophy and theory is received, have been crucial. But the formation and roles of intellectuals within literary and political contexts are nationally very different. It has often been observed that the social role of the intellectual in the United States is neither as vital nor as self-conscious as in Europe. Perhaps we serve different needs. Historically, intellectual life in France has had, in its international aspect, links to imperialism; in Italy to immigration. We (in the United States) have been more often, mere consumers. Furthermore, it may well be, as Gramsci observed, that certain of the functions of intellectuals in relation to national life in countries like Italy and France, is served by the relative homogeneity of our two-party electoral system. Kristeva's work remains obsessively involved in national history and literature; her views (and recently Macciocchi's) of the avant-garde and its politics are overwhelmingly French. This is not to say that they are unusable or irreducibly foreign.

Theoretically, the questions of subjectivity, identification, cultural morphogenesis and "crises of reason" and social practice are relevant and even pressing. What I would insistently argue is that our historical dispersiveness, intellectual pluralism, independence as intellectuals from parties, etc. which seem attractive and even avant-garde after certain tired European political debates should be understood as contradictory and not leading naturally or necessarily to some transnational identification with dissent. What I have tried to suggest is that such questions might be focused in an intellectual framework that would be informed by foreign contexts, and reflective of the differences and difficulties of our own.

Still, the conditions of historical and national contexts do not fully contain "post-feminism" or put it by any means to rest. As it has emerged lately, it seems a kind of sign of the times. As a signifier, it is shifty and elliptical. It comes, often, emptied of much history and women's work. At worst, it identifies with institutional and discursive power that women as a group, even the many exceptional women theorists, do not have. At best, "post-feminism" marks a discursive and theoretical impasse that may release new strategies and narratives that may be, however provisionally, utopian and affirming. For now, the conflations and dispersiveness of "post-feminism" must be read as significant effects: traces not only of a scattered sibylline puzzle of the future, but here and now as part, in these times, of reflux and change, of the ideological handwriting on the wall.

Notes

1. "Post-structuralism", as well, can be read in a fuller historical sense as "condition", rather than "ism", "theory", or institutionalized doctrine. See Philip Lewis, "The Post-structuralist Condition", *Diacritics*, Vol.12, pp.2-4. His outline of the historiality of structuralism as a tale yet to be told (p.24) parallels the task I see on the "post-feminist" horizon.

2. For an important recent discussion of these problems of "Travelling Theory", see Edward Said's article of the same name in *Raritan*, Vol. I, Spring 1982, pp.41-67. For the "time-space shuttle" between American and French contexts, Alice Jardine, "Introduction to Women's Time" in *Signs: Journal of Women in Culture and Society*, Vol.7, no.1, pp.4-12; also the introduction by the editorial collective to "Feminist Readings: French Texts/American Contexts", *Yale French Studies*, no.62, pp.2-18.

3. Maria-Antonietta Macciocchi, "Le Post-Féminisme", *De la France* (Paris, 1977).

4. As a young student in 1943, she worked within the clandestine, antifascist, communist organization in Rome, leaving after the war to become a political organizer in Naples and the South. In the late forties, she came to prominence as a journalist and editor of *Noidonne*, a political journal for women. In the 1950s, she travelled and wrote on politics and culture in China, Iran and Algeria, and was given the editorship of the house organ of the PCI central committee. In the 1960s, she became the European foreign correspondent for *l'Unita*, the party paper, and was arrested by the Franco regime while reporting on the miners' strike in 1964. In 1968, she was reporting from Paris and travelling to Italy as a candidate (successful) for office as Deputy to the Italian Parliament from Naples. In the 1970s, Macciocchi began to publish, first and extensively, in France; by 1977 she was out of the PCI and publishing no longer in *l'Unita* but in *Tel Quel*. She has served most recently as a member of the European Parliament and on the faculty of the University of Vincennes.

5. *Lettres de l'Intérieur du Parti* was published in France in 1970 without Althusser's replies; Italian edition (Milan, 1969).

6. Macciocchi, *Après Marx, April* (Paris, 1978); Italian edition (Milan, 1978). The title refers to the "events of Bologna" in 1977.

7. "Je me déclare plutôt pour un féminisme à visage humain (et qui ne commence pas au-dessous de la ceinture)." *De la France* p.IV. (Translations mine unless noted.)

8. "Nous naviguons déjà dans l'estuaire du Post-Féminisme, les voiles flasques. Pourquoi (se) mentir," *Ibid.*, p.I.

9. I recognise the dangers here of paraphrase in my production of Macciocchi but her own travesty of Feminism is so quick and high-spirited that short of reproducing the entire text, it seems at cross-purposes (mine and hers) to slow it down with long quotations.

10. *De la France*, p.V.

11. This argument against "assembly-line abortions" and "multinationals of Reproduction" as playing into the rationalizations of Capital is associated with the late Pier Paolo Pasolini who is seen here as persecuted by the "historical feminists". "Les Féministes historiques volaient lui arracher les yeux: un homosexuel, un pervers, un anti-féministe". As I remember the debate, the attacks on Pasolini as a homosexual who as such supposedly had no right to speak of reproduction came from prominent male intellectuals, not feminists.

12. *De la France*, p.III.

13. "... la Mère du féminisme historique coincide avec la pure et simple hallucination du désarroi enfantin ..." *De la France*, p.XI.

14. Each of these projects has its own narrative. For French philosophy, see Vincent Descombes, *Le même et l'Autre: Quarante-cinq ans de Philosophie Français* (Paris, 1979). For a discussion of the politics of 1977 in Italy in relation to theorizations of "implosion" and power, see the introduction to Jean Baudrillard, *Dimenticare Foucault*, by Pietro Bellosi (Milan, 1978); Renate Holub, "Towards a New Rationality, Notes on Feminism and Current Discursive Practices in Italy", *Discourse: Berkeley Journal for Theoretical Studies in Media and Culture*, No.4, pp. 89-107, discusses the tensions between the critical establishment and new Left discourse on modes of rationality as they powerfully eclipse and silence the theoretical voice of feminism to which they are indebted.

15. Julia Kristeva, "Women's Time", translated by Alice Jardine and Harry Blake, *Signs: Journal of Women in Culture and Society*, Vol.7, no.1, pp.13-35.

16. *Ibid.*, p.33.

17. Catastrophe theory is derived from topology, a branch of mathematics; it seeks to explain discontinuity and divergence and has been applied to many biological and social sciences. It is the invention of René Thom, *Structural Stability and Morphogenesis*, trans. D. Fowler (New York, 1975). Catastrophe theory in its application to the human sciences is mentioned in various contributions to Claude Lévi-Strauss's seminar, *L'Identité* (Paris, 1977).

18. Kristeva, "Un nouveau type d'intellectuel: le dissident", *Tel Quel*, No.74, 1977, pp.3-8.

19. *Ibid.*, p.7.

20. Quoted by Leon Roudiez, "Introduction" to Julia Kristeva, *Desire in Language* (New York, 1980), p.10.

21. Macciocchi, *Éléments pour un analyse du fascisme* (Paris, 1976).
22. Kristeva, *Desire in Language*, pp.237-270.
23. Kristeva, "Women's Time", p.17.
24. René Thom, p.317.
25. *Ibid.*
26. Elizabeth Hardwick, *Sleepless Nights* (New York, 1979).
27. "Intellectuals and Power, A Conversation between Michel Foucault and Gilles Deleuze", In *Language, Counter-memory, Practice*, ed. Donald F. Bouchard, trans. Donald F. Bouchard and Sherry Simon (Ithaca, New York, 1977), p.209.
28. *Ibid.*, p.216.
29. *Ibid.*, p.206.
30. Marilyn French, *The Women's Room* (New York, 1977), p.471.

THE HORRORS OF POWER:
A CRITIQUE OF 'KRISTEVA'

Jennifer Stone

I don't like party lines. They make
for intellectual monotony and bad
prose.

Susan Sontag's caricature of feminist discourse in her *Salmagundi* interview of 1975 goes to the heart of female dissidence. Her belated remark - after a long history of anti-feminism - also establishes her as an influential precursor to Julia Kristeva who shares her uneasiness with feminist politics. Individualists both, they kept their distance from the women's movement and muttered their female asides within a larger body of politicised writings.

In the last ten years, the work of Kristeva has circulated in translation among Anglo-American feminists. The accumulation of texts, regulated by the author function, 'Kristeva', has attempted to challenge some of the pieties of feminism. Her stance is one of intervention, and her work should be read as a text in process where the last words reconstruct the meanings of what was said before. What is of interest is not whether her writings will stand the test of time, but what they tell us about the political conjunctures in which they were produced. Can one make sense of their popularity and dispersal among women in view of their antagonistic position?

European fascism is the signifier around which Kristeva's texts converge. She has continually revised her polemic which now extends to a critique of marxism as well. In many respects her texts have been misread by Anglo-Saxon cultures where parliamentary democracy operates differently from European political engagement and confrontation of the Left and Right. Aspects of her work have certainly been misappropriated by the *avant-garde* faction in the U.S. women's movement. (A rare exception is the recent critical response by Gayatri Spivak who gives Kristeva very short shrift indeed [*Critical Inquiry*, vol.9, no.2, September 1982, pp.269-72].) I shall attempt to contextualise Kristeva's Continental flair within Europe, and then to map her translation. British socialist feminists have contributed by being guarded in their response. Their caution has a history which is relevant to the politics of theory. A chart of Kristeva's discursive trajectory is of special interest since she has betrayed the small radical potential she once showed. Her latest book in English, *Powers of Horror: An Essay on Abjection* (New York: Columbia University Press, 1982) is the starting point of my critique.

It may be worth stating that I do not intend to suppress the history of my writing of this paper: a draft was presented at the Essex Conference in a session where three women, with links to Amherst, used Kristeva in their arguments. Retroactively. the session was named 'the Kristeva session', although it had not been consciously planned as such, and nor had there been communication beforehand on this topic by the panelists.

Kristeva featured in Toril Moi's paper, and did emerge as a focus of feminist attention at the conference. This was as symptomatic as it was inevitable in view of the vogue. The debates at the conference have influenced sections of the paper written after the event. An edited form of this piece was commissioned as a book review for the *Village Voice Literary Supplement* (*VLS*). I have retained my voice of a South African/ British feminist in the U.S. as a pedagogic device for the sake of American students who are not aware of the British discussions. I have chosen not to fictionalise the place from which I speak this paper and I have left in the racy colloquialisms of the conference talk and of journalese on purpose. The effect, I hope, will be to communicate the flavour of Kristeva's latest book, since my language is a conscious pastiche of her style and concerns. I have minimised the scholarly apparatus on this occasion and I supply a selected bibliography of her work in English to which I refer. Rather than split academic hairs, I decided to make an example of Kristeva since I believe it will be instructive for a feminist politics of theory.

Julia Kristeva, like Alice in Wonderland, has stepped through the looking-glass. What she finds behind is her self, reflected in Louis Ferdinand Céline's abject image of womanhood:

Women, you know, they wane by candle-light, they spoil, melt, twist, and ooze! ... The end of tapers is a horrible sight, the end of ladies too, ...

This new book, *Powers of Horror*, collaborates with Céline's misogyny. Absolutely spellbound, Kristeva does not distance the reader from his 'derisive femininity', but emits a gruesome new theory of abjection which is supposed to suck us in. Bow down to the Powers of Horror!

Kristeva should know better than to dispense her former Leftist followers this fascination with oppression. She once was a fugitive from subjugation in all its forms. A cosmonaut of theory, her intellectual jetsetting began in Bulgaria from where she fled to France. She thought she had escaped the monologue of social fascism for the dialogue between Marx and Freud in post-68 France. After she had caught up with what had happened in de Gaulle's Parisian capital, where the riots of '68 had led to a Renaissance in Radical Theories, Kristeva soon became bored with what she called French 'predictability' and she began to look farther afield. In search of an 'anarchic outbreak within Marxism', she came up with nothing less than Chinese women. Roland Barthes, who accompanied her on her trip to China in 1974, soon lost patience with her misguided venture, but she was to write a book, *About Chinese Women* (1977). In China, it appears that she found little more than a repetition of Stalinism which she thought she had abandoned in Bulgaria.

After cruising through Mao's China, she arrived wide-eyed in - of all places - New York, in 1977. Away from the lassitude of Paris, and from the fetters of Peking, she said that she now appreciated the democratic pluralism of the U.S. Despite the resilient way in which American capitalism is able to recontain everything radical, she was knocked out by New York's ethnic differences and by the *avant-garde* 'underground' she happened to encounter in Soho's arty lofts. Liberated from restrictive dialogue, she coined the term '*polylogue*' to describe the cultural Babel. She expressed her bizarre excitement with passion: 'I felt as though I were in the catacombs of the early Christians'(!). She thought she had found the future of the Revolution in the perverse and polymorphous freedoms of New York. She had finally arrived in the Bagel capital of Frenchified manners. Kristeva, the *parvenue* of theoretical ideas, the late-starter, here confused the carnival of sexual revolution with the artifices of Disneyland - her naïve gesture was appealing but ominous. Her serious misreading of power in the U.S. surprised some of her followers who reserved judgement, waiting to see where her belated tripping would take her next. Her itinerant flirtations with different modes of production - from the Asiatic to the Post-industrialist - had indeed prepared the ground for this her latest book: *Powers of Horror* is a realisation of her readers' worst fears.

There are three main divisions in this book: an outline of 'abjection'; a review of traditional anthropology and of the Old and New Testaments; and another critique of Céline. The text, despite appearances, has no system and the three parts have no linking rationale. The book is no more than a series of different essays, cobbled together, without any sign of logic. The logic was imposed retroactively when, after the publication of the book in France in 1980, she published an essay on abjection (*Tel Quel*, 91, Spring 1982, pp.17-32). This revisionary essay clarifies some of the strange thinking in the introduction to the book, 'Approaching Abjection', and it might have been included as an Appendix to this English translation.

What on earth is 'abjection'? Her new theory requires some labours of explanation. Kristeva argues throughout that she is taking leave of her masters, Freud and Lacan, in order to explore her recently conquered realm of abjection. Not subjection, or objection, but Abjection. In a flight of fancy which now has become increasingly familiar to her readers, she decides to territorialise a new zone of the unconscious, where the self is an abject, instead of a subject or object. She thinks this condition can explain why it is we love to hate. She invents this incredible foreign location of abjection in the same way as she discovered a New York which most New Yorkers would not recognise. This happy state of being abject is what she calls a form of borderline psychosis. Kristeva, whose latest profession is practising psychoanalysis, returns - with a vengeance - to Freud. She defines borderline psychosis in classic terms, as a state where the analysand takes all language quite literally - metaphorical symbols and real events or things become indistinguishable for this patient. In this scenario, say, castration is believed really to occur. She adds that borderline psychosis is the condition of artistic discourse and thus she, like all poets, is psychotic. Abjection leads to writing and creativity:

> Contrary to hysteria, which brings about, ignores, or seduces the symbolic but does not produce it, the subject of abjection is eminently productive of culture. Its symptom is the rejection and reconstruction of languages.

Her new theory, it can be argued, also shares in the borderline psychosis she defines, since she misreads Lacan, and takes both him and Freud quite literally! In doing so, she qualifies herself clinically as a borderline psychotic - an abject, according to the rules of her couch game.

Kristeva's new theory of abjection also reinforces traditional patriarchal and sexist notions about the repulsiveness of the female body. That man is always fascinated with it, we know. But do we have to give him terrible realist reasons for his repulsion and to justify and titillate his distaste by spreading the viscous sight across the page? Kristeva recalls that Céline devoted his doctoral thesis (1924) to the early obstetrician, Ignaz Semmelweis, a specialist in puerperal fever - the infection which develops during childbirth. She deciphers Céline's identification with the Hungarian doctor who practised in Vienna in the middle of the 19th century:

A foreigner, a solitary, on the fringe of the profession, insane in the end, persecuted by everyone, the inventor of obstetric hygiene, had what it takes to fascinate not only those suffering from obsessions but, more deeply, those who fear decay and death at the touch of the feminine.

Kristeva writes that the abject is a compound of abomination and fascination, sex and murder, attraction and repulsion. The pinnacle of abjection, she claims, is Céline's prostitute, with the bleeding sore of her loving body reduced to a wound in the ass. She quotes Céline: '"She was pulling at her dressings, she was chucking them all around, all over the floor, cotton, bandages, shreds ... Boy, what laughing in the joint".'

Kristeva is here adding to her earlier opinions of Céline in *Polylogue* (1977), and much of this new theory is a tedious repetition of arguments in *La révolution du langage poétique* (1974). *Powers of Horror* not only repeats the ideas of her earlier writings, but these now assume rather curious proportions in the light of her newest book. A short survey of her past work may situate her new theory and illuminate her aberrations ahead.

Once an eminent post-structuralist, Kristeva's analytic instruments, like some other recent gods and goddesses, have failed. After the delirium of structuralist science, the radical chic tools of semiology have come under criticism for their complacent claims to truth and objectivity. Kristeva's own peculiar version, '*sémanalyse*', has not worn well, and has not protected her from the generalised Nietzschean crisis in reason of the late 70s (represented mainly by the work of Deleuze and Guattari). Her semiology was unable to deliver us from the Horrors of Power, so she might as well join up with the schizopoliticians and talk about the Powers of Horror. Her latest book is no horrid echo of Sade, no cheap sado-maso job, but a serious essay, with come-on chapters like 'Something To Be Scared Of', and 'Suffering and Horror'. (Other titles are ripped off from the anthropologist, Mary Douglas's book, *Purity and Danger: An analysis of the concepts of pollution and taboo* (1966): for example, 'From Filth to Defilement' and 'Semiotics of Biblical Abomination'.) Whenever theory is used to explain the repellent, it runs the risk of promoting it.

In contrast with her earlier work, *Powers of Horror* also shows that she has taken leave of her feminist senses. She once looked as if she would chart new directions in feminist theory with her notion of the 'semiotic'. She departed from orthodox linguistics and stretched her models by developing a radical theory of female carnival from the Soviet semiotician Bakhtin's reading of Dostoyevsky. She got away with her explanation of how a literary text is feminised and ruptured by its internal carnival or dialogic moments, and marxists soon adapted her theory of revolutionary poetic language in Mallarmé, Joyce, Artaud and Céline, to make sense of radical ruptures in unsovietised Europe. In the early 70s, she was associated with sensible models of signifying practice and production, even though her idiosyncratic definition of a female 'semiotic' was a little hard for conscientious semioticians to stomach. Kristeva had expanded the quite innocuous meaning of their term which refers to the production of meaning by a sign system, and had given it a special female, and oddly enough pre-linguistic content. For traditional semiotics, meaning is produced in the linguistic arena of symbol, but for Kristeva, the semiotic was linked to the rhythmic, gestural, non-verbal and pre-linguistic elements of the female body. Modernist male texts, she claimed, were revolutionised by the eruption of these so-called female elements.

It is this interest in female signification that has made Kristeva more recently the darling of the *avant-garde* in the U.S. women's movement.

In the marketplace of feminist ideas, the journal *Signs* has promoted her as a representative of the latest Parisian fashion. Kristeva's 'antifeminism' and 'gynocriticism' is placed alongside the more usual women's wares. Another journal of contemporary criticism, *Diacritics*, rarely fails to mention Kristeva somewhere. That essence of intellectual balance, *Critical Inquiry*, has also given space to her contentious views. With *Powers of Horror* topping the *VLS*'s alternative bestseller list, Kristeva's media exposure has never been higher, nor more puzzling since she hawks a brand of post-feminism which most socialist feminists in England regard with deep suspicion. Since 1978, a group of British socialist feminists of the no longer extant Marxist Feminist Literature Collective have been debating Kristeva's politics and possibilities for feminism. The verdict was not good and more recently, at a conference on *The Politics of Theory* at Essex University in 1982, her dubious case was re-opened. Kristeva's work is no longer in women's interests.

Early on, it was apparent that her female semiotic was unacceptable to socialist feminists who feared her essentialism since she was advancing a theory which only with difficulty could be distinguished from reactionary views of the female body. By privileging the maternal uterus ('*chora*') as the site of production of revolutionary noises, Kristeva was positing the female body outside of social discourse. Traditional marxism is wary of giving value to an essence which pre-exists social intersubjectivity and it could not endorse a theory which suggested that the pre-constituted female body is able to interrupt social discourses. Instead, marxists argue that the female body is an effect of discourse and needs to be reconstructed through discourses which challenge and interrupt conventional sexist views of the body. They disagree with Kristeva's notion of liberation which implies that there is a pre-existent and already fully constituted female subject inside dying to get out. Socialist feminists argue that the new woman is an effect of new social discourses and practices which re-articulate common-sense notions of femininity. Besides, Kristeva's celebration of irrational female elements smacked of proto-fascism. Even socialist feminists did not always detect Kristeva's fascist whispers which in this latest book have become a primal scream.

Kristeva has also abandoned her former feminist stance by returning wholeheartedly to Freud. Her re-assertion of Freudian orthodoxies ignores the way feminists in psychoanalysis have criticised Freud's legacy. There is a sophisticated school of psychoanalytic theory in England, as represented by the journal *m/f*, and the work of Juliet Mitchell and Jacqueline Rose. Mindful of feminist responses to Lacan's revisions of Freud, they have explored the radical potential of Lacan's project. Kristeva has made the error of returning to Freud with a sincerity that outdoes Lacan's. Lacan returned to the master-text only to establish his own reading of Freud as the masterly one.

Kristeva re-cycled into Freudian orthodoxy is unaware of her own intertextuality in relation to Freud. She produced the concept of intertextuality in her early work in order to explain how a text is never self-sufficient, but always written in relation to a precursor text. This model itself is ultimately Oedipal, as Harold Bloom's *The Anxiety of Influence* (1974) can explain. In the early 70s, Kristeva was merely regarded as an intertextual structuralist who assaulted bourgeois original genius by showing his borrowings from other figures. The unconscious of her theory of intertextuality is now readable after abjection as just another version of Oedipus. How does Kristeva distinguish herself from Lacan and what does she add to Freud so that she can invent abjection?

Lacan returned to Freud as a strategy to deal with conservative ego psychologists who do not understand the revolutionary consequences of

Oedipus. Lacan's version of Freud is a theory of such intense subjective
alienation that it prevents one from ever assuming the coherence of a
unified self. Any deodorised version by ego psychology with its notion
of a fully integrated and normal self repudiates Lacan's Freud. For
Lacan, the mirror stage is the only moment in the subject's evolution when
there is a fiction of imaginary wholeness, where the other is mistaken for
the self. What Kristeva decides to do in her theory of abjection is to
get behind Lacan's mirror, to what she claims Freud named, but never
elaborated, primary identification. She complements Freud's theory, she
says, by calling this pre-subjective place, abjection. She returns
uncritically to Oedipus and takes literally Lacan's convenient mirror
metaphor. The effect of her literal reading - in keeping with borderline
psychosis - is that she gives Freud's text an empirical and 'scientific'
presence. Kristeva returns to Freud and so authenticates him, while
Lacan stages a return to Freud and so explodes him.

In *Powers of Horror*, Kristeva treats Lacan's fictional scenario of
the mirror phase as if it were an empirical stage of the subject's development. At this moment, in Lacan's view, the subject has yet to become conscious of loss, of the separation from the mother and of the sacrificial
but symbolic law of castration. From Lacan's perspective, the imitation
of the mirroring other is narcissistically perfect. Yet for Kristeva,
this fabulous existential tale was not enough. She claims that Lacan's
mirror phase, like Freud's secondary identification, can be substituted
by something even more ecstatic and perfect, primary identification where
the body is abject, rather than caught in the web of intersubjectivity as
subject or object. As abject, the body waits in suspense for the paternal
metaphor, daddy of the ideal-ego. What Kristeva's embroidered story does
not acknowledge is that it is itself yet another story, a retroactive
fiction which her theory rewrites after the assumption of identity, in
order to compensate for the painful process of becoming a social self.
Lacan's lesson is that this self is fragmented, and that it can only 'know'
the origin it seeks, after it has become a so-called self, that is, retroactively. What Kristeva does is present this nostalgic prior space of
abjection as if it is a real place in the evolution of the ego and as if
it can be re-presented objectively in language. She does not apparently
realise that her realism is misplaced, or that she has invented this wonderful abject terrain in language. There is no such space as abjection,
it is nothing more than a discursive effect, the result of her wild imagination. What her newest theory gives the reader is an alternative myth
of coherence to that of Lacan. She presents an utterly selfish wholeness
which dispenses with his mirror metaphor and takes itself quite literally.

Where is the reality of the abject found? Kristeva claims here and
elsewhere that literature is the site *par excellence* of abjection, which
is a euphemism for incest. If you are sufficiently oedipalised to want
to screw a certain woman known as mommy, then write from your imaginary.
Give her your text as a substitute for her castrated phallus and restore
your umbilical loss by reconstructing the imaginary conditions of abjection. Back to the womb where you were wholly mommy and phallic mommy was
wholly you. For Kristeva, the writer is one who separates, like the
father, at the same time as he touches, like the son and lover, even
taking the place of the feminine. She claims that the text is a more or
less satisfactory fetish because of its undecidability - one need never
assume a gendered identity - gender can simply be written away. This is
the land of abject opium eaters where ambivalence is a way of life which
avoids the neurosis of socialisation, of separation and of identity.
Abjection re-incorporates the neurotic into the sanity of the womb.
Kristeva calls society paranoid and with her theory of abjection exchanges
history for carnival and stamps on memory.

The anthropological dimension of her analysis sits very uneasily on her Lacanian introduction. After her adventure in psychoanalysis, Kristeva then à la Lévi-Strauss and Mary Douglas tells us how she sees horror in the raw. On her long voyage to the end of this dreadful night, when she goes where she thinks Freud has never been, she decides to augment her version of purified Freud with a dirty and dangerous (literary) supplement. She asks: 'Why does corporeal waste, menstrual blood and excrement, or everything that is assimilated to them, from nail-parings to decay, represent - like metaphor that would have become incarnate - the objective frailty of the symbolic order?' Unless one thinks Freud was literal about his Totems and Taboos, her fascination with repulsion is too full of gory details to have any theoretical status. She describes with relish how the subject gives birth to himself,

... by fantasizing his own bowels as the precious fetus of which he is to be delivered; and yet it is an abject fetus, for even if he calls them his own he has no other idea of the bowels than one of abomination, which links him to the ab-ject, to that non-introjected mother who is incorporated as devouring, and intolerable. The obsession of the leprous and decaying body would thus be the fantasy of a self-rebirth on the part of a subject who has not introjected his mother but has incorporated a devouring mother.

All then is not so beautiful in her vision which has faltered and tripped over the obscene body of the mother. Mommy is also a Monster. She is difficult to grasp because she is divided into good and bad. This split (theorised by Melanie Klein) is symbolised, for Kristeva, by the pregnant woman who is both self and other. The uncanny slippage of her identity makes the domestic figure of homeliness frightening, and ultimately a paradox, unhomely. For Freud, the term '*Unheimlich*', translated as 'the uncanny' sums up the experience of oscillating between the familiar and the terrifyingly exotic. Such is mommy whom we both love and hate. The site of mommy's hideous castration - the narcissistic scar - is what Kristeva claims is her power. This is the horror which exercises power, the power of her little horror.

Kristeva's neo-orthodox Freudianism has grave consequences for socialist and feminist politics. She never challenges the way the self is constituted in patriarchal society, but formally legitimises the classical Freudian model. Rather than being interested in why her authors return to mother, we should ask why Kristeva condones this homesickness. Instead of questioning the kindergarten of Oedipus, or of rewriting the history of a long mistake, she reinforces the myth of Oedipus. Female subjugation to phallic Law is naturalised and made to seem inevitable.

When Céline catches sight of his mommy's mess, he displaces his desire onto foreigners, and Kristeva writes: 'A ballerina is the most perfect example of it, preferably a foreigner - the opposite of the mother language, without language if need be, all sensitivity and acrobatics.' It is Céline who gives birth to Kristeva, the voyeur of foreign parts. She quotes from a letter of Céline in the chapter, 'Those Females Who Can Wreck The Infinite':

And a pagan on account of my absolute adoration of physical beauty, of health - I hate sickness, penance, morbidity - ... madly in love - I say, in love - with a four-year-old girl at the height of gracefulness and blond beauty and health - ... America! the feline nature of its women! ... I would give all of Baudelaire for an olympic swimmer! There's not a penny's worth of rapist in me - but I am a voyeur to the death!

Pederasty creeps in during this regression to abjection because, Kristeva states, the body of the child defers man's abject encounter with the feminine sex. In the child, she claims, the sexual component, being everywhere, is actually nowhere. The pre-pubescent child is therefore safe for the voyeur, her genitals are made invisible by this naïve theory of abjection. Kristeva finds that Céline has manufactured a French version of Lewis Carroll's Alice - a carnivalesque counterpart in the abject wonderland. Kristeva thinks that her own and her author's aggressive writing will turn incest inside out and bankrupt the power of the father. Carnival is supposed to be a cover-up of incest, 'when the sister becomes her brother's daughter' - an indefinite journey into the blue. But Kristeva fails to orphan the unconscious and she is still boxed in by Oedipus.

Kristeva justifies male abhorrence at the sight of the female genitals. She endorses his ghastly phallic fear instead of digging it out at its root. It is only in a culture where Freudianism is hegemonic that her defence makes any sense: the reason why the phallus is elevated to the status of a privileged mark of sexual difference is that orthodox Freudianism does not challenge the concept of 'disavowal'. For Freud, disavowal is the turning away from the terrible sight of castration which produces ambivalence. The sexual pleasure in looking, Freud's '*Schaulust*', includes the meaning of being afraid to look at what one sees, of being ashamed of it. An acceptance of the truth of disavowal leads to the domination of the phallus in western culture: the phallus becomes the only measure of genitality, not simply one of the marks of sexual difference along with breast, beard, clitoris, etc. Kristeva reproduces Freud's boring hierarchy in her map of male sexual disgust - Freud's cynical 'a hole is a hole'. She is not aware of the overriding phallocentrism of her theory. Her prose keeps us women down ... under. She rips the scar open, instead of showing that it doesn't exist except in the male imaginary of erectile tumescent presences. We can do without her surgery, or even without her deft needlework when she tries to use her ambiguous words to sew together the gaping abject wound.

For an ambiguous word to mean several things at once is not news to masters of irony. That the word '*propre*' in French, connotes both 'clean' and 'own' should not have presented problems for the translator, Roudiez, who hints that English may not be as rich in connotations as French. If Kristeva told him that she meant both, then he has no need to apologise for a cumbersome instead of a narrow and anchored translation. What does warrant apology is Kristeva's mania for cleanliness, which like the 'housewife psychosis' of Dora's mother in Freud's case history, leads to aberration. Kristeva states blandly that Céline causes the abject to exist in his prose. Exactly! His discourse produces horror, rather than reflects it as she is wont to imply. She complains that Céline doesn't clear up his mess. But then nor does she. All women, writes Céline, are housemaids at heart. In her efforts not to make her psychoanalysis the 'housemaid of psychiatry' (Freud), Kristeva venerates the abject. She writes that 'urine, blood, sperm, excrement ... show up in order to reassure a subject that is lacking its "own and clean self". The abjection of those flows from within suddenly become the sole "object" of sexual desire ...'. Kristeva over-compensates with filth. A critique of the dualist structure of Kristeva's thought is not necessarily moralistic or puritanical. It simply points out that her ambivalence is neurotic, since her dichotomy of abjection - the oscillation between subject and object; murder and sex; abomination and fascination - is a Freudian paradigm for neurosis.

To oppose Oedipus is to transcend Freud and to show the way desire can be produced without Oedipus. Oedipus is just another legend in a set of many, whereas Anti-Oedipus demolishes Oedipus's claim to encompass the whole production of desire. For Kristeva, Oedipus is the only bedtime story she knows how to tell ... I mean, watch. Her brand of voyeuristic masochism doesn't explode the boundaries of gendered identity, as a more radical recipe might - it simply confirms woman's time and woman's limits. Kristeva's writing is fetishistic, that is, it is a substitute object which aims at replacing the 'lost' phallus in the form of a phallus. Her phallomorphic text may make the law of castration universal for all genders, but it still confirms rather than questions that Law.

Kristeva's intellectual and political 'smut' is no direct challenge to the pure and normal male world. It is so predictable that it doesn't raise any questions about what we already know. Freud gave us an adequate anatomy of the laws of patriarchal society and its effects on the structures of the unconscious. That patriarchy stinks does not mean that Freud's theory does. But unlike Kristeva, feminists should aim to theorise beyond Freud, and as a consequence, eventually beyond the likes of her.

The latest Kristeva is not interested in explaining the way meanings are produced according to marxist paradigms, nor in advancing a politics of rupture as were her earlier selves. Instead, she has finally chosen mysticism as the route out of the endless dichotomies of Hegelian thought with its oppositions between slave and master, and attraction and repulsion. Kristeva's major focus on Céline in *Powers of Horror* leads nowhere. She whitewashes him in her chapter, 'Neither Actor nor Martyr'. It won't be the last time that the so-called modernist *avant-garde* will be mistaken for the voice of Revolution. Whilst none of us wants to be a vulgar marxist, one cannot but reduce Céline to the race and class moments of his texts. Céline, the proto-fascist Jewbaiter and quintessential modernist, may well be textualising his mother's body in prose, but he certainly is not a revolutionary in any radical language of desire. In the chapter, 'Ours to Jew or Die', Kristeva perverts the futurist faith in spontaneous action which inspired the fascist *squadristi*. She lends their devil-may-care attitude (*menefreghismo*) a sordid credence. Céline's political pamphlets, when read in a 1980s context, may seem to be divorced from the social conditions which led to their emergence and which made their racist programme possible. But if one considers the historical place of production of these anti-semitic writings, one cannot miss the signs to the factories of genocide. Forty years on, in post-modernist modernity, their fascist edges are blunted but they are not revolutionary documents by any means, despite Kristeva's efforts. She tries to displace attention from his politics to the quality of his war chronicles.

She portrays Céline as the greatest hyper-realist of war and massacre since all his narratives converge on scenes of death - his *Bagatelles for a Massacre* (1937). He does not give news accounts, she enthuses, but 'a vertiginous, apocalyptic, and grotesque evocation of ecstasy before death'. One gets the eerie feeling that she might have liked a peep-hole to the gas-chambers, when she writes:

> Céline tracks down, flushes out, and displays an ingrained love for death, ecstasy before the corpse, the other that I am and will never reach, the horror with which I communicate no more than with the other sex during pleasure, but which dwells in me, spends me, and carries me to the point where my identity is undecidable.

She seems to gain considerable pleasure from the holocaust echoes in a harrowing passage of dismemberment in Céline's *Death on the Instalment Plan* (1936):

> He sticks his finger into the wound ... He plunges both hands
> into the meat ... he digs into all the holes ... He tears
> away the soft edges ... He pokes around ... He gets stuck ...
> His wrist is caught in the bones ... Crack! ... He tugs ...
> He struggles like in a trap ... Some kind of pouch bursts ...
> The juice pours out ... it gushes all over the place ... all
> full of brains and blood ... splashing.

Stuck in her abyss of abjection, and attracted by the ritual soilings, Kristeva cannot make head or tail of this all. She has no political or ideological bearings when faced with Céline's cadaver. She actually states that she is choosing the literary over the ideological, and one must wonder if she really thinks they can be separated like this. She adds that she does not think social realism is up to describing horror. She forgets her Reich, and even our Sontag, in her hypnotic and nauseating fascination with fascism. In the wish for apocalypse now, she preaches catastrophe and the conflagration of all ideologies - as if any traveller can get beyond the gravity of her own. In Kristeva's case, her ideology does not vanish but evidently pulls her down. She gets tied into knots when she tries to separate her own irrationalities from fascism's. With the evil of banality, she associates castration with fascism and talks about the way Fascism and Nazism tapped an economy of suffering. With nothing new to say, she asserts that fascism was not touched by theory or reason. Well nor is she here.

Kristeva's naturalistic regression to the maternal space duplicates fascism's refusal to deal with history, difference or dynamism in any other terms except repression. Her chapter, 'In the Beginning and Without End' is a signal of the way history is excluded from the fascist social utopia. The populist discourse of fascism gives an illusion of national unity. Kristeva's abject illusion of wholeness of self is just as grandiose as Mussolini's equation of fascist Italy with glorious ancient Rome - her social paranoia is clear. By exploiting vulgar Freudianism to talk about fascism, she is oedipalising the reader and author to fantasise not being oedipalised: this contradiction requires the law of Oedipus to make it meaningful. Her rhythm is circular, not liberatory. Her reaction against the totalising Oedipal triangle only serves to reconfirm the privileged status of its psychic totalitarianism. She is ambivalent and has no political directions, no tactics to adopt. Her radical war is over and she no longer markets a ruptural strategy but stands and gapes at the culture of narcissism.

Not only has she done a complete disservice to Freud and Lacan in *Powers of Horror*, but she has also parted ways with French feminists and the former comrades, Foucault and Derrida. The latter have remained in touch with revolutionary and feminist principles even if they have reconstituted and deconstructed their sanctities along the way. Foucault and Derrida don't tour totalitarianisms on the lookout for socialist examples - they are their own example of a radical discursive practice. Their analysis stays political, not moral as Kristeva's has become. She unwittingly has now joined the ranks of the French New Philosophers, grouped round Glucksmann and Bernard-Henri Lévy whose book, *Barbarism with a Human Face* (1977), has become a cult for the renegades from Communism. They adopt a wishywashy humanism, since they believe that 'without a certain idea of man the State soon surrenders to the whirlpool of fascism'. Yet to be an 'anti-barbarian intellectual' does not mean that you are civilised. That there is widespread discontent with the 'fragile and uncertain tools with which to decide political questions' also does not mean that we should all become writers of treatises on ethics, as Lévy recommends. What does Kristeva's new position lead to? Her passage to the New Philosophers' camp erases her as a viable political guide and results in a general intellectual scandal, when one considers her early radical promise. This crisis is not hers alone, but is the crisis in historical materialism. In this regard, we learn that Kristeva's *Powers of Horror* has nothing to say.

Kristeva has now taken up her place on the list of radical disaffections which have resulted from so-called Soviet 'confrontations'. Events like Afghanistan and Poland rock the nuclear missiles in their silos, and produce radical wills and testaments. Like Susan Sontag before her, and Nadine Gordimer after, Julia Kristeva has come out against Communism which she also mistakes for Fascism with a Human Face. Sontag plans to rewrite the history of the Left - whatever's left - and Gordimer swops her novels for a long and eloquent essay on the morbid symptoms of living in the Interregnum, between capitalism and communism, in *The New York Review of Books* (vol.xxix, nos.21 and 22, January 20 1983).

Milan Kundera, the Czechoslovak favourite of both Sontag and Gordimer, writes that Marxism is not a belief, but a pragmatic device, that is, a revisionary practice. As a belief, it is doomed and bound to disappoint. They may have missed his point. Debates about Marxism are relative to whether one is a casualty of capitalism or not. If, say, one is a Black South African, then capitalism signifies Barbarism with a Pale Face. Sontag, Gordimer and Kristeva have no real scars to bind - they have yet to learn to struggle.

In *Powers of Horror*, Kristeva has told a mean tale, full of sound and fury, not signifying nothing (for how could it?), but of negligible significance unless you have a taste for neo-orthodoxies and for hob-nobbing with dissidents. What is instructive is not the story she tells, but her telling the story now. *Powers of Horror* is written for those who are so ambivalent about politics that they get off (*jouissance!*), like Kristeva says she does, 'dancing on a volcano'. Her political confusions blow her text apart. Her contemplation of the sublime beauty of literature - as she puts it - will never cancel out our existence as political beings. The struggle against power, writes Kundera, is the struggle of memory against forgetting. In laying bare the powers of horror, Kristeva has forgotten power's horrors. Our task still is to transform the Horrors of Power.

SELECTED BIBLIOGRAPHY OF BOOKS AND ARTICLES

IN ENGLISH BY KRISTEVA

Books

About Chinese Women (London, Marion Boyars, 1977).

Desire in Language: A Semiotic Approach to Literature and Art, edited by L. S. Roudiez (New York, Columbia University Press, 1980).

Articles

J. Kristeva, M. Pleynet and P. Sollers, 'The U.S. Now: A Conversation', *October* 6, Fall 1978, pp.3-17.

'Women's Time', *Signs*, vol.7, no.1, Autumn 1981, pp.13-55.

'Psychoanalysis and the Polis', *Critical Inquiry*, vol.9, no.2, September 1982, pp.77-92.

THE MOTHER TONGUE

Jane Gallop

I have come to England to speak about my book. An apparently simple statement of purpose for a somehow terrifying task. England may be precisely where it is impossible to speak of my book, to speak of that book as mine.

'My book': the phrase reeks of possession, self, identity, property. I choose to speak of 'my book' although such a gesture seems wrong or lazy, finally self-indulgent, self-involved. Self-involvement seems particularly suspect in a Marxist context: seems bourgeois, seems American. Yet it just might be that the self which would possess this book is most effectively called into question through the agency of something I could call England (or maybe even Marxism, but hopefully I will get to that).

Certainly, in order to move beyond possession, I should use the title and avoid referring to 'my book'. Yet that is no easy gesture, but rather takes me to the heart of my difficulty. My book has two different names. In Great Britain it is called *Feminism and Psychoanalysis*; in America its title is *The Daughter's Seduction*. The American title is the British subtitle and vice versa. I named the book *The Daughter's Seduction*. My British editors changed it, against my wishes. The American editors, who bought the book from the English press, changed the title back, without consulting me.

Except for the title page and cover the two editions are identical. The American book thus actually has two titles: one on the cover and title page; the other in the running heads at the top of each page. Even in the British version there is some slight question about the title. In the introduction, in either edition, there are three mentions of the book's title, all in italics. The first two call the book *Psychoanalysis and Feminism*; the third refers to it as *The Daughter's Seduction*.

The book comes back home to America, bearing the name I gave it, and yet, now, that very name has become somehow alien, marked by difference, no longer the book's title, but the book's American title, carrying, for me, always a thought of the difference between England and America, the return of a difference never adequately recognized.

Were the difference simply understood as representing two countries, that would ultimately be assimilable to, easily represented by the standard concept of foreignness, by the familiar move which projects anxiety about self-boundaries into xenophobia. According to Freud, projection is a gesture by which internal disturbances are perceived as originating externally because it is easier to defend against external threat. The difference between the American and English editions is a blatant, histrionic version of some quieter internal difference. In any edition, the book has, in some small way, two different titles, an internal disturbance to identity, which is most comfortably represented by mapping it onto the space between England and America.

In order to talk about the agency of England upon my book, let me here introduce the Lacanian terms 'imaginary' and 'symbolic'. When I consider a book to be commanded by its author's conscious intentions, that is an imaginary construction of writing. In the imaginary register, I might talk about my book, might consider it my possession, would presume it said what I intended it to say, that I generated and authorized its meaning. In that imaginary register I would resent, be angered by, and oppose any alienation of my book, any violation of my intentions, any understanding which considered the book to signify other than what I intended. However, when a book is published, in the public domain, its meaning cannot be commanded by the author, but is at large, abroad, in circulation. This is what Jacques Lacan calls the symbolic order. In the symbolic order the author is one reader among others. Her reading may be better than most, better than any other, but it is not definitive.

It might even be said that the violation of authorial intention which inevitably accompanies circulation of the work can operate as a means for the author to get at what she cannot hear, what she is blocked from receiving because of the self's defensive borders, what is unavailable to her through the agency of the wish to call the book 'mine'. The intrusion of otherness into one's discourse produced by publication might function according to a psychoanalytic model. The subject must come to recognize his own drives which are insisting unbeknownst to him, in his discourse. That recognition is reached through the mediation of the analyst's interventions into his discourse. Breaking up my imaginary embrace of my book, what I have called England represents the site of the intrusion of the symbolic order.

What has this to do with feminism? With women? Women, in a structuralist, feminist analysis, are seen to be 'in circulation'. Lévi-Strauss sees society as an exchange of women, and calls this the symbolic order. Men exchange women. Feminism has decried our alienation, our expropriation into circuits of exchange. Feminists have demanded control, autonomy over our bodies, our selves. Our outrage is not unlike that an author feels when his book is altered for and by the market.

In the Introduction I wrote: 'The notions of integrity and closure in a text are like that of virginity in a body. They assume that if one does not respect the boundaries between inside and outside, one is "breaking and entering", violating a property. As long as the fallacies of integrity and closure are upheld, a desire to penetrate becomes a desire for rape. I hope to engage in some intercourse with these textual bodies that has a different economy, one in which entry and interpenetration do not mean disrespect or violation because they are not based upon the myth of the book's or the self's or the body's virginal wholeness. But rather upon the belief that, if words there be or body there be, somewhere there is a desire for dialogue, intercourse, exchange.'

The contribution of what has been called structuralist psychoanalysis has been to recognize the autonomous self as an illusion, as an imaginary function, whereas actually, or in the symbolic, the self is, from its very constitution, already alienated in an intersubjective network, a system of exchange, a kinship structure, a place in the public domain. The self is constituted, if we follow Lacan's notion of The Mirror Stage, as a fictional representation, always already altered through the mediation of the other's gaze. The self is constituted as an exchange value.

In Chapter 6, in a discussion of Luce Irigaray's *Ce Sexe qui n'en est pas un*, I wrote: 'assertion of one's uncontaminated selfhood is no practical way out of the circuit [of exchanges]. Alienation is the necessary obverse of the self's integrity. Violation would lose its meaning and its attraction were the body no longer represented as "virginal-solid-closed, to be opened with violence". The economy of phallic desire is subtended by a notion of woman as property belonging to the man whose name she bears, and the penetration of her? his? body is an act of breaking and entering. Even if a woman's body were her own, the problem/attraction of rape would not disappear. The social self (self tainted by the world) is grounded in the specular self (assumption of the fictionally solid, cohesive body - total shape, well-defined and firm). Alienation/violation cannot be avoided without calling into question the specular self, the fictional unity of the body. The answer to woman as property is not the restoration to woman of her body, her self.'

The difference between the imaginary fiction of a closed, autononomous self and the symbolic inscription of the subject in exchange, that difference which is internal to each subject, has been projected onto the difference between men and women. Women are exchanged, possessed; men appear to command that process. Yet a Lacanian reading could answer that we are all in exchange, no man is autonomous, and thus the female position is less illusory, less imaginary, closer to the structural human condition. Or to use a Lacanian turn of phrase: we are all castrated, whatever organs we might possess. This has, I believe, some affinities with a Marxist critique of the psychological self of bourgeois ideology. The subject is determined by his place in history, her relation to the means of production, rather than by individual, monadic psychology.

Whereas American ego psychology would hold up the autonomous self as ideal, thus making man, phallic man, the measure of all things; Lacanian psychoanalysis asserts the inevitability of castration, health as the assumption of castration, so making castrated woman, the subject always in exchange, in circulation, so making woman the measure of the human. A feminism based upon the autonomous self as ideal will believe the illusion of men's autonomy and will demand a like autonomy, uncontaminated selfhood, untainted by market economy, embracing man the measure. However, if feminism believes every subject is always in exchange, always in intersubjective chains, it will denounce the illusion of phallic autonomy and revalue woman's position, the position assigned women by projection, revalue traditional feminine psychology with its emphasis on connectedness rather than individualism. Which is not to say that woman should remain in an inferior position but that the inferiority of that position should be questioned. That we must expose and question a mechanism by which an internal threat to self is projected onto the difference between men and women.

What if rape itself, prime target of feminist outrage, were the projection of man's internal violation, of an internal sense of compromised self, which becomes projected in the violation of a woman, becomes externalized as an assertion of the opposition: autonomous male/expropriated female? Then the insistence upon woman's integrity, upon the sanctity of her bodily autonomy, could only fuel the anxiety about self-boundaries that makes a man want to violate the boundaries of the other.

Must we claim unalienated self, body, labor? Or should we rather denounce and undo the reigning illusion that projects alienation onto one class and represents and rationalizes another as in command?

In an attempt to assume that symbolic order, to affirm the inevitable alienation of my work, I would like to approach this book as reader, rather than author, to try to actually read it rather than presume I know what it says. My method of getting at it, the means of disrupting my complacent proprietary sense, is attention to that which surprises me, that which is not recognizably mine.

One word shocks me; one word is least receivable; one word, in fact one letter, most violates my command. In Chapter 6, in a parenthetical aside where I reflect upon my relationship to Irigaray, I read: 'Irigaray is not just my sister-rival; she is my Daddy, my Mummy. And when she is at her best ... I love her and get scared not knowing where the boundary lies between her and me.' 'Daddy', 'Mummy' are written with capital initials. Not objective kinship terms, they are the proper nouns by which the little girl calls her parents. Something infantile, primal, and familial erupts and disrupts the more theoretical, objective discourse. Yet the effect is, after all, willed, theatrical, controlled. The real uncanny is the word 'Mummy', the letter 'u' which changes the 'Mommy' I too cutely wrote to the British 'Mummy'. Into that most familiar parenthesis, parent-thesis, into that cozy, domestic aside, the foreign word intrudes.

Lacan relates the imaginary register to the pre-Oedipal, unmediated dyadic relation between infant and mother. In the Lacanian version of Oedipus, it is the symbolic order, the structure of language itself, which keeps the child and mother from merging. Lacan's third Oedipal term is not the real father, who might jealously prohibit the infant and mother's embrace, but the Name-of-the-Father, the name, even Mommy as name rather than bodily presence, the linguistic kinship structure which locates every term in intersubjective circuits of exchange. To have my most private name for my most primal other edited is to encounter the symbolic order which structures even the most intimate relations according to socioeconomic laws of exchange.

Once any dyadic relation is understood as between a self and an other, a me and a you, then the structures of differentiation, the structures of language, function as a third term defining the relation of the other two, defining infant and mother, speaker and addressee as me and you. The undifferentiated maternal body becomes the other, becomes the interlocutor, occupies the linguistic function of second person. Rather than a unique presence, the proper noun is reduced to the replaceable shifter 'you'. According to Lacan, the truth is to be found in the letter, even though the letter kills. The 'u' in 'Mummy' speaks the truth of kinship as interlocution and exchange even as it chills by replacing the close, warm body of the mother with a foreign corpse wrapped in the Oedipal bandages of language.

From the imaginary point of view, for Mommy to be mummified is an irrevocable tragedy, an irreparable loss. However the last sentence of the parenthesis reads 'I love her and get scared not knowing where the boundary lies between her and me.' The imaginary mode is not idyllic but terrifying, life-threatening. It is the symbolic order of differentiation, the loss of immediate bodily union with the mother, that allows the self to be in the world. To the extent that this is a plea for boundaries, even if a theatricalized plea, then the appearance of a foreign word, an opening into otherness and reminder of borders, represents a relief.

From the imaginary point of view, we assume that what the infant really wants is the inalienable possession of Mommy, the right to call her 'mine'. Perhaps this imaginary perspective is structurally, in the structures of our sexual dialectic, male. Freud says, in the New Introductory Lecture 'Femininity', that 'a boy's mother is the first object of his love and she remains so too ... in essence, all through his life.' 'Woman's destiny', I wrote in Chapter 5, 'is to become her husband's mother'. 'A marriage is not made secure', writes Freud in 'Femininity', 'until the wife has succeeded in making her husband her child as well and in acting as a mother to him.'

On the other hand, the little girl, early on, before her Oedipal moment, gives up her mother and transfers her love to her father. From a Lacanian perspective since the Oedipal father is not the real, but the name, could we not see this transfer as an embrace of the symbolic order? The little girl desires what I might call here the mummification of Mommy. That is, she seeks some mediating structure to allow her to differentiate her self, to limit and bind Mother and maintain her within bounds. The loss of Mommy is not a loss but a gain for it opens the closure of the family and lets in history, lets in the world.

My phrase 'I am scared not knowing where the boundary lies between her and me' prefigures Irigaray's *Et l'une ne bouge pas sans l'autre*, a little book I consider in Chapter 8, in which the narrator pleads with an interlocutor she calls 'Mother': 'Continue to be also outside ... I would so much like that we both be here. That the one does not disappear into the other or the other into the one.' In that same chapter, as a way of working through the paralysis of the mother-daughter relation, as a way of working beyond my fix on Irigaray, I introduce into the book Julia Kristeva and her consideration of the phallic mother. My discussion of Kristeva occasions the only other apparition of the uncanny 'Mummy'.

I wrote that Kristeva, in one of her articles, 'posits a continual, analytic vigilant dissidence to any order as the necessary position for the intellectual. In this context she speaks of exile as dissidence and goes on to consider exile a necessary condition to attain to the irreligious state from which one could always be in opposition to any homogenation. The exile, by being in the place where she is out-of-place, always represents a heterogeneous exception to the constitution of the homogeneous group. And of course, she reminds us "I speak a language of exile". Kristeva is a Bulgarian living, working and writing in France and in French.'

At this point in the chapter I nervously reflected on my relation to Kristeva the exile: 'I grope to assert my right to be a "dissident" without leaving my homeland and my native language, trying to arrange an interpretation of my position as one of exile too. Me too. Just like Mummy. My feminism and my psychoanalysis are French although I am American. My exile is even more profound because I speak a foreign language in my native language. America itself is become a foreign country for me.'

Language never is an expression of self: always alienated, it always derives from the place of the other. One could, then, say that the subject is always speaking a foreign language. Nonetheless, the subject has internalized the laws of his native language to the point of forgetting their extrinsic and arbitrary rule over him and his needs so that the experience of speaking a literally 'foreign' language can force the subject into an awareness of the symbolic dimension. The foreign exile is thus in a position to disrupt the closure of the imaginary order, of the homogeneous family, of bourgeois ideology, by recognizing and asserting the structuring grammar of exchange.

Although the speaker of a foreign language is in a position to remember the symbolic, a foreign language cannot insure one's dissidence. Speaking a foreign tongue, one is apt to believe that the relation to language would be different if only one could speak one's 'own' language. Just as the castration intrinsic to self is projected onto the difference between male and female; so the alienation structurally internal to language is projected onto the difference between foreign and mother tongue. In the sexual dialectic, woman must live the more radical, symbolic position, must live her self (and not the other) as in exchange, as castrated. The female, dissident position in the language dialectic would fall to the speaker who is forced to live her native language as foreign, who undergoes the linguistic mummification of Mommy.

There is, then, a remarkable consistency of purpose between my assertion of the foreignness of my mother tongue and the appearance of the word 'Mummy'. However, I am forced to notice that my experience of exile at home is not where I expected it, not where I planned and claimed it. I chose to locate my exile in the France in my America. But an exile can never be willingly chosen. The difference between French and English may be a more blatant, exotic, and ultimately more comfortable, version of a quieter difference internal to the English language. (Linguistically, can we ever forget either the Norman Conquest or the American Revolution?)

By emphasizing the opposition between France and America - French and American psychoanalysis, French and American feminism - this book avoids a more radical, because more intimate, foreignness, an alienation which I will momentarily locate in England inasmuch as England functions as a third term whose relation to the dyad France and America the book never confronts.

In the introduction I read: 'The fourth chapter returns to Lacan's twentieth seminar, this time reading it to the accompaniment of Stephen Heath's feminist critique ... A British reading of Lacan ... reimposes notions of the gap between Anglo-American and French feminism. Across this gap jumps the spark of desire that ignites *Feminism and Psychoanalysis*.'

The last sentence does not read right. Originally the sentence read: 'the spark of desire that ignites *The Daughter's Seduction*'. Desire might ignite a seduction, but could desire ignite 'Feminism and Psychoanalysis'? British intervention ruins the elaborate, sexy metaphor but may, after all, serve to avenge a violence quietly perpetrated in the preceding sentence: 'A British reading ... reimposes notions of the gap between Anglo-American and French feminism.'

In the flash of a sentence, 'British' becomes 'Anglo-American'. A hyphen silently plugs a gap. The broad Atlantic is as nothing as we pause to contemplate the width of the Channel. As the spark plug metaphor reminds us, a gap is necessary for desire. Desire, or difference, between England and America is blocked, barred, resisted. Assimilation makes exchange impossible.

From the beginning of this book, from the beginnings of the book, long before I came to England, long before I had an English editor, England posed a problem. The book begins, the book began, with a reading of Juliet Mitchell's *Psychoanalysis and Feminism*. On page 1 I wrote: 'Her boldness stands in fullest relief in America ... Following both the developments of psychoanalysis and the course of feminism peculiar to different countries, she sets up a "descending scale of opposition by feminists to Freud" and finds the greatest opposition in America, most interest on the continent, with England in between. So it seems fitting that Mitchell, one of England's best-known feminists, should take on the project of importing the continental feminist interest in Freud, in an effort to combat the American opposition to psychoanalysis.'

The first page clearly highlights Mitchell's position as English and contrasts it with the American position. Then in a sentence that bridges pages 1 and 2 we read: 'Although, at one point she mentions

Scandinavian feminists, she is, in fact, leaning not upon a general continental but upon a specifically French feminism.' It is thus not until the second page that French feminism, that France, is mentioned. The paragraph then concludes: 'Having based her undertaking upon a certain French feminism, Mitchell speaks up within the generally anti-Freudian atmosphere of English-speaking feminism ... for a serious reading of Freud.' Once France is introduced into the discussion, England and America are blithely merged into the amalgam 'English-speaking feminism', ignoring the distinctions clearly articulated on page 1, distinctions never again mentioned in this book.

My major objection to my British title is that I fear my book will be mistaken for Mitchell's. I had already entitled the first chapter simply 'Psychoanalysis and Feminism', in italics, naming the chapter after the book to which it is devoted. So now throughout the first chapter of what no longer feels quite like my book, at the top of the pages, I am met with a distressing specter. Above the left-hand sheets I read 'Feminism and Psychoanalysis': at the top of the right-hand pages is 'Psychoanalysis and Feminism'. I cannot immediately tell which is 'my' book, which belongs to 'the other woman'.

One side is the mirror-image of the other. Here then is the Mirror Stage of the book. The Mirror Stage, as Lacan describes it, is the moment of constitution of self through a process of anticipatory identification with a mirror-image or an alter ego. The as-yet-untotalized self anticipates its maturation through an identification with a totalized image. In this case, the nascent book constitutes itself through identification with the finished book. According to Lacan one of the traces of the specular constitution of the self-image is the reversal of left to right order in images of the double. Relations to the double, elaborates Lacan, are marked by aggressivity since the double threatens to expose the fictionality of identity, based as it is upon an alienated and premature identification.

Although I boldly admit my identifications and boundary confusions with such exotic continental figures as Irigaray and Kristeva, there is no such self-reflection upon Mitchell, only the mirroring imposed by the accidents of publication.

Another accident forces me out of my sphere, out of the reassuring confines of my imaginary. I am invited to a conference in England. I have much resistance to coming, approach with anxiety and ambivalence. I arrive in England via Paris, spending but a day there, for no good reason. Psychologically, it seemed easier to come to England if I went to Paris first, as if it were France that was closer to America.

What do I fear in England? What lurks here that threatens my imaginary mastery as author? I do not, of course, know. Reading my book cannot tell me that, since it is erected upon the *méconnaissance*, the misprision of England. I have come here to expose myself to an English difference; I have come here, full of trepidation, to lay myself open to your intrusion.

I do have one clue as to what England might represent. In a recently published article by Elaine Showalter called 'Feminist Criticism in the Wilderness', I read: 'English feminist criticism, which incorporates French Feminist and Marxist theory but is more traditionally oriented to textual interpretation is also moving toward a focus on women's writing. The emphasis in each country falls somewhat differently: English feminist criticism, essentially Marxist, stresses oppression: French feminist criticism, essentially psychoanalytic, stresses repression: American feminist criticism, essentially textual, stresses expression. All however, have become gynocentric.'

The paper I have just presented, like the book itself, is essentially textual and psychoanalytic, American and French in Showalter's geography. In my occlusion of England, of England as a difference, I have excluded Marxism, banished oppression, from my imaginary. What can I say about the relation of my work to Marxism? I am in no position to say anything. Yet I am in a position, here in England, at a Marxist conference, I am in a position where something must be said. I have placed myself in this position, in the hope, perhaps, that you will say something. If Marxism can intrude into the cozy dyad *Feminism and Psychoanalysis*, it will be, perhaps, through your intervention. If, as I said to begin, I have come to England to speak about my book, it was to speak in this context, in this intersubjective dialectic, to this interlocutor, to this other. I do not speak simply to express my 'self' and defend myself from your intrusion. To paraphrase *The Daughter's Seduction*: 'I hope to engage here in some intercourse that has a different economy, one in which entry and interpenetration do not mean disrespect and violation because they are not based upon the myth of the book's or the self's or the body's virginal wholeness. But rather upon the belief that, if I have come to England to speak about my book, somewhere there is a desire for dialogue, intercourse, exchange.'

KLEINIAN PSYCHOANALYSIS AND
THE THEORY OF CULTURE

Michael Rustin

The purpose of this paper is to explore the relevance of Kleinian and other object-relations theories in psychoanalysis to the understanding of culture. In particular, it will be argued that this psychoanalytic tradition can contribute to a socialist and humanist view of culture, and to its much-needed remaking after some years of fashionable theoreticist attack. (1)

One enters, in seeking to explore the relevance of psychoanalysis for cultural studies, a field already densely populated by impenetrable thickets of Lacanian interpretations of Freud, and their application to the theory of culture. One had hoped it would be possible to set out some clear comparison between absorption of Freud's work within this semiotic and post-structuralist debate, and work undertaken in recent years within the 'English school' of object-relations psychoanalysis, which has also given some attention to aesthetic matters. This turned out, however, to be easier said than done. There are many difficulties in understanding the work that is being done in cultural studies under the influence of Lacan, and while it may be useful to make some observations about it from my different perspective, it would be presumptuous to pretend that this is a thorough or rigorous critique. The fundamental difficulties stem from divergences in theoretical and philosophical presuppositions between the Lacanian reading of Freud and most psychoanalytic work undertaken in Britain. But since, in general, the opening of cultural theory in Britain to influence stemming from continental sources - structural linguistics, semiotic analysis, discourse theory - has been fruitful in opening new terrains to theoretical investigation, there is every reason to give close and receptive attention to the interpretation of psychoanalytic theory offered within this framework.

This is especially the case given that this 'reading' of Freud appears to fill a number of important gaps within the theoretical debate. The problem Freud's work seems to address in such a richly textured way is the construction of the individual subject through cultural discourse. It offers the promise of doing this in a way which can escape an unwelcome polarity: on the one hand the reduction of the individual to a point of intersection of social roles, a mere bearer of social forces. Such a sociologically determinist view of the individual is particularly difficult to sustain in the field of cultural studies, where so much emphasis is traditionally given to the individual particularity of experience, sensibility, etc., though this has not impeded valiant efforts by Marxist structuralists to attempt just this reduction. On the other hand, the Lacanian reading of Freud also appears to escape the problems of positing a 'human nature', whose fixity and universality would then contradict the whole programme of demonstrating the historical and social construction of culture, and of the subject itself. In this reading of Freud both the

---

I would like to thank for their written comments on this paper, Ian Craib and Margot Waddell.

'subject' and 'culture', both the individual and society, are problematised. The subject is seen, following Freud, as a script in continuous process of articulation, a point of contact between an unconscious nature and the only partially definitive constraints of culture and language. And while in this reading some elements of 'culture' can be seen as repressive and ideological representations of a supposedly 'natural' subjectivity, other kinds of cultural work can be seen to reflect upon cultural codes themselves, to disrupt through contradiction and polyvalency, and to make unconscious desire available to reflection and thus, perhaps, political action.

It is the convergence discovered between Freud's account of the transformations of unconscious thought through 'condensation' and 'displacement' in *The Interpretation of Dreams* (Harmondsworth, 1976) and the structuralist account of the basic figurative elements in language and literature, defined by Jakobson as metaphor and metonymy, which has made possible this programme of a parallel analysis of subject and culture, since the same mechanisms appear to be involved in the formation of both. Lacan's formulation 'the unconscious is structured like a language' asserts this dependence of inmost subjectivity on the cultural process, just as the converse programme of psychoanalytic investigation of culture asserts the unconscious (or desire-rooted) dimensions of culture. The earlier concerns of 'Marxist psychoanalysis' are absorbed into this new discourse, in the sense that there is still beneath the texture of cultural analysis an idea of infinite desire blocked and repressed by social arrangements, while the Oedipus Complex is seen in this new account particularly as a mechanism of reproduction of patriarchy.

One problem in relating Lacanian work to the object-relations tradition is their different philosophical presuppositions. One of Lacan's main tasks was the naturalisation of Freud's work within a predominantly Hegelian and post-Hegelian philosophical tradition. Since Freud's work was not originally conceived in these terms, there is a double problem of translation: first that undertaken by Lacan, and second that undertaken by those seeking to understand Lacan's work from a British cultural setting largely shaped by empiricism. Desire is an example of a concept which in the orthodox psychoanalytical tradition has rather concrete empirical referents (signifying states of feeling or instinct, and their imagined or real objects), but which, as Lacan's Hegelian version of the id, becomes a more abstract disposition. It did not need the particular indulgences and difficulties of Lacan's personal style to make this philosophical recoding of psychoanalysis a daunting task.

There is, however, something rather extraordinary about an attempt made to incorporate Freud's work into cultural theory in England which almost exclusively relies on this double transformation, while largely avoiding direct acquaintance with psychoanalytic work undertaken in Britain in the same fifty year period. Even more odd is the fact that this British 'object-relations' work has had some influence on Lacan and his associates, and that there are some convergent elements in their approaches to the psychoanalytic tradition. There is a strange xenophilia involved in this pattern of intellectual transmission, and there cannot be much doubt that it is not helping the cause of psychoanalytic influence in English culture.

One major cost of this routing of all messages via Paris has been the disconnection of psychoanalytic discussion in cultural theory from its proper base in clinical work. This disconnection is also probably a doubly-amplified one, in that one has the impression that in his last years Lacan, like Laing in England, had tended to cut himself off from the psychoanalytic community and orient himself instead towards a broader cultural circle not professionally engaged in psychoanalysis. So those whose psychoanalysis is learned mainly from Lacan, and from Freud's classic texts, are removed not only from current psychoanalytic work in their own culture, but even from the greater part of psychoanalytic work in France. A small knowledge of the work by those influenced by Lacan - such as Laplanche, Pontalis, and Maud and Octave Mannoni - suggests that the loss is serious, and that the two fields of British and Lacanian-influenced French psychoanalytic discourse are less distant from one another than a reading of Lacan alone would lead one to think. A parallel comes to mind in the field of Marxist theory and history. Here, writers such as E. P. Thompson have forcefully urged the importance of empirical historical work to any living Marxism, and while his arguments have called in question the value of 'theory' *per se*, it has been a source of strength to Marxist studies in Britain that there has been a continuing practice of historical research. The analogue of empirical research in the psychoanalytic field is the clinical practice of psychoanalysis. Psychoanalytic theories have developed not mainly through textual elaboration, but have been formulated and tested in relation to experience of analytic cases. This was Freud's own procedure (together with his self-analysis which, however, appears to be even less attractive as a model to his modern interpreters) and has been the basis of the development of psychoanalytic understanding ever since.

The costs to any proper understanding of psychoanalysis of this divorce from case material are so great as to threaten to doom into sterility the whole project attempted by Lacanian cultural theorists in Britain. It seems also that the efforts to relate Freud's ideas to the various problematics of linguistics and semiotics have taken precedence over the detailed study of the development of Freud's own work. A rather small number of Freud's texts are repeatedly cited to make some key points, but one has the sense that it is a reading of Lacan's reading of Freud, not a reading of Freud, that is the decisive source. Althusser's 'reading' of Marx led many others to read Marx for themselves; there is less evidence that this has been happening in the instance of Freud. This lack of interest in the internal development of Freud's work (a development which is very helpfully set out in, for example, Richard Wollheim's *Freud* (London, 1971), and Donald Meltzer's *The Kleinian Development* (Perthshire, Clunie Press, 1978)) may go some way to explaining the lack of curiosity about the evolution of his ideas in the last forty years.

A second major problem with this Lacanian interpretation of psychoanalysis is its classical orthodoxy, a consequence of its dependence on certain texts of Freud. This orthodox model excludes many important unconscious phenomena from study, with serious consequences for the analysis of culture, and also with serious moral and political implications. What in effect has happened is that the empiricist individualism of Freud's own early account (Freud's 'pleasure principle', and instinct theory) has been translated into a quasi-Hegelian vocabulary of desire (for recognition by the other), but with an unchanged core of tragic contradiction between desire and its impossibility of social fulfilment. Antony Wilden has pointed out in *The Language of the Self* (Baltimore, 1968) the implicit connections between Lacan's early work and Sartre's. In this model, it seems impossible to conceive of subjects who are related to others without being inevitably part of some relationship of mutual imprisonment. The emphasis in the reading of Lacan on the 'mirror stage' brings out a related connection with this Sartrean perspective. The 'me' fixed in the definitions of the other by the forms of language and culture is in inevitable contradiction to the 'I' of unconscious and repressed desire, in close parallel to the contradiction of 'being in itself' and 'being for others' expounded in Sartre's work. Such models - they are also to be found in the 'I' and the 'me' of

symbolic interactionism in the work of Cooley and Mead in the United States
- have the effect of contrasting an inauthentic 'social self' with a
potentially real (even if unknowable) inner self. This model provides
only for oscillation between the imprisonment of human beings by social
and cultural structures, and the temporary lifting of these structures,
either in revolution or in the necessarily ungeneralisable practice of
avant-garde art. Some more inherently social concept of man is essential
to any socialist vision.

There are in fact two crucial developments from Freud's own later
work which need to be central to the assimilation of psychoanalysis into
cultural theory. The first of these is the shift from a 'bio-energetic'
and topographical model of the mind, conceived in terms of instinctual
energies and more or less mechanical structures, towards a more phenomenological account. What is meant by phenomenological account is that the
model of the subject's mind held by the analyst attempts to map the mental constructions experienced by the subject. While theoretical models
are used by object-relations theorists (in this there can be agreement
about the unconscious being the key theoretical object of psychoanalytic
science), these models attempt to represent, in a generalising and systematic way, the phenomenology of the subject, more closely than is the
case with Freud's topographical accounts. This does not displace explanations in terms of flows of energy and its discharge, or of mental structure, but complements them in order to map the subject's own inner
experience. A number of important developments in the substantive theory
of the mind, and in analytic method, are associated with this shift
towards a more phenomenological approach. The second development is the
evolution of substantive theory involved in the concepts of 'object-
relations'. What is involved here is the idea of an internalisation by
the subject of mental images of the parental figures, and the foundation
of the personality on a persisting fantasy relationship to internal and
thus unconscious 'internal objects'. Klein found that the earliest
experiences were of 'part-objects' - fantasies of the breast and nipple for
example - which were continuously split and fragmented by the operation of
violent feelings of love and hate. A mental picture of the mother as a
whole person was only gradually put together in the infant's mind,
through the mother's capacity to contain the anxieties of the infant and
to mitigate its frustrations through both physical care and emotional
understanding. The model of the internal world which results from this
account is one composed of different 'parts of the self' related to different internal objects. These 'objects' will be associated with different bodily functions, will have different dispositions towards the
infant (persecuting, caring, abandoning, etc.) and will be fantasised in
relation to each other, the infant's fantasies of its parents' sexual
relations being a very early feature of development according to Melanie
Klein. The anxieties involved in these experiences of 'parts of the
self' are dealt with in this account by a variety of mechanisms, of which
the classical process of 'repression' described by Freud is only one.
Whereas Freud's mechanism of repression describes the censorship and
inhibition of forbidden feelings, Klein developed additional concepts of
'splitting' and 'projective identification', by which unwanted feelings
were displaced into other persons and objects, which were then invested
with qualities which derive from unconscious fantasy. This was not only a
process of fantasy attribution, but also of the actual pushing of feelings
onto others, making them experience aspects of the self in order to
relieve the self of mental pain. This idea of parts of the self, and its
internal objects, being projected into others leads to a heightened concept of the unconscious dynamics of family interaction, and of the role
of fantasised internal worlds in the making of marital and parental relationships. The containment of projected parts of the infant self by the

mother is held in this account to be crucial to the infant's development, and to its capacity to re-introject and integrate its conflicting feelings and internal objects. This concept of projective identification has been the most important in the Kleinian development, and has especially furthered the understandings of primitive psychotic states of mind, in which fragmentation of the self and its internal objects is a crucial phenomenon. Particular attention has been given to the experience of the counter-transference, whereby analysts are able to study the mechanisms of projective identification through understanding of feelings evoked in them by the transference. The underlying model of the self employed in this view is not merely one of desires bound to certain categories of object, or narcissistically bound up in the self, but of a mental structure understood as an unconscious representation of the self related in fantasy to others. These others are conceived primitively as part-objects but also, in more developed states of mind, as persons.

The Oedipus Complex is of course one such product of unconscious fantasy, and one ground for asserting that the 'object-relations' model is a development of Freud's own work. But Klein revised Freud's view, discovering 'Oedipal' preoccupations with parental intercourse at a much earlier stage of development than Freud assumed. These were linked in her view to the development of the 'depressive position' and to the recognition of the other as a whole and other person. Oedipal anxieties therefore occur in conjunction with intense and sometimes violent fantasies about mother's body, and are dealt with not only by means of repression (so central to the Lacanian account), but also through the mechanisms of splitting and projective identification. The Kleinian model generally draws attention to earlier stages of development, through which the differences between self and other are constructed, notably in the theory of the 'paranoid - schizoid' and 'depressive' positions. These, together with the early Oedipal anxieties associated with the depressive position, are located initially in the first few months of life, not, as in the case of Freud's Oedipus Complex, in the third and fourth year. This suggests that a capacity for fantasy and thought is developed in the infant prior to the development of language, and is therefore inconsistent with Lacan's view of language as the precondition of the development of the differentiated self.

These models of Klein's describe the integration of the sense of the self as a reciprocal of the development of awareness of the mother (or mother-figure) as a whole being. The initial fragmentation of experience as a series of physical sensations and powerful emotions (love, hatred, terror and anxiety) is resolved, through the 'containment' of these experiences by the mother, into a continuing sense of self and other which can survive these extremes and discontinuities of feeling. The infant's sense of its own body is formed through its mother's handling of it, and its transmuting of potentially catastrophic sensations and boundaries into ones through which a continuing sense of self can survive. (The significance from this standpoint of the Leboyer approach to childbirth is that it seeks to initiate from birth this tender approach to the experience of 'difference'.) The infant's sense of the benignness and reliability of the world is dependent on its caretakers' ability to attend to and mitigate its frustrations. Its sense of the meaning of love and hate, and of the possibility that the former feelings will in the end take precedence in its infant scheme of things over the latter, depends on the containment both of its own and of its parents' negative feelings in their mode of caring for the baby. Klein describes how in the first few months (and later in recurring re-livings of this developmental 'position' throughout life), the infant comes to perceive the mother as a 'whole object' combining good _and_ bad qualities, vulnerable to its

attacks, and needed and loved even in its apartness and difference from
the infant. Following this, the infant must encounter the reality of two
parents, and of other babies made or potentially made by them, and of many
other kinds of 'otherness' in the lives of its parents. Many kinds of
identification of the self with these parents, and as possible objects of
these parents' love or hatred, are possible as an outcome of these stages
of development.

What are formative, in this account, are the fantasised internal
objects which represent the parent figures in the mind of the child. These
internal objects may be cruel or kind, strong or weak, fragmented or whole,
related to each other in love or hatred, and the self will be fantasised
in different identifications to and relationships with them. This account
does not imply that the mental stages of the infant's life are a direct
precipitate or imprinting of the real-life behaviour of its parents. On
the contrary, the inner-world of the child has its own structure and
dynamics, and constitutional factors in the infant as well as part experiences of the parents will interact in its development.

It is important to stress that in the 'object-relations' account
the elaboration of fantasy about the parents in the inner world of the
child precedes the development of what Freud called 'repression', and
involves other means than unconscious censorship of dealing with anxiety.
In order to deal with mental pain, arising from bad qualities in the self
and its objects, and also from vulnerability and dependence, the self
will organise its experience through unconscious fantasy, redistributing
dangerous or unwanted parts of its self and its objects in accordance with
the demands of its inner world. Psychoanalysis provides a scene for these
transferences (the operations of envy, greed, idealisation, projective
identification) as well as the Oedipal jealousies and identifications with
which orthodox Freudians remain preoccupied. The work of psychoanalysis
consists of seeking to make conscious the internal world of the analysand,
and above all to make conscious and thus relieve the anxiety and mental
pain inseparable from it. Clearly, in the Kleinian account, negative
emotions, especially of envy and jealousy, are given great stress, and
are often perceived as the primary source of resistance to analytic
understanding. There are important differences between Kleinian and the
large group of 'middle group' analysts ('middle group' signifying a non-
aligned tendency influenced to some degree by Klein but not committed to
all her ideas especially those concerning the importance of envy:
Winnicott is perhaps the most representative figure). But from the point
of view of consideration of the work of the 'British school' of psychoanalysis, the large measure of agreement on these early phenomena of
object-relations experienced in fantasy is most significant, and contrasts with the continuing dominant emphasis on the later Oedipus
Complex by the Lacanians and other orthodox Freudians.

These differences of view can be very clearly grasped through a comparison of Lacan's much-cited paper on 'The mirror stage' (published in
English in *New Left Review* 51) - one of the main foundations of Lacanian
cultural theory - and Donald Winnicott's paper 'The Mirror Role of
Mother and Family in Child Development', republished in his *Playing and
Reality* (1971) which, incidentally, acknowledges the influence of Lacan's
paper. For Lacan, it is the actual mirror-experience, the self constituting itself by looking at itself, which is the crucial stage of
development. The roots of subjectivity lie irredeemably in this account
in the experience of Narcissus and self-regard. This is then transposed
into the self as perceived by the Other, in a move not unlike that
achieved in Cooley's symbolic interactionist account of a 'Looking Glass
Self' in which, to similar effect, a social 'me' is counterposed to a
primary but inaccessible I. In Winnicott's account, on the other hand,

the face in which the baby first sees itself is its mother's not its own. It learns about itself as capable of being loved, or of causing fear, distress, or repugnance, through observing its reflection in the face and mind of another. Winnicott suggests that we subsequently interpret what we see in the mirror in the light of how we have seen ourselves in this human mirror, and in the regards of those many others who are significant to us. The literal mirror is not a primary experience of the constitution of the self, and when it becomes so, as Winnicott and the legend of Narcissus suggests, it is because something has gone wrong with our sense of ourselves in our inner dependence on the love of others. (2)

Lacanians argue that it is precisely the 'fixing' of the perception of the self by the other (and its categorisation in language) which creates a tragic space between the plasticity of desire of the inner self, and its thinkable forms of expression. In this sense, the 'mirror-stage' can be taken (though it is not clear from the original paper that this is what was meant) as a metaphor for the positioning of the self in culture, and its inevitable self-recognition as such, as a self-for-others. The contribution of structuralist theory to this model is that this self-for-others becomes not merely the contingent product of specific social interactions as in Sartre's work, but reproduces the categories and roles of a definite social structure (for example its categories of gender).

Both object-relations and Lacanian accounts agree that the self is constituted by a process of interaction, and both would also agree on the inevitable sacrifices of possibility and repressions of desire inherent in this process. But the object-relations tradition stresses also the potentially creative elements of this interaction, the realising of potential through mutual recognition (e.g. of mother and baby), as well as its loss through denial. The utopia of infinite desire is on this view a pointless projection of primary narcissism onto the world, and cannot constitute a conceivable standard of what might be. The self cannot be constituted except through others - this is not a metaphysical catastrophe, but man's social nature - and our concern should be to understand the more and less benign and creative forms which this social process can take.

It must be said that a very large amount of cultural theory seems to have been misconstructed on the premises of Lacan's 'The mirror stage'. Christian Metz's influential 'Psychoanalysis and Cinema', for example, in *Screen*, Vol.16, No.2 (1975) (which has the merit of being an unpretentious and intelligible piece of writing) depends on this largely erroneous premise. On the strength of 'The mirror stage', the cinema is attributed the functions of the subject-constituting mirror. The theory of the child's relation to the Oedipus Complex leads to the equating of cinema-viewing with voyeuristic observation of the parental couple. The theory of castration anxiety and its displacement into fetishism leads to Metz's view of excessive attachment to the techniques of the cinema as a kind of fetishism. Well, no doubt identifications of a narcissistic type, voyeurism and fetishism can all be found as important phenomena in regard to the cinema, but as a whole account of the relation of the cinema to the unconscious this displays all the marks of its disastrously narrow and schematic origins. There are many different forms of identification with whole and part-objects, besides narcissistic ones. Many other interests and identifications can be expressed by looking at others, besides voyeurism focused on the parental couple. Symbol formation is about many things, other than fetishistic displacements of the lost phallus. A psychoanalytic account of film or of other arts needs to take account of many more unconscious processes and states of mind than these. And indeed of a rather different range of symbolic activities than fetishism, if it is not to be reductionist and denigrative of art, in its effects.

Kleinian psychoanalysts, like the Lacanians, have given great importance to the development of symbolism and the capacity for thought in recent years. Kleinians agree with Lacan in locating the origins of symbol formation in the experience of what they call 'the absent object' (which seems to translate as the 'imaginary Other' in Lacan). But because of the way in which Kleinian approaches have developed through the psychoanalysis of children, and are based on hypotheses about the mental state of clearly pre-verbal children in the first months of life, the emphasis is not primarily on language *per se*, but on symbolic representations of the internal world which are most commonly interpreted through the child's play and through visual symbols as well as language. (Indeed, the provision of a set of toys, including invariably different sizes of human figure, and of drawing materials, is a basic technique of child analysis.) It was argued in an important paper by Hanna Segal that the development of a capacity for symbol formation was related to the attainment of the 'depressive position' - that is, the capacity to internalise the mother as a 'whole object' in her absence, and to achieve the integration of conflicting feelings in the mind. W. R. Bion has subsequently discussed, in the brilliant series of papers published as *Second Thoughts* (London, 1967), the phenomenology of more primitive mental states, in which thoughts are (as Freud earlier put it) indistinguishable from the objects which they represent, and are projected and exploded in fantasy rather than being used as the materials for 'linking' experiences and objects with one another.

This combination of attention to the phenomenology of infantile experience, and to the importance of the mother's role in thinking and retaining and modulating feelings for the child, has given rise to a key concept in later Kleinian work (influenced especially by Bion and Meltzer) - that of containment. (3) The parent figures need to be actual containers, in emotional experience, for the angry, greedy and frightened feelings of their child. Most commonly, Meltzer has pointed out, the mother's role is to contain the anxieties of the baby and the father's is to contain the anxieties of the mother, but there are many possible divisions of labour. The internalisation in fantasy of the parent figures will give prominence to their capacity to be satisfactory or unsatisfactory containers, of which mother's body is a powerful and basic image, and of which a house is a common symbolic transformation in play. The role of symbolism and of language itself is also to contain and to bind feelings. The failure to achieve a primary level of integration - the capacity to experience both the self and other as persisting, whole, and related beings - will be reflected, so these analysts have discovered, in failure in the capacity to symbolise, in schizophrenic and autistic states.

The development of symbolic capacity is seen in this tradition not merely as an aspect of repression, as the means by which the subject is inscribed in society through the cultural definitions of the other and especially of patriarchy. It is on the contrary through symbolisation that the infant learns to achieve a continuity of experience, both of his own existence and of the mother's. Winnicott's paper 'Transitional Objects and Transitional Phenomena' (4) describes an early stage in the development of symbolic capacity in which the baby's illusion of mother or the breast, not clearly differentiated from itself, is transferred to a bit of blanket or cuddly toy which is then able to represent something comforting for the infant. This might be described as a primitive symbol, developed before the capacity clearly to discriminate symbols from what they stand for (through language for example) has evolved, and used with special intensity at moments (such as going to sleep) when the child needs an illusion of not-being-separated from mother. This early symbolisation is not of the phallus (though Winnicott uses the term 'maternal phallus'), or of a fetish, least of all of a 'subject' defined by culture,

but of aspects of the primary figure of attachment in the child's life.
The role of symbolisation in achieving both differentiation and
relationship (linking) of the experiences of the self and others, makes
it a crucial element in development. The relationship of symbolism to
the containment of anxiety (separation, disintegration, disappearance,
destruction, abandonment, jealousy, envy, and greed are sources of
anxiety for the infant and therefore reasons for symbolic activity) gives
symbolic capacity a critical importance in the development of the subject,
but of a rather different kind than that proposed in the Lacanian tradition. Bion goes so far as to hypothesise an epistemophilic instinct - a
primitive desire for understanding - parallel to the primitive emotions
of love and hate. It is through understanding (symbolic representation,
linking, containment) that the self is able to contain and resolve
anxieties, and to achieve progressively greater capacities for differentiation. The internal objects that will shape the forms of symbolisation
will depend on the transactions between the internal and external worlds
of self and caring figures. The mental world can be composed of punitive, feeling-less, ravaged internal objects as well as relatively benign
fantasies of parents and babies. (Some infants have been known to attribute the natures and relations of parents and babies to every animate
and inanimate object in sight, almost as soon as they could speak.) No
doubt the _forms_ of symbolisation will vary too, in ways.which correspond
with definite states of the internal world. Bick, Bion, Tustin, Meltzer
and others, as well as Winnicott in somewhat different terms, have already
undertaken some of this exploration in relation to psychotic and autistic
states of mind among children. The point is that to understand symbolisation, from the findings of psychoanalysis, as the primary instrument of
growth and development, leads to a very different approach to culture
from that which interprets symbolisation and language mainly as the
instrument of repression; of the imposition on to the desiring subject of
categories which necessarily mis-represent and distort its unconscious
wishes. That is a metaphysic of inevitable alienation, however little
these anti-humanists may own the term, a psychoanalytic and linguistic
reassertion of a world of almost universal Being-for-Others or Bad Faith.
From this (in this world view) only the *avant garde* (and perhaps the
psychotic) can escape, in the few cracks that can be opened in the her-
metic structure of 'realist', or mirror-like cultural representation.

Interestingly, one of the passages most frequently cited by Lacan
and the Lacanians, the Fort! Da! (Gone! Here!) section in *Beyond the
Pleasure Principle*, where Freud describes a fifteen-month-old child's
game with a cotton-reel in which he throws it away from his cot and pulls
it back within sight, is also important in the genesis of the object-
relations approach to symbol formation. Freud, in his delightful and
memorable piece of observation, is led to think about the child's game
as an instance of repetition compulsion which he regards as not explicable
by the pleasure principle, and which he later relates to a sort of law of
entropy or regression to a state of stasis which he called the death
instinct.

The cotton-reel game is important to Winnicott and the Kleinians,
however, as an instance of early symbolisation of the absent mother,
through play. The cotton-reel's disappearance and reappearance (under his
own control) provides reassurance to the infant. This space, neither the
real mother, nor hallucination, but illusion or symbol, is crucial to
growth and development in Winnicott's view, and is parallel to his idea
of the transitional object. For Mrs Klein, the cotton-reel is a symbolisation of an internal object, and she suggests that there is an element
of depressive anxiety (evoked by the child's fear that he has harmed the
mother and caused her absence) which is being overcome through this game.

The child's subsequent discovery, in Freud's account, that his own image too can be made to appear and disappear in a mirror, and his excitement in conveying this to the mother, shows the child learning to generalise his idea of absence as something temporary, seeing himself as absent and returned in his mother's eyes, as he has just observed the cotton-reel gone and come back with his own. It is interesting in this example, in relation to our earlier discussion of 'The mirror stage', to see that the mirror probably has its strongest meaning as a representation of mother's regard, baby gone and returning being a way of showing mother that baby has gone and returned for her. We see in this example the infant self learning to hold onto a feeling of the internal reality of its loved others, and of itself, even when they are not physically present.

Freud's example has been significant in a number of ways in this tradition. It demonstrated the fertility of direct observation of babies which has since become a major element in analytic training. It suggested the relation of the development of symbol-formation to the absence of the mother, and to the child's capacity, depending on its state of emotional development and actual experience, to cope with the anxieties arising from this. It indicated the role of play and non-verbal symbolisation, as well as words, for children, which subsequently became a central insight in the development of the 'play-technique' in psychoanalysing children. It also showed the importance of symbol-formation (and, as Freud said, repetition-compulsion) as a means of dealing with anxiety. The child is able to hold onto a reality that is symbolised in a form of play that he would be in danger of losing contact with without such a representation: its anxiety is thus contained by its game. It is for this same reason that a child analyst might draw charts to represent analytic holiday periods, and help a child to visualise its break with a sequence of coloured squares.

The Fort! Da! game is also very important in Lacan's work. There is some convergence in the sense that the example also illustrated for Lacan the relation of symbol-formation to absence of the mother, prior to the experience of the Oedipus Complex. But whereas in the object-relations tradition one can point to the cotton-reel example as just one early empirical observation followed by innumerable others from the analysis and observation of children, in Lacan's work it appears to be the canonical case, from which much theory is then constructed. Wilden comments that 'if Freud has not reported the Fort! Da! it would have been necessary to invent it, since it plays the role of necessary "myth of origins" in Lacan's theory', and he points out how much weight is rested by Lacan on this single instance in the development of his concepts of the Imaginary and the Symbolic. The example appears to be used by Lacan for purposes of a philosophical recoding of Freud's work, not to suggest any new empirical investigation. The contrast between the various discussions of this observation (including Freud's own) not least in their relative clarity and intelligibility, seem to me to be a powerful testimony to the perverseness of the choice of Lacan as a major point of entry to psychoanalysis, for those at least with easy access to writings in the British psychoanalytic tradition.

It remains for me to summarise the most important differences between Lacanian and object-relations theory in their implications for cultural studies, and also to indicate what their respective political implications might be. For reasons of space, these will have to be stated briefly.

Lacanian cultural theory seems to me to be pessimistic and élitist in its political implications, as well as academic in its practice. Culture and society are conceived as inherently repressive (rather than, in their essence, as both repressive and as the only positive means of realisation conceivable). Emphasis is given to this metaphysical state of being and to the restricted possibilities for particular individuals - through psychoanalysis or in other ways - to transcend these limits in more-or-less momentary ways, rather than to the historical and particular conditions of repression, The emphasis in Lacanian-influenced cultural theory is on the generally ideological character of cultural forms, as bearers of imposed social categories, illusory ideas of subjective agency, and mirror-like identifications of the self with imposed definitions. To this is contrasted a practice of deconstruction (5) in criticism and in art, for which only the most highly educated and informed (and perhaps some marginal individuals) have the capability. The social vantage point from which this theory is advanced is mainly that of academics, educated and privileged out of any broader relationship to their wider society. One might say that the elitist pessimism of the Frankfurt School is echoed in these modern writings, but without that intellectual generation's historical tragedy as a justification. There have of course been positive features in the exposure of British cultural studies to more theoretical traditions evolved on the Continent, and the attention to ideology in modern cultural theory reflects the real power of the communications industries in late capitalism. But the creation of these various theoretical discourses has served other purposes than the advancement of a more comprehensive and sophisticated Marxist theory of culture. What from one point of view can be seen as a sustained attempt to extend serious consideration to popular cultural forms, from another can be seen as their academicisation, as a process of incorporation into quite traditional and hierarchical academic procedures, of cultural forms and their audiences to which intellectuals should have a different kind of relationship. Leavis' influence led to a more positive and committed cultural practice - notably in education - than most contemporary Marxist theory. One reason for this is that the Scrutiny group maintained, especially in its earlier years, the view that a particular English literary tradition carried a discourse of moral dissent from dominant social values, and also that it gave an imaginative possibility to potential life forms different from those which were actually realised for the majority. Limited, non-conformist, humanist and 'untheorised' as this vision might have been, it at least provided some positive grounds for a cultural commitment against that of the ten dominant classes and their cultural representatives. Whereas a theory of ideology and demystification, in the context especially of vanishing beliefs in the socialist potential of the working class, leads to a Frankfurt School style of pessimism, or even to a Nietzschean recourse, in desperation, to negative understanding as the only defensible standpoint and pleasure. The attack on 'humanism' and 'moralism' as ideologies, even though initially presented as the implication of a scientific materialism, also has unnoticed echoes of Nietzsche's own attack on the ethical as a form of illusion. (6) The fact is that the intellectual difficulty and frenetic fashion-changes in this discourse are related both to its theoretical presuppositions (which require a ceaseless critique of unreflective ideology) and the social location of its practitioners. In a highly competitive and stratified intellectual environment (competition is between both individuals and coteries) theoretical sophistication and cosmopolitanism is a distinct competitive resource.

Work in the object-relations tradition on the other hand, remains largely confined to the field of pscyhoanalytic clinical work, and few recent attempts have been made to think out its relevance for other fields. (7) Lacanians have attacked the 'biologism' of Klein, and this is an aspect of a more general rejection in these quarters of positions held to be essentialist or humanist. I have argued elsewhere that attention to the biological substructures of human life, and the limits and

preoccupations which they necessarily impose on cultures should be no
more exceptionable for socialists than Marx's attention to the material
preconditions of life, which in any case derive from biological needs.
The distinctive contribution of object-relations theory has been its
attention to the preconditions of development in human infancy, providing
understanding of a formative stage of life, neglected in most socialist
discussion. This account depends on the interrelationship of conditions
which are biologically given with those which are social and cultural in
origin; neither aspect of this interaction can be neglected in the study
of socialisation without serious confusion.

A second fundamental difference from the Lacanian perspective lies
in the emphasis in the object-relations tradition on the containing (Bion)
and facilitating (Winnicott) properties of cultural and social forms,
including those of the family, as well as their repressive and alienating properties. For anyone trained in the psychoanalytic tradition,
this must be a matter of emphasis and not of contradiction, since both
dimensions are central to its account of development. But the distinctive value of the object-relations tradition is its attempt to discriminate between conditions favourable to growth and development and those
inimical to it.

One may as well grasp the nettle at this point and say that Kleinian
and related approaches to psychoanalysis can contribute vitally to the
reconstitution of humanism on a theoretically coherent basis. The
'subject' is described in this account as only gradually individuated, and
as continually enmeshed in unconscious projections and projective identifications with others, into adult life. There is no prior postulation of
a given individual, and the internal and external others in the individual's experience are also constitutive of his or her identity. Nevertheless, there is a concept of the differentiated and individual subject as
a goal of development, with capacities for thought and feeling as primary
attributes of successful growth. I have argued elsewhere that the postulation of an inherently social man, nurtured by others and with the capacity to create and nurture actual and symbolic others as its 'normal'
fulfilment, is a potential foundation for a socialist universalism, which
cannot be said for the juxtaposing of abstract desire to inevitable cultural alienation.

Symbolic processes are central, in the object-relations as in the
Lacanian accounts of the formation of the self. In both, it is mental
pain and loss which provoke and necessitate thought and symbolic representation. For object-relations theory (both Winnicott's and in the
Kleinian tradition) this symbolic activity, shared and supported by others,
is seen as the precondition for growth, not necessarily as an imposed and
alienative misrepresentation and displacement of unconscious desire.
Cultural forms are one mode of containment and facilitation for this
growth, through life, and their availability to all as living forms is
therefore central to the possibility of a good society.

Critical life experiences will recur and need to be surmounted in
most if not all individual lives, over generations - loss and mourning
for example - and such mental and emotional experience must be symbolised
and given its due human value in literature and art. Cultural artefacts
can therefore properly be understood in terms of the central human
experiences to which they give representative form. Some element of
human commemoration and celebration (and not only of the struggles of
classes) cannot therefore be missing from any socialist view of culture.
If this is currently a point of difference between 'socialist' cultural
theorists and 'liberal humanists' (it certainly seems to be in practice,
if not in theory), then on this point liberal humanism is right. The
understanding achieved in relationship with another represented by

psychoanalysis is one such valuable contemporary model of cultural process, combining as it does the experience and toleration of intense mutual feeling with the attempt to think about and represent these states of feeling and mind in words.

Object-relations theory is at this point better adapted to the recognition of the dynamics of individual life-crises, and their representation in literature and art, than to the understanding of more broadly social or historical phenomena. The main immediate resource that a psychoanalytic approach can provide for cultural studies is its capacity to disclose meanings derived from states of object relations in the individual's inner world, in cultural forms which may have a different manifest meaning. Our experience in responding to cultural forms (as well as that of making them) derives from inner unconscious experience and its symbolisation. Inappropriate and reductive 'psychobiography' sometimes arises from psychoanalytic 'readings', but it is what is represented in the work and not its author which should be their subject. An educational conclusion which can be drawn from the relevance of psychoanalysis is that there is need to create learning settings which give space to the experience of feeling as a primary element of understanding. Psychoanalysis here gives a more explicit and theoretical form to a familiar precept of Leavisian criticism, whilst this emphasis on feeling is a dimension which much recent critical discourse seems to have rejected.

There is, however, a more difficult but also necessary task, which is to relate these 'unconscious' perspectives to the specifically social and historical aspects of cultural forms. How, that is, are the experiences of the inner world differently formed and represented in different 'sociological' or class contexts? A psychoanalytically-informed cultural theory will have to address these problems, but it must be admitted at this point that its derivation from contemporary clinical practice provides few resources for this. Indeed, the historical differentiation and placing of psychoanalytical ideas has not proceeded far within its own principal clinical domain, let alone in such wider applications. What is perhaps needed to begin this work are analyses which connect the representation of unconscious experiences (inevitably mainly of the inner world of individuals) with their wider social determinations and representational forms. This may be best attempted at this stage through the consideration of particular works.

FOOTNOTES

1. This paper develops an argument already attempted for a broader area of social theory in an article 'A Socialist Consideration of Kleinian Psychoanalysis' which was published in *New Left Review* 131 (1982).

2. Margaret Rustin has pointed out to me how in a girl of ten she has observed the 'mirror' in which the child continues to prepare herself for the world (in getting ready for school, for example) remains her mother's gaze, and not an actual mirror. And later, adolescents will provide this 'mirroring' for each other, in a social process of preparing a presentable appearance for themselves. Actual mirrors may be something we learn to use rather late, *faute de mieux*, in an individualist culture.

3. This emphasis in later Kleinian theory on the concept of containment can be taken as an index of a wider process of feminisation of psychoanalytic theory which I think that this tradition has accomplished.

4. In D. W. Winnocott, *Through Paediatrics to Psycho-Analysis* (London, 1975).

5.   The development of a coherent body of theory may not be as closely
linked with socialist purposes as was earlier thought by critics of
empiricism. Recent American post-structuralist work indicates that liberal
as well as socialist positions can be elaborated in explicit theoretical
terms. The left does not now seem to be winning this intellectual battle.

6.   A further hidden affinity of post-structuralist theory with Nietzsche
arises from the consequences of a thoroughgoing relativism. If all values
are historically constructed, and ethical or philosophical justifications
(of the kind Marx attempted through his concept of 'species being') are in
principle rejected, then differences can be resolved only by arbitrary fiat
(existential choice), by mechanical materialism, or by recognition of the
overriding imperatives of power. A related point about Nietzschean influence was made in Peter Dew's critique of Foucault at this Conference.

7.   Peter Fuller's work on the visual arts is an important example to the
contrary, as was that of Adrian Stokes. Interesting examples of literary
analysis in this psychoanalytic tradition are essays by Ella Freeman
Sharpe in her *Collected Papers on Psychoanalysis* (1950), by Hanna Segal in
her *The World of Hanna Segal: A Kleinian Approach to Clinical Practice*
(New York, 1981), and by Lisa Miller (on *King Lear*) in the *Journal of
Child Psychotherapy*, Vol.4, No.1 (1975).

A REPLY TO MICHAEL RUSTIN: KLEINIAN PSYCHOANALYSIS AND THE THEORY OF CULTURE

Graham Seymour

Michael Rustin's project, both in the preceding paper and in the article to which he refers in *New Left Review*, 131, (1) can be summarized as an attempt to constitute a humanist socialism for 'cultural studies' which would have a 'theoretically coherent basis'. This project has a number of distinguishing features: most prominently an unproblematized notion of 'culture' (2) allied with an argument for the displacement of continental structuralism in general and Lacanian psychoanalytics in particular. In its place is proposed a specifically 'British' variant of psychoanalytic discourse which is centred upon the work of Melanie Klein and the 'British School' of 'object-relations' theorists. This argument is not without appeal, highlighting as it does the difficulties involved in coming to terms with much 'structuralist' and 'post-structuralist' work on what is called the 'human subject' from the perspective of an Anglo-American empiricism. The supposed distance of such 'cosmopolitan', but ultimately 'arid' theoretical sophistication from the 'fundamental questions of human nature and needs' leads Rustin to draw the following conclusion:

> Lacanian cultural theory seems to me to be pessimistic and elitist in its political implications, as well as academic in its practice.

It is thus to the psychoanalytic work of Melanie Klein and her followers that Rustin turns for the theoretical coherence that will underpin the political project of securing a 'socialist universalism' that would be relevant to the field of 'cultural studies'. This theory will be used to achieve a new understanding of those 'central human experiences' to which 'cultural artifacts ... give representative form'.

Before considering exactly what kind of theoretical coherence Klein is to bring to this renascent humanism, and before going on to argue that Rustin's rejection of Lacan's work is based upon a number of misinterpretations brought about by weaknesses in the Kleinian position, I would like to make one strategic point about the project as a whole. Since 1968, the overall movement of broadly socialist 'cultural analysis' has been directed towards a critical re-negotiation of the problems of 'language', of 'representation' and of 'ideology' in general, as they affect what can loosely be termed 'internalization'. The kind of political impetus that could mobilize wide sections of the Parisian populace in May/June '68, and which give such rapid rise to the forms of direct democracy, fell foul not only of the repressive apparatus of the French State, but also of the 'internal', or better unconscious, structures of subjectivity. The economic intrication of sexuality and private property and the more than recalcitrant religious and familial ideologies that Gaullism was able to re-invoke gave to the infamous slogan 'I take my desires for reality, because I believe in the reality of my desires' a particularly hollow ring. The realisation that desire itself was not necessarily a liberating force, but rather, one which was equally liable to participate in conservative structures, gave rise to the need to understand what was seen as its specifically limited function. (3) By way of response, 'socialist cultural analysis' has developed the tactics of critical dis-intrication of power-relations; of deconstruction of theological meaning structures and of psychoanalytic de-mystification of sexualities. But the transition from a critically reflexive theorization to the deployment of new arguments in the fields of strategic and limited ideological exchange, has, with the notable exception of feminism, not been successfully achieved. There exists, in short, a 'gap', a political hiatus between the critical/theoretical response and the exigencies of the current situation - a 'gap' which is already open to exploitation by the 'New Right'. (4) It seems to me that Michael Rustin has identified this gap with some accuracy - albeit in terms of 'culture' - and his project is thus aimed at filling it. However, his proposals for a 'socialist universalism' are curiously anachronistic: a 'theodicy' of pain and evil with which to confront the world; a set of 'fundamental beliefs' that would somehow correspond to the natural needs and capacities of men' - as though such needs were the ahistorical constants of a fundamental human condition forever chained to an unchanging 'biological or natural substratum', (5) and an optimistic stress on 'the egalitarian force of an emphasis on human capacities for feeling'.

I wish to argue that Rustin's humanist empiricism effectively returns 'cultural analysis' to the ideology of the fifties by calling upon notions of psychic 'growth', the 'integrated' self and the 'realized' individual - reproducing a Leavisite dissolution of politics into the morality of the 'mature', 'responsible' and 'caring' person. This latter connection is not a gratuitous one, for Rustin himself draws the parallel with the kind of analytic activity he wishes to advocate.

> One might say that the actual practices of criticism - which the Leavisites say should be based on a kind of emotional and empathetic sensitivity explicated through language - and analysis, which has some of these same prescribed qualities, are not all that far apart.
> (*NLR*, p.89).

This connection can be used to point up both the political and theoretical flaws that the project embraces. There is first of all the question of Leavisite morality which Rustin wishes to see Kleinian theory validating as a fundamental of human nature:

> I would summarize this (Kleinian) body of work as offering a view of human beings which in an intense and unusual way assumes them to be moral in their fundamental nature. (*NLR*, p.80).

> Kleinian theory uniquely ascribes moral and altruistic capacities to human beings in its theoretical model of them ... (*NLR*, p.81).

> What is unusual is its attribution of moral capaity to its subjects as their essential nature. (*NLR*, p.81).

This is the necessary centre of Kleinian humanism as Rustin sees it. But to make the step from asserting the 'inherently social' structure of human identity - upon which the political claims of the project rest - to the ascription of moral capacity as a fundamental of human natures is to slip into idealism. It shifts the starting point in the construction of subjectivity away from 'the assumption that social relationships are always primary ' by re-discovering a 'moral'capacity for social identity or 'relatedness' - what other 'object-relations' theorists have called an 'ego-potential' (6) - that would be present at birth. What this inherent capacity amounts to is the pre-supposition that the human infant is born with the psychological structure of a self - even in its early undifferentiated state - already in place, and that the processes of psychic 'growth' will then take place in a 'developmental' fashion. But on this 'ego-potential', wherein 'organism' collapses into 'identity', rests not only the essentialist attribution of 'moral and altruistic capacities', but also the inherence of the category of individuality - isolated from its social and material determinants - in the form of an innate capacity for differentiation. This conflation appears where Rustin argues for the subject's 'innate concern for the well-being of the other, at a very deep level, ...' (*NLR*, p.81) without appearing to realise that if such an 'innate concern' is to be founded in 'the earliest lack of differentiation between self and other' then not only must the potential for that differentiation be pre-supposed - in the psychological form of some 'early ego' - but also that this same form precedes the fact of its social construction by setting itself up as an essential of the emergent individual human identity. This is in fact the main flaw in the Kleinian theory upon which Rustin bases his argument for 'theoretical coherence' and the single most significant point of divergence from Freudian theory. For Melanie Klein, the 'early age' has a sufficient presentiment of unity (the ego comprises the unifying or 'binding' functions of consciousness upon which identity is based) to experience anxiety in the form of a threatened disintegration. It is then led to defend against this anxiety by developing the mechanisms of 'projective identification' and 'splitting'. For Freud, these ego processes have a secondary status, dependent upon the initially narcissistic formation of the ego (Lacan's 'Mirror Stage') that is set in motion between the ages of 6 and 18 months. But for Klein they have a primary status. Hanna Segal makes the point as follows:

> Klein ... contends that there is enough ego at birth to experience anxiety and to use a defence mechanism. She does not (like Freud) speak of an organism deflecting, but of a primitive ego projecting, the death instinct ... the early ego, as she conceives it, is also capable of primitive phantasy object relationships. (7)

Freud, on the other hand, is categorical that this cannot be the case,

> I may point out that we are bound to suppose that a unity comparable to the ego cannot exist in the individual from the start. (8)

To suppose that such a unity could exist, even in potential, actually removes the grounds for the whole psycho-sexual conflict upon which psychoanalytic theory is based. By closing the gap between the domain of the body and the disciplines of sociality, the dynamics of ego-functioning re-centre human subjectivity around a core of individual consciousness while marginalising the radically 'impersonal' activities of the unconscious.

> ... there is a concept of the differentiated and individual subject as a goal of development, with capacities for thought and feeling as primary attributes of successful growth.

One of the major theoretical disadvantages of the developmental perspective with regard to 'cultural studies' is the specifically limited conceptualization of language that its unilinear chronology gives rise to. The Manichean opposition of hate and love, of anxiety and containment/reparation that is projected in the teleology of the ego, entails not only the disavowal of the distinction between 'self' and 'other'

with which it operates (viz above), but it extends this disavowal to
include the effective distinctions between 'self' and 'environment';
'subject' and 'culture' and ultimately 'subject' and 'language'.
These distinctions, presented and maintained through such concepts as
'the subject's mind', or the notion of 'the subject's own inner experience', correspond to the empirical nature of the project, with its
implicit assumption that it is possible to operate with an unproblematic distinction between subject and object. Within this framework,
the subject's capacity for speech is confused with language itself, so
that the pre-verbal infant is in some paradoxical way either 'outside-
of' or 'before' language - yet nevertheless able to respond to the interpretation of 'visual symbols' by the Kleinian analyst. In this
sense of a subject which precedes language, speech itself is reduced
to a voluntarist - or in the terms used, 'moral' - capacity for symbolization. Such a capacity, which entails the development of the
ability to re-present 'part-objects' as 'objects', and finally as
'persons', depends upon a notion of language as an extension of 'mothering'. (9) If the quality of 'mothering' which the child receives is,
to use Winnicott's term 'good-enough', it will achieve a sufficient
level of integration to be able to 'use' language to differentiate between its 'self' (empirical subject) and its 'others' (empirical object). Language itself then takes over the mother's 'nurturing' role
by continuing to make available the 'containment' of the 'central
human experiences' in the form of 'culture'.

> Cultural artifacts can therefore properly be understood
> in terms of the central human experiences to which they
> give representative form.

In this scheme, the empiricist objectification of both subject and object puts such an insupportable weight upon the mothering role on one
hand, and liberal culture on the other, as to endanger their immediate
collapse into an index of normalization:

> Most commonly ... the mother's role is to control the
> anxieties of the baby and the father's is to contain
> the anxieties of the mother ... The role of symbolism
> and of language itself, is also to contain and bind feel-
> ings. The failure to achieve a primary level of inte-
> gration - the capacity to experience both the self and
> other as persisting, whole, and related beings - will be
> reflected ... in failure in the capacity to symbolize,
> in schizophrenic and autistic states.

This is perhaps the most disturbing aspect of Kleinian empiricism, which,
in failing to come to terms with the full implications of lanugage, (10)
grants covert authority to the analyst to decide exactly what constitutes
an experience of the self as 'persisting, whole and related'; or indeed,
just how much 'openness to deep emotional experience of others' a 'whole
person' can take.

In turning to consider Rustin's arguments against Lacanian theory
as they are outlined in the preceding paper, it seems appropriate to recall Lacan's criticism of the Kleinian school as being 'incapable of even
so much as suspecting the existence of the category of the signifier.'(11)
For while Rustin makes only the most cursory of references to the linguistic mechanisms of metaphor and metonymy,there is no attempt whatsoever to
come to terms with what must be the central aspect of Lacan's theory -
namely his 'theory of the signifier', without which the major part of his
contribution to Freudian theory is lost. It should also be pointed out
that none of the conceptual categories that Lacan introduces into psycho-

analytic theory are really discussed either: the topological triad of the Imaginary, the Symbolic and the Real; the Other; the objet a; the law of the Father; the gaze; even the phallus appears subject to its customary confusion with the penis. In this context, I would like simply to focus attention on the two well-known instances of Lacanian theory - the 'Mirror Stage' and the 'Fort-Da' game- that have been selected for consideration.

Both of these interventions by Lacan seem to me to offer materially based explanations for the establishment of subjective processes that are effectively pre-supposed by Kleinian theory. The 'Mirror-Stage' constitutes an attempt to establish in what way the mechanisms of the ego are formed while the 'Fort-Da' game provides an account of how the young child is first able to situate itself in relation to the processes of representation. But in his discussion of the 'Mirror Stage', Rustin actually pre-supposes the existence of that which Lacan is trying to account for. A pre-existent self is posited, which would then recognize/ constitute itself at a given moment in development by seeing itself in the mirror. Looked at from this angle, it is not surprising that Lacan's theory seems to make no sense:

> For Lacan, it is the actual mirror experience, the self constituting itself by looking at itself, which is the crucial stage of development. The roots of subjectivity lie irredeemably in this account, in the experience of Narcissus, and self-regard. (12)

Leaving aside the point that the 'Mirror Stage' does not actually require the child to see itself in an empirical mirror, (13) its main point is to give an account of the initial formation of the ego - the matrix in which it is shaped. This being so, there can be no ego or 'self' already present to recognize itself. What occurs is a mis-recognition in which the child is identified with the virtual image that it has correlated with the movements of its own body. 'The function of méconnaissance that characterizes the ego in all its structures', (14) is the product of an effective identification with the image - be it auditory, tactile or visual - that comes about through the fantasy of coherence and bodily control that its appearance provokes. The pleasure that the child experiences via this fantasy, which is in fact alien to its original experience of discordant sensation and lack of motor-coordination, situates a primary Narcissism not, as Rustin would have it, at the 'roots of subjectivity', but at the roots of the ego. The 'self' in this account, that is to say the psychological unity upon which a social identity is premised, is not only a secondary development, it is founded upon what is better called a 'mis-identification ' - a movement towards a point of coherence that is strictly virtual or 'fictional'. Consequent upon this position it needs to be stressed that there is no 'potentially real (even if unknowable) inner self' of the variety proposed by symbolic interactionism, which would then be contrasted with the 'inauthentic "social self"' represented by the ego. That is to say, there is no 'true' self to be represented by the grammatical 'I', or to be alienated in the inauthentic 'me'. The Lacanian concept of the subject is not an analogue for the 'total personality' or 'realised' individual, but a concept in the strict sense of the term: the designation of a space which the individual attempts to fill and the result of a process of positioning by language which is continually disruptive of the motives of consciousness. The 'subject' occupies a social relation that transgresses the bounds of individual subjectivity:

> The subject goes well beyond what is experienced 'subjectively' by the individual. (15)

A relation which re-asserts the transindividual structure of the unconscious

> The unconscious is that part of the concrete discourse, in so far as it is transindividual, that is not at the disposal of the subject in re-establishing the continuity of his conscious discourse. (16)
>
> It is a question of re-centring the subject as speaking in the very lacunae of that in which, at first sight, it presents itself as speaking. (17)

At the basis of Lacan's argument is a theory of language which is double-edged: a theory which accounts for the continuously provisional structure of all forms of human identity by emphasising the disruptive force that haunts their power to impose a reality.

The importance of Lacan's discussions of the 'Fort-Da' game rests upon their attempt to explicate how the child begins to make its entry into the symbolic order of language by considering one of its first and most tentative trials of speech. (By 'speech' is meant the child's efforts at representing itself in language - here by using the alternating phonemes 'Fort' - 'Da' - rather than the simple use of sounds or words as 'markers', with which early speech is often confused.) Here again, this is pre-empted in the Kleinian account in favour of a 'prelinguistic' symbolization (play) of an empirical reality (the child's continued existence as a 'self') that has been threatened by the anxiety provoked by the mother's absence:

> The child is able to hold on to reality that is symbolized in a form of play that he would be in danger of losing contact with without such a representation: its anxiety is thus contained by its game.

The problem that is avoided here is that in order for a child to be able to hold onto a reality - by symbolizing it - or indeed to lose contact with it - by failing to symbolise it - it would apparently have to have some idea of what might constitute a reality in the first place. At the very least it would need to be able to situate itself in relation to the presence and absence of objects. From the child's point of view, for the mother to be simply 'gone' is not the same as her being 'absent'. For Lacan, the 'Fort-Da' game is related to the child's perception that there can be 'something missing' in its world. The game then dramatizes the child's attempt to recover this lack - which its mother's departure has precipitated - by using the alternation of phonemes to situate both the presence and absence of objects, with the help of the cotton reel, in relation to the 'something missing' from which it desires to disassociate itself. Jacqueline Rose outlines the process as follows:

> Lacan ... states that symbolization turns on the subject as absence ... (it) starts, therefore, when the child gets its first sense that something could be missing; words stand for objects, because they only have to be spoken at the moment when the first object is lost. (18)

But behind the processes of symbolization there is no empirical reality to be excavated, held onto or lost, threatened or contained. There is only that which eludes symbolization altogether - a residual black hole at the heart of the object world which Lacan calls the Real and which grants to discourse its materiality. Faced with that particular difficulty, Freud only had the confidence to hope 'that internal objects are less unknowable than the external world'. (19)

NOTES

1. Since the *NLR* article 'A Socialist Consideration of Kleinian Psychoanalysis' represents a broader development of the same theme, I have taken the liberty of quoting from it in making this reply.

2. This seems to me to present an insuperable barrier to the attainment of any overall theoretical coherence within the framework presented. The lack of any rigorous conceptual understanding of 'culture' as an object of theoretical investigation obscures two major problems which remain unaddressed. Firstly, neither 'culture' nor 'cultural studies' comprise any kind of cohesive or unified field of study or set of practices. The extent of the diversity involved is clearly indicated by Stuart Hall in his introduction to *Culture, Media, Language*, (Birmingham CCS, 1980) - which also provides a way of situating the present debate. Secondly, nowhere is it made clear how the proposed empiricist approach could distinguish between 'culture' and 'language' in its account of the social construction of the 'human subject'.

3. 'If, in the register of a traditional psychology, stress is laid on the uncontrollable, infinite character of human desire - seeing in it the mark of some divine slipper that has left its imprint on it - what analytic experience enables us to declare is rather the limited function of desire. Desire, more than any other point in the range of human possibility, meets its limit somewhere.' Jacques Lacan, *The Four Fundamental Concepts of Psychoanalysis* (London, 1977), pp.30-31.

4. 'The liberal in all of us would like to keep sex and politics apart. But it is not possible. Human sexuality concerns encounters not between organs, but between persons; relation between persons are the stuff of morals; and morals, through the shared concept of "justice", seek dramatic confirmation and support in law (not to enforce them is to make the good look fools). Moreover, law and culture reinforce each other: culture is underpinned by law, and law, at bottom, is simply culture in the guise (or as the radical would have it, the disguise) of necessity.' R.A.D. Grant, 'The Politics of Sex', *The Salisbury Review*, p.2.

5. The question of 'biological substructures' and 'human needs' is throughout subjected to some confused thinking by Rustin (*viz NLR*, 131, pp.79-80). For while he stresses the importance of accounting for the inter-relationship of 'biological' and 'socio-cultural' conditions he grants to the former an unwarranted pre-eminence, suggesting that the 'biological substratum' *imposes* 'limits and preoccupations' upon cultures whereas it is precisely those 'limits and preoccupations' which define what a given culture will recognize as biological need.

6. 'Naturally, we have to remember that at birth there is no ego in a conscious sense, but there is a psychic self with ego potential, out of which the sense of self-hood can gradually grow' (Harry Guntrip, *Psychoanalytic Theory, Therapy and the Self* (1977), p.57).

7. Hanna Segal, *Klein* (1979), p.114.

8. Sigmund Freud, 'On Narcissism: An Introduction', *Standard Edition*, vol.XIV, p.77.

9. A partial explanation of the expression 'mother-tongue'?

10. In this 'chinese box' theory in which language is the largest container, it is noticeable that the nurturing role ascribed to the mother effectively masks the exercise of patriarchal authority, be it within the family, or in 'culture' at large.

11. Jacques Lacan, *Ecrits* (London 1977), p.272. This same criticism is cited by Christian Metz in 'The Imaginary Signifier', *Screen*, vol.16, no. 2, p.17 and in *Psychoanalysis and Cinema* (London 1982) p.6 .

12. The best rejoinder to this conflation of the self with the subject is perhaps as follows: 'where the subject sees himself, namely where that real, inverted image of his own body that is given in the schema of the ego is forged, it is not from there that he looks at himself' (*The Four Fundamental Concepts of Psychoanalysis*, p.144).

13. 'The idea of the mirror should be understood as an object which reflects - not just the visible, but also what is heard, touched and willed by the child' (Lacan, 'Revue Française de la Psychanalyse', 1949, cited in J. Mitchell and J. Rose *Feminine Sexuality: Jacques Lacan and the Ecole Freudienne* (London, 1982), p.30.

14. *Ecrits*, p.6.

15. *Ibid.*, p.55.

16. *Ibid.*, p.49.

17. *The Four Fundamental Concepts of Psychoanalysis*, p.83.

18. *Feminine Sexuality*, p.31.

19. Sigmund Freud, 'The Unconscious', *Standard Edition*, vol.XIV, p.171.

POLITICS, PEDAGOGY, WORK: REFLECTIONS ON
THE 'PROJECT' OF THE LAST SIX YEARS

David Punter

This paper is about educational practice: about the specificity of the teaching of English in higher education as that task appears in the present context. It is also about the dangers of collusion, as they may come to affect a left-wing intelligentsia. I want to stress at the outset that 'collusion' does not mean that there is no possibility of progress in the politicised practice of the teaching of literature; but I assume that innovations, new ways of attempting what Foucault calls the 'insurrection of subjugated knowledges', (1) will inevitably bear the traces of those older knowledges which bear the imprint of state sanction and are embedded in the processes of state power, and that it is necessary to distinguish and foreground those traces if we are to take part in an enlivening practice in the course of which new meanings can be produced. I assume that there are specific functions in British society which the teaching of English has been traditionally structured to discharge, functions inscribed in pedagogic mode itself; the question for us is about what those functions might now be and, assuming that they are functions which serve to help with the postponement of the terminal phase of capitalism, how we might dislocate literary education from the overall system of discourses and knowledges into which it is inserted.

That Foucauldian discourse can also be translated, I believe, into a discourse based on the kind of psychoanalysis of group dynamics flowing from the work of Melanie Klein and Wilfred Bion, in which case the questions might be these: what are the meanings which the 'group' of literary intellectuals holds for society at large? What meaning of the 'literary' is that group being obliged to introject and reproduce? And, within that, what role are Marxists like ourselves being asked to take up? (2) What kind of symbol are we, here and now in the Essex conference as a continuing sub-system? It seems to me that these are the kinds of question to which we ought to be able to give an answer, because, after all, we are skilled in the reading of symbols: it is our trade. And although they are not the only questions which could be asked within this framework, they do touch in significant ways on unconscious process.

I want to tread a rather convoluted path in this paper; and I want to stress that it is a sequence of hypotheses, to be tested. The circuitousness is necessary because the teaching of literature over the last six years has been to a large extent drained. There are, of course, specific examples of political progress - the formation of the Literature Teaching Politics group, the publicisation of new pedagogic modes (3) - but for the most part I assume that the politicising task which we attempt in the course of our teaching now is a very difficult one. I am reminded of Philip Larkin's comment that 'Life is first boredom, then fear': (4) certainly that corresponds to the trajectory of many students, as they come to study English in universities, polytechnics, colleges. They find that what is provided has little to do with the socio-psychological reasons which have drawn them to the reading of literature in the first place; they find, because the site of literary study has been to a large extent evacuated of certain kinds of unconscious material, little interest in listening to shadow controversies; and they then become submerged in the terror of potential unemployment, a terror which, I fear, will become coupled with a resentment against the incapacity of the 'humanities' to protect them from economic and personal catastrophe, and will thus multiply the levels of politically motivated philistinism in the society of the future. I want at this point to throw in a comment from Foucault, the relevance of which to my argument will, I hope, become clearer later:

> The essential political problem for the intellectual is not to criticise the ideological contents supposedly linked to science, or to ensure that his own scientific practice is accompanied by a correct ideology, but that of ascertaining the possibility of constituting a new politics of truth. The problem is not changing people's consciousnesses - or what's in their heads - but the political, economic, institutional régime of the production of truth.
> It's not a matter of emancipating truth from every system of power (which would be a chimera, for truth is already power) but of detaching the power of truth from the forms of hegemony, social, economic and cultural, within which it operates at the present time. (5)

Althusser and others have said that educational practice is the major ideological state apparatus, around which many others cluster. (6) There are three questions we need to put on our continuing agenda:

1) what specific functions does the higher teaching of English habitually discharge on behalf of the State?

2) in what ways can we see the forms of educational practice in English as reproducing or representing the relations of production in the social formation at large?

3) by what means does this specific educational practice provide itself with a 'store of energy' which can be deployed in the service of state interests?

The first two questions are conventional within an Althusserian framework: my justification in adding the third, more psychopolitical question comes again from Foucault who, in the course of discussing the relations between 'structure' and 'event', says that:

> The problem is at once to distinguish among events, to differentiate the networks and levels to which they belong, and to reconstitute the lines along which they are connected and engender one another. From this follows a refusal of analyses couched in terms of the symbolic field or the domain of signifying structures, and a recourse to analyses in terms of the genealogy of relations of force, strategic developments, and tactics. (7)

In working on this particular form of practice, we are dealing not only with the production or inhibition of knowledges, but also with the distribution of powers, and the powers at stake in 'English' are of a very complex kind. (8)

Essentially, I believe it is possible to formulate the 'crisis in English studies' in terms of a crisis in pedagogic mode: the forms in

which we teach - tutorial, lecture, seminar - promulgate a series of
substitute gratifications, for all participants, and provide an unconscious substratum of conservatism which acts as a countertext to our
efforts, such as they are, to radicalise the 'canon'. (9) While those
modes remain unaltered, the authority structure which underpins the
educational practice cannot be opened to challenge, and our messages
are drowned in the wash of background noise which begins each time one
of us, or one of our students, sets foot in lecture-room or study. For
the most part, we are reduced to playing out fantasies of leadership
and 'membership' which have no relation to the necessity for political
change, and yet we remain unwilling to carry out the experiential examination of primary (unconscious) process which might unfreeze the
structure. It would be cheering to believe that this is to depict a
discourse, a practice, to which we as Marxists are tangential, to consider that we have learnt, at least to an extent, the lesson Foucault
teaches us about the death of the universal intellectual:

> For a long period, the 'left' intellectual spoke and was
> acknowledged the right of speaking in the capacity of master
> of truth and justice. He was heard, or purported to make
> himself heard, as the spokesman of the universal. ... Some
> years have now passed since the intellectual was called upon
> to play this role. A new mode of the 'connexion between
> theory and practice' has been established. Intellectuals
> have got used to working, not in the modality of the 'uni-
> versal', the 'exemplary', the 'just-and-true-for-all', but
> within specific sectors, at the precise points where their
> own conditions of life or work situate them (housing, the
> hospital, the asylum, the laboratory, the university, family
> and sexual relations). ... This is what I would call the
> 'specific' intellectual as opposed to the 'universal' in-
> tellectual. (10)

Brave and optimistic words, and to some extent true. The major modification in educational practice, it seems to me, over the last six years
has indeed been an increased attention to work, to the active transformation of the text in the course of the production of meaning. There has
been some desacralisation of the text; some realisation that mere 'discussion' may not be the final goal of education; some attempt to realise
an intimacy with textual workings, so that some of the alienation in the
process may be squeezed out. But the evolution of a new educational
practice has encountered many problems, and here I want to foreground
three of them, as the crucial obstacles to pedagogic progress: the problem of phallomorphism, the controversy about subjectivity and the question of the production of theory itself.

My views on phallomorphism as it affects and deforms educational
practice will doubtless be controversial, and may well appear to some
archaic, since my attempts to wrestle with it have not got beyond the
1977/8 'debate', in the pages of *Ideology and Consciousness*, between
Luce Irigaray and Monique Plaza. I can summarise this debate in a few
quotations. Irigaray cites Lacan as complaining: 'I beg [women] on my
knees to tell me what they want and they tell me nothing'; (11) this,
according to Irigaray, is because Lacan 'situates himself in the functioning of language and of desire in which women cannot say anything,
and in which he cannot hear them, even if they were to begin to speak to
him. ... he cannot bear that someone else speaks anything but his
truth as he describes it'. Men cannot hear women because the 'grid'
through which we hear functions to exclude, and in particular to exclude
the many-voiced: we remain deaf to the refusal of phallomorphic unity
which Cixous characterises:

always more than one, diverse, capable of being all those
it will at one time be, a group acting together, a collection of singular beings that produce the enunciation.
Being several and insubordinable, the subject can resist
subjugation. (12)

Thus for Irigaray, the power of women is a 'something else being kept
in reserve': 'in hysteria there is always a power in reserve at the
same time as a power which is paralysed'. (13) Plaza's objection to
this characterisation of women as absence, as silence, as the conditional is doubtless well-known:

by projecting women in a conditional way, by arguing from
her present non-existence, we remain prisoners of our own
oppression ... It is here: in the society in which we
live, and now, that we must situate our reality as women,
and not in the timeless splits of our body or of our
essence. (Plaza, p.8)

According to Plaza, Irigaray 'closes us in the shroud of our own sex,
reduces us to the state of child-women; illogical, mad, prattling,
fanciful' (Plaza, p.31), by refusing the category of women as also the
general-individual, and she cites Irigaray thus:

'She' is indefinitely other in herself. It is doubtless
because of this that she is said to be capricious, incomprehensible, fanciful, agitated ... Without going so far
as evoking her language, where 'she' sets off in every
sense without 'him' locating the coherence of any sense.
Contradictory words, a little mad for the logic of reason,
inaudible to those who listen with ready-made grids, with
a code already worked out.

For Plaza this is merely an extension of the 'patriarchal chain', which
arose 'after the emergence of feminism. That is, after women's oppression by the social system was recognised. It consists in invalidating
this discovery, in channelling women's research into a perspective
which allows the concealment and perpetuation of patriarchy' (Plaza,
p.32).

I may seem to have moved away from educational practice: let me
bring myself back through my own experience. A few weeks ago, I was
involved in planning a workshop on the teaching of English in tertiary
educational institutions. (15) The workshop has happened before, and
has been to a large extent staffed by men. Already, in the three years
of its operation, an orthodoxy has emerged, built on several premises.
The principal premise is that the primary task of the workshop is to
get the members to engage in literary work on their own authority; thus
that the function of the staff is to provide them with opportunities to
do that, rather than to instruct. The techniques we have used have thus
consisted largely in methodological demonstration and practice. I proposed a method for a specific pair of sessions on ideology and myth,
which entailed a series of 'exercises' designed to alert members to the
latent content of cultural myths, advertisements and so on, and at the
same time, I hoped, to engage with their own rememorations of myths and
legends. My justification was that, if we are to de-mystify the learning process, we need to offer precise tasks, to define detailed kinds
of work to be attempted, rather than moving within the vague coordinates of traditional 'teaching'. A female colleague later proposed a
working method for a session on gender and writing, which consisted, as
far as I could see, of no method at all; the point of the session would
be for her to produce certain women's texts, and a discussion was then

to ensue. This looked to me like a regression, but it did not look like that to her; she thought rather that the kind of method I was proposing was phallomorphic, insofar as it set out a controlled discursive system. I have no idea what the solution is to that; but clearly one consequence of the analysis of phallomorphism in society is coming to be that many kinds of work are themselves being revealed as phallomorphic. To the extent that this is so, the very innovations and demystifications attempted may be collusive: that is to say, they may collaborate in the reduction of literary work to the 'technical', rather than opening the discourse to change, and may collaborate in a sexual deadlock.

My second instance concerns subjectivity, and in my mind there is the article in the first issue of *Literature Teaching Politics* in which a group of students report on their experience of being exposed to two different teaching methods, one characterised as post-structuralist, the other as subjectivist, and assert the value of the former at the expense of the latter. (16) I cannot say I formed a very detailed impression of post-structuralist teaching method from the article; but in any case, my concern is with the other side of the coin, with the role of 'subjectivism' in teaching, and with the possibility that here too we are reaching an impasse.

Subjectivist teaching practice, as used by David Bleich at the University of Indiana and others, focuses on the actual responses students have to works of literature. (17) Underpinning it is a world-view which is curiously parallel in places to the '"Copernican" revolution' which Catherine Belsey talks of in *Critical Practice*. (18) The premise is that epistemologies of objectivity have been undermined; that the text as text needs now to be seen within a complex of relations, which will include, and indeed be based on, the student's actual perception of the text, which will in turn be based on features of earlier psychological development. Thus the function of teaching becomes the liberation, and validation through negotiation, of those perceptions, in the course of which the student is enabled to take on his or her own authority for critical practice. The role of the teacher becomes the optimisation of conditions in which that transfer of authority can take place. (19)

The Marxist polemic against this kind of method bases itself on the importance of not treating subjectivity as an unproblematic unity, and of focusing attention on the historical constitution of the subject: (20) but it seems to me that here, as with the problem of phallomorphism, there is an issue of strategy. As far as educational practice is concerned, as distinct from critical practice, the installation of subjectivity can be the origin of a revolution. The redoubled authority of text and teacher as traditionally established, a refraction of the mediated surveillance systems of political control, cannot be simply taken as an available site for the investigation of the construction of subjectivity; that way, I suggest, subjectivity as a category falls again under the sway of the Absolute Subject, and the individual experience is one of being lost in the discourse. It is, paradoxically, only through the experience of attempting to own an element in that discourse, through the experience of feeling towards personal authority, that the limits and obstacles of ideology can be disclosed. Obviously those limits are already present in the ambiguities of the phrase 'transfer of authority'; but they will remain unexamined, and hence reproduced by specific intellectuals in their sites of work, unless the travails of the becoming-of-the-subject are available within practice.

My suggestion is that, in both these areas, <u>critical</u> sophistication can lead to a <u>pedagogic</u> collusion with established lines of authority;

distributions of power become validated by a confusion of discourses, and this rests partly on the undoubted fact that Foucault's statement about the emergence of the specific intellectual is in fact a project rather than an accomplishment; for instance, most academics still base their own claim to authority on work assumed to be in the public arena - books, articles, conference papers - rather than on their location and power relations within their institutions; thus students become spectators on a far-away struggle, which to them will appear as a struggle of shadows, rather than participants in a local struggle for their own power as women and men, and as agents within the teaching/learning process. One result of this is the familiar nostalgia for the university, which has converted so many professional echelons into awful imitations, and which rests on the disparity between goal and achievement so painfully felt in what we proffer as student life.

And I would say that the same confusion affects the third of my instances, the production of theory itself, in several different ways. Here, it seems to me, we continue to proceed as though the universal intellectual were the receiver of our messages, as though, while knowing at least that we are no longer in the business of turning out gentlemen of leisure, we are nonetheless engaged in the construction of the intelligent reader of literature, on his or her guard against ideological operation, able to view the world of representations with a discriminating eye and to maintain within the realm of commodities a poised awareness of the capitulations offered in the name of the literary. This is for the most part a self-regarding fiction, which has its psychological origin in a type of mirroring: the preferred objects of our educational practice are very like ourselves. To an extent, there has been some justification for this while the flow of students into academic life still existed; that is now effectively, as we all know, dammed. In fact, the individuals whom we educate are going to occupy a variety of positions in the social formation: they are going to become, perhaps, social workers, probation officers, recreational managers. (21) Where is the theory which takes its own realisations seriously, and attempts to interpellate the real subjects of its discourse?

It seems to me that this kind of argument finds us as Marxists in a very uneasy position. The only model on offer for how literary education might relate to this heterogeneous bundle of roles is one which we take to be discredited: that somehow a history and habit of reading might 'humanise' the professional. An alternative would be that semiotics really is what it has for so long claimed to be, a totalising science: but if this is so, most educational practice remains fatally ungeared to it. And the hiatus rests, of course, on deeper ambiguities: ambiguities about whether, actually, we want to produce a form of education which may in turn be placed at the service of oiling the social wheels more smoothly. My suggestion is that Marxist theory colludes with capitalist design by refusing to examine the concept of education for competence; and that in doing so, it is collaborating in producing a student body increasingly characterisable as cynical, increasingly engaged in proficiency of reading as a mere qualification of a pseudo-universal kind.

Under these circumstances, the opportunities for the local redistributions of power slip by: the revelation of the fraudulent in literature and culture becomes an end in itself, while the practical development of those skills which might be used to 'read' the social formation is ignored. Here Barthes stands as an important example: since his death critics of right and left have crowded round to bestow those ambiguous laurels which simultaneously crown an unrepeatable achievement. (22) Yet what was important about *Mythologies* had very little to do with the analysis of specific cultural examples, everything to do with the possibility that here was, and is, a text which offers precisely the potential for method: that the <u>writing</u> of Barthesian analyses would be of the essence of good educational practice, and this pretty much regardless of grasp on the complex conceptualisations of myth which, in effect, serve as the book's guardian angels, warning off the reader and sealing the text as moment.

My point is that these issues of difference - gender, subjectivity, theory - need to be inserted into educational practice in terms of specific strategies; not as shadow-struggles for observation, but as the sites for specific methods, for unless they give rise to methodology they serve merely as the means for reproducing in the educational realm those crucial divisions which act as the major practical obstacles to social change. Like post-nuclear ghosts enmeshed in a struggle of fantasies, we thus become the symbols for the way in which interpretation itself is being 'ghosted', made into the unreal, by the expansion of an obscenely reductive concept of 'technique'. As literature returns to the condition of commodity, interpretation becomes redundant, and even the older functions of a literary education become superfluous. As society no longer needs to shore up any pretensions to culture, so it is turning literary academics to a new use, and forcing us to collude in the atrophy of agency.

I want to offer you, as a text for the times, *Fahrenheit 451*: and to run through some work which I have done with students on unravelling the unconscious process of that text, because I believe it throws light on the societal and cultural project which education, and specifically literary education, is being called upon to serve, and thus on the position which we as educators are being pressured into occupying. The technology and futuristic projections of *Fahrenheit 451* may have come to seem old-fashioned, but this does not affect the way in which the text as myth lives on and contributes to laying down tracks into the imaginary future. I begin from a quotation near the end, where Granger is talking to Montag and welcoming him to his new life in exile:

> When I was a boy my grandfather died, and he was a sculptor. He was also a very kind man who had a lot of love to give to the world, and he helped clean up the slum in our town; and he made toys for us and he did a million things in his lifetime; he was always busy with his hands. And when he died, I suddenly realised I wasn't crying for him at all, but for all the things he did. ... He was part of us and when he died, all the actions stopped dead and there was no one to do them just the way he did. He was individual. He was an important man. I've never gotten over his death. (23)

The old association of the name 'granger' with the husbandman of the Lord, the good tenant-farmer who makes the most of his talents, discloses the affinities between Granger's grandfather and Montag, 'Saint Monday', holy relic of a world before the enclosure of space and time. In that world, we are told, the skill of shaping could move and distribute itself freely down the channels of power: sculpting and town planning were fused in a universal concept of 'good works'. Yet the <u>books</u> which are the central topic of *Fahrenheit 451* have an uneasy relation to this concept of communicational flow, and this is the site of irresolution in the text: channel for experience, and also blocking artefact, the book is not a direct means of transmission but a double symbol. 'They weren't at all certain that the things they carried in their heads might make every future dawn glow with a purer light, they were sure of nothing save that the books were on file behind their quiet eyes, the books were waiting, with their pages uncut, for the customers who might come by in later years, some with clean and some with dirty fingers' (Bradbury, p.148): transmission into the present is thus subordinated to the demand for a channel direct from past to future, and what is encoded is the fear that the present is too tarnished to allow for revelation. The only way to escape societal surveillance is through a separation: the conscious contents of the mind can be allowed to remain trivial - must remain trivial if they are not to be detectable by the probes of authority, the deadly scenting of the Mechanical Hound - provided we can cheer ourselves up with the thought that, below the surface, in people like us, the wisdom of ages is stored, un-conscious, providing the source for an unimaginable future educational practice.

The literary thus hides itself and sulks; (24) but in fact, it has already been taken over, reduced itself willingly to quantification under the thin guise of quality control. Montag is asked:

Do you know why books such as this are so important? Because they have quality. And what does the word quality mean? To me it means texture. This book has pores. It has features. This book can go under the microscope. You'd find life under the glass, streaming past in infinite profusion. The more pores, the more truthfully recorded details of ·life per square inch you can get on a sheet of paper, the more 'literary' you are.
(Bradbury, p.82)

But this is a capitulation in the discourse of data storage, and the text knows it: only in the future can we do anything with the streaks on the tulip except number them, and in the meantime the text must pass the time on the shelf of a human library. Secrecy and the existence of an élite of 'Voluntary Nobility' become the mirroring response to the freemasonry of the firemen: (25) what is thus enacted is the academy, cheated of access to power, turning into a temporary consumer, absorbing back into itself the sweetness and light which a blackened world rejects. In *Fahrenheit 451*, the controlling wish is for the validation of the unaccompanied word, for the refusal of the hieroglyphs of commercial and political persuasion represented in the televisor and the White Clown; the text realises that what is proposed can therefore be nothing less than a change in the processes of time and space, a switch from the domestic interior and the programme note to the wilderness of unsurveyed leisure.

What Foucault can be taken to suggest is that this opposition should be seen as a reflection of the ways in which, operating in our own minds and bodies on behalf of the sources of state power, we exercise surveillance over ourselves, in the name not of repression but of specific distributions of pleasure. The new mechanism of power, according to Foucault, is 'constantly exercised by means of surveillance rather than in a discontinuous manner by means of a system of levies or obligations distributed over time. It presupposes a tightly knit grid of material coercions rather than the physical existence of a sovereign'. (26) Within this system, it is obvious that the televisor represents the tightly knit grid, without loopholes; what is less obvious, because it is partly suppressed by the text, is the significance of the books (the sources of our own authority as academics). The charge of pleasure connected to the book, to the naked text, is here associated with, I believe, a wish for a return to the older system of sovereignty and domination. The book, indeed, is apparently freed from time: it can be picked up and put down, parts of the memory can be rerun at will. But over this illusory freedom, which is also the illusory freedom we offer our students, hovers the domination of established concepts of culture, the internalisation, particularly strong in teachers of English, of an allegiance to simple textuality which is feudal in its intensity, no less slavish in its resistance to change. (27)

And the pleasure of the unaccompanied text in *Fahrenheit 451*, itself a convenient training in humility and self-denial, is caught up, as we might predict, in an unarticulated set of gender assumptions: what female reliance on the televisor is said to effect is the breakdown of the family, but what lurks behind this is an unacceptable challenge to male authority, and it is this which Montag flees to be with a new Rosicrucian 'brotherhood', leaving the women to an endless round of coffee mornings. It is only the male, we are told, who can be truly scorched by the flames of experience: their heat is contrasted with the steady white light of the screen, and we are invited to collude in a masculine but sexless resurrection. After the cataclysm,

> The other men lay a while, on the dawn edge of sleep, not yet ready to rise up and begin the day's obligations, its fires and foods, its thousand details of putting foot after foot and hand after hand. They lay blinking their dusty eyelids. You could hear them breathing fast, then slower, then slow ... (Bradbury, p.155)

Womb envy is evidenced in the tucking away of the seeds of the future, the return to a modified 'tribal' vision where male obligation is rendered palatable by a clutching of creativity to the masculine self in a Hemingway-esque projection of hunting and poetry, from which women are excluded as they are excluded from the real academies. Here, all the books are garnered away from the dangerous city, but the passivity of the televisor is in the end merely replicated by the passivity of continuous and pointless rememoration, an endless wandering in search of the lost secret of reproduction and birth. The text turns in on itself, and the fear of the complexity of knowledges is drowned in a 'child-like' sleep, in a space without organisation or direction.

I offer this brief account as a literary and symbolic parallel to the processes of collusion in resistance to change within the institution, and it touches on the three areas I've already mentioned: the insistent phallomorphism of the options for survival on offer, the dismantling of subjectivity through symbolic severances within the psyche, and the locking away of ideas about literature because, in this terrible present, we cannot risk the strategies through which they might be made available.

A symbolic structure to do with the displacement of desire and agency can be detected at the root of various of the institutions and practices in which the 'literary' is housed, and I suggest that this relates to an unconscious wish within the wider society, which has to do with the renunciation of responsibility for complexity, and with a set of fictions (lies) about ideological transparency. Which brings us, inevitably, to the Falklands. (28) I don't want to talk about the obvious ways in which myths of heroism have been invoked to justify murder, but just to make some fringe points. It seems to me clear that the Falkland Islands, symbolically, are these islands: a small pair of islands off a hostile mainland. Among other things, we have been hitting back at the imminent Latinisation of the Common Market; while, of course, also rerunning old movies of the Second World War. For the false virility which has been the basis of our actions in the South Atlantic has not, in this way, previously been tested: Britain has taken its international stance, for centuries, on being uninvadable, but that is a stand-off. The dreadful event, the invasion of home earth, has not happened; now, in the Falklands, that invasion can be experienced vicariously and punished vicariously.

What the Falklands have enabled us to play out is a primitive enactment of international affairs, and one which we would prefer: just as we choose to believe that affairs at home would be so much simpler if it were not for the 'illicit' cabals of mainland Europe, so we blithely behave as though destabilisation of the Argentinian regime is none of our business, despite what were at times obvious risks of other border conflicts flaring up if the Argentinian air force became too depleted. The image of Clydeside workers cheerfully buckling down to unpaid overtime now the emergency is really here is a ready alternative to thinking too much on the problems of leisure: Space Invaders on a grand scale, with occasional epilepsy an acceptable risk.

Above all, the Falklands have been used to remind us of the fiction that Britain is a country where communication is free and true: despite the delays in news, we have been fed with an endless succession of information, in the attempt to persuade us that knowledge, here, is uncensored, that it flows freely through the untrammelled air as the navy sails below cloudless skies. (29) Not for us the murkier aspects of a Vietnam, of a war where, tucked out of sight, Western armed forces demonstrate that military imperatives may pale and be forgotten in the jungles. Everything is seen from the air, in two careful dimensions: like Treasure Island, the Falkland Islands are presented as the simple, empty territory, in which stockades can be erected and fantasies of new beginnings, before the population explosion, be played out in a fixed economy of ships and planes. Foucault makes the point that the most significant recent changes in the structuring of power came at the point when governments decided that, in order to govern, they needed to know facts about population: (30) the Falklands provide a simple set of equations, equations of life and death, of strength and weakness, away from the muddle of wrecked planning and resource starvation which characterises our inner cities. We all know now that the cost of HMS Sheffield would build 200 secondary schools, or four brand-new hospitals, but the numbers game and the war of principle cannot be allowed to intersect.

Let me try to bring this material back to the question of educational practice in a number of different ways. Plaza makes this comment on 'Other'-ness:

> The Other is always the negative of the One, the Same. The notion of Difference necessarily founds the constitution of a dominant referent (the Same) and a referred dominated (the Other). It is to be feared insofar as it implies the idea of a hierarchy when it orders social relations. It consists of a double movement: it accords primacy to one term that it erects as a norm and casts the other into the negative, the monstrous. (Plaza, pp.13-14)

War, of course, is the system in which this absolute domination of the Other appears in its most naked and violent form: the Other as monster, as fiend, and, of course, as dirty, mired in the freezing swamps of the Falklands (which simultaneously, of course, are portrayed from our point of view of the islanders as a haven). But in the realm of educational practice, there is also a casting of the Other, and a set of assumptions about possible relationships. Cixous talks about it in connexion with the theatre, although she uses the more ambiguous and, for us, more helpful term 'poet' to characterise the super-agent on the scene of suppression:

The poet behaves with regard to his audience like the
leader (as described by Freud) with regard to a primary
horde: he deprives it of the real world and plunges it
into a place of violence, where he moves it, tortures it,
impassions it - in short, makes it dance to the tune of
his pipe. This great paranoid encounters virtually no resistance since he is assisted by the servant-stagehands.
No more theatre, no more real. What is left is the imaginary and its magical, wicked, ephemeral aspects, the paltry
offerings of the fantastic, insofar as it is alienating:
for the 'spectacle' doesn't give the poor, swindled spectator his <u>own</u> phantasms to enjoy. (Cixous, p.400)

This seems to me to be a good account of the meaning of the 'spectacle'
of the Falklands, and in that realm the nature of the mysterious 'servant-
stagehands' is obvious; but it is also a description of communicational
charisma which operates through all the levels of discourse, through
all the practices of power. In the case of educational practice, it is
a description of non-participatory work: and here, as in various other
registers, the servant-stagehands are harder to see as they scuttle
about their business, for they are largely internalised. It is elements
within our own historical subject-positioning which encourage us, and
our students, to put up with forms of education which rely on the transmission of spectacle, and which thus transmit further into the body of
society an ineradicable blend of fear and pleasure in our experience as
primary horde, as lecture audience.

I mentioned in my prospectus that among the levels of discourse I
wanted to consider was the Essex conference itself, but I have only one
comment to make; and that is that the function of this sub-system has
become, it seems to me, subordinated to the demands of the situation
Cixous describes: that is to say that under the guise of productive work,
the real text of the conferences, like that of most educational estab-
lishments, is one of consumption. The institutions, perhaps we say,
provide us with a bad diet: but a fix of sound discourse will correct
the imbalance. Also, of course, there is a relativisation of the institutional: alongside the real institutions, where we might form embat-
tled minorities, there is the shadow institution, in which preconcep-
tions can be shared, and the whole difficult labour of constantly re-
forming the shapes of the generations can be avoided.

There is, clearly, a mark of 'difference': that the Essex conferences in some way provide a countertext. But the modes, the lecture
and the overcrowded seminar, with their particular shapings of unconscious process, remain the same; the concentration of fantasy around
charismatic leadership - with, of course, the inevitable requirement
that the leader will also commit a satisfying temporary suicide during
question time - remains, and the possibility of collaborative, socialist
work remains a project for the far horizon. What is in my mind as I
think of those possibilities is, I believe, a parallel within educational
practice to some thinking in the realm of critical practice. I am reminded particularly of Belsey's book, and of the fact that, when she
reaches a point in it which seems to me parallel to the point I have
reached in this paper, two things happen: a concept appears, that of the
'interrogative text', and a name appears, that of Brecht. (31)

About the concept of the interrogative text, I have some doubts: I
would prefer to speak of an interrogative critical practice, within which
the text will figure as an element in a system. And I would like also
to speak of the possibility of an interrogative educational practice,
which could not be the same, but which would perform parallel functions:

beyond the imperative and the affirmative modes, the instructional and the knowledgeful, a mode which would provide opportunities for the formulation of questions; but the difficulties are great. Brecht's relevance is in terms of the foregrounding of estrangement: in the most obvious sense, perhaps, in the offering of a silence to be filled, rather than of a continuous series of primary and secondary 'texts' to be juggled. In case this might seem a trivial matter, a final quotation from Foucault:

> The intellectual 'par excellence' used to be the writer: as a universal consciousness, a free subject, he was counterposed to those intellectuals who were merely competent instances in the service of the State or Capital - technicians, magistrates, teachers. ... This process [of recent change] explains how, even as the writer tends to disappear as a figurehead, the university and the academic emerge, if not as principal elements, at least as 'exchangers', privileged points of intersection. If the universities and education have become politically ultrasensitive areas, this is no doubt the reason why. And what is called the crisis of the universities should not be interpreted as a loss of power, but on the contrary as a multiplication and reinforcement of their power-effects as centres in a polymorphous ensemble of intellectuals who virtually all pass.through and relate themselves to the academic system. (32)

It is that 'relate themselves to' which I would want to seize on, and which I believe we as Marxists need to elaborate. We are all familiar with the doubleness of ideological operation; in the process of forming a world, albeit full of contradictions and half-effective operations, ideology also produces us as subjects, and in this case as Marxist intellectuals, also, no doubt, full of contradictions and half-effective operations. To do transforming work on the ideological clearly involves taking on both sides of this dialectic: not only interrogating the text, but also interrogating our own subject positions and the histories which have formed them. In this sense, the interrogative mode of educational practice would be one within which our own positions, our capitulations, our insertion into the academic, would have to become available to discourse; but there is a strong resistance to such a process, no less strong on the Left than elsewhere - stronger in one sense, in that this kind of exploration can be categorised as a naive psychologising. And there is another problem with the educational which does not have to be tackled in the course of critical practice, which is that the 'text' itself is broader: it encompasses not only the verbal but also the gestural, the messages delivered through us to our students by our behaviour, and the resistance we may have to opening that up as a field for interrogative discourse.

'He or she is alternately interpolated', says Belsey, describing interrogative critical discourse, 'drawn in to the events, and distanced, pulling out of the fixity of ideology and into active critical debate' (Belsey, p.94). This could also be taken as a general description of the desired educational activity, and of the estrangement which could be built into it to avoid the deathly pull of the obvious. What I am trying to suggest is, with Brecht, that the deployment into the 'interrogative' implies transfer of authority in order to produce the conditions for the resurrection of suppressed knowledges, revision of the subject-positionings available for action; a consequence would be that the fatal pull into positions of self and other, leader and primal horde, would be put into flux, held away from fixity. In some ways, this manifestation of the interrogative mode can be begun in quite small ways, and indeed must be if we are to resist the phallic attractions of the global: for instance, the competitive and gender-determined model of inquisitor and answerer can be broken up temporarily by various kinds of manipulation of grouping. The false naturalness of the transition from information-giving to questions can be foregrounded by providing opportunities for enquiry into the experiential: what does it feel like to have been on the receiving end of this one man's discourse for over an hour? What subject-positions have been available for me during this particular bit of practice? What fantasies of dominance and suppression are being played out in this scenario? What social divisions are being reproduced in this discourse, and what lies behind them? And, and this is my final point, what kinds of closure are effected in educational practice? How can I stop without ending? (33)

NOTES

1. Foucault, 'Two Lectures', in *Power/Knowledge: Selected Interviews and Other Writings 1972-1977*, ed. C. Gordon (Brighton, 1980), p.81. Most of the Foucault references in this essay are to *Power/Knowledge*, which seems to me the most politically useful of the available texts.

2. I am trying here to refer to the concept of 'group culture' developed especially in W.R. Bion, *Experiences in Groups and Other Papers* (London, 1961), and to its heuristic roots. See Bion's references (p. 191) and especially Melanie Klein, *Contributions to Psycho-analysis, 1921-1945* (London, 1948).

3. See, for instance, some of the work in *Yale French Studies*, No.63 (1982): *The Pedagogical Imperative: Teaching as a Literary Genre*, although here it is not so much the modes which are new as the authorisation to describe and reflect upon them.

4. Larkin, 'Dockery and Son', in *The Whitsun Weddings* (London, 1964), p.38.

5. Foucault, 'Truth and Power', in *Power/Knowledge*, p.133.

6. See Althusser, 'Ideology and Ideological State Apparatuses', in *Lenin and Philosophy and Other Essays*, trans. Ben Brewster (London, 1971), pp.127-128, 136-149. Cf. Althusser, *Politics and History*, trans. Brewster (London, 1972), pp.62-63, and *For Marx*, trans. Brewster (London, 1977), p.234.

7. Foucault, 'Truth and Power', in *Power/Knowledge*, p.114.

8. I have gone into greater detail about the unconscious structure of pedagogy in my 'University English Teaching: Observations on Symbolism and Reflexivity', *Glyph: Textual Studies* (forthcoming).

9. I was conscious, when giving this as a lecture, that the conference baulked at my denigration of changes in the canon: my argument, though, would be that to focus exclusively on the content of that presented is further to articulate the levels of reification, and that it is the mechanism of presentation (of 'presence') itself which thus continually eludes our attention, resulting in a leaking away of the truly political.

10. Foucault, 'Truth and Power', in *Power/Knowledge*, p.126.

11. 'Women's Exile: Interview with Luce Irigaray', *Ideology and Consciousness*, No.1 (May, 1977), p.71.

12. Cixous, 'The Character of "Character"', *New Literary History*, V, (1973-4), 387.

13. Irigaray, *Ce sexe qui n'en est pas un* (Paris, 1977), p.136; quoted in Monique Plaza, '"Phallomorphic Power" and the Psychology of "Women"', *Ideology and Consciousness*, No.4 (Autumn, 1978), p.28.

14. Irigaray, *Ce sexe qui n'en est pas un*, pp.28-29, quoted in Plaza, pp.31-32.

15. In the series organised by DUET (the Development of University English Teaching Project). See John Broadbent, 'Untwisting All the Chains', *Quinquereme: New Studies in Modern Languages*, IV, 2 (July, 1981), 225-230; and 'That Melodious Noise', *Studies in Higher Education*, VII, 1 (1982), 35-45.

16. See Glyn Fry, Nicola Powe, Paul Vernell, 'Politics, Teaching, Criticism', *Literature Teaching Politics*, No.1 (1982), pp.50-57.

17. See Bleich, *Subjective Criticism* (Baltimore, Maryland, 1978); also Bleich, 'The Identity of Pedagogy and Research in the Study of Response to Literature', *College English*, XLII (1980), 350-366.

18. Belsey, *Critical Practice* (London, 1980), pp.130-137.

19. This is a radical simplification of Bleich's epistemology and procedures. See especially *Subjective Criticism*, pp.213-237.

20. See, of course, the seminal arguments of Marx and Engels against Bauer and others in *The Holy Family*, in *Collected Works* (London 1975-), IV, 5-211, and more importantly against Stirner in *The German Ideology*, in *Collected Works*, V, especially 193-314.

21. More probably, they are not going to be employed at all, and are going to experience at first hand the vicious contradiction at the heart of the bourgeois concept of leisure.

22. See, for instance, Peter Conrad, 'Images of Mortality', *The Observer* (14th Feb. 1982), p.32. This is not an obituary but a review of Barthes, *Camera Lucida: Reflections on Photography* (1981), and is structured as a thinly-veiled threat against those who might presume to 'use' Barthes' perceptual framework.

23. Ray Bradbury, *Fahrenheit 451* (London, 1954), p.149.

24. Here I am indebted to the other members of the UEA English Studies Group (Jonathan Cook, Diane DeBell, Thomas Elsasser and Su Kappeler), and to our work on the politics of the contemporary literary.

25. The reference is to Harold Monro and Maurice Browne, *Proposals for a Voluntary Nobility* (1907), referred to by I.F. Clarke in *The Pattern of Expectation 1644-2001* (London, 1979), as 'one of the most pretentious declarations in the history of utopian literature' (p.215). The significance is that it is (male) fantasies of this type which have fostered the life of the 'academy' from Plato to Monro's mentor, Wells.

26. Foucault, 'Two Lectures', in *Power/Knowledge*, p.104.

27. The continuous imagistic string which runs through Rosicrucianism, freemasonry and their many avatars underlines the false premise of a masculine enlightenment descending from above; its most relevant figure is the Senior Common Room.

28. Some of these comments arise from work done with John Broadbent in connexion with DUET (see note 16 above).

29. The contradiction between opacity and transparency is a resonant one: cf., e.g. T.W. Adorno, 'Cultural Criticism and Society' in *Prisms*, trans. S. and S. Weber (London, 1967), pp.17-34; and Adorno and Max Horkheimer, *Dialectic of Enlightenment*, trans. J. Cumming (London, 1973), pp.120-167.

30. See Foucault, *Discipline and Punish*, trans. A. Sheridan (Harmonds-worth, Middx., 1977), e.g. pp.105-228.

31. See Belsey, pp.92, 125-129; it is significant that Cixous similarly turns to the example of Artaud (p.399).

32. Foucault, 'Truth and Power', in *Power/Knowledge*, p.127.

33. It is odd that I did not succeed in delivering this 'ending' in lecture form; there are many inversions of 'ouverture' and closure between oral and written modes.

THE FREEDOM OF THE CRITIC AND
THE HISTORY OF THE TEXT

L.A. Jackson

(One Principle of a Diachronic Semiology)
1. Radical Structuralism

I want to begin with de Saussure's theory of the sign. (1) This was originally presented by a linguist, to linguists - philologists, in fact - and was intended as a foundation and framework for, and a suggested generalisation of, linguistics; which is one reason why it readily becomes vacuous, and easily subject to all kinds of Derridaean distortion, when the linguistics is left out. However, it was presented seventy years ago; and there is a case for updating the linguistics a little. The older linguistics saw language as a finite repertory of structures and elements: it saw meaning as a system of oppositions within a finite set of signs; and its main theoretical activity was labelling rather than explanation. Modern generative models define languages by finite sets of constitutive rules, specifying infinite sets of structural possibilities; they see meaning as a matter of complex semantic relations; and they seek theories that will offer explanatory adequacy. (2)

The new linguistics offers a much better pattern for a general structuralism than the old; and an insight into the precise sense in which freedom and creativity - the traditional attributes of the human subject - may be postulated of what is after all a biological organism in the material world. It is possible to see the structure of the human mind as an interlocking set of competences - i.e. finite systems of internalised constitutive rules - which define the space of possible action and recognition. The model here is linguistic competence. When I learn the grammar - the set of constitutive rules - of my language, I learn in consequence how to construct an infinite set of possible sentences; and the grammar thus specifies the full range of my freedom and constitutes my creative power, in uttering and recognising sentences, while staying within the bounds of that language.

My freedom to utter and recognise sentences has not in any way been limited by my learning the language; on the contrary, it has been constituted by my learning the language; if I hadn't learnt the language, I wouldn't have the freedom to speak or recognise any of it. (In this way, constitutive rule systems are quite different from prescriptive ones.) More exactly (though the point is more difficult to express) the "I" that is free to speak the language has been partially constituted by incorporating that language. By obvious extension, we can say that the "I" has been totally constituted by the incorporation of all the rule-systems socially available in the milieu in which the biological individual develops; along of course with a memory - an internal representation of the unique life-history of that individual. These rule-systems specify between them the total potential freedom of the "I" that they partially constitute.

Any one such system - e.g., London middle class English of 1982 -

will be historically and socially specific; will indeed be an internalisation of a historically specific and local society, in one of its objective aspects. All such systems will be biologically limited by the capacities of the organism - Homo Sapiens - that internalises them, and this will limit the range of societies, out of those logically possible, that the organism can enter or form. History, however, in two senses - the history of the individual and the history of the world - will determine the actual society the individual enters, and the actual individuality he has; as well as the limitations, both actual and apparent to him, upon his freedom.

A general structuralism of this kind poses many problems - not least that of relating historical changes of the rule systems, with the human actions which on this model necessarily occur within the rule systems, and yet bring historical change about (presumably by their material effects within the material world). But it still offers, I think, the best current hope of reconciling the biological, the sociological, and the cultural or mentalistic frameworks of discussion, all of which we need if we are to have any hope of understanding the human world. Yet this promising line has not been pursued by radical structuralists; and there are three main reasons for this.

The first is what can only be described as a neurotic fear - understandable, perhaps, in those in reaction from the Hegelian tradition, but very bewildering to the rest of us - of the resurgence of metaphysics. The metaphysics of presence plays the same part in the work of Jacques Derrida (3) as does sin in some seventeenth century Divine. Constantly detected, repented of, and banished, it as constantly reappears in undreamed of forms. Only, this obsession seems to lead Derrida into (philosophical) sin: namely, bad arguments based on misrepresentations and puns. The second reason I would call neurotic Marxism; a Marxism constantly haunted by the fear that it is not being materialist enough, as if that were a kind of disloyalty to the workers. Combine these two, and you get a reluctance to postulate any abstract entity whatever. From this point of view, even physical science becomes 'mechanical materialism' and is halfway to idealism and metaphysics; and it is quite impossible to talk about language; you have to speak of 'productive linguistic practice' and such like. The third reason, also neurotic, is a species of anarchism, haunted by the fear that to admit any set of fixed structures or rules, even constitutive ones, is to accept a prison for the self they constitute, and an essentially conservative brake on radical social change.

Driven by these religious doubts, post-structuralists have come to replace the rational development of structuralist theory within human ethology, psychology, and formal sociology by a mystical procedure known as "questioning the sign"; and that has been used to excuse an oversimplification, or an actual misrepresentation of Saussurean linguistics, and a whole series of bad arguments for drawing unlikely philosophical and critical implications out of it. Thus, Derrida misrepresents Saussure's warning to philology students, that what they need to study is the spoken language not the written, as a metaphysical claim for the privileging of the inner voice. On this quaint fancy he founds his most celebrated erection: the logocentric tradition of Western thought. Coward and Ellis (4) kindly simplify linguistics for us by collapsing the language/speech, synchronic/diachronic, and paradigmatic/syntagmatic oppositions into one; thus identifying the history of a language (period, say, twenty centuries) with the speaking of it (period, say, twenty seconds); a particular example, perhaps, of the Utopian illusion common amongst post-structuralists that one can make changes of a historical order in the existing cultural codes by making quick modifications in one's cultural or linguistic practices now.

Several writers pick up with apparent approval Saussure's unfortunate implication that Frenchmen cannot tell the difference between sheep and mutton because they have only one word for both. One writer (5) allows Lacan to persuade her that when you label two identical doors "Ladies" and "Gentlemen" you create a difference in social reality - without stressing his point that you need a preexisting social rule to make it happen, and certainly not noticing the underlying reasons for the existence of that social rule. The valuable point that it is entry into the symbolic code system that transforms the biological organism into the human individual is vulgarised into the claim that we learn to realise ourselves as (thinking) subjects by using the pronoun "I" in (grammatical) subject position - presumably the counterpart to this claim is that we learn to see ourselves as (material) objects by using the pronoun "me" in grammatical object position.

Arguments like this rest on puns. I would like to argue that the pun plays too large a part in our reasoning in this field, for that reasoning to be taken seriously; and Derrida has made it a staple of his argument. Puns should be left to schoolboys. And, more generally, jokes (especially in-jokes) should be the ornament of an argument, not its substance; unless we really want the argument to be taken as a joke. Perhaps we do.

But the most basic error, which lies at the foundation of all further argument, and also of much refusal to argue seriously, within the poststructuralist tradition, is the selection from Saussure of the one element - his theory of meaning - which can be shown to be flat wrong - in the strong sense that it is logically inadequate for the purposes for which it is put forward.

This theory is that meaning is simply a reflex of the differences between signifiers in a system of signifiers. As Jakobson pointed out in 1942, (6) it is merely a generalisation of the way in which phonemes signify. All /t/ signifies is (not /d/ and not /k/ and not /g/ and not /p/ and not ...) and so on until we have exhausted the full list of phonemes. And, as he went on to point out, the generalisation is intuitively wrong; no other signs in language, not even grammatical category markers (let alone words) signify in just this way; they may oppose each other, and limit each other's meaning, but they also stand for something. Radical structuralists reject the intuition that signs must stand for something; really radical ones reject the notion that signs consist of signifier and signified, and accept only the signifier: the play of differences among signifiers, they say, is all. This is a view that gives a somewhat vertiginous quality to structuralism; our anti-metaphysics leaves us in an ontological void, with nothing but signifiers to hold onto.

But setting the ontological question aside, there are three awkward logical questions to face if we adopt this theory. First, in Saussure's system a <u>signifier</u> is by definition the material part of a package called a <u>sign</u> whose immaterial part is the <u>signified</u>. What has no signified is by definition not a signifier; so the least that radical structuralists need is a new definition. Second, Saussure and Jakobson agree that the phoneme is a sign that signifies pure difference; but this claim hardly makes sense. There is an alternative formulation that covers the facts perfectly: phonemes <u>are</u> the minimal (perceptual or articulatory) sound units in language, and having different phonemes is what makes the difference between one signifier and another. On this view, phonemes themselves are not signs at all. Radical structuralism has based its theory of all signs on an analogy with something that is not a sign.

The third objection is very mundane. Difference-semantics will not work. Words in a language have very complex meaning-relationships, known to every native-speaker, and learnt when language is learnt. These have to be represented in any dictionary that describes the speaker's knowledge of his language - that is, any descriptively adequate dictionary. Take, for example, a simple kinship term like "aunt". This has a derived, honorific sense; its primary sense, however, is precisely:

"sister of father or mother"

and this is what the dictionary must represent. How it should represent such a sense - what primitive elements it should use, and how they should be combined - is a matter determined by one's theory of meaning; but this theory of meaning must, for explanatory adequacy, be compatible with some descriptively adequate dictionary.

Now within a system of pure differences - that is, one in which the only primitive logical relationship available is that of exclusion - the only sense we can represent is:

"aunt is not sister, is not father, is not mother..."

with this list continuing throughout the vocabulary system, till we get to:

"... is not panther, is not motor-cycle, is not Karl Marx..."

But this is absurd.

I suspect that most people who talk about "pure difference" don't really mean what they say; they are thinking of differences within subgroups of signs, and admitting hierarchies of signs, etc; in fact they are tacitly assuming quite a complex semantic theory. But even the most complex difference semantics will still fail to capture the sense: "sister of father or mother", since this contains two irreducible and probably primitive relationships - the logical relationship "or" and the linguistic relationship "of", as well as three vocabulary items.

For our description of word meaning to be able to represent such a complex sense as this, our theory of meaning will have to postulate such primitive elements as these; in effect it will postulate the elements of a meaning-world; a world of elementary concepts and relationships that is much simpler, and less rich, than our everyday common-sense world; but still one that would be logically impossible to construct using a semantics of differences alone.

Because this is a logical impossibility it does not help if we make the standard radical move of those who do not believe in abstract objects like "languages", and talk, perhaps, of "creating meaning by the play of difference between signifiers in linguistic, or discursive practice" (or something of that kind). It is still logically impossible, while we confine ourselves to pure difference, that we should ever create the meaning of the word "aunt". And if we can't do that, we are not going to have much luck in creating the meaning of more complex words, like, say, "Marxist", or "semiotician".

If we really want to explain how complex concepts are created in discourse, we need to recognise the existence both of the formal rules that define languages - in a broad sense, grammatical rules - and of further rules that govern the use of language in discourse: in particular, the way in which it is possible for a later part of a discourse to make what is called anaphoric reference to an earlier part. Here is an example:

I had a cup of coffee on the table, but someone doused a
cigarette in it. The coffee tasted nasty.

In this discourse, the phrase "the coffee" acquires that complex meaning
which is represented in the language by the whole expression:

the coffee which I had a cup of on the table and which
someone doused a cigarette in.

It is precisely because of the structure of the language that I am
able to construct (a representation of) this complex concept; it is not
unreasonable to say that I use the language according to pre-existing
rules to construct a complex concept incorporating an earlier concept
within a new framework. This is, I think, a typical example of the way
in which new concepts generally are formed; and doubtless they could not
be formed unless there were some rule-governed representational system
to form them in. It seems, however, mystifying and unhelpful to refer
to such a system as a "writing", or to a concept as a "text".

It is obviously not true that to form such a concept one must go
through the linguistic process here illustrated. One might form it by
seeing the cup of coffee; seeing the cigarette doused in it; and tasting
the horrid mess; without linguistic processes being overtly employed at
any stage; though, tacitly, some encoding process must be, and the relation of this encoding process to language is simply not known. It is
clear that we can in fact combine linguistic and non-linguistic sources
of information; which suggests that there is some level of representation
at which both are similarly encoded; and it is perhaps at this level of
representation that one should speak of "concepts".

This talk of "levels of representation" is a bit vague; but it ought
to be said that it is not in the least idealist. I am a crude mechanical
materialist and a cultural materialist; and I hold that actual cups of
coffee exist, and are different from representations of them. For a
materialist, rules and representations are stored in material form in the
brain in exactly the same sense that computer programmes are stored in
material form in a computer - for example, as magnetic traces on a floppy
disc. Indeed, all culture could be seen as a set of modifiable 'computer
programmes' used by the organism for reproduction and survival, and the
materialist interpretation of history could be given a corresponding sense:
social structures, internalised in each generation as socio-cultural rules,
are modified in the course of history in accordance with material needs.

2. The Writerly Scientist: Misreadings in Barthes

There is obviously a loose analogy between the building up of a complex concept in discourse by anaphoric reference, and the way in which a
work of literature derives part of its meaning by referring back to earlier
works of literature or to literary conventions derived from them. It would,
however, be mystification to subsume these processes under the same technical term - intertextuality, perhaps - and thus avoid the necessity of
giving detailed analytical accounts of both. These processes are not, I
think, mystifying; they are complicated. Thus - to refer only to one
linguistic aspect of literary convention - we may have uses of language
which are imitations for aesthetic purposes of uses of language which are
characteristic of different social occasions or of different social milieux,
and we have to keep all these distinctions clear.

Julia Kristeva (7) claims that linguists will fail to explicate the
complexity of the act of signification unless they adopt a semiotic framework. In my experience this warning sign ought to face the other way
round. Many post-structuralists readily adopt a semiological framework,
but they fail to explicate the complexity of the act of signification

because they don't put any linguistics in it. Instead, they (4) talk
happily about "the productivity of meaning from a system of differences".
Derrida has a lot to answer for here.

Many of the complexities of literature, however, are not linguistic
at all; indeed they are not exclusively semiological. Consider, for
example, that important negative achievement of the critical theory of
radical structuralism, the attack on the naturalness of the conventions
of bourgeois realism, based on an attack on the naturalness of naturalness
itself. (5) The idea is, that what seems natural is merely unconscious
convention; the novel's constant appeal to what seems natural is an appeal
to unconscious convention. The exclusively semiological basis of this
attack weakens it in the following two ways.

First, "common-sense" functions on many non-linguistic levels. It
is not just that the most important features of, e.g. sexism, are not in
the uses of masculine and feminine pronouns. Any form of semiology offers
a clumsy way of talking about, say, social stereotyping offered as naturalism; and is constantly likely to carry the suggestion that we could alter
the stereotype itself - which is, likely as not, deeply built into actual
social practices - by altering the way we represent it.

Second, and more important, semiological insights undermine, or
underpin, not merely realism, but all literary modes and all equally; an
attack based on them lacks historical specificity and is to that extent
inferior to vulgar Marxist approaches of the Stalinist era - Caudwell,
for example. There is no easy passage from an ahistorical philosophical
position - a critique of naive realism, for example - to an ahistorical
critical position - a critique of "expressive realism". Literary conventions are purely conventional, and involve no truth-claims; any literary
convention is compatible with any philosophical position. But it is not
true that any literary convention will work at any point in cultural
history.

One obvious difference between literary conventions and linguistic
rules is that the former are much less insulated from socio-historical
change. A synchronic system of independent literary conventions is, in
many cultures including our own, very difficult to isolate for study.
Works of literature are engaged in a continuous modification of the
literary conventions derived from past literary work, in the course of
responding to present social reality; and at the same time they take their
meaning from their present use of those conventions. One has, then, an
essentially diachronic semiology, in which the conventions governing a
dominant art-form are related in a very complex way both to its own past,
and that of art in general, and to the intellectual practices and value-
systems of the period of its dominance.

It is thus still the case that the most powerful exposure of the
conventions of the novel, say, is a historical study of their origin:
Ian Watt's book, for instance. (8) To oversimplify: Defoe, writing for
dissenters, had to disguise an extravagant romance about the creation of
a two-man civilisation on a desert island, as a record of fact, using
police-court evidence techniques to do so; because dissenters disapproved
of fiction, but felt improved by fact. They did not necessarily disapprove
of improving moral allegories: Bunyan, for example. But they might very
reasonably have disapproved of an immoral allegory, like the one at the
heart of *Robinson Crusoe* - if they had recognised it, consciously, as
such.

Realism did not permit them to recognise it; and thus was instituted
what might be called the bourgeois lie at the heart of the novel - at the
heart, for example, of *Pamela* and of the successor novels, *Cecilia*, *Pride*

and Prejudice, right down to *Lady Chatterley's Lover* which are in continuous historical dialogue with it - on a realistic surface, that the reader can accept consciously, disguising an unacknowledged allegory operating directly on the unconscious, and carrying powerful ideological stereotypes.

It is strange that from the French left intelligentsia comes a movement that effectively disjoins criticism from historical control. One crucial weakness of the critical theory of radical structuralism has been the treatment of Roland Barthes' intensely personal anarchistic approach to criticism - however disguised as pseudo-science in his early work - as exemplary; (4,5) so that we are left with this recommendation as the only alternative to some feared idealist closure: read productively to create endless alternative meanings; but be sure to make frequent ritual reference to signifiers. This is to recommend dilettantism; an energetic lack of seriousness in approach to literature, and one only possible for an elite of specialists with leisure; therefore unMarxist.

This is a harsh judgement, so I shall try to justify it by a summary analysis of S/Z, which is the model-work of the genre. (9) The left-wing credentials of Barthes' system seem to lie in the claim that the "writerly" reader is a worker: that is, a producer, rather than a consumer of the text. I am sure this claim would seem a sick joke to a manual worker, and I don't propose to discuss it. In my view, Barthes is adopting the same position as the mass reader under capitalism: that a book is neither a classic, representing past civilisation, nor a communication, from some person, but rather a commodity, whose producer is effaced, and which the purchaser may use as he likes, and misunderstand as he pleases. Barthes is, however, much more ingenious in misunderstanding than is usual.

It is also nowadays customary to see S/Z as a deconstructionist work that subverts its own theories. It is not clear to me why this is a good thing to do. As one might gather from part one of this paper, I don't take this framework seriously, or even frivolously, and I shall interrogate S/Z from what a deconstructionist might see as a position of relentless metaphysical closure - i.e., I shall ask whether its claims are true, interesting, important, etc., and whether it fairly represents Balzac's text.

Barthes refuses to look at the overall structure of the text, instead dividing it into 561 artibrary lexia, and checking each against five codes. He also scatters the book with general discussions of narrative, often insightful. The result is a book which has the air of being at once systematic, theoretical, and immensely rich. But the system, the theories, and the riches are not related to each other.

Barthes is not actually testing the absurd theory that a fictional narrative consists of a linear sequence of lexias, each communicating according to the five codes, and that the 5 x 561 matrix that results specifies the total meaning of the narrative. But that is the only theory that this particular systematic structure is appropriate to test.

Nor does this matter much, since the theories are not offered in testable form anyway; they are really bright ideas; one is in the company of McLuhan rather than Chomsky. There are also rich insights, and others less impressive - the book seems to contain every single thing that occurred to Barthes and his pupils, about this one short story, in a two year seminar - but they are not organised in any way. (Barthes prides himself on this, and I imagine his followers would think it terroristic even to try.) And the simple linear way in which the book is organised, following the narrative of *Sarrasine*, prevents any higher organisation from arising.

It is clear that Barthes did not make his book systematic because he was systematically testing a theory. He made it systematic because, at this stage of his career, he liked the rhetorical effect of systematicity. At earlier and later stages of his career, he liked other effects: a scientificity arid to the point of being castrating in the period of *Elements of Semiology*; and in his later work, an erotics of the text which, in its continuous willed production of fantasy objects, becomes masturbatory.

I now propose to show that Barthes' elaborate procedures have one foreseen, and one quite unforeseen effect. The foreseen effect is to justify productive misreading - in particular, an illuminating hypertrophy of Balzac's castration symbolism. The unforeseen effect is to hide, both from Barthes and his followers, a gross, crude, and oversimplifying misreading - in effect, a replacement of the story by Barthes' castration complex.

I don't mean by this that Barthes has added new subtleties and Freudianisms that a reactionary critic might question. I mean that he has offered a crude account of the story that doesn't fit the text, and ignores what Balzac wrote.

Barthes says that the narrator in *Sarrasine* offers his mistress a contract of prostitution: a night of love for a story. She agrees; but the story turns out to be about castration; repulsed by this, she breaks her contract with him.

None of this happens in Balzac's story. No such contract is made, and therefore none can be broken; and the lady's motive for not proceeding with her love affair is not the one Barthes ascribes to her.

Balzac shows the narrator having reached a certain stage in a love affair; he is permitted to take his mistress to a party. He wishes to be admitted to the next stage, when he will be permitted to attend her in private, at her home. He uses the promise of the story to achieve this. When he tells the story he hopes, of course, to end in the lady's bed; but he hopes it in the sense in which any lover does; he hopes to impress her sufficiently for her to accept him as a lover. Unfortunately, the story that he tells carries with it a moral, that one is all too likely to be deceived in love; the object of love is likely to be unworthy, as Zambinella was, appearing to be a woman, but in fact being a castrato. The lady takes this point; and decides to play safe, and stick to Christian virtue.

That is Balzac's story - the one in the actual text. It is obviously better than Barthes' story; for one thing, it is just plausible. Why did Barthes substitute his own story for the original? He may, of course, have simply not noticed what the text said; though he did spend two years reading it. In that case one is entitled to suggest that his critical method is like a very elaborate suit of armour that is too heavy to fight in. Alternatively, he may have wished to substitute a crude story for one that seemed to him over-refined; presumably as part of a fight against bourgeois standards. But this is no more than an oppositional gesture. It is no more than cocking a snook.

Any real opposition to the standards Balzac is embodying would have to start by recognising what they are. (After all, Marx and Engels did!) To refuse to read the story (while pretending one has read it more carefully than anybody else in the history of criticism) is to engage in a fantasy of opposition; in which, I am afraid, Barthes has had a substantial readership accompanying him.

3. Judging within History

Bourgeois criticism in the twentieth century has produced two antithetical attitudes to history - those of the critic and those of the scholar. The critic - new, Leavisite, or whatever - writes from his own sensibility and uses history as a source for background information; the scholar tries to replace his own sensibility with an artificially cultivated historical one. The post-structuralist syntheses, insofar as Barthes makes a fair example of the critical work within them, offer an anarchist freedom to propose alternative interpretations: which leads to triviality and insignificance.

But the freedom of the critic is only a special case of freedom of action within history. That the human subject is socially constituted does not mean that it does not exist, nor that it is not free to act in the future; only that it cannot be free of the past. Freedom is always now; and is the freedom of a subjectivity formed within history. Such freedom the writer - or, collectively, the writers - of works of literature had once in the past, and exercised it; that is now part of history, and it is the same history that the critic himself lives in, since history has only happened once. The critic has no freedom to change that history (either the history of the text, or of his own mind) but he has freedom to act, and every free decision constitutes an interpretation of history. (If I leave the Labour party, I am reinterpreting my - and its - historical significance.) Since the literary work is a unique event in history, the critic's interpretation of it is controlled by and controls his interpretation of history as a whole; and this depends on his underlying political commitment.

I will give two illustrations. The first is the case of Aeschylus and feminism. As recent visitors to the National Theatre will have noticed, and as my own students have been informing me for some years now, Aeschylus was anti-feminist; he wrote in favour of the suppression of women's rights; a fact that few critics have thought important enough to mention for two millennia or so. His god Apollo, influenced by concern for Athenian property rights, offers the astounding legal fiction that a woman is not related to her child; she is merely the vessel that stores the father's seed. As a student acidly pointed out to me, with, I think, perfect correctness, that has been the essential position men have taken for the past two thousand five hundred years, in respect of property rights, control of the family, etc. etc.

It seems that to be a feminist now is to revalue the historical significance of Aeschylus. This is not because the critic's stance as a feminist can change any fact about Aeschylus. But to be a feminist is, quite justifiably, to rewrite the whole of history showing the oppression of women as a major theme; and this general revaluation of history is what licences the new view of Aeschylus. Nothing else would. A feminist who had no interest in history would presumably merely find the antifeminist aspects of Aeschylus distasteful. That would be the pure critic's attitude. The pure scholar, on the other hand, would forget she was a feminist and imagine she was Pericles. A Barthesian would show us that the text of Aeschylus, suitably manipulated, is feminist, in addition to all the other things that it is; and none of them would matter, more than anything else. The historically aware critic - who, like any other politically committed person, has a commitment within history as she conceives it, to change the course of history - finds Aeschylus far more of an ally than some hypothetical Greek feminist might be, since he helps to reveal the course of history that she wishes to change.

My second example, which I can only present in very abbreviated form,

arises out of the three hundred years war over the status of Milton.
Paradise Lost itself offers a Christian historicist view of history;
that is to say, it offers the view that God arranged history to have
a definite and intelligible moral pattern which Milton undertakes to
set out. Emphasis on such a view was of course a mark of the Puritans;
Royalists tended to stress that society had a definite and intelligible
moral pattern - a hierarchical one, which was in principle fixed by
God. *Paradise Lost* stands in a curiously ambiguous relationship to
the historical conflict - the English Civil War - in which that difference of historical theory was worked out; since it tells the story of
an unsuccessful rebellion against a God portrayed as an absolute monarch
at the head of a great hierarchy. Generations of critics have been uncertain whether Milton was against rebellion like his God, or for it
like his devil; and this doubt arises, not just from a knowledge of
Milton's life, but directly from the text.

That civil war, our last, settled the main lines of political combat
to the present day. Thus it is still possible to map present-day political differences onto those of the civil war, though not onto those of,
say, the Wars of the Roses. (In recent years both intelligible propaganda and popular entertainment have been based on this fact: the film
Winstanley, various National Theatre programmes based on the historical
work of Christopher Hill, a popular thriller by Anthony Price.) But in
fact it has always been possible to interpret contemporary politics in
this way - consider, for example, Macaulay's unselfconscious appropriation
of Milton as a party supporter, and the detailed presentation of Milton as
party hero in J.R. Green's *Short History of the English People*. It is fair
to say that, for three hundred years, no account of Milton - even if ostensibly a literary-critical one - has been politically innocent.

The main twentieth century battle - the famous one - was fought between conservatives and conservatives: those like C.S. Lewis (10) who
wished to appropriate Milton for a theocratic authoritarianism ("The Fall
is simply and solely Disobedience - doing what you have been told not to do;
and it results from Pride - from being too big for your boots, forgetting
your place, thinking that you are God.") and those who wished to damn him
for a rebel and a liberal. Of the latter, T.S. Eliot (11) saw deeply
enough to say frankly that the Civil War had never ended; and that often
judgement of Milton rested on interpretation of that. But even Eliot saw
this problem not as a condition of critical judgement, but as a difficulty
in the way of critical judgement. It is one of the curious features of
this great paper battle, that both sides were compelled by their literary
principles to deny that they were judging on political grounds; or even,
more generally, on the grounds of disliking "Milton's ideas". But it can
be shown that they were, even in the least plausible case, which is Dr.
Leavis's treatment of Milton's verse; (12) and I shall demonstrate this
immediately.

Leavis's treatment of Milton's verse is the least plausible case for
interpretation as political criticism, for two reasons. The first is that
Leavis deliberately structured his argument to exclude any such charge.
Elsewhere, in the comparable case of Shelley, he makes this point explicit;
here, he makes a more general exclusion:

"if we can and do read poetry, then our objection to Milton,
it must be insisted, is that we dislike his verse".

The case against is going to be a narrow and technical one, based solely
on response to verse; and this promise Leavis fulfils. Only by analysing
the grounds for Leavis's judgement of particular types of verse would we be
able to relate this narrow technical judgement to wider positions; and here

the second reason operates to bar us; Leavis is careful, as a matter of
principle, not to base his critical judgements on an appeal to abstract
principles of any kind. He appeals, instead, to consensus; to a consensus of the suitably qualified: the "we" of the quotation I have given;
and the nearest he ever comes to general theory is to offer a theoretical
defence of this antitheoretical stance, in an article - *Literary Criticism
and Philosophy* - republished in *The Common Pursuit*.

It follows that, if we wish to look either for political, or for any
other general intellectual bases for Leavis's judgements, we must do it
by way of a sociological analysis of the consensus to which he appeals:
who, we ask, is "we"? And what we shall uncover here is academic politics,
and a conflict between the standards of a rentier, and a rising professional, middle class. I shall not pursue this sociological path, but will
attempt instead, despite Leavis's own opposition, to extract general standards from his text. As a first step I note a significant gap in the argument of *Milton's Verse*. Extensive illustration is given of the qualities
of this verse: its "heavy rhythmic pattern, hieratic stylisation, ...
swaying ritual movement ... steep cadences." No reason is given for
supposing that these qualities are bad; so that it is open to an opponent -
to C.S. Lewis, in fact - simply to accept the Leavisite description of
Milton's style, and add: "I like it!"

Now Leavis also gives abundant hints, and some illustrations, of the
verse style of which he would approve ("subtlety of movement ... the play
of the natural sense movement and intonation against the verse structure
.. 'natural', here, involves a reference, more or less direct, to idio-
matic speech ...") One is inclined to ask here: "Whose idiom?" - but in
this chapter, one is not told, and the assumption is, that it is anybody's
idiom. However, we can establish precisely whose idiom is in question if
we examine the immediately preceding chapter of *Revaluation*, for there we
are told, not just what relationship between verse and speech is desirable,
but where you learn it, and what it tells you about the civilisation behind. Here is Ben Jonson - I give a small fraction of Leavis's extensive
quotation, and follow with Leavis's comment.

> "Come leave the loathed stage,
> And the more loathsome age: ...
>
> ...   Leave things so prostitute,
> And take the Alcaick lure;
> Or thine own Horace or Anacreon's lyre; ...
>
> ...   But when they hear thee sing
> The glories of thy king,
> His zeal to God, and his just awe o'er men:
> They may, blood-shaken, then,
> Feel such a flesh-quake to possess their powers
> As they shall cry, 'Like ours,
> In sound of peace or wars
> No harp e'er hit the stars,
> In tuning forth the acts of his sweet raigne;
> And raising Charles his chariot 'bove his Waine.'

> "His Horace and his King associate naturally: the Court culture of
> that 'sweet reign' provided the grounding in actuality of Jonson's
> ideal civilisation."

So the secret is out; the value of the verse, as one might expect, is
in the fact that it embodies a fine civilisation; and, as one might not
quite so confidently expect, that civilisation is to be found in King
Charles's court. Leavis is, a little earlier, perfectly explicit about

this:

"What it" (a poem by Carew) "represents is something immeasurably finer than, after the Civil Wars and the Interregnum, was there - was there at all, by any substitution - for the mob of gentlemen who wrote with ease; it represents a Court culture (if the expression may be permitted as a convenience) that preserved, in its sophisticated way, an element of the tradition of chivalry, and that had turned the studious or naively enthusiastic Renaissance classicising and poetising of an earlier period into something intimately bound up with contemporary life and manners - something consciously both mature and, while contemporary, traditional."

What has this to do with politics? Well, everything; it is to put it bluntly, Royalist propaganda. So is the comment on Jonson's very crude piece of court flattery. And, from where I stand, it looks as if the first casualty of that propaganda is critical truth. No one would guess from Leavis's comments that Ben Jonson's plays were better than his masques; or that the court had any damaging effect upon his talent (one thinks of Jonson furious at a civilisation that preferred Inigo Jones's stage scenery to his words).

But there is no dishonesty in Leavis. Political commitment of this kind operates deep beneath the surface of the mind and controls the direct literary response that validates the superficial literary judgement. Hence the honest critic never has any choice about his critical judgements.

One of the most impressive things about Leavis is the way in which his critical judgements of literature build into an impressive account of the history of English civilisation; and that history then validates, systematically, the individual judgements. In the end, his views are just as much part of a closed system as those of a theorist might be; but it is a historical, not a theoretical system; and it is a history with the value judgements left in; specifically, history seen as the long defeat of high civilisation by mounting barbarism. The verse of the line of wit directly embodies - we have Leavis's word for it - the values of high civilisation. What does that of Milton embody? In the first place, the heavy emphases of Republican political rhetoric - the hammer blows that brought that civilisation down. The conscious grandeur that insists that we have, not an intimate personal story to tell, but something world-historic. The latinate syntax that recalls - as does the imagery and the epic form - the standards of an older, higher, Roman civilisation to bring them in judgement on a present one. (And of course recalls also, as Leavis sourly points out, Milton's own international political propaganda.) It is these that Leavis - that "we" - dislike; and "we" are the new conservatives who have despaired of our own civilisation and want to preserve whatever of human value seems to be left, or reconstructible, of the seventeenth century's.

Milton has now been appropriated for Marxism, and is playing a part in the ideological revolution probably more significant than that of Barthes. This is not because of any change in Milton; his revolutionary implications have always been there. But the critics have had to reinterpret half English history in order to perceive them. The appropriation of Milton by Christopher Hill seems to me neither more, nor less legitimate than his earlier appropriation by Lord Macaulay. What concern me are the similarities in the process.

It would be surprising if Marxism offered a less deep ground for value judgements than - to use T.S. Eliot's phrase - Whiggery. What I cannot understand is how any critic who had once committed himself to any position in relation to the historical process that contains literature, can escape from the control of that commitment in his relation to literature alone. I conclude that any critic who sees literature as a field for the display of skill in multiple interpretation is likely to show a similar exhibitionist ambiguity in relation to political commitment too.

Behind the semiological stance, the endless questioning of the sign, there is often, I think, a desire for transcendence: specifically, a desire to transcend history, or at least to escape from one's own historical situation, and from that of the text. The subtitle of this paper offers the promise that at least one principle of a diachronic semiology will be proposed. Here it is. History only happens once; and both author and critic live, therefore, within the same history. This principle is obvious; but its implications are quite far-reaching.

FOOTNOTES

1. F. de Saussure, *Course in General Linguisites*, McGraw Hill, 1966.

2. N. Chomsky*, *Topics in the Theory of Generative Grammar*, Mouton, 1966. *Reflections on Language*, Fontana, 1976.

3. J. Derrida*, *Writing and Difference*, Routledge, 1978. *Of Grammatology*, John Hopkins, 1976.

4. R. Coward and J. Ellis, *Language and Materialism*, Routledge, 1977.

5. C. Belsey, *Critical Practice*, Methuen, 1980.

6. R. Jakobson*, *Six Lectures on Sound and Meaning*, Harvester, 1978.

7. J. Kristeva, 'The Semiotic Activity' in *Screen* Reader 2, 1981.

8. I. Watt, *The Rise of the Novel*, Chatto, 1957.

9. R. Barthes*, *S/Z*, Hill and Wang, 1974.

10. C.S. Lewis*, *A Preface to Paradise Lost*, Oxford, 1942.

11. T.S. Eliot*, *Selected Prose*, Penguin, 1953.

12. F.R. Leavis*, *Revaluation*, Chatto, 1936.

* References have been kept down in number; what is really presupposed, in the case of the authors starred, is the whole range of their work or some large part of it.

IN DEFENCE OF REDUCTIONISM

Ian H. Birchall

La vie est plus simple.
(Zola on Stendhal) (1)

A

This paper is intended as a polemical - and hence necessarily one-sided and schematic - intervention in the debate about the sociology of literature. It is directed against one trend in previous Essex conferences; the attempt to combine Marxism with various brands of structuralism and post-structuralism. While making no claim to be countering a single homogeneous position, I shall illustrate my argument with reference to papers from previous conferences and to recent books by Terry Eagleton and Catherine Belsey. (2)

To begin - where else - with F.R. Leavis, who comments that in the thirties a lecture on 'Literature and Society' would have had as its main themes: 'the duty of the writer to identify himself with the working-class, the duty of the critic to evaluate works of literature in terms of the degree to which they seemed calculated to further (or otherwise) the proper and pre-destined outcome of the class-struggle, and the duty of the literary historian to explain literary history as the reflection of changing economic and material realities.' (3) Leavis certainly wouldn't have got that at Essex, however much he might have disapproved on other grounds.

And that, I would argue, is a pity. In my view the main attraction of the sociology of literature is that it is subversive, and that in particular, it subverts the notion that literature is autonomous from politics.

Ever since Theophile Gautier launched the idea of 'art for art's sake' in a vicious polemic against the followers of Fourier and Saint-Simon, (4) the idea of the autonomy of art has been a component of conservative ideology.

Ever since the government of Louis-Philippe instructed Edgar Quinet to remove all reference to 'institutions' from a proposed lecture course on 'The comparative literature and institutions of Southern Europe', (5) the sociology of literature has embodied a subversive potential. That this potential is often dismissed as an unjustified 'politicisation' is simply indicative of our impoverished notion of what constitutes politics.

Yet in much recent writing, even from avowed Marxists, an attempt to link the literary and the political is often denounced as 'reductionist'. In the discussion of literary theory the term 'reductionism' has acquired the same negative connotations as 'economism' and 'workerism' in a more narrowly political discourse. Pierre Macherey has suggested that 'the identification of literature purely and simply with the interests of a class' might logically lead to book-burning. (6) Yet if reductionism is as dead as is often claimed, it is surprising that so much energy still needs to be devoted to burying it.

Moreover, the argument has repercussions for politics as well as for literature. Colin Mercer, who in 1977 told us that what Baudelaire offers in his poetry is "another history" (7) returned in 1978 to argue that 'Fascism was not the "emanation" of a particular class or class fraction.' (8)

I want, therefore, to begin by tracing the political origins of some of the theoretical arguments we have gone through, to argue that there is indeed a 'politics of theory' too often concealed by theoretical discourse itself.

B

For a quarter of a century after 1928 Marxism was generally perceived as synonymous with Stalinism. Yet in effect Stalinism transformed Marxism into something indistinguishable from bourgeois ideology. When Zhdanov urges that the task of writers is to "struggle against all the remnants of bourgeois influence on the proletariat, against laxity, frivolity, idleness, petty-bourgeois indiscipline and individualism, greed and the lack of conscientiousness with regard to collective property" (9) we are dealing with a clear expression of class ideology with echoes of the Protestant ethic.

The process of 'deStalinisation' after 1953 raised a new set of problems. For that profoundly humanist document, the Kruschev 'secret speech' of 1956, decades of repression could be explained by the fact that "Stalin was a very distrustful man, morbidly suspicious". (10) Those who were not satisfied by such a formulation were left with the problem of how to explain the fact that an apparently socialist economic base had been accompanied by a political superstructure of unparalleled repression. Two possibilities were available: either to examine more closely the socialist credentials of the economic base, or to argue that the traditional base/superstructure model was inadequate and that a less deterministic, more mediated relationship between the two must be posited. In political terms at least the latter path raised less problems.

It is in the context of these arguments that a new wave of work in the sociology of literature emerged. The key texts of the new period are Goldmann's *Le Dieu Caché* (1955), Williams' *Culture and Society* (1958), Fischer's *Necessity of Art* (1959) and Sartre's *Critique de la Raison Dialectique* (1957-60), to which the work of a host of minor figures such as Garaudy could be added. All of these are either direct products of the debate in the international Communist movement, or else, consciously seek to relate to it; all propose a more complex relationship between literature and society than the reduction of text to class criteria that had characterised the Stalin era.

Thus Goldmann develops such non-class criteria as 'genius' and insists on a continuity between Marxist humanism and the values of the progressive bourgeoisie. (11) Williams tries to draw out the contradictions in the account of the base/superstructure relationship in British Marxism of the thirties and to show how that Marxism related to an earlier Romantic tradition. (12) Fischer seeks the roots of art in magic and in the unchanging characteristics of human nature, and deliberately blurs the lines between socialist and non-socialist art. (13) Sartre's attempt to revivify Marxism by an existentialist focus on the individual situation is summed up in the celebrated epigram: 'Valéry is a petty-bourgeois intellectual, of that there is no doubt. But not every petty-bourgeois intellectual is Valéry.' (14) This body of work opens the period in which we are still working; it is the well from which we still drink, even if we also spit into it.

It is in this context that the work of Althusser must be seen. Althusser must be understood, not as an autonomous subject, but as constructed by the contradictory discourses of the French Communist Party. And constructed, moreover, with a function. As Jacques Rancière has shown, Althusser's job was to provide a bridge between the Party and critical leftist elements of the intelligentsia, while at the same time maintaining the authority of the Party in strictly political matters. (15) As a result we find a number of distinct and sometimes contradictory strands in Althusser's thought:

i) a continuity with certain key themes of Stalinism. The radical break between Marx and earlier thought and the treatment of Hegel are taken straight from Zhdanov's 1947 lecture 'On Philosophy', (16) while the essay on 'Contradiction and Overdetermination' is an explicit defence of the theory of socialism in one country. (17)

ii) a concept of the 'relative autonomy' of different parts of the superstructure. This is directed against a notion of totality which Althusser sees as 'ultraleft', (18) and moreover, is explicitly intended to deal with the problem of Stalinism: 'Nonetheless, all that is said about the "cult of the personality" very precisely concerns the realm of the superstructure, that is, of State organisation and of ideologies; it concerns, moreover, in general this realm alone, which in Marxist theory we know to possess a "relative autonomy" (which explains very simply, in theory, that essentially the socialist infrastructure was able to develop unscathed during the period of errors affecting the superstructure.)' (19)

iii) an attack on what Althusser sees as the 'humanist' distortion of Marxism; in political terms a defence of the Party's hegemony against the influence of such thinkers as Sartre.

iv) an insistence on the 'autonomy of theory'. While this meant a rejection of the Party's right to dictate a line on scientific matters (as in the Lysenko affair) it also implied a situation in which Party intellectuals had the right to independence in working in their own fields so long as they did not challenge the authority of the Party in the strictly political sphere.

These positions had certain obvious implications for the 'relative autonomy' of literature, and were developed in the anti-humanist literary theory of Pierre Macherey's *Pour une Théorie de la Production Littéraire* (1966).

C

The main lines of the Althusserian position were developed, subject to certain tactical modifications, before May 1968. The events of May served to propagate Althusserian Marxism around the world, but also opened up a whole new complex of political and theoretical issues.

The three basic tenets of Marxist politics can be summarised as follows:

i) the primacy of the class struggle and the objective historical role of the working class;

ii) the view that the state is a weapon of one class against another and the consequent necessity of smashing the bourgeois state in any transition to socialism;

iii) the necessity for a centralised vanguard party bringing together

the most conscious and militant elements of the working class
alongside revolutionary intellectuals.

In the late sixties and seventies major social and theoretical
developments called all these tenets into question:

  i) a number of factors challenged the traditional Marxist view of
  the historical role of the working class:

   a) the emergence of a militant student movement;

   b) the rise and fall of Maoism with its insistence on the
   revolutionary role of the Third World peasantry and its
   consequent populist implications;

   c) the re-emergence of the womens' movement, leading to the
   difficult attempt to establish a synthesis of Marxism and
   feminism.

  ii) the classic Marxist doctrine of the state came under attack from
  opposing sides during the seventies:

   a) the seventies saw the rise and fall of so-called 'Eurocommunism' in the Communist Parties of France, Spain and Italy.
   This argued for the replacement of the single act of smashing
   the state machine with a phased series of captures and transformations of sections of the state, and a greater emphasis
   on the ideological rather than the repressive functions of
   the state;

   b) while Eurocommunism has attempted to dilute Marxism, the
   influential work of Michel Foucault has rejected the 'entire
   political discourse' of Marxism as leading to the Gulag, (20)
   and has replaced it by the notion of a disembodied and omni-
   present 'power'; instead of the strategic focus of the capitalist state, we are told that 'from state to family, from
   prince to father, from the tribunal to the small change of
   everyday punishments, from the agencies of social domination
   to the structures that constitute the subject himself, one
   finds a general form of power, varying in scale alone.' (21)

  iii) the challenging of the Marxist focus on proletariat and state
  had drastic consequences for political practice. As Rancière
  points out, if the class struggle was 'everywhere, then no-one
  needed to put themselves out.' (22) He cites a French academic
  who explained that he was in the Communist Party because it was
  the 'only organisation that didn't require him to be active.'
  (23) Althusser's attempt to unite theory and practice ended
  with the pathetic spectacle of a life-long Communist writing
  articles in the bourgeois press complaining that a Stalinist
  party functioned in a Stalinist manner. (24) For those who
  rejected party organisation altogether the picture was no
  better. For Foucault political intervention was simply one good
  cause after another, the endless debilitating round of demonstra-
  tions, statements and press conferences.

D

The intellectual development described up to this point has been
predominantly French. Many of its themes can be understood only in the
context of the peculiarly prolonged and tortuous process of deStalinisation in the French Communist Party. The PCF leadership in 1956 supported
the Molotov faction in the Russian party, and hence downplayed and even
denied the existence of the Kruschev revelations. (25)

It is, of course, right that we should take whatever is useful from recent French theory, but we should beware of being too deferential towards it. For the history of the French left since 1968 has been one of the triumph of open reformism over its rivals. The PCF has been outmanoeuvred and forced into a humiliating subordination to the Socialist Party, while the revolutionary left that in 1968 was a beacon for the whole advanced world has lost a good part of its support and largely collapsed into tailing Mitterrand.

In Britain Stalinism has always been a relatively marginal current in the labour movement, and hence the crisis of Stalinism was also relatively peripheral, despite Edward Thompson's continuing readiness to 'man the stations of 1956'. (26) But the crisis of the British Communist Party did give birth to *New Left Review*, the most influential journal of Marxist theory in Britain. And it was *New Left Review*, in two major articles by Perry Anderson (*Origins of the Present Crisis* and *Components of the National Culture*), (27) that developed an account of the alleged theoretical backwardness of the British labour movement. This account has undoubtedly had a widespread effect on the development of British Marxist thought in the seventies. Terry Eagleton prefaces *Criticism and Ideology* by declaring that for a Marxist aestheticism 'to intervene from England is almost automatically to disenfranchise oneself from debate. It is to feel acutely bereft of a tradition, as a tolerated house-guest of Europe, a precocious but parasitic alien.' (28) There are, of course, real issues here, but I find it hard to accept that such deference is appropriate in a revolutionary thinker.

More generally, I would argue that those who have pioneered the propagation of Althusserian and post-Althusserian thought in England should ask two questions of themselves:

  i) have they not underestimated the traditions and potential of the British Labour **Movement** (not the Labour Party), and overestimated the achievements of the French left?

  ii) is there not a danger that a body of theory, developed in relative autonomy from practice, and transplanted into a culture which lacks the political conditions that gave rise to it, may by its apparent irrelevance actually reinforce the distrust of theory that does exist in many sections of the British labour movement?

E

For any sociology of literature the question of the relation of literature to ideology must be central. But I would argue that the model of ideology taken over from Althusser and his co-thinkers has not been particularly fruitful in confronting that question. The reasons for this are basically political.

In *The German Ideology* Marx and Engels offer a proposition on which a theory of ideology can be constructed: 'The ideas of the ruling class are in every epoch the ruling ideas'. (29) For Althusser, however, this starting-point presents certain difficulties. For if it were to be applied to Russian society it would leave him with two alternatives: either that there is no ideology in Russia, which is, to say the least, implausible; or to say that there is a ruling class in Russia, which would be politically embarrassing. Hence Althusser has developed a more elastic notion of ideology. He has argued that 'ideology ... is indispensable in any society' and that only an ideological conception of the world has been able to imagine societies without ideologies. (30) Catch-22 indeed!

As a substantive proposition Althusser's argument seems to me to be on a level with the claim that socialism is impossible because of human nature - something that can be refuted only by future practice. But its implications for a theory of literature are interesting.

It is always salutary to be reminded of the pervasiveness and tenacity of ideology, to be reminded, in Catherine Belsey's words, that we 'cannot simply step outside it'. (31) Yet the danger of this approach is great. For if all literature is caught under the net of ideology, we are left with a 'pessimism of the intelligence' which offers no strategy for struggle. Chapter Four of Terry Eagleton's *Criticism and Ideology* contains many perceptive insights; but the overriding impression is one of the cancer of organicism working its way into every cell of English literature from Arnold to Yeats.

The second political component of Althusser's account of ideology is what Alex Callinicos has called his 'ideologism', the fact that ideological relations assume a central explanatory role in his work. As Callinicos points out: 'This "ideologism" has political effects. Althusser's discussion of the superstructure quickly focuses on the ideological state apparatuses - the institutions which sustain the dominance of the ruling class primarily through "consent" rather than "force". This analysis can easily be used to justify a political strategy based upon the assumption that the working class and its allies can win control of the ideological state apparatuses first and thereby attain political power without any violent confrontation with the capitalist state machine. Santiago Carrillo invokes this text in support of just such a strategy in his book *Eurocommunism and the State*.' (32)

To be fair, Althusser has commented that 'the material existence of the ideology in an apparatus and its practices does not have the same modality as the material existence of a paving-stone or a rifle'. (33) It is nice to know that he sees the difference between a school and a machine-gun, but some major problems remain.

For if ideology is given so much ground to occupy, we inevitably end up talking about ideology in a highly generalised and abstract manner. The formulations Althusser develops in his 'Letter on Art in Reply to André Daspre' refer to 'art' and 'ideology' as general undifferentiated categories. (The proviso that 'I mean authentic art, not works of an average or mediocre level' (34) is singularly useless, since it takes for granted a judgement we might have hoped for some guidance in making.) This is a long way from Marx's reference to the 'ideological forms in which men become conscious of this conflict and fight it out'. (35) Texts by Brecht and Patience Strong do not relate to ideology in the same way. What we need is a model that shows how some texts transmit ideology and some challenge it, while others do both at the same time.

F

Yet another aspect of the Althusserian model of ideology reinforces its pessimism as to the possibility of radical literary practice. This is its theory of the subject, namely that ideology encourages individuals to see themselves as autonomous agents rather than participants in a history without subject. Now of course Althusser is right to reject a naive voluntarism, just as Marx argues that 'men make their own history but not of their own free will'. (36) If human beings' actions could be reduced directly to their intentions, there would be no problem of ideology - and no need for politics. Yet voluntarist individualism would scarcely seem to be the main threat at the present time. Foucault has argued that the analysis of *énoncés* 'does not pose the question of the speaker', (37), and Barthes has said that 'to give a text an Author is to impose a limit on that text, to furnish it with a final signified, to close the writing'. (38)

This suppression of subjective intention renders problematic any claim of objective interpretation of the text. Macherey tells us that 'the necessity of the work is founded on the multiplicity of its meanings', (39) while Barthes insists that 'to interpret a text is not to give it a meaning ... but on the contrary to appreciate what plurality it is made of', (40) while Derrida talks of disqualifying 'the hermeneutic project postulating the true meaning of a text'. (41) Even if all of them reject the notion that a text can mean anything one likes, they are on a slippery slope that leads in that direction.

Of course the proposition that the text may have a meaning which goes beyond or even contradicts the explicit intentions of the author is one that is well established in the Marxist tradition, and can be traced back to Engels' celebrated letter to Margaret Harkness where he contrasts Balzac's personal political views with the picture of society contained in his work. (42) I want to argue, however, that most Marxist writing in the post-Stalin period has taken the reaction against a Zhdanovite direction of artistic practice to such a point that it has abandoned the whole problematic of partisanship in art. Lenin's attempts to recuperate the dead Tolstoy have been discussed and rediscussed at the expense of the much more complex and interesting relationship between Lenin and the live Gorky. (43)

As a result, those writers who consciously aligned themselves with the working class have got something of a rough deal from recent Marxist writing. One example is the treatment of various British writers of the inter-war period in Terry Eagleton's books. 'While Meyerhold and Piscator were at their peak,' we are told, 'English theatre was dominated by the grandfather of all naturalists, George Bernard Shaw ... there is no English Brecht.' (44) The false individualist posing of the issue - 'an English Brecht' - is allowed to obscure both the positive features of Shaw (prized by Lenin and Brecht) and the various workers' theatre movements. Orwell is presented as the representative of the 'Lower-Middle-Class Novel' in an essay which makes no mention of *Homage to Catalonia*. (45) The left being thus disposed of, the field is now clear for the claim that 'most of the agreed major writers of the twentieth century - Yeats, Eliot, Pound, Lawrence - are political conservatives who each had truck with fascism'. (46) With friends like that, writers of the left scarcely need enemies.

This is not to argue for an uncritical attitude towards any writing claiming to be on the left, nor is it to argue that there is nothing to be gained from a study of reactionary writers. What is true, however, is that the concept of commitment, which was central to the cultural debates of the early New Left in Britain, has largely disappeared from more recent discussion. And on the problematic of commitment we still have more to learn from Sartre than from Althusser or Derrida. (I am aware that quoting Sartre at Colchester is a little like wearing a Dicky Valentine badge at a Clash concert.)

For in talking of the death of the author and the self-producing text, we neglect to see that all writing derives from a choice. Writing is one political practice among others; the left-wing poet who opts to write a poem rather than planting a bomb or canvassing for the Labour Party has made a choice among possible practices and confronts the criterion of efficacity. The career of Victor Serge, who at various conjunctions opted for Literature or for political activism would make an illuminating study in this regard. (47)

The notion of commitment also has an application for the reading of texts from the past. Thus a recent text for students on Zola's *Germinal* tells us that the strike is a 'virility drama', (48) and the most authoritative study in English on the same author tells us that 'the dark, airless galleries below ground were the perfect symbol for the deep-buried corridors of the unconscious mind'. (49) Against such mystifications, with all their implications for the present, we have a responsibility to insist that the cause of strikes is exploitation and that work down the pit is a degrading reality; and to cite in our support our knowledge of Zola's commitment, that he knew exactly where he stood and what he was doing.

G

One of the main features of the insistence on the 'relative autonomy' of the text from its class base has been the attention given in recent work to the question of language. Behind the difficult attempt to discover a theory of language compatible with Marxism stand two key texts, one openly acknowledged and constantly invoked, the other far less often named but equally present. The former is Saussure's *Course in General Linguistics*, (50) the latter Stalin's *Concerning Marxism in Linguistics*. (51)

Saussure's contribution to the establishment of a science of linguistics is not in question; what may be doubted are the alleged radical implications of his work. For if we attempt to develop Saussure's method beyond the narrow field to which he himself applied it we find, firstly a downgrading of history, and secondly a theory of meaning which, if not itself idealist, certainly opens the door to idealism.

The scientific value of Stalin's attack on the linguistic theories of Marr can be rapidly dealt with, but the rejection of the view that language forms part of the superstructure was of great political significance. Stalin takes time out in his polemic to attack the Proletcult, (52) supposedly dead nearly thirty years before; behind the figure of Marr stands the spectre of ultra-leftism; for if Stalinism employed the rhetoric of the class criterion, Stalin was all too aware that if the class argument were taken seriously it could undermine the whole structure of his ideology. Althusser, who hails Stalin's pamphlet as a revelation, is equally clear that it is directed against leftism and the Proletcult. (53)

The main theme which has emerged from the preoccupation with linguistic theory has been the stress on the materiality of language, a notion which has certain problematic implications.

One aspect of this is the delight in word play, in puns and anagrams, which runs through the work of Lacan and Derrida and their followers. Inasmuch as this is harmless fun no-one could begrudge it them. But it seems intrinsically unlikely that there is anything subversive about puns which were so popular among the Victorian bourgeoisie. And there is a bolder exploitation of the materiality of language in the average cryptic crossword than in anything I have understood of Derrida. Indeed, it is arguable that our pleasure at recognising a pun (that is, in realising that the same signifier can refer to two distinct signifieds) derives precisely from a sense of reassurance that language is fixed and comprehensible, let alone the sense of satisfaction that we are clever enough to understand Derrida's trilingual puns.

More important is the potential political implication. As Terry Eagleton has pointed out: 'In rematerialising the sign, we are in imminent danger of de-materialising the referent.' (54) To insist that words are as material as anything else may lead to a politics that is all words and no action. Once again we encounter the 'ideologism' of Eurocommunism. The most tragic avatar of the doctrine was the slogan of the Chilean Communist Party in 1973: 'Collect signatures against civil war'. (55)

This is not to dismiss everything that Althusser and Derrida have to say about the reading of texts. The value of their insights may be tested in empirical studies of particular texts. But a certain danger of formalism persists, perhaps most clearly seen in the evolution of Roland Barthes. Like Elvis Presley, Barthes did his best work in the mid-fifties and spent twenty years getting worse. Barthes' *Mythologies* is a major contribution to the study of ideology, which combines a detailed and perceptive concern for the forms in which ideology is embodied with a genuinely materialist view of social conflict. ('The real problem is not to find out how to stick cherries into a partridge, it's to find the partridge, that is to say to pay for it.') (56) In Barthes' later works the clear focus on social conflict is lost and the study of ideology collapses into the multiplicity of meanings.

H

The accusation of formalism must be wielded carefully. More than one paper at previous conferences has defended the work of the Russian Formalists. Certainly the relation between the Formalists and the Bolshevik revolution was a complex and contradictory one. (Shklovsky, for example, fought both with and against the Red Army.) (57)

And certainly no serious theory of radical literature can neglect the importance of form as an active factor in achieving the purposes of the text. Yet within this recognition there is an ever-present danger of overestimating the subversive potential of form alone. Most participants in Essex conferences have aligned themselves with the formal innovations of modernism rather than with classic realism. But in some cases the claims made on behalf of modernist texts are excessive. Thus Terry Eagleton argues:

'When Samuel Beckett concludes *Molloy* by telling us: "It is midnight. The rain is beating on the windows. It was not midnight. It was not raining", he brazenly reveals the virtuality of his enunciation, exposes the text as a machine for producing pseudo-statements. It is in such doubling of the text, such raising of the parody to the second power, that "literary" works may perform productive operations upon the ideological. For if an English chauvinist were able to say: "The Irish are inferior to the English. The Irish are not inferior to the English", it would not merely be a matter of adopting another position: it would be a question of discovering something of the nature of positionality itself, its production of a closure constantly threatened by the heterogeneity of language.' (58)

Leaving aside the fact that the argument is based on a misquotation of Beckett's text, (59) I find this very hard to follow. The power of anti-Irish racism in British society is very deep, and if its protagonists are to be cured they will need sterner treatment than being required to talk nonsense.

In the last resort, then, I would argue that the Bolshevik critics of Formalism were correct. In Trotsky's words: 'The Formalist school represents an abortive idealism applied to the questions of art. The Formalists show a fast ripening religiousness. They are followers of St. John. They believe that "In the beginning was the Word". But we believe that in the beginning was the deed. The word followed, as its phonetic shadow.' (60)

I

The alignment with modernism among most participants in Essex conferences has meant an attitude of distrust towards the realist tradition. In a paper on film which had applications to other genres, Colin MacCabe challenged the epistemological bases of realism: "film does not reveal the real in a moment of transparency, but rather ... is constituted by a set of discourses which (in the positions allowed to subject and object) produce a certain reality". (61) Catherine Belsey has argued that realism is a 'predominantly conservative form'. - 'The experience of reading a realist text is ultimately reassuring, however harrowing the events of the story, because the world evoked in the fiction, its pattern of cause and effect, of social relationships and moral values, largely confirm the patterns of the world we seem to know.' (62)

More serious is the attempt to co-opt Brecht as an adversary of realism. Brecht's critique of the theatrical illusion is extremely significant and pertinent, but it does not involve a rejection of realism. Brecht laid claim to the concept of realism, while seeing the necessity to 'cleanse' it. And among the characteristics of realism Brecht lays down 'writing from the standpoint of the class which offers the broadest solutions for the pressing difficulties in which human society is caught up'. (63) It is on this point - the proletariat as the holder of the truth about society - that Brecht converges with his old adversary Lukács, and it is on this basis that a defence of realism can be developed.

And realism needs to be defended, notably against the mystification developed by Barthes in S/Z, where he argues that 'realism (badly named or at least often badly interpreted) consists, not in copying the real, but in copying a (painted) copy of the real'. (64) Nothing could be more calculated to encourage the complacency of the reader than this perpetual deferment of reality.

To take an example, once again from the arch-naturalist Zola. In the five years before Zola's *Germinal* was written, several other novelists (Talmeyr, Maisonneuve, Guyot) wrote novels of mining life. In them all we find similar themes - the pit-disaster and the strike. But to relate Zola's text to others' texts (which he may or may not have read) rather than to the reality he sought to encounter is precisely to divert attention away from the facts that coal-mines are dangerous and that oppressed miners will resist.

J

To summarise: I have argued that the concept of 'relative autonomy' is a hangover from the epoch of deStalinisation and that the sociology of literature should now give greater attention to relating texts to their class base. This would imply a revival of the idea of partisanship and a defence of realism against formalism. To conclude I shall suggest what practical conclusions may be drawn from this analysis.

In his book on *Walter Benjamin* Terry Eagleton devotes a couple of paragraphs to the tasks of the Marxist critic with which I largely agree. (65) The only pity is that the rest of the book seems to be about something quite different.

Most of the participants in this conference are established within academic institutions (and presumably will spend a good deal of their time in the next few years trying to stay there). Our political tasks clearly begin there.

Catherine Belsey argues that 'there is always a danger that a radical literary criticism will simply create a new canon of acceptable texts, merely reversing old value judgments rather than questioning their fundamental assumptions'. (66) Yet to create a new canon would be no small achievement, especially if it were embodied in the material apparatus of the syllabus. It would certainly be a worthwhile task to get Zola, Robert Tressell and Victor Serge implanted in a few more syllabuses - and while contrary to Macherey I don't advocate book-burning, I should not be heart-broken if, say, Ezra Pound and Jane Austen got squeezed out. To promote suppressed radical writers, and to recuperate those radical writers who have been co-opted and rendered anodyne by bourgeois criticism - these are more urgent tasks than yet another Marxist reading of an established conservative author.

But there are other tasks outside of academic institutions. The whole experience of Stalinism and Zhdanovism has distorted the argument about the relationship between cultural practice and political organisation. There are a whole number of questions to be reopened here.

One such question is that of the Proletcult. Anathematised by both Stalin and Trotsky, the project has been dismissed with contempt. Yet we might recall that in 1920 the Proletcult was operating 300 workshops with 84,000 members. (67) Victor Serge describes what the Proletcult actually meant: 'The Vagranka group in the Rogoysko-Simonovsky suburb of Moscow is made up of sixteen workers who write for the press. Perkati-Polé, an old Bolshevik writer, a forgotten man, blind and dirt poor, gathers them in his comfortless lodgings and teaches them how to get rhythm into their verse and prose. There are not enough chairs; they crouch in a circle on the floor. They arrive smelling of tar, machine oil, and metallic dust.' (68)

We need a theory which can incorporate this experience, but also bring it together with more contemporary cultural practice. After all, if revolutionary art is being produced in Britain today, it is coming from the Specials, the Jam and the Clash. The most successful recent experience of bringing together political organisation and cultural practice was Rock Against Racism. In constructing such a theory we need to turn first to the early years of the Communist International. Lenin's correspondence with Gorky, and Trotsky's comments on fellow-travellers (69) still have relevant lessons. More recently the work of Lukács and Sartre raised important questions about the relations of party and writer, of literature and class-consciousness. The answers were often wrong, distorted by the vagaries of Stalinist politics, but at least the questions were posed. With Althusser, Barthes, Foucault and Derrida such questions don't even get asked. And above all, we need to make the fact of class more central. Whatever else Valéry may have been, he was certainly a petty-bourgeois.

FOOTNOTES

1. Zola on Stendhal in *Les Romanciers Naturalistes* (1881).

2. T. Eagleton, *Marxism and Literary Criticism* (Methuen, 1976); *Criticism and Ideology* (Verso, 1978); *Walter Benjamin* (Verso, 1981); C. Belsey, *Critical Practice* (Methuen, 1980).

3. F.R. Leavis, *The Common Pursuit*, (Peregrine, 1962), p. 182.

4. T. Gautier, *Mademoiselle de Maupin* (Garnier-Flammarion, 1966), pp. 25-60.

5. H. Levin, *The Gates of Horn* (Oxford U.P., 1966), p. 23.

6. P. Macherey, 'Problems of Reflection', in F. Barker et al (eds), *Literature, Society and the Sociology of Literature* (University of Essex, 1977), p. 52.

7. C. Mercer, 'Baudelaire and the City:1848 and the Inscription of Hegemony', in F. Barker et al (eds), *1848: The Sociology of Literature* (University of Essex, 1978), p. 227.

8. C. Mercer, 'Gramsci and Grammar', in F. Barker et al (eds), *1936: The Sociology of Literature* (University of Essex, 1979), Vol I, p. 74.

9. Address to the First Congress of Soviet Writers (17.8.34) in A. Zhdvanov, *Sur la Littérature, la Philosophie et la Musique* (Editions Norman Bethune, 1972), p. 5.

10. 'N.S. Kruschev's Secret Speech', in D. Jacobs (ed), *The New Communist Manifesto and Related Documents* (Harper Torchbooks, 1962), p. 101.

11. L. Goldmann, *Recherches Dialectiques* (Gallimard, 1959), pp. 59, 14.

12. R. Williams, *Culture and Society* (Penguin, 1963), pp. 258-75.

13. E. Fischer, *The Necessity of Art* (Penguin, 1963), pp. 13, 220, 202.

14. J-P. Sartre, *Critique de la Raison Dialectique* (Gallimard, 1960), p. 44.

15. J. Rancière, *La Leçon d'Althusser* (Gallimard, 1974), pp. 33, 49; 202-8.

16. Cf. A. Zhdvanov, *op cit*, pp. 42, 58.

17. Cf. L. Althusser, *Pour Marx* (Maspero, 1967), p. 93.

18. Cf. L. Althusser, *op cit*, p.12; Rancière, *op cit*, pp. 62.4.

19. L. Althusser, *op cit*, pp. 247-8.

20. M. Foucault, 'La grande colère des faits', *Le Nouvel Observateur*, 9.5.77.

21. M. Foucault, *The History of Sexuality* (Pelican, 1981), pp. 84-5.

22. Rancière, *op cit*, p. 138.

23. *ibid.*, p. 137.

24. L. Althusser, 'Ce qui ne peut plus durer dans le Parti Communiste', *Le Monde* 24-27.4.1978.

25. Cf. 'The Kruschev Speech, the PCF and the PCI', R. Miliband and J. Saville (eds), *The Socialist Register 1976* (Merlin), pp. 58-60.

26. E.P. Thompson, 'The Peculiarities of the English', in *The Poverty of Theory* (Merlin, 1978), p. 88.

27. *New Left Review*, nos. 23 and 50.

28. *Criticism and Ideology*, p. 7.

29. K. Marx and F. Engels, *The German Ideology* (Lawrence and Wishart, 1965), p. 60.

30. *Pour Marx*, pp. 242, 238.

31. C. Belsey, *op cit*, p. 62.

32. A. Callinicos, *Is There a Future for Marxism?* (Macmillan, 1982), p. 78.

33. L. Althusser, *Lenin and Philosophy* (New Left Books, 1977), p. 156.

34. *ibid*, p. 204.

35. K. Marx, 'Preface to a Contribution to the Critique of Political Economy' in *Marx Engels on Literature and Art* (International General, 1974), p. 85.

36. K. Marx, 'The Eighteenth Brumaire of Louis Bonaparte', in *Surveys from Exile* (Penguin, 1973), p. 146.

37. M. Foucault, *L'Archéologie du Savoir* (Gallimard, 1969), p. 161.

38. R. Barthes, *Image-Music-Text*, cited in Belsey, *op cit*, p. 135.

39. P. Macherey, *Pour une Théorie de la Production Littéraire* (Maspéro, 1969), p. 96.

40. R. Barthes, *S/Z* (Editions du Seuil, 1976), p. 11.

41. J. Derrida, *Eperons* (Flammarion, 1978), p. 86.

42. In *Marx Engels on Literature and Art*, (Progress, 1976), pp. 116-7.

43. Cf. V.I. Lenin and M. Gorky, *Letters, Reminiscences, Articles* (Progress Publishers, 1973).

44. *Walter Benjamin*, pp. 94-6.

45. 'Orwell and the Lower-Middle-Class Novel' in *Exiles and Emigrés* (Chatton & Windus, 1970), pp. 78-108.

46. *Marxism and Literary Criticism*, p. 8.

47. Cf. V. Serge, *Memoirs of a Revolutionary* (Oxford U.P., 1967), especially p. 262.

48. C. Smethurst, *Emile Zola: Germinal* (Edward Arnold, 1974), p. 38.

49. F.W.J. Hemmings, *Emile Zola* (Oxford U.P., 1966), p. 193.

50. F. de Saussure, *Course in General Linguistics* (Fontana, 1974).

51. J.V. Stalin, *Concerning Marxism in Linguistics* (Irish Communist Organisation, 1968).

52. *ibid*, p. 24.

53. *Pour Marx*, p. 12.

54. T. Eagleton, 'Aesthetics and Politics', *New Left Review 107*, p. 22.

55. H. Blanco, 'Chilean Workers meet Rightist Threat', *Intercontinental Press*, 11.6.1973, p. 707.

56. R. Barthes, *Mythologies* (Editions du Seuil, 1970), p. 130.

57. V. Shklovsky, *Mayakovsky and his Circle* (Pluto, 1974), p. xvi.

58. *Walter Benjamin*, pp. 125-6.

59. Cf. S. Beckett, *The Beckett Trilogy* (Picador, 1979), p. 162, which reads 'Then I went back into the house and wrote. It is midnight. The rain is beating on the window. It was not midnight. It was not raining.'

60. Trotsky, *op cit*, p. 183.

61. C. MacCabe, 'Theory and Film: Principles of Realism and Pleasure', in *Literature, Society and the Sociology of Literature*, p. 61.

62. C. Belsey, *op cit*, p. 51.

63. B. Brecht, 'Against George Lukács', in Bloch, Lukács, Brecht, Benjamin, Adorno, *Aesthetics and Politics* (Verso, 1977), p. 81-2.

64. *S/Z*, p. 61.

65. *Walter Benjamin*, pp. 97, 113.
66. C. Belsey, *op cit*, p. 103.
67. M. Slonim, *Soviet Russian Literature* (Oxford U.P., 1967), p. 34.
68. V. Serge, 'Is a Proletarian Literature Possible,', in J. Ehrmann (ed), *Literature and Revolution* (Beacon Press, 1970), p. 143.
69. Cf. L. Trotsky, *Literature and Revolution* (Ann Arbor, 1960), pp. 56-115.

THE TRAJECTORY OF *SCREEN*, 1971-79

Antony Easthope

> What does the proletariat expect of
> its intellectuals? That they dis-
> integrate bourgeois ideology.
>
> Brecht (cited *Screen*
> Summer 1974, p.123)

For nearly ten years from 1971 the film magazine *Screen* was the most important theoretical journal concerned with aesthetic discourse in Britain. (1) It continues to be an important journal, though now its concern is specifically with cinema, and its implications are not generalisable in the way they once were.

I mean to defend the theoretical trajectory marked out by *Screen* not only as compatible with traditional Marxist criticism but as a valuable extension of it and one widely available for appropriation in other areas, such as literary studies and art history. I shall defend the trajectory in a modified form, that is, with some of the excesses of *Tel Quelism* filletted off. This is justifiable because there never was a homogeneous, doctrinaire 'Screen theory'; there was rather a developing coherence assembled piece by piece from a number of contributions in the same problematic. For this reason I shall avoid naming names and try to let the argument speak for itself. I'll begin with a brief round-up paragraph on the institutional aspects of the journal.

A major influence on the *Screen* problematic was Althusser's essay on Ideological State Apparatuses. There is an irony therefore in the fact that the *Screen* project was nurtured in the bosom of the state. From 1971 the journal was published by the Society for Education in Film and Television, an independent body with a grant-in-aid from the British Film Institute. As well as *Screen*, there was *Screen Education*, explaining theory in a more popular form and engaged on its own account in a useful analysis of popular culture. *Screen* successfully penetrated British intellectual life in a series of practical forms: regional groups, reading groups (such as that in Manchester), the BFI summer school, *Screen* readers' meetings in London, weekend schools both in London and the provinces, the film 'event' at the Edinburgh Film Festival. At one point in 1977 *Screen* had nearly 1200 subscribers. Through various personnel, and also the connection with state capital at the BFI, *Screen* was involved with the avant-garde and independent film production. The editor of *Screen* was Sam Rohdie from 1971-74, Ben Brewster from 1974-76, Geoffrey Nowell-Smith from 1977-78. Of the internal politics of the Editorial Board, a politics which led for example to the 1976 resignations, I know nothing. The success of *Screen* was shaped in part by the leadership of the personnel involved, just as its decline after 1978 was due in part to their withdrawal. A very significant feature of the leadership was the high proportion of women in it. There were other external influences on the problematic. One was the films that came out in the early 'seventies (*Screen* preferences were Godard and Oshima). Another was the seemingly endless stream of new names that arrived across the Channel each quarter. Moving out from a basis in Russian Formalism, Brecht and Althusser, *Screen* was able to introduce Metz, Bellour, Lacan and Kristeva, all hot from the bookshops of Paris. For example, Metz's 'The Imaginary Signifier' appeared in *Communications* no.23 in May 1975 and was translated for *Screen* in Summer 1975.

Relentlessly academic, never reluctant to engage in intellectual terrorism, *Screen* developed its own high theoretical style. In 1976 I heard a leading practitioner give a brilliant analysis of a recent American film. At the end someone stood up and proved that the last shot of the film was not a point of view shot as the analysis had claimed. After a pause, the practitioner replied, 'According to the inexorable logic of my theory, that fact is impossible'.

The *Screen* Problematic

Before giving a synchronic outline of the *Screen* problematic, I need to say something about its diachronic development. By taking as its object cinema it won at a stroke two related advantages denied to traditional work in literature and art history. It escaped entirely 'a cultural ideology'based on 'a differentiation of "high" from "low" culture, such that the "good object" is identified as Literature, as distinct from "popular fiction"' (Spring 1976, pp.103-4). At the same time it bypassed the whole question of authorship. As a way to get beyond *auteurisme*, film studies at the end of the 'sixties had already pushed forward into the questions of genre and iconography. In its early period (1971-74) *Screen* drew on and drew together three main areas of work: Althusser's theory of ideology from the ISA's essay, Brecht's criticism, film theory from the Russian formalists. The search was on for an account of film 'language' - in the work of Christian Metz it was believed this could be found (Spring and Summer 1973, double issue on Metz). A second period, the heroic days of 1974 -76, was inaugurated by Metz' essay on 'The Imaginary Signifier', (Summer 1975). Making as much use of Juliet Mitchell's *Psychoanalysis and Feminism* (1974) as of the then untranslated French originals, *Screen* drew on Lacanian psychoanalysis to describe and explain the kind of subjective position offered to the reader by a kind of cinema. A third period (1977-1979) evidences faltering and uncertainty, an uncertainty induced above all by the work of Hindess and Hirst. It is my intention later to argue that this loss of faith was premature, misguided and unnecessary.

In its mature development, the *Screen* problematic was concerned to theorise 'the encounter of Marxism and psychoanalysis on the terrain of semiotics'. (2) Film was to be understood as a specific signifying practice. To quote:

> 'signifying' is the recognition of a language as a systematic articulation of meanings; 'practice' refers to the process of this articulation, to the work of the production of meanings, and in so doing it brings into the argument the problem of the relations of the subject within that work; 'specific' gives the necessity for the analysis of a particular signifying practice in its specific formations (which is not a commitment to some 'purity') ... (Summer 1974, p.128).

The aim is to think together cinema as triply determined: 1, semiologically; 2, ideologically and historically; 3, subjectively.

1. The semiological determinant of film was seen to lie in its specific materiality as signifier. 'A text is structured primarily at the level of the signifier' since 'it is the ordering of the signifiers

which determines the production of the signifieds' (Spring 1976, p.19). It is a 'fundamental axiom of a materialistic aesthetic' that 'style is a producer of meaning' (p.20). The work of the Russian Formalists had shown that the stylistic devices of literature were not mere vehicles for meaning but constituted its very literariness. Metz had shown that there were five matters of expression in film: 'phonetic sound, written titles, musical sound, noises, the moving photographic image' (Autumn 1975, p.23). *Screen* meant to analyse these apparently formalist devices of cinema. And so it did, providing close, detailed and thorough investigation of deep focus, lighting the point of view shot. Since this is all specific to film I shall say no more about it except to mention one important essay in the area. This shows how the separate materialities of the matters of expression are synchronised, constructed into a homogeneity and unity in the classic realist film ('The Politics of Separation', Winter 1975/76).

2. Most traditional Marxist analyses of aesthetic discourse share with bourgeois criticism a prime concern with 'content', differing only in treating 'content' as ideology. Basing itself on Althusser's later account of ideology, the *Screen* problematic understood film not just in terms of the ideological signified, 'the province of a traditional "content analysis"', but through its 'ideological operation'. (3) The emphasis on 'form' rather than 'content' is consistent with and extends the previous recognition of the materiality of the signifier. Just as each Althusserian practice (economic, political, ideological, theoretical) was a transformation and an act in the present, so film is theorised as signifying practice. It is not to be grasped in any sense as a reflection of a meaning which pre-exists it, but as an active transformation or work or operation producing meanings in relation to the reader. Moreover, to term film signifying practice explicitly acknowledges its relative autonomy as a practice for which the others are necessary but not sufficient conditions, a practice historically determined in the last instance by the economic. This stress constantly surfaced in the work of *Screen*, for example in the close studies of studio production at Ealing (Spring 1975) and Columbia (Autumn 1975).

3. The ideological operation of film was understood as subjective in providing a position for the reader, and it was in this area that the project was most original, moving well beyond its Parisian antecedents. Besides Lacan, and besides the already developed conception of film as materially specific, there were two points of departure for theorising 'the relations of the subject' within the work of the text. One was Althusser's progressive definition of ideology at a deeper, more pervasive and less conscious level until by 1969 it had become equated with the function of the ego itself, that which is socially constituted to misrecognise itself as constitutive: the subject is produced historically so that I 'see' myself as a free agent, an autonomous self. The other came from recognition of the cinema (typically Hollywood) as economic practice. Bourgeois cinema sells a commodity not in the form of a consumable object (a packet of cigarettes) but as a ticket giving you the right to sit in a seat for a performance. So Metz says that 'the cinematic institution is not just the cinema industry (which works to fill cinemas, not to empty them), it is also the mental machinery - another industry - which spectators "accustomed to the cinema" have internalised historically and which has adapted them to the consumption of film' (Summer 1975, pp.18-19). Hollywood markets forms of pleasure. Analysis of pleasure and pleasures can only be undertaken with the aid of psychoanalysis.

Thus a paper on Brecht ('Lessons from Brecht', Summer 1974) brings into relation commodity fetishism and Freud on fetishism. Brecht distinguishes between a play which reveals its own production and invites an audience into a critical attitude, and a play which tries to conceal its production and seeks an empathic response. Freud's example of a fetish significantly includes both an object and looking at it - a 'glance at the nose'. (4) He argues that the fetish is produced for a (male) subject as a substitute for the lack of a penis in women, a structure of disavowal therefore. The *Screen* paper claims that in classic realist cinema:

> The structure of representation is a structure of fetishism: the subject is produced in a position of separation from which he is confirmed in an imaginary coherence (the representation is the guarantee of his self-coherence) the condition of which is the ignorance of the structure of his production, of his setting in position. (Summer 1974, p.106).

On this showing, realist cinema provides narcissistic gratification for the ego, specifically the pleasures of scopophilia and mastery.

The structuring of the ego in 'imaginary coherence' calls on Lacan's distinction between the imaginary and the symbolic. In the realm of the imaginary, language is understood 'in terms of some full relation between word and meaning', while in the symbolic it is understood in terms of the syntagmatic and paradigmatic chains by whose operation the signifier makes meaning possible. Thus, 'as speaking subjects we constantly oscillate between the symbolic and the imaginary - constantly imagining ourselves granting some full meaning to the words we speak, and constantly being surprised to find them determined by relations outside our control' (Autumn 1976, p.13, p.14). The drama of the subject is defined in terms of the absence opened in the subject by the non-semantic materiality of the signifier; 'the imaginary is then the consistence of the subject images set up to fill the lack; the symbolic is made of gaps, divides, and effects - "causes" - the subject in that division' (*sic*, Winter 1976/77, p.55). The *Screen* problematic draws several implications from the Lacanian conception. 1. The subject does not exist outside or prior to discourse but is constituted as an effect within discourse in a specific relation of imaginary and symbolic. 2. Since there can be no signified without a signifier, there is no imaginary coherence for the subject without an operation of the signifier in the symbolic to bring about this coherence. 3. A textual institution such as classic realism works to disavow the signifier and so produces a position for the reader in which the signifier is disclaimed by various strategies.

One important device for disavowal establishes a hierarchic relation between two levels of discourse in the realist narrative text. It works also in literature and is illustrated from George Eliot's *Middlemarch*. At one level of discourse characters speak directly from their partial and inadequate understanding of their situation. On the basis of this inadequacy a second discourse can function as a metalanguage making the claim that the text 'has direct access to a final reality', the truth (Summer 1974, p.10). The operation of such devices in the classic realist text (novel or film) 'ensures the position of the subject in a relation of dominant specularity' (p.12). The realist text exacts a logic of contradiction that 'produces a position for the view but denies that production' (Autumn 1976, p.17). This formulation advances Althusser's later concept of ideology but also reaches back to the Brechtian critique of realism.

Through its concern with psychoanalysis *Screen* was able to relate its project to sexuality and the politics of feminism. An essay on 'Visual Pleasure and Narrative Cinema' (Autumn 1975) argues that psychoanalysis has an obvious interest for feminism because it helps to face 'the ultimate challenge: how to fight the unconscious' (p.7). The paradox of phallocentrism is that it depends on an 'image of the castrated woman to give order and meaning to its world' (p.61). Phallocentrism denies that masculine and feminine can be defined positively and reciprocally, each the other of the other; in its representations it aims to identify masculine with the active and the symbolic presence of the phallus, feminine with the passive and the absence of the phallus. The image of woman is bound into this structure twice over. She both produces the threat of castration and is fixed in place of that lack; she opens the wound her passivity as an object serves to close.

Developed from Lacan's account of the gaze and the look, of being and having the phallus, this analysis makes possible an understanding of the dominant specularity of classic realism (Hollywood) as sexist. Quite simply its visual strategy is to treat 'Woman as Image, Man as Bearer of the Look' (p.11). If a male wish for the phallus as full presence encounters the feminine as lack, then woman always represents castration anxiety, an unpleasure from which 'the male unconscious has two avenues of escape' (p.13): either mastery by 'investigating the woman, demystifying her mystery' (p.13) or fetishistic scopophilia which 'builds up the physical beauty of the object, transforming it into something satisfying in itself' (p.14). Hence classic realist cinema works through: (a) a plot which uncovers knowledge of the truth; (b) visual plenitude which disavows its own production. In sum: 'the image of woman as (passive) raw material for the (active) gaze of man' is demanded by the ideology of the patriarchal order and 'worked out in its own favourite cinematic form - illusionistic narrative film' (p.17). This mode of representation is historical since in it the camera is used as a 'mechanism for producing an illusion of Renaissance space' (p.18).

Its analysis of classic realist or illusionist cinema led *Screen* to stand firmly on the side of modernism in the Marxist debate over realism versus modernism. An extrapolation of the *Screen* problematic endorsed avant-garde cinema, for if illusionist cinema by disavowing its own productivity confirmed the reader in his or her own self-presence, it seemed to follow that the self-reflexive text, one displaying its own productivity, would exhibit the self as socially and subjectively constructed, so opening the possibility of alternative construction and political change. There came about a classification of texts into four kinds: complicit, progressive, formalist, radical. A complicit text reiterated classic realism; the same with a radical content was progressive cinema (or television - 'Days of Hope'). If the signifier is revealed (shots of the camera etc.) but 'the breaking of the imaginary relationship' is treated as 'a political goal in itself' (Autumn 1976, p.21), this is 'ultra-leftist' or formalist cinema ('Materialist Film', Gidal), limited to 'an aesthetics of transgression' (*ibid.*, p.108). If however there is work at a deeper level, work on 'the operations of narrativisation' and so on 'the constructions and relations of meaning and subject' (as for example in Oshima's 'Death by Hanging', see Autumn 1976, pp.108-112), then this is radical cinema.

The classification was never so explicit in the *Screen* problematic. Though suggestive, it is the least defensible area and I shall move straight to criticisms of it. The first is that if illusionist cinema is pleasurable (for reasons that were psychoanalytically explicable), then anti-illusionist cinema must be unpleasurable. One article contains the ominous if ambiguous side-heading 'Destruction of Pleasure as a Radical Weapon' (Autumn 1975, p.7). A more comprehensive objection is made by Constance Penley in an article on 'The Avant-Garde and its Imaginary' that deserves to be much more widely read. (5) In drastic summary the argument is that there is always an imaginary, since for the speaking subject the only alternative to a more or less coherent ego is psychosis, and that the apparently deconstructive and self-reflexive avant-garde text provides its own imaginary pleasures in the form of epistemophilia (the model being something like: 'My ego is so strong I can make sense even of this'). The article implies the need to look for distinctions between kinds of imaginary. If the classic realist text offers the reader a position as absolute or transcendental ego, other texts may work to relativise the reader's position. They would not aim to destroy the imaginary (that way lies madness) but rather to set the ego in place relative to its semiological, social and subjective construction.

Objections, Modifications, Defence

Having tried to give a relatively unmediated exposition of the *Screen* problematic, I shall now qualify and defend it under five headings: Reflectionism, Formalism, History, Subjectivity, Knowledge. The last two excited the most controversy - and figured prominently in the demise of *Screen* - so they will detain us longest.

1. Reflectionism By taking up film through the Althusserian concept of signifying practice, as transformation and production of meanings, *Screen* broke decisively with a reflectionist problematic. It anticipated the widespread recognition that the reader should not be seen as 'a consumer, but a producer of the text'. (6) In the passage on Greek art Marx demonstrates how such art depends on the ideological configuration of Greek mythology, which in turn is determined by the ancient mode of production. That is not the problem. The difficulty is the pleasure it produces in him now, reading Aeschylus in his room in Victorian London. There are practices - economic, political - in which signification is not dominant as well as signifying practice, in which it is. Signifying practice differs in the degree to which it can be produced and reproduced transhistorically. A sixteenth-century sword and a sixteenth-century sonnet are both products of history; both can be used in 1982. But the special 'productivity of language' (7) ensures that the sonnet can be 'used' in many more and more different ways than the sword. It may be that the aesthetic text has to be thought in two separate problematics: in one as the product of history, in another as the product of the reader in a determinate reading.

2. Formalism Even though its primary concern with the signifier in no way denied that the signified was ideological, *Screen* was nevertheless attacked for 'formalism'. (8) As well as formalism there is an error of 'contentism', and I suggest *Screen*'s attention to the level of the signifier in aesthetic discourse is fully appropriate. For all discourse it is the case that there can be no signified without a signifier and that 'the represented exists as an effect of a process of signification'. (9) But concern with the signifier is especially pertinent for aesthetic discourse since it is specified by the work/play of the signifier. Poetry, for example, 'has rules which govern the ordering ot signifiers independent of the signified: metre, rhyme, etc.' (Spring 1976, p.19). The *Screen* problematic is correct to regard these not as 'embellishments' but as stylistic devices producing meaning. In a way entirely compatible with traditional Marxist criticism the problematic opens for interrogation whole areas of textual production that

such criticism has generally abandoned as 'merely' formalist and so left invisible for political critique. To keep the example of poetry and metre: iambic pentameter, the traditional metre of the English poetic canon since the Renaissance, is not some harmless decoration but is a materialist basis for the poetic discourse and integral to its ideological significance and operation. (10) The *Screen* problematic is widely generalisable and brings into political question all literary, graphic and musical forms, indeed aesthetic forms altogether.

3. History Most critiques of the *Screen* problematic from a left perspective (I don't know of any from the right) were unhappy with the way history was theorised. Stuart Hall, for example, says that in the 'Screen theory' the politics of ideological struggle were reduced exclusively to a problem 'around "subjectivity" in the Lacanian sense' and the formation of this subject was envisaged as "trans-historical and trans-social". (11) This is a misunderstanding, though one the pages of *Screen* did little to disperse explicitly. It was always claimed that concern was directed at a specific signifying practice, one that was also specific 'in a given socio-historical situation' (Autumn 1976, p.109). This sense of the historical was never conjunctural, and the account of single texts (progressive, formalist, etc.) as a means of local intervention is very weak, as I've already suggested. *Screen* did not take the single text as its scale. It drew on the Metzian account of cinema as an institution and on texts in their aggregate in and across a mode of representation. Classic realism extends back from twentieth century cinema into the nineteenth century novel (George Eliot) and into a tradition of visual representation which began with the devices used for 'producing an illusion of Renaissance space'. The problematic was firmly historical in its account of modes of representation as historical on an epochal scale. Though exemplified in terms of cinema, classic realism is a mode of representation coterminous with bourgeois society, a mode working to sustain a position for the transcendental or Cartesian ego - the bourgeois ego therefore. The essay on 'Narrative Space' (Autumn 1976) traces the origins of cinematic realism back to Quattrocento perspective and to a representational economy by which this construction of space is unified with narrative forms to ensure the dominant specularity of the subject, always maintaining a position for the reader as though they were 'outside and looking in' (like god). If we withhold the attribute 'historical' from this account, we'll have to deny it to *Capital* as well.

4. Subjectivity Historical materialism treats individuals 'only in so far as they are the personifications (Träger) of economic categories'. (12) The *Screen* problematic early on recognised that aesthetic discourse introduces the question of subjectivity as an immediate and pervasive concern, one therefore that could only be effectively theorised by 'a historical materialism that has integrated the scientific revolution inaugurated by Freud and psychoanalysis' (Editorial, Summer 1975, p.5). Surely there is a necessary step forward here. Psychoanalysis makes it possible to examine how texts work through pleasure and unpleasure within an explanatory framework that aims to be materialist. Its Lacanian development enables the position of the subject to be grasped as ideological. And it problematises gender and sexuality in relation to signifying practice. [This last properly requires a separate paper. There is a whole 'other history' of *Screen* to be written, one that would take in both the inadequacy of the reply to Lesage's attack on the phallocentrism of *Screen*'s use of the concept of fetishism (the reply appealed to 'the thesis of bisexuality', Summer 1975, p.85) and the degree to which amends are made in the critique of Lacan in 'Difference', Autumn 1978.]

5. Knowledge In method the *Screen* problematic broke completely with the tainted ideological complicities of literary criticism, what Raymond Williams refers to as its 'perfect and virtually unbreakable circle'. (13) It was helped to do this partly by taking cinema as its object, partly because it took over from Althusser an opposition between ideology and science: if cinema was ideological, the consequent analysis of cinema would be scientific, a theoretical practice, attempting to construct systematic understanding of film, For Althusser science is a process without a subject, and the extent to which *Screen* developed a theoretical knowledge of film can be judged from the way all the separate pieces in it transcended their authors to become part of an impersonal coherence, a collective discourse, a form of knowledge. If there is a subject for this process, one might note that the pleasures promised to it were very much those of mastery and the pleasure of knowing. Was that not why people worked so hard for and at the journal? And was it not when these pleasures were delegitimated - when belief in the possibility of knowledge was undermined - that the *Screen* trajectory swung round its apogee and into decline?

Retrospectively *Screen*'s theoretical coherency may be understood as a version of 'Post-Structuralism Phase 1', a phase signalled most vividly by Barthes' *S/Z* (1970). Around 1977 the *Screen* project faltered. It did so in ways which are importantly generalisable and relate to what may be referred to as 'Post-Structuralism Phase 2', a phase marked by the ascendency of Foucault and Derrida, and a realisation that 'no metalanguage can be spoken'. (14) In *Screen* it took a particular form: a crisis over the subject as effect of discourse, a crisis in epistemology inaugurated by the work of Hindess and Hirst.

1. 'Subject position' The *Screen* problematic assumed that a systematic understanding of film could be reached by considering how a position for the reader was 'inscribed in the film' (Winter 1975/76, p.61). The confidence derived from a firm rejection of belief in any transcendental subject and a firm adherence to the Lacanian conception that subjectivity was constituted as an effect of the discourse which included it. 'Subject position' was theoretical, not actual: 'In themselves the cinematic codes implied in the film text are not capable of producing an unambiguous reader'; at stake was only 'the implicit reader', 'an ideal reader, one who completely conforms to the supposed intentions of the text' (Autumn 1972, (15)). Six years later Paul Willeman's essay of Spring 1978 pointed out what had always been known but had been disavowed:

> there remains an unbridgeable gap between 'real' readers/ authors and inscribed ones, constructed or marked in and by the text. Real readers are subjects in history, living in given social formations, rather than mere subjects of a single text. The two types of subject are not commensurate. But for the purposes of formalism real readers are supposed to coincide with the constructed readers. (p.48)

Arriving here, the trajectory of *Screen* neatly recapitulates that of Russian Formalism. This began as an attempt to define literariness, came to describe this as an effect of the text (defamiliarisation), and was then overtaken by the knowledge that what defamiliarised in 1918 didn't do so in the same way in 1928, that it was not possible to limit what a text might mean to an actual, historically situated reader.

The issue of the necessary non-coincidence between inscribed and real readers returns us to the same difficulty as may be resolved by recognising two problematics for the text, one as product of history, one as product of the reader. Only now the distinction is between the reader as product of the text and the reader as product of history. And even if reality is assigned to the reader rather than the text, there are serious problems about doing much with this real reader. David Morley has collected various audience responses to the television programme 'Nationwide'. (16) However well these correlate with group and class, they fall under the shadow of an objection made by the same Paul Willeman in developing Vygotsky's theory of inner speech ('Cinematic Discourse - The Problem of Inner Speech', *Screen* no.3 1981). There are four levels of discourse, writing, speech, inner speech, the unconscious. Each is different with its own effectivity, and some so different they contradict each other. The problem for work on the actual response of the real reader is simply stated: granted the four levels of discourse, which counts as the actual response and why?

A text presents itself only as writing. Differences produced in different readings must always arise from a basis in the identity of the text. An article in *Screen* subsequent to Willeman's of Spring 1978 argued that 'to hold that a given text is "different for everybody" is as much the end of any consequent political analysis and practice as to hold that it is "the same for everybody"' (Autumn 1978, p.104), the text being a common ground on which difference is defined and experienced. Unless we dematerialise the text into an infinitely pluralist play (after the fashion of Deconstruction), the text will retain an identity in difference - these signifiers in this syntagmatic order and not others - a materiality that resists any single reading in which it is constructed.

What the Spring 1978 reminder about subjects as real readers in history brings out is another problem that had been masked by *Screen*'s use of Lacan. It was assumed quite correctly that the subject is constructed as an effect of discourse and, again correctly, that there is no 'experience' of the text (or anything else) outside a system of representation. From this it was supposed that a position for the reader was inscribed by the filmic text with the <u>same degree and kind</u> of effectivity that a position is assigned to the <u>subject by other discourses</u> and systems of representation. This view ignored the status of most film as <u>fictional</u>. An essay in the later *Screen* reasserted 'the manifestly obvious and anciently attested fact that there is a difference between the real and its representation' (Spring 1979, p.126), a difference registered in the way specific discourses have contrasted forms of relation to the extra-discursive. Hollywood's classic realism shares with all aesthetic discourse the status of being fictional, which means that it should not be read as referring to the extra-discursive. (This feature is not absolute, an essential inherency of the text but rather devolves on a text from the discursive ensemble: in America in 1938 Welles' radio broadcast of Wells' 'War of the Worlds' <u>was</u> read referentially). In the other direction, it is precisely the fictionality of the aesthetic text, marked in it by repetition and condensation of the signifier, that invites plural readings for it in a degree to which the referential text does not. Analysis of the subjective operation of fictional texts is more valuable as a way of studying texts than for its account of how any such text is actually received. If you reject reflectionism and admit the reader as producer of the text, where else is there to go?

2. <u>Knowledge</u> By 1977 the air around *Screen* was thick with epistemological anxiety. The project got off the ground in 1971 in the assumption that it was a theoretical practice that would produce systematic knowledge of film. Hindess and Hirst's *Mode of Production and Social Formation* (1977) was thought to deny this possibility altogether. 'What

can we know of objects in the real world except through discourse, which necessitates the involvement of a subject?' (Autumn 1977, p.124). The objection was posed more radically in Paul Willeman's essay: 'there is no "pure" imaginary to be opposed to the symbolic (or in Althusserian terms: science)' (Spring 1978, p.63). He pointed the way to a retreat from the very possibility of knowledge into Foucauldian interventionism: 'The production of readings, and hence of criticism and theory, is always a more or less well calculated intervention in the "battle of ideas"' (p.57), a battle in which the only criterion for ideas was their political effectivity. If systematic knowledge of film had been an object of desire endlessly escaping beneath the *Screen* problematic, from now on it became a bad object. Among the many causes for the decline of *Screen*, I would estimate loss of faith in its own methodology as primary.

There was no need to take this path. Rightly understood, the work of Hindess and Hirst aimed only to rid Althusser's epistemology of a residue of absolutism. While insisting that knowledge of an object is constructed in relation to the subject, Althusser retained a form of epistemology in general by supposing a general relation of adequacy/ inadequacy between thought and the real ('a relation of adequacy or inadequacy of knowledge'). (17) In rejecting epistemology in general Hindess and Hirst were not rejecting the possibility of knowledge of reality but only the belief that knowledge is only knowledge if it can have some absolute guarantee. Paul Hirst has summarised the position as follows:

> There are no general criteria of adequacy or truth ... We would argue that discourses and practices do employ the criteria of appropriateness or adequacy (not of epistemological validity) but these practices are specific to the objectives of definite bodies of discourse and practice. (18)

There is then 'no knowledge process in general' (*ibid.*), only different discourses of knowledge operating with specific criteria of adequacy. Knowledge is not absolute (whoever thought it was?) but relative in four respects: to the theoretical problematic of its construction, to the object it seeks to construct but which resists that construction; to the subject who is brought into position to read the discourse as referential; relative finally in that it cannot be 'referred up' to some absolute epistemological guarantee for its validity. Historical materialism can well survive with this conception, and in fact a Marxist criticism is stronger for not trying to defend an epistemological position that is indefensible and need not be defended.

If this argument is right, it may seem surprising in retrospect that the *Screen* trajectory missed the gap in the hedge. It looks as though it got blocked here - as elsewhere - by overgeneralising the Lacanian account of the subject-in-discourse (symptomatic of this is Willeman's attack on Althusserian science in terms of the imaginary against the symbolic). The error, as so often with genuinely original work, comes in the form of overtotalisation, an error Stuart Hall points out as that of giving 'Lacanian psychoanalysis an exclusive, privileged, explanatory claim'. (19) It was not an error integral to the *Screen* problematic. While trying to give a fair representation of the long march from 1971 to 1979, I've taken the opportunity to discard some unnecessary baggage. I think we are now left in possession of a valuable supplement to traditional Marxist criticism, one which brings into explanatory relation issues of aesthetic form, ideology, subjectivity and sexuality. It is still there waiting to be exploited, rethought in terms of the specificity of other signifying practices, music, painting, and literature.

Fig. 1 J.-B. Greuze, *La Mère Bien-aimée*.

Fig. 2 Thomas Gainsborough, *Landscape with a Woodcutter Courting a Milkmaid*, 1755.

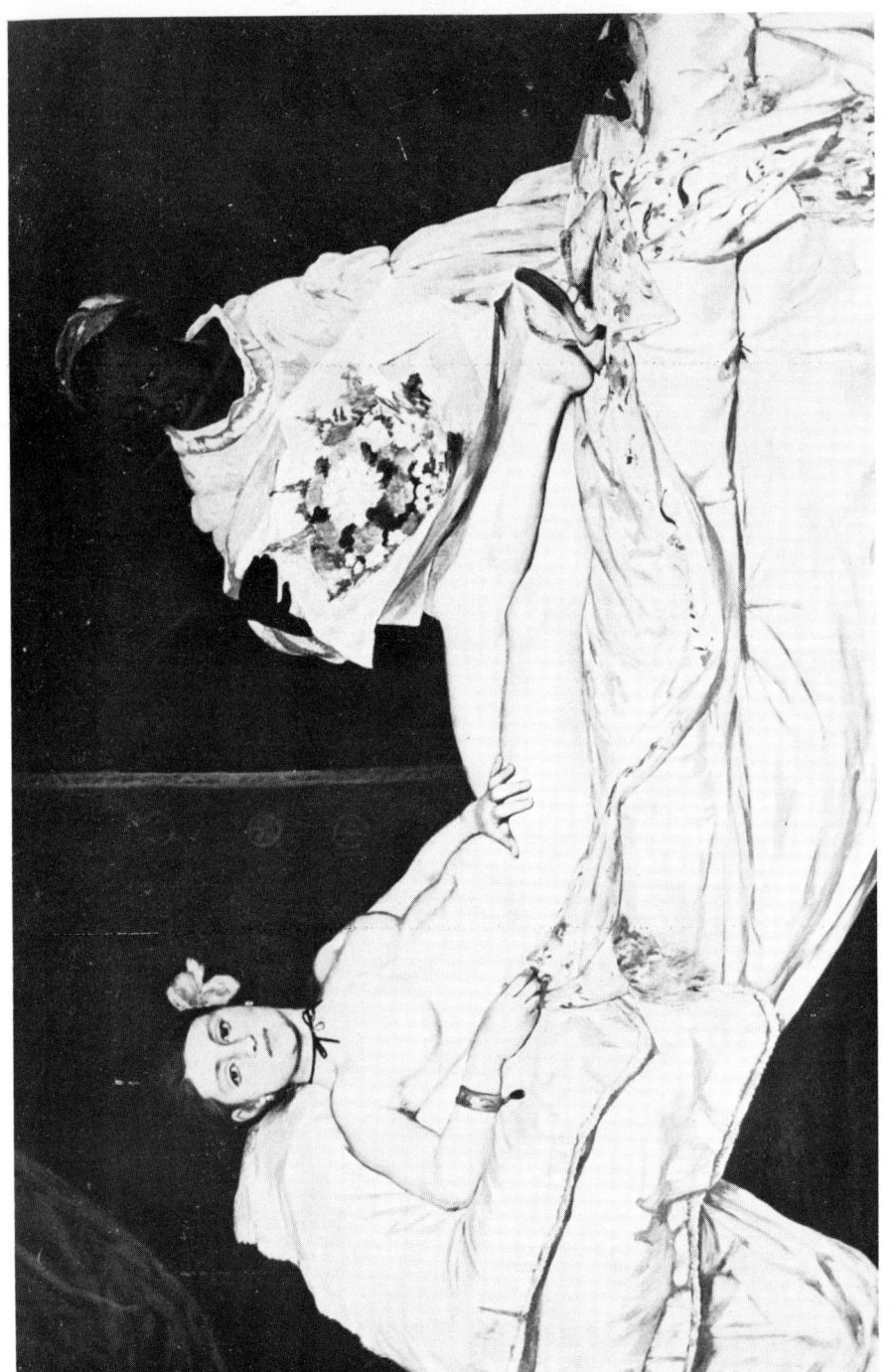

Fig. 3 Edouard Manet, *Olympia*, 1863.

Fig. 4 Edouard Manet, *The Nymph Surprised,* 1861.

Fig. 6 Advertisement for *Clairol* hair colour.

Fig. 5 Edouard Manet, *La Serveuse de Bocks*, 1879.

Music is an especially inviting territory. Western harmonies were invented with the Renaissance and stay dominant until at the beginning of the twentieth century they are challenged by (for example) atonal and serialist forms. The Western system, which claims to derive naturally from acoustic reality, must be a bourgeois form, susceptible to semiological and idelogical analysis. Is the horizontal axis of melody syntagmatic? And so is harmony paradigmatic? What position for the subject is offered by the harmonic system? Someone interested - and competent in musicology - can pick up the trail from Adorno, Chanan and Middleton. (20).

FOOTNOTES

1. There have been a number of critiques of the *Screen* problematic. See: A. Britton, 'The Ideology of Screen', *Movie* No.26 (no date), pp. 2-28; K. McDonnell and K. Robins, 'Marxist Cultural Theory: the Althusserian Smokescreen' in *One-Dimensional Marxism*, ed. S. Clarke et al., (London, 1980); T. Eagleton, 'Aesthetics and Politics', *NLR*, No.107 (Jan-Feb 1978) (for a reply to this see, A, Easthope, *NLR* No.110 (July-Aug 1978), pp.95-6); S. Hall, 'Recent Developments in theories of language and ideology: a critical note' in *Culture, Media, Language*, ed. S. Hall et al., (London, 1980) (also D. Morley, 'Texts, readers, subjects' in the same volume); J. Woollacott, 'Messages and meanings', in *Culture, Society and the Media*, ed. M. Gurevitch et al., (London, 1982). T. Lovell's book *Pictures of Reality: Aesthetics, Politics and Pleasure* (London, 1980) may be read as a sustained critique of the *Screen* problematic.

Some of the best critiques, however, appeared in *Screen*'s own pages. See: J. Lesage, 'The Human Subject - You, He, or Me,', Vol.16 (Summer 1975), pp.77-83; E. Buscombe, C. Gledhill, A. Lovell and C. Williams, 'Statement, Psychoanalysis and Film', Vol.16 (Winter 1975/6), pp.119-130; R. Williams, 'A Lecture on Realism', Vol.18 (Spring 1977), pp. 61-74; I. Chambers, J. Clarke, I. Connell, L. Curti, S. Hall, T. Jefferson, 'Marxism and Culture', Vol.18 (Winter 1977/78), pp.109-119; N. Garnham, 'Subjectivity, Ideology, Class and Historical Materialism', Vol.20 (Spring 1979), pp.121-133.

I have cited essays in *Screen* by date and page. A full list with authors appears below.

I am grateful to two other members of the Manchester S.E.F.T. Reading Group (1977-1981), Rob Lapsley and Mike Westlake, for comments on this paper.

2. S. Heath, '*Jaws*, Ideology and Film Theory' in *Popular Television and Film*, ed. T. Bennett et al., (London, 1981), p.201 (this essay first appeared in *The Times Higher Education Supplement*, 26 March 1976).

3. *Ibid.*, p.200, p.201.

4. See S. Freud, 'Fetishism' in *On Sexuality* (Harmondsworth, 1977).

5. C. Penley, 'The Avant-Garde and Its Imaginary', *Camera Obscura*, No.2 (1978), pp.3-33.

6. R. Barthes, *S/Z*, (London, 1975), p.4.

7. S. Heath, 'Language, Literature, Materialism', *Sub-stance*, No.17 (1977), p.71.

8. T. Eagleton, *op.cit.*, p.23.

9. P.Q. Hirst, *Law and Ideology* (London, 1979), p.68.

10. See A. Easthope, 'Problematising the Pentameter', *New Literary History*, Vol.XII (Spring, 1981), pp.475-92.

11. S. Hall, 'Recent Developments', *op.cit.*, p.159, p.160.

12. K. Marx, *Capital* (London, 1970), p.21.

13. R. Williams, *Marxism and Literature* (Oxford, 1977), p.45.

14. J. Lacan, *Ecrits* (London, 1977), p.331.

15. B. Brewster, 'Notes on the Text "John Ford's Young Mr. Lincoln" by the Editors of Cahiers du Cinéma', reprinted in *Screen Reader 1* (London, 1977), p.160, p.162.

16. See D. Morley, *The Nationwide Audience* (London, 1980).

17. L. Althusser and E. Balibar, *Reading Capital* (London, 1975), p.87.

18. P.Q. Hirst, *op.cit.*, p.21.

19. S. Hall, 'Recent Developments', *op.cit.*, p.160.

20. See: T.W. Adorno, *Philosophy of Modern Music* (New York, 1980); M. Chanan, 'The Trajectory of Western Music', *Media, Culture and Society*, Vol.3 (July 1981), pp.219-42; R. Middleton, '"Reading" Popular Music', *U203 Popular Culture*, Unit 16 (Open University Press, 1981).

Volumes of *Screen* cited:-

C. MacCabe, 'Realism and the Cinema: Notes on Some Brechtian Theses', v.15, n.2 (Summer 1974), pp.7-32.

S. Heath, 'Lessons from Brecht', v.15, n.2 (Summer 1974), pp.103-128.

C. Metz, 'The Imaginary Signifier', v.16, n.2 (Summer 1975), pp.14-76.

J. Lesage, 'The Human Subject - You, He, or Me,' v.16, n.2 (Summer 1975) pp.77-83.

B. Brewster, S. Heath, C. MacCabe, 'Comment', v.16, n.2 (Summer 1975), pp.83-90.

R. Bellour, 'The Unattainable Text', v.16, n.3 (Autumn 1975), pp.19-27.

L. Mulvey, 'Visual Pleasure and Narrative Cinema', v.16, n.3 (Autumn 1975), pp.6-18.

E. Buscombe, 'Notes on Columbia Pictures Corporation 1926-41', v.16, n.3 (Autumn 1975) pp.65-82.

C. MacCabe, 'The Politics of Separation', v.16, n.4 (Winter 1975/76), pp.46-61.

P. Wollen, '"Ontology" and "Materialism" in Film', v.17, n.1 (Spring 1976), pp.7-23.

K. Tribe, 'Appropriation/Recuperation', v.17, n.1 (Spring 1976), pp.102-109.

C. MacCabe, 'Principles of Realism and Pleasure', v.17, n.3 (Autumn 1976), pp.7-27.

S. Heath, 'Narrative Space', v.17, n.3 (Autumn 1976), pp.68-112.

S. Heath, *'Anata mo'*, v.17, n.4 (Winter 1976/77), pp.49-66.

G. Skirrow, 'Language and Materialism', v.18, n.3 (Autumn 1977), pp. 121-132.

P. Willeman, 'Notes on Subjectivity', v.19, n.1 (Spring 1978), pp.41-69.

S. Heath, 'Difference', v.19, n.3 (Autumn 1978), pp.51-112.

N. Garnham, 'Subjectivity, Ideology, Class and Historical Materialism', v.20, n.1 (Spring 1979), pp.121-133.

P. Willeman, 'Cinematic Discourse - The Problem of Inner Speech', v.22, n.3 (1981), pp.63-93.

C. MacCabe (Summer 1974) and L. Mulvey (Autumn 1975) are reprinted in *Popular Television and Film*, ed. T. Bennett et al. (London, 1981).
S. Heath (Autumn 1976) is reprinted in S. Heath, *Questions of Cinema* (London, 1981).

NATIONAL LANGUAGE, EDUCATION, LITERATURE

Renée Balibar

Although the title sounds quite broad and general, what I intend to offer is, in effect, a brief historical survey of very precise and concrete facts.
But, first of all, I wish to make clear, as briefly as possible, what is the scope and place of "my research works", of "my articles" and "my published books", using, for so doing, one or two French textbooks. I've selected these books among other works of critical analysis, because they are currently used as reference books in French Higher Education. Indeed my personal views are not what is to be considered; What I am concerned with is to propound the terms I'm using, i.e. "National French", "fictional French languages", "colinguistic practice" and "grammatisation", with a view to raising certain problems regarding the relation of literature to literacy.

As a preliminary caution, I wish to let you know that I won't be taking into account the Review *Praxis* (issue No.5 of 1981) entitled 'Art and Ideology' and published by the Praxis Study Group in Art and Society at the U.C.L.A. In that issue the problems of the materialist criticism of literary texts are very well explained, especially with regard to my work, in the first article signed by Claude Bouche. One reason is that such a publication, of importance in itself far beyond my own published books, cannot be dealt with in a few lines only. Rather I have deliberately situated my contribution within the professional context of French School Education - which however does not prevent me from thinking that positions such as those expounded in *Praxis No.5* have a great international future. The talk I'll give here is precisely intended to show that the French language and French literature exist only in association with English language and literature in their historical apparatuses.

I had two books published in 1974: *Le français national (The National French Language)* and *Les français fictifs (Fictional French Languages)* (both Paris, Hachette;littérature). This was in a series created by Althusser, "Analyses", in which three titles only have been published: *Positions*, by Althusser, and my two books. In 1977 the Editions du Seuil (in their series "Pierres vives") published *Histoire littéraire*, "the history and the interpretation of the fait littéraire" by Gerard Delfau and Anne Roche. Delfau (who was responsible for the chapter dealing with *The Fictional French Languages*) discusses the "theory of ideology" which Althusser launched, and he considers that *Fictional French Languages* is:

> an initial assessment of Althusserism as far as literary criticism is concerned, both on account of the application, on specific works, of the working hypotheses contained in Althusser's article on "the State Ideological Apparatuses", and also because of the long introduction written by Etienne Balibar and Pierre Macherey, essentially focused upon the theme of "Literature as an ideological form". (1)

I don't wish to enter into a controversy about the words "application of Althusser's working hypotheses", which seem to give primacy to theory over actual literary practice. I'd rather take up the following sentence:
> Let's confess our perplexity in front of the meagreness of the results attained. (2)

I'd like to make a note of the extensive "benefits expected" - in Delfau's own words - either by himself or by Althusserians, ranging from "restoring the capacity of Marxism for opening up onto the social sciences" to "throwing a light, in passing, upon the Marxist position on art". Delfau is disappointed by "the timidity" of "the Althusserian school" in comparison with
> the great adventure of criticism, that of a man like Sartre who got engrossed in Flaubert to the point of almost losing some of his own identity. (3)

One feels at liberty to have a different view on critical venturesomeness! Nevertheless Delfau considers that the best Althusserian works - the most convincing ones, he says, being mine - restore to the work of art
> part of its autonomy. From being "pure reflection" [of reality], the work of art becomes the place and state of a specific form of class struggle fought within the sphere of influence of "the State Ideological Apparatuses", namely: academies, salons, schools, universities, etc. (4)

I am keeping in mind that, in connection with my books, Delfau recognizes the existence of an "ideological formative action" in which literary fiction takes shape; a specific formation that cannot occur without apparatuses or institutions. The linguistic aspect of that formation will be recognized later, but it was overlooked by Delfau, although the titles of my books did announce analyses concerning "French", first of all, and the historical struggle in the field of language.

In 1978 a textbook widely circulated in Higher Education - *La Critique (Criticism)* by Roger Fayolle (A. Colin, Series 'U', 2nd edition, entirely revised) makes favourable mention, among the "currents" of Marxist criticism, of
> the research works undertaken and published under the leadership of Renée Balibar, which represent the most important contribution [...] in that direction [the direction shown by Althusser's analysis concerning ideological apparatuses and formative actions].
>
> The point here is to lead us to understand the illusions on which our habitual conceptions and practices of what we call " literature " are based. Are we not inclined to recognize the presence of literature only providing that we exclude and cast out into some mechanically separated exterior region, the relationship of literary effects to education and the history of schools, to the national language and the history of that language, to the struggles among social classes and the history of those struggles? (5)

Having said this, Fayolle wonders how to extend such methodological principles to those centuries that preceded the nineteenth. Besides, he thinks that the research work accomplished by Marxist literary critics (e.g. Barberis) often differs from that "*avant-garde* methodological prospection".

Let me point out, at this point, that it is mostly those presenting my work (whether Delfau and Fayolle, or Etienne Balibar and Pierre Macherey) who have concerned themselves with general Marxist theory. My only pretension has been to introduce the history of literary production into the history of the national language, in fact, to call back to mind that French literature is written in French, and that the creative work of writers moves in the field where institutions and linguistic apparatuses interplay; which, of course, falls within the province of historical materialism and ties up with Marxist research on the State and ideological formative actions.

In 1979, Nathan published *Sociocritique (Sociocriticism)*, a collection of texts presented at a Symposium organized by the University of Paris-VIII and New York University. In that book Jacques Dubois describes "the literary institution" which, since the Revolution of 1789, has been giving literary practice its twofold character: official and sacred. Dubois mentions my book *Fictional French Languages* and adopts this phrase:

> Thus literature appears to us as being submitted, in most cases, to a threefold determination: linguistic, educational and imaginary.

And he concludes:

> As it is strongly articulated, this thesis strengthens the basis one wishes to give to the institutional analysis of literary practices. It has the special merit of inscribing the set named "literature" within a concrete pattern of historical determinations, and, in the last resort, of relating it to a State power. We believe however that, by subordinating that set "massively" to the educational apparatus, it leads to the paradoxical consequence of eliminating the specific apparatus instituting literature, and of neglecting the role it plays. (6).

Perhaps, in order to understand better the special function of the literary institution, we only need to bring out the role of the linguistic apparatus within the educational institution. But I won't carry on any longer with such abstract considerations, and I'm now going to set out a few results of recent research.

I hope that, in doing so, my notions about the relationship between the French fictional languages and the national language, as well as the concept of colinguistic practice, won't deserve the blame expressed in the famous phrase: "What is simple is not accurate, and what is complex is incomprehensible."

The English may not be aware of the historical event called *Les Serments de Strasbourg*, the compacts of Strasbourg, which took place in the ninth century, more precisely, on February 14, 842. Theoretically, the French should have heard about it when in primary school. Anyway, I think I have drawn conclusions (that have been unpublished so far) from the history of the French language and the general history of the early Middle Ages in Europe.

Here is a summary of the facts, according to F. Brunot:

> Two sons of Louis the Pious (who died in 840), Louis the Germanic and Charles the Bald, in revolt against the pretensions of their brother Lothair, had just won the battle of Fontanet (841) over the latter. As the war was not over, they met in Strasbourg, on February 14 842, to strengthen

their union and they pledged themselves to an alliance with
each other. In order that the armies who were present might
be witnesses of their solemn compact, Louis the Germanic
swore his oath in the language of his brother and of the Franks
from France, i.e. in French "Roman" (late vulgar Latin), and
Charles repeated the same oath as his elder brother in the
Germanic language. And in their turn, the soldiers swore too,
in their respective languages.

A historian of the time, Nithard, himself a grandson of Charlemagne, recorded those oaths, the original copies of which he
may have had under his eyes, in his *History of the divisions
between the sons of Louis the Meek* (Louis le Débonnaire).
... We are presenting below a facsimile of the page of the
unique manuscript (from the end of the tenth or beginning of
the eleventh century) which has preserved, with Nithard's
chronicle, this text, the first one written in French and one
of the first written in old German.

[...] In 860 peace was proclaimed at Coblentz, in French "Roman"
and in Germanic, but the phrasing of the declaration has not
come down to us.

F. Brunot translated the contents of the compacts into present day
French. I'm giving here an adaptation of it in English:

The phrasing of the king's oaths:

For the love of God and for the common good of the Christian
people and of ours, from this day on, as long as God gives
me knowledge and power, I will support my brother Charles
with my assistance and in all things, as one must justly
support one's brother, provided he does the same for me, and
I shall never make any arrangement with Lothair that, depending on my will, may be to the detriment of my aforesaid
brother Charles.

The phrasing of the soldiers' oaths:

If Louis keeps his pledge to his brother Charles, and Charles,
my lord, for his part, does not keep his, in the event of my
being unable to dissuade him, I, for one, shall not lend him
any help, nor shall any one I shall be able to dissuade from
doing so. (7)

The spontaneous interpretation of present day Europeans is suggested
by the way the above story is told: Louis the Germanic had expressed himself in "Roman" (i.e. French of *langue d'oïl*, Northern French) - it is
suggested - in order to be understood by Charles the Bald and his "French"
army; and Charles the Bald had expressed himself in Germanic to reciprocate. The "soldiers" are supposed to have warned their respective kings
that they would abide by the compact, if necessary against their lord.
And such is indeed the meaning laid down by the teaching of French
history since 1880 in Republican France. This is a fabulous historical
misinterpretation; a wonderful ideological vision of things, of vital
importance in the nineteenth century and still so nowadays in modern
French society. Let's now have a look at the real state of affairs in
the ninth century.

According to the historical documents, the first Carolingian kings
spoke Germanic "Francique". Neither Charlemagne nor his grandsons Louis
the Germanic and Charles the Bald spoke rustic "Roman". So it was not
in order to be understood by his brother that Louis the Germanic took
his oath in the "Roman" language. He must have recited a text he had

learned by heart, or repeated word after word of a text whispered to him,
a text totally strange and unfamiliar in the centuries old noble practice
of the two kings' family. Neither did Louis the Germanic utter his solemn
oath in Roman so as to make himself clearly understood by an army that
would have been "French". The two parties present represented, each one
under the king, two sets of vassals, singly bound according to personal
vassalic pledges. On the two sides, the powerful lords, no doubt the
spokesmen of their inferiors, would also have spoken Germanic "Francique".
As for the lower class of vassals - down to the men-at-arms who had no
vassals of their own and ruled only over the peasantry and the serfs on
their small estates - they had multilingual and confused oral practices;
they were able to speak in rustic language with the Galloroman of various
conditions, in the territories inherited by Charles; and they could, also,
on occasion, speak with the men-at-arms of the opposite party. Far from
having established a direct communication between the participants in the
Strasbourg alliance, the proclamation of the oaths in the form of a two-
fold speech delivered in vernacular languages by the two kings must have
created some obscurity and originated new distances. Thus some aims were
effectively attained, so effectively that nowadays such a situation seems
natural.

What aims? This is the point where the clerks come in. The clerks
of the royal chancelleries were not gathered on the field with the men-
at-arms; they were not standing on the dais with the kings. They were
penmen and not swordsmen, and they had discussed at length among themselves the alliance between Louis and Charles against Lothair; they
were dignitaries of the Church, relatives of the kings and experts in
law and in rhetorics. Then the specialists of both courts had drawn up
compacts, composed of exactly symmetrical phrases, and they had worked
out the staging of a sacramental event: the outcome of long experience
in a centuries old apparatus.

In the ninth century, in the Carolingian kingdoms, churchmen,
"clerks", were in possession of their heritage ("cleros" in Greek) which
set them apart and gave them their share of power: the exclusive control
of the written word, and consequently of teaching, recording, translating. This monopoly had been instituted since the Church was recognized
by Emperor Constantine in the territorial divisions of the Roman Empire.
Thus the bishops' administration had duplicated the administration of
local magistrates, in written official Latin. At the time of the inva-
sions, the Church had become more rural, and had preached the gospel in
vernacular languages, in accordance with the different lands: Irish,
Galloroman, Anglosaxon, Germanic. The Church was recognized anew as an
official power by the Merovingian Franks who wished to cast their con-
quests into the Galloroman administrative moulds, and again by Charlemagne, two centuries later, when he tried to establish his centralizing
power. And all that time the Church had managed to keep up its classical
Latin, a factor of universality, while developing its local linguistic
implantations. Only the Church had the power to channel down the doctrine and the law from the Scriptures into oral commentaries and injunc-
tions in the vernacular languages.

That power was used in an original way by the clerks of Strasbourg
to consolidate their heritage and, at the same time, the heritage of the
kings. They reversed the translating operation which, until then, they
had performed only from the written Latin text into various oral vulga-
rized versions. They produced two written texts in two tongues derived
from oral languages, in such a way that each one of those texts might be
rendered with rigorous accuracy in the other and in Latin, thus giving
versions of the same discourse. We won't go into the details of the

operation but we'll just point out what it was aiming at: it aimed at creating two state languages as valid as Latin for diplomatic recording, and distinct from each other as signs of two different lands.

In fact the spoken languages typical of territorial divisions had already been recognized by the Church for the evangelization of populations (Council of Tours, 813, one year before Charlemagne's death). In Strasbourg, those languages became symbols of the territories inherited by Charlemagne's grandsons: to one went the lands where the people obeyed in Germanic, to the other the lands where the people obeyed in Roman French. And from then on the changes brought about by apportionments and vassalage obligations could not affect the situation. The *King's Language* was present within stable linguistic boundaries controlled by bishops and abbots as well. A few years after the Compacts of Strasbourg, Charles the Bald took advantage of the linguistic channel of the bishops whom he asked to make his royal edicts known to the people in the people's tongues.

This brings us back to the power of the kings. They were the ones that gave to the phrasing of the oaths, when it came through their charismatic lips, the value of a sacred sign. In accordance with their divine right, the kings of Strasbourg recognized each other as being entitled to set as a national language the distinctive language of the land each one had inherited. If, as it happened, neither of them had ever spoken the French language in that manner, since they were ignorant of the various Roman dialects, the inauguration, the consecration and the acknowledgement of the new linguistic practice were all the more revealing of their power. Each set of vassals swore loyalty to the sharing out that had been accomplished, expressing himself in the language of his own king. The vassalic pledge put each subordinate under an obligation to defend personally the sacred linguistic boundary. There was an immediate political consequence: in spite of the Treaty of Verdun (843) which gave Lothair a third intermediate kingdom, the Strasbourg alliance entered into by the two kings succeeded in depriving the land of Lorraine of the linguistic sign which would have been the mark of its personal unity.

Thus the Compacts of Strasbourg closely associated two apparatuses (royal and clerical) and three tongues (a classical one and two new ones) with very precise functions: to legitimate and to separate. Since 842 the national French tongue has preserved its classical Latin dimension and its modern foreign dimension. I have coined the term colinguistic practice to designate that historical association.

Now we'll see what the rightly named French Revolution of 1789 created in the structure of its apparatuses and its languages, in opening up the era of Republican French, that is, School French - after the eras of clerical royal French, and of university royal French, and of academic monarchical French. By the same token, we'll see the strategic place occupied by literature in the history of a national language.

Everybody knows that the Revolution of 1789 changed institutions in France; that it abolished feudal rights on the land; that it abolished the King's power by divine right; that it created middle-class property rights, and the right to vote for the citizen's participation in the government of the nation. But the revolution in the State language has not been studied seriously enough, i.e. the abolition of the divine right of the king's language, and the creation of a state language common to all citizens.

In 1789, the *Declaration of Rights for Man and the Citizen* Article XI proclaimed:

The free communication of thoughts and opinions is one of
the most precious rights of Man; any citizen then can speak,
write and print freely.

The right to free expression was linked to the right of all citizens to
State Education (Article XXII of the Constitution of Year I). The practice of the national language which used to be the privilege of the king
and the literate belonged, from then on, to all citizens from the first
level of the new schooling system.

That revolution in the language assimilated the right of expression
to the right of communication. For privileges imply power of authoritative expression, whereas the right to writing, in a republic, presupposes
the sharing of the power of expression so that linguistic exchange in
communication can have a character of equality.

Far from legislating in the air, all the Declarations, Reports and
Decrees issued on free communication by the revolutionary Assemblies
were accompanied by an abundant publication of books, newspapers, periodicals of various types, etc.; what historians have called a "deluge of
papers". It is for intellectual convenience that the revolutionary principles have been stated in the first place through the medium of phrases
in institutional texts. We cannot ignore the fact that those phrases
could not have existed without playing a role in the field of practice.
Among the papers printed at the time it is of interest to bring to light
a text the practical importance of which has not been sufficiently recognized.

In 1790, during the campaign which preceded the elections for the
Legislative Assembly, there took place the publication of *La Bibliothèque
des Villages (The Library for Villages)* of Arnaud Berquin, a series of
small booklets which were issued every month from July 1st onwards.

The subscription to the ten volumes delivered by post
in all villages, postage paid, amounts to 6 *livres*. Each
volume sold separately, 12 *sols*.

Each booklet contained several short narratives or dialogues imbued with
the tenets of the *Society of the Friends of the Constitution*.

The Happiness of Country Folk
M. Rancey, Matthieu

M. Rancey - Well, Matthieu, how are things with you?
Matthieu - Oh, sir, do you really have to ask? Things are
            always bad with people in our station. Happiness
            is not for us.
M. Rancey - Who is it for, then, can you tell me?
Matthieu - That's a question you may very well ask, gentlemen from the town.
M. Rancey - So you think we are happier than you people are?
Matthieu - I'd like to see you lead our life for just a
            month. You would soon see what you yourselves
            would have to answer.

At the end of the story, the farmer, won over to the new ideas, gets involved in political life:

- Look, M. Rancey went on, take this piece of writing that a
worthy member of the National Assembly has just addressed to
his fellow citizens, read the pages I marked [...] Matthieu
took the paper home with him and, after having read it with
attention, transported with joy, he ran and communicated it
to the parish priest who immediately summoned the inhabitants

of the village to read it to them. [...] All the country
people renewed in their hearts the oath they had already
taken: to maintain a constitution so favourable to their
felicity, at the risk of their lives.

In another story in the *Library for Villages*, Arnaud Berquin presents three farmers, three brothers, two of whom are sinking into routine, whereas the third one is in favour of new things: potatoes, artificial meadows, the teaching of writing and arithmetic. This man, Julian, has to face hardships:

> For the mayorship of his village, in preference to him, they had elected a worthless intriguer who had gone as far as paying a fortune to buy votes all over the district.

But in the end:

> There is no doubt that, in the next election, Julian will be made one of the administrators of his district. I even know of many people who intend to make him become a member of the next legislature, in which I am confident that he will distinguish himself by his disinterestedness, his love for the public good, the extent of his knowledge in rural affairs, and the soundness of his views about all sorts of things. ("Honour", 5th vol.)

What was the circulation of those small booklets? What was their impact upon the population? I shall deal with this later. May I remind you that, at the beginning of the French Revolution, only a small number of the literate were capable of writing after they had been trained in Latin grammar and rhetoric in *Collèges* by ecclesiastics, then in the king's language in public offices, at the Court, in the Academies. In the *petites écoles* of the parish schools, when reading was taught, it was to decipher A and B in the Latin text of the Lord's Prayer and Hail Mary, or to make out as a whole such signs as *'Au Cochon Rôti'* (The Roasted Pig), *'Au Lion d'Or'* (The Golden Lion), in fact *'Au lit on dort'* (You sleep in a bed at an inn, here). As a rule in the first electoral campaign of the revolutionary period, the parish priests would normally serve as interpreters into the provincial vulgar languages, when they were in favour of *les lumières* (enlightenment); or else there were some beneficient worthies, some wealthy farmers like Matthieu. All media of expression, oral or written, being meant to establish discriminations and hierarchies, any literate who wanted to write in order to address the new citizens on an ideal equal footing, had to invent a medium for communication, coin a style, write in a fictional French that could get over obstacles. A text for revolutionary propaganda had to hold the attention of the citizens at whose approval it was aiming, by calculating the risk of being misunderstood or betrayed - or else given an advantage - by its translations and by gossip.

Under such conditions, the texts which were trying to establish revolutionary communication come, I think, under three main types of style which correspond to as many attitudes, as many ideological and political camps. Some texts proceeded with a wealth of Franco-Latin rhetoric; others in a fictionally spoken coarse style; others in a fictionally simple conventional French, which was the case with the *Library for Villages*.

It is paradoxical that those revolutionaries that were the most advanced in the political field on account of their republican spirit (the Jacobins, the Montagnards of the Convention) were the weightiest latinists, conservative in the field of rhetoric, users of high-flown language, unable to get away from their own writing habits, with the exception

of the great tribunes, the leaders of parties in the Assemblies, who
often fired the spirit of the people of Paris who had come to listen
to them, thanks to their theatrical personalities, their voices, and
the dramatic circumstances of the great Days of the Revolution. There
is nothing inexplicable in this if one remembers that, for the most
part, they were lawyers and they belonged to the middle class, and they
were convinced they must use the trump card of their literary education
against the old nobility and the courtiers. In the most successful
cases they attained their aims and made the great abstract texts of
Declarations, Reports, Decrees, when their grandiloquence yielded to
the demands of juridical precision. Later Stendhal, the novelist, was
to make famous this modern literary style when he tried to write "*comme
le code civil*" (like the civil code).

The camp that adopted the '*poissard*' (fishwife) style (the term
used at the time) was, in the beginning, that of the counter-
revolutionary propagandists who published several series of lampoons
in 1790, *The Acts of the Apostles*, full of dialogues that make the Parisian rabble speak fictitiously, and that dragged the people's representatives through the mud. Coarse words then created a link between illi-
terate aristocrats whose swearwords, in the absence of well-argued
speeches, scandalized the Assembly, on the one hand, and, on the other,
the workers from the central food market of Paris, with, in between,
characters of all conditions who delighted in violating all interdicts.
Quite soon, that enormous mass of potential support came from the readers for whom the journalists of the extreme-left wrote, in the publications of the *Père Duchesne*. Most of the time, Father Duchesne and his
imitators in Paris or in the provinces, had no difficulty outclassing
the productions of the extreme-right. The leftist journalists had a
great variety of linguistic means at their disposal, ranging from classical Latin to the languages used in salons and in trades. They also
had newer and stronger ideas. After the Revolution, in the reign of
Louis-Philippe, Balzac, the novelist, was to write a serial, *Les
Paysans (Country folk)*, for a rightist paper, and he created a fright-
ful image of rural classes, by making his fictional rustics speak the
'*poissard*' language of the Parisian revolutionary lampoons. Such are
the complexities of literary realism!

Finally there was the third camp, that in which Berquin's *Library
for the Villages* is to be situated from a linguistic point of view.
That is the camp that was banking upon State education and that was intended for well-to-do farmers who were capable of taking advantage of
changes in the way of tilling their lands, and, in the long run, for
all the citizens that had been through primary schooling. Berquin was
a first-class journalist. He belonged to the staff of the *Moniteur
Universel*, the best of the period, and he also wrote in *La Feuille
Villageoise (The Village Sheet)*, a publication which had a very high
run and an extensive circulation in all the newly created '*départe-
ments*', at the beginning of the French Revolution. He was also close
to the staff of *La Feuille du Cultivateur (The Husbandman's Sheet)*,
an organ for the popularization of agronomic science, a link between
the most enlightened of the farmers and members of the former *Societies
of Agriculture* for the propagation of knowledge. During the terrible
years when it was so hard to provide the population and the army with
food supplies, the *Feuille du Cultivateur* was to publish articles about
fodder plants, the three-year rotation of crops, etc. while it also discussed the problems of the nomenclature of plants, tools and farming
skills. For in that domain as well as in others, nothing could be improved in communications without an effort to standardize the language.
It should be remembered here that it was possible to subscribe to those

booklets issued by Berquin "in all post-offices". The *Library for Villages* marked the end of the chapbooks of the former regime, and the beginning of the written informative literature centralized and circulated thanks to modern means of transmission.

Letters, orders and money had to be sent to Paris, at this address: Rue de l'Université No.28, at the *Bureau de l'Ami des Enfants* (the Office of the *Children's Friend*). That site was the very fulcrum of the lever that was to uplift the world, the place where a new French language was being created in another colinguistic practice. But to sum up the process briefly, it is now necessary to comprehend its European dimension, and, first of all, to go over to England.

Ten years earlier, in 1778, there had appeared in London the first primer for learning the language, an instrument directly suited to the needs of children from aristocratic and higher middle-class families. A sort of book that relegated hornbooks and ancient alphabet primers to an archaïc past. A sort of book too which does not belong to utopian literature as do those written by the theoreticians of education. That book was *Lessons for Children*, the work of Anna-Laetitia Aikin-Barbault. Anna-Laetitia was then 34 years old and belonged to a family that was perfectly typical of liberal culture in England: they were important cloth merchants, then great scholars in the world of large-scale European trade and of the classical humanities, great dissenters excluded from certain official ecclesiastical offices, interested in education and together founders, with other most distinguished men, of Warrington Academy (1757). Anna-Laetitia made a name for herself as a poet, the writer of Odes. Some learned men have considered that she was wasting her talent in *Lessons for Children*, then in her *Hymns in Prose* (1781). The latter work was meant to provide texts for the first steps in religion and moral education in the English tongue, in parallel with biblical texts. But those books aroused a tremendous interest among the general public. They were immediately translated into other European languages and were constantly republished. They created a universal demand in middle-class families. Mrs Barbault opened a school in Palgrave, which soon became a place famous for training gentlemen of a new type. Her brother John was to be, at the same time, a physician, a humanist, and the literary editor of the *Monthly Magazine*, and the founder, in association with his sister and his daughters, of *Evenings at Home* (1793-1796), recreational and educational publications. Years later, Lamb, in a letter to Coleridge, made the remark that because of Mrs Barbault and her imitators, geography and natural history had replaced old wives' tales for children.

Arnaud Berquin, born in Bordeaux, made a name for himself in London as well as in Paris, at that same period, as a writer of Elegies and Romances. He belonged to the same generation as Anna-Laetitia Aikin-Barbault, the two Chéniers, Germaine Necker de Staël, Joachim-Henri de Campe. He immediately adapted *Lessons for Children* into French. He founded a periodical publication, *L'Ami des Enfants*, made up of narratives and dialogues which were so well suited to the foundation of teaching French within families that it established a new French word, a common noun: a 'berquinade', that was to designate that kind of writing for more than a century. *L'Ami des Enfants* was in its turn translated into English, very successfully. Berquin, without creating a school as Mrs Barbault had done, became the friend and adviser on pedagogical matters to liberal-minded important men and distinguished families, such as Malesherbes. He was considered as a possible tutor for the primary education of the heir apparent to the throne, at the beginning of the Revolution, a future position he was hindered from filling on account of his death in 1791. The German Joachim-Henri de Campe, born in 1746, was a year older than Berquin and two years younger than Mrs Barbault. He was a European lexicographer and humanist, Adviser for Schools to the Duke of Brunswick. He wrote the *Small Instructive Library for Children* (1779-1784) or *Hamburg Almanach for Children*, and he rewrote Defoe's novel under the title of *Young Robinson* (Hamburg, 1780), the starting point of the book's universal fame in modern times.

On the one hand, these new books were widely introduced among the national-international aristocratic upper middle-class circles. They were even intended to revive the elite descended from the *'ancien régime'* thanks to their boldly realist views on education and instruction. But on the other hand, they impugned the old structure based on privileges. Their aim was to share the means of expression in the State language with the lower classes. Those who were literate believed they could establish general communication by providing every child with the means to appropriate, through practice, the grammatical rules followed when writing in the national language. In their minds, *Evenings at Home*, by winning for itself a wide public, was in keeping with the development of a new type of public spirit: "The morality they inculcate is not that of children merely, but of men and citizens." The French Revolution provided the political circumstances for that evolution of ideas, with the possibility of carrying them out. Grammarians, philosophers, teachers, journalists from all the European capital cities often became, in Partis, honorary citizens of the French nation. That was the time when Berquin started canvassing in the French style of *L'Ami des Enfants*, in the election campaign for the Constitution.

The national-international aspect of the new instructive publications is evident. It has been one of the fundamental structures of European colinguistic practice, since the Compacts of Strasbourg. But here, from the outset, the mutual translations of foreign languages from one into another excluded the authority of a Latin model. In *Lessons for Children*, Barbault created images of every day life in an English house in the country. For instance in the Lesson entitled *Tea-Time*:

> Bring the tea-things.
> Bring the little boy's milk.
> Where is the bread and butter?
> Where is the toast and the muffin?
> Here is some bread for you.
> Little boys should not eat butter.
> Sop the bread in your tea.

It would never come to anybody's mind to try and translate this type of discourse straight into Latin. On the other hand, it is of interest to find out how the linguistic and culturally distinctive features of the English tongue can pass into French, e.g. in the following 'new translation illustrated with pretty printed pictures' (edition of Geneva and Paris, 1854):

> Apportez le thé.
> Apportez le lait du petit garçon.
> Ou est le pain et le beurre?
> Ou sont les rôties et les gauffres?
> Voici du pain pour vous.
> Trempez votre pain dans votre thé.

- a translation in which the Swiss consciousness could not write such nonsense as *"les petits garçons de doivent pas manger de beurre"*. However, in the *Library of Villages*, English readers will be able to recognize at once a fictional French farmer named Matthieu with double *t* like

Matthew in English, a man from the middle classes named Rancey (= Ramsay in English), and an episode pertaining to British mores (the farmer stakes his best cow in a bet) which would be a preposterous fantasy in French. From then on, everything which, in the colinguistic practice of previous days, had stemmed from an imaginary fed on Latin mythology (*Telemachus*) and on Roman history, was to be the product of modern folklore, mostly Anglosaxon.

Now the same linguistic revolution that had invented general communication between all citizens, invented State Education with different '*Degrés*' (levels, grades). Latin, which had been discarded from the common training for written expression in the national tongue, had gone away through the door and came back through the window. It survived under a different form in the '*Degré Secondaire*' (at the high-school level): it was no longer spoken or even fluently written but it was, as it still is nowadays, essential to the appropriation of really rationalized, really theorized comparative grammar; and it is essential, as well, for the appropriation of European culture, founded as it is on Greco-Latin classical literature and on comparative criticism, both having firm roots in the history of 'Western' European peoples.

In *Lessons for Children*, Barbault showed the family of a wealthy landowner, Mr Dodwell, and one of his farmers, Matthew. The farmer is the target of Roger's, Mr Dodwell's son's, jeerings: he smells of manure. But the landowner takes advantage of the occasion to educate his son, to make him see that manure earns a man his bread - which Latin does not - and, besides, that it brings income to the owner of the land. So it is a duty to honour the farmer and his manure, especially when one possesses the invisible power conferred by the knowledge of Latin.

The English grammarians, journalists, literary men of a new type, were bringing to the linguistic revolution the centuries-old experience of their education based on the official English version of the Bible. In the same way, the Germans had been using Luther's Bible for a long time. But the French élite could bring in the Port Royal Grammar (the work of their dissenters) and the *Traité des Tropes* (the *Treatise on Tropes*), as well as an aristocratic language which was extremely sophisticated as far as effects of "simplicity" were concerned (e.g. in the Romances written by Arnaud Berquin the "*poète de salon*"); and finally the double volume of Franco-Latin Elementary Grammar of Lhomond for the lower forms of secondary schools (the Convention subsequently took the French part of that school grammar and had it used separately in Primary Schools). Modern French literature has always been less 'credible' than English when in fictional plain style; but it has constantly invested anew the national French language with the classical Latin heritage.

In the exposition of historical facts and in the synthetic views I have been submitting to you, literature has often been mentioned. And it is a fact that the practice of a written language recognized and taught by the State, cannot be dissociated from literary practice. Training in written expression cannot take place except in the presence of texts, considered as examples, which are the starting point and the final result of abstract work. These texts are made up by grammarians according to their theoretical needs in particular cases. But as soon as a global intuition of the discourse is required, grammarians draw their material from large-scale verbal structures by which a language idealizes its entity, and by its own means only, recreates the equivalent of reality as it has been experienced. The imaginary dimension is vital, even and especially when the grammatical exercise imposes its conventions. Thus sentences like "Bring the tea-things" and "The Earth is blue like an orange" have a two-fold existence. Once as examples of simple sentences having to do with literacy, that is to say examples of simple communication, of elementary grammatical convention in a republican situation; secondly, as linguistic imaginings, having to do with literature written in fictional English, in fictional French, dreaming it is establishing or cutting communication.

Most of the time, in present day France, nonsensical terms or phrases function as a way of asserting the solidity of instituted syntax, paradoxically and all the more forcibly, by creating daydreams, rather than by appealing to common sense. In fictional French "the Earth is blue like an orange", the incongruity of the terms "blue" (like an orange) makes the syntactic structure authoritative, for only that structure is capable of making the sentence stand up, i.e. capable of writing French. But through the breaches opened up by the imaginary, there sneak in all the individual phantasms linked with the appropriation of the written language. The three-fold determination of literary production mentioned at the beginning of this lecture: linguistic, educational, imaginary, is to be found on the plane of subjective experience, on the border line with the unconscious, as much as on the plane of the state institutions. Far from stifling art, general scholarization generalizes literary practice; it creates, in every individual, the frustrations and the delights of the power of expression in the State language, that is to say the conditions of literary calling. "Poetry must be made by all": a fictional French phrase coined by Lautréamont in the reign of Napoléon III, which has become more and more expressive of literary ideology in a republican situation.

With that phrase I will conclude considerations that were only meant to attract attention to the complexities of the linguistic practices which create simplicity in national languages. To take leave with the help of a concrete quotation, I wish to pay tribute to that great writer in the English language, Anna-Laetitia Barbault. In one of her "lessons", she has described the death of a hare that a pack of hounds has just hunted down. I would like this text to become the symbol of the primary school readers, so vigorous and so full of hope, which have been captured, devoured, digested, forgotten by all European children:

> Then the hounds come up and tear her and kill her. Then, when she is dead, her little limbs, which moved so fast, grow quite stiff, and cannot move at all. A snail could go faster than a hare when it is dead and its poor little heart that beat so quickly, is quite still and cold; and its round full eyes are dull and dim; and its soft, furry skin is all torn and bloody. It is good for nothing now but to be roasted.

FOOTNOTES

1. G. Delfau, A. Roche, *Histoire Littérature. Histoire et Interprétation du Fait Littéraire* (Paris, 1977), pp.299-300.

2. *ibid.*, p.300.

3. *ibid.*, p.302.

4. *ibid.*, p.303.

5. R. Fayolle, *La Critique* (Paris, 1978), pp.200-203.

6. C. Duchet (ed.), *Sociocritique* (Paris, 1979), p.171.

7. F. Brunot, *Histoire de la langue française* (Paris, new edition 1968), vol.I, pp.143-195.

BIBLIOGRAPHY

Each page of the paper could well carry numerous notes and bibliographical references. We list here a small number of books which were particularly useful.

R. Balibar, *Le français national* and *Les français fictifs* (both Hachette-Litterature, Paris, 1974) (both out of print); and in preparation: *La République des lettres*, to appear in the series 'Pratiques théoriques' published by Presses Universitaires Françaises.

Marc Bloch, *La Société féodale* (Albin Michel, Paris, 1939, new edition 1968).

Jacques Le Goff, *Pour un autre Moyen-Age* (Gallimard, Paris, 1977).

Histoire de la langue française (new edition A. Colin, Paris, 1968) under the general editorship of Ferdinand Brunot (vols.1-13). Vol.14 - to appear in 1983 - will include (chapter 2.2) "*L'école de 1880. Le français national: républicain, scolaire, grammatical, primaire*, by Renee Balibar.

Perry Miller, chapter XII "The Plain Style" in *The New England Mind* (Macmillan, New York, 1939; new edition Beacon Press, Boston, 1968).

Betsy Rogers, *Georgian Chronicle. Mrs Barbauld and her family* (Methuen, London, 1958).

THE BOUNDARIES OF HEGEMONY

John Oakley, Roger Bromley and Sue Harper

The following pieces appearing under a common title are not the product of a shared programme of research. Nor is there any theoretical framework consciously elaborated. There is, however, a marked similarity of interest and approach which comes from some of the themes developed in the Cultural Studies course at Portsmouth. This is best indicated as an attention to the analytical and empirical character of what is usually referred to as the 'middle strata' - especially at its less advantaged levels. Reference is especially to times before, during, after World War II. The theoretical and conceptual issues recently raised in discussion of this area have emphasised a need to examine, within the limits set by the analysis of productive relations, the place of cultural practice in the definition of class, or class-fractional, boundaries. Of special concern, therefore, is the place of fiction in the differentiation of the middle strata and also its place in the consolidation of such solidarities as 'the nation' or 'the people' which frequently assist in the process of class formation or dissolution but are not coincident with it. It is believed: (1) that the substantial ambiguities of relation and function which differentiate the phenomenon of the middle strata are complexly consonant with specific features of both canonic and popular fiction; (2) that many fictional components, appearing in works primarily addressed to these strata, and alluding to social order and to threats to that order, derive from an earlier structural complexity relating landed gentry to capitalism in the last century. The values of the aristocratic conduct of the estate and of professional (including literary) vocation are assimilated within an ethic of pure duty. This, incorporating various modalities of honour and ritually subject to Byronic violation, becomes a resource for the expression of ambivalence at quite other boundaries of the social system. Investigation of pre-war 'middle brow' novels and the costume melodrama of British cinema in the 1940s has been supported by work on Victorian figures such as Lytton and on the carriers for the transmission of such resources for the symbolic representation of boundary (e.g. the 'Anglo-Irish' clerisy).

THE BOUNDARIES OF HEGEMONY

John Oakley

(This is an attempt to establish briefly the concerns mobilised under this title. There is no great claim to originality, and so, as the footnotes would be disproportionately numerous, they have been excluded.)

This project explores how the resources of fiction may contribute to systems of meaning which sharpen or occlude the identity of social groups. It is especially concerned with how such resources are frequently generated or reinforced at the periphery of the social system or in areas of structural insecurity or ambiguity. Fictional resources are expressive of these fields of social action in consequence of their other purposes. However, that some kinds of idiom seem selected for this task and others not, has consequences for their substantial survival in any function. This raises issues as to why certain idioms perform this work; also why, when initially they seem to have 'belonged' to a particular group, they cease to identify or be identified by such origins, and either become increasingly abstracted or generalised, or reappear to identify another group entirely. By contrast, it also raises issues of why other idioms might be excluded, to be reactivated should boundaries need to be withdrawn: or be impoverished, yet nevertheless function to identify less visible groups. Where structural lines are not represented in predictable, legal, or traditional terms, where the trend of the system is toward the volatile or complex, fiction will have a role to play in organising the experience of complexity. It may be especially equipped to qualify those elements of the culture which negotiate the structural uncertainty with reinforced rigidities - although, in turn, fiction will also respond to such an ascetic pressure. To do this, fiction may operate like a school where the social actor learns to appreciate complexity; to judge, say, the success or failure of a protagonist's realisation within a web of societal and cultural forces. Otherwise, it may be like a ritual, where fiction mythically represents a threat to a social margin and the social actor is the spectator of its symbolic containment.

It is necessary to distinguish some different levels at which fiction may operate for this purpose and then some features of its mode of operation. Such a contribution may be of two interrelated kinds. The first is where limits are determined through productive or juridical relations or functions but where phenomenal boundaries are secured at lines defined by cultural practice. For example, the mechanism of capitalist production, of rent, profit, wage, is sustained by relations and functions such as class, class-fraction, class-alliance, intellectuals, the state etc. These are analytically identifiable in instances like: landed rentier; mercantile and industrial capitalist and his

repressive apparatuses; productive/non-productive and mental/manual
worker. On these bases, is constructed a phenomenal story of landed
gentry, older/newer and urban/rural propertied, government and management, advantaged/disadvantaged labour, to the visible character of
which fiction will have contributed. The second is where the definition of the group is primarily achieved through cultural practice alone.
This may like fiction itself, or science, thought, or various objects
or beliefs, be expressive of society incidental to more apparent purposes; or may be one of those systems of meaning which exist solely
for such expression but which are not directly derivable from an analytical base: e.g. interest; honour; nation; people etc. But as all
social groups in some degree define each other within society as a
whole, fiction will in fact clearly contribute at all levels by contri-
buting at any one of them. As implied, it may be a special strength of
fiction that it can express and resolve a measure of conflict present
at levels other than the cultural, and within the cultural level itself,
either in an educative (canonic), or in ritualist (popular) way.

Because the identity of social groups is necessarily relational,
to heighten the identity of one is normally to diminish that of another.
To establish limits is to extinguish an entity potentially greater or
smaller. For the coherence and solidarity of a class-alliance to be
accentuated, it must be at some expense to elements of class or class-
fraction which make it up. Similarly, the refinement of a common code
of honour - an exemplary component in such a consolidation - may be at
the expense of particular codes of professional or aristocratic honour.
Contrariwise, effects which emphasise the difference inherent at class
or fractional borders, which, for example, stress the autonomy of the
landed gentry or the specificity of a code of aristocratic honour will
be at the expense of any wider commonality. However, the issues are
not simply those of greater and smaller but concern function and relation. Thus while cultural and juridical factors may consolidate the
solidarity of landed gentry to other propertied or administrative
groups, they cannot simply obliterate the contradiction held to exist
between capitalist land ownership and capital. If there, it must be
both expressed and resolved. Similarly, one definition of interest,
honour, nation or people cannot simply absorb another; forms are needed
to enact the tension. They will do this at more than one level at once.
While the contrast in style of life of older as opposed to newer capital
may be more apparent than the different functions of mercantile and
industrial capital, the cultural identity of a bourgeoisie will need to
symbolise and concentrate both levels of difference within a necessary
unity - and in such a way as it can take in other cultural opposites
such as public/private etc. So one level, or facet of a level, has
often to negotiate contraries or difference in relation to another and
therefore to articulate unity/plurality and centre/periphery.

The unity/plurality especially in mind is that of the hegemonic
bloc dominant in Britain by the middle of the last century where a
number of strata coalesce, but where the kinds of dominance exercised
from within the bloc, and its external and internal boundaries are
ambiguous. Evangelical Christianity provided a measure of unified
culture ("whenever lines are precarious, we find pollution ideas coming
to their support" Mary Douglas). This culture also has a complimentary
complexity and plurality, the elements of which seem - but only seem -
directly to allude to, or to belong to, the several classes or groups.
The criteria for inclusion or exclusion of cultural elements is controlled
by this unity and the necessity of defining its limit. It is controlled,
in addition, by the need also for a manifest variety of cultural identity.

Evangelical Christianity, from a focus on sexuality and gentility, pervades both religious and secular attitudes, even those (of, for example, the Benthamites and Tractarians) to which it is ostensibly hostile. Comparably, it selectively appropriates the discourse of political economy or romanticism. It dominates, partially externally, 'residually' or 'emergently' distinctive cultures at the margins of the bloc: e.g. that of the landed gentry. It follows from this that the cultures over which the hegemony is imposed (as distinct from realistic or symbolic testimony to their existence within the dominant culture) have to be reconstructed as objects of research - being scarcely, or only partially, visible. This is more the case for those substantially within the bloc than for those (e.g. of the working class) more identifiably beyond it. It is especially the marginal cultures perceived as 'residual' by the dominant yet also to be a source of that 'energy attributed to the boundaries and the less structured areas', which require this recomposition; e.g. those of the patrician Regency or Victorian Ireland.

Cultures may be distinguished in various, not immediately consistent, ways. Reference has been made to residual, dominant and emergent culture; canonic and popular culture; literary as opposed to other cultures. Such analytical oppositions are tools for identification and reconstruction. The fictive aspect of a dominant culture may, for instance, reveal both canonic and popular work. The recognition of this may, in turn, suggest "distinct" literary cultures. George Eliot and Lord Lytton seem equally to inhabit a dominant culture. The first has more value than the other but is not simply a superior version of the same thing. Different forms are involved and, in a way, different literary cultures. These are not wholly within the dominant, but establish a relation with the residual i.e. the Augustan resonance of the narration in *Middlemarch* or the prose version of the Regency verse romance as novel-form in Lytton. A difference - indicative of value - would be the perception of the archaic in George Eliot, and value is an element in the analytically dichotomous social functions peculiar to canonic and to popular fiction. The polysemic resonance of the canonic novel of moral education is linked to images of society as a system. As implied, the education is one in how an individual is to be realised in and through such constraints. Such a novel requires its ideal readers actively to judge; to assess the moral and educative resources of social groups, the needs for and limit of vocation, and to weigh the assessments of the protagonists themselves. For the reader of Lytton, matters are not so much actively judged as seen to be decently done. Here the ritual - like function is seen in plots which enact a danger to virginity/gentility, but where the danger can also be mobilised as a power when realigned with the pursuit of duty. But the strength of such powers lies in their instability; they could go elsewhere.

The marginalised aristocratic culture provides resources which because of their origins, serve to consolidate the larger unity and actually to lessen the identity of the culture in which they have their source. The unity is secured because the destructive potentiality (to violate a precarious social integrity) is felt to be real. Both the wrongly accused, who returns from exile to harness his renewed Byronic energy to the conduct of the estate, and the rightly accused who is 'compost', share in the ritual of the margin. So the aristocratic popular novelist (one who provides a fiction enforcing the values of 'the people') is such because he is aristocratic; but his aristocratic achievements are then free to interpret ambiguities beyond those arising from land and capital. It may be that an agency in this mobility arose from their transfer into the Anglo-Irish terror novel. A Protestant minority in a Catholic country become, said Weber, a 'people of the book'. They become, perhaps, the carriers both of literacy and of anxiety about ambiguity. Some cultures of the puritan diaspora (e.g. those of the Church of Ireland, or of American Unitarianism) evolved in such a way as to allow for the symbolic expression of their ambiguous awareness of their boundary with a native people or a natural wilderness which informs both popular and canonic fiction - including the privileged ambiguity of literary modernism. Thus, certain groups at the periphery, such as the protestant clerisy of nineteenth century Dublin, contribute disproportionately to literature. The affinity between anxieties felt over ambiguities at the borders of meaning and of society, becomes a resource for defining the structural ambivalences of the metropolitan culture - although, in this case, they served also to define aspects of a national beyond its periphery. The power at the pale is real. Pretension or escapism do not explain why the middle strata are identified through the cultural legacy of the landed classes. Rather society has invented resources to express structural uncertainty and these are transmitted from one boundary to another.

THE BOUNDARIES OF HEGEMONY
Components of the Middle Way

Roger Bromley

Introduction

This paper is a report on some preliminary findings which form part of work in progress in which it will be established that certain forms of fiction writing, with class-specific core themes of discourse, became popular in the period in question. Analysis will be based both on the locating of these core themes and on the recognition of 'the structural contradiction which arises whenever a dominant culture seeks to incorporate, and include, within its boundaries, the people'. (1) In other words, even if these fictions foreground and actively signal, for instance, the dissolving of class antagonisms by a rhetoric of personalisation, this does not mean simply that alternative meanings, images of dispossession and evidence of subordination, are finally neutralized. Despite the primary narrative effects of coherence (using the devices of realism to furnish references from the 'real world'), ideologies actually operate in a state of disorder as part of ongoing social processes. What is proposed for this period is that a whole number of discourses together constituted a complex field of conflicting forces whereby what was, initially, socially peripheral (the articulation of certain fractions of the middle strata with the interests of the working class, invested particularly, but by no means exclusively, in the Labour Party) became symbolically central.

It is the role of specifically 'middlebrow' social fictions in the circulation of cultural and ideological symbols which forms a substantial part of the larger research. 'Middlebrow' was the term used in the period; for reasons which should become clear I would like, provisionally, to call them 'intermediate fictions'. How, in fact, these discourses performed the precise function of lowering real class contradictions and of reconstituting, on a fictional level, relatively coherent narratives which served as the horizon of 'popular' experience will form part of the task of analysis. This analysis will be concretely related to the role of the middle strata, and its various positional ideologies, in the hegemony and leadership of the 'popular alliance', the formation of the 'people', in the period leading up to the Labour Party victory in 1945.

In this period the middle strata were articulated through a host of cultural and ideological signs which had the double effect of simultaneously guaranteeing difference (from the working class) and yet also dissolving this difference figuratively through images of service, or stewardship, representation, identification and conscience. The idea of politics as 'a moral vocation' was stressed in the writings of Tawney, and the image of a secular puritan is one which frequently occurs, linked with a suspicion of worldliness. In fact, it could be argued that a secularised form of a particular religious legacy is inscribed in the syntax, images and vocabulary of the political rhetoric of the period: a characteristic mode of expression in the labour movement and in those fictions of social melodrama with their 'religion of the heart'. This adds to the sense of the diverse and contradictory sources of the fragile political and cultural 'alliances' which marked the course of politics at that particular moment. It was a specific and complex process, often drawing upon many formative influences, originating in the middle strata and often non-socialist in motivation, which served to justify and to mobilise the strategy of social reconstruction. What became, ultimately, ascendant modes of rhetoric have to be considered in the context, and contest, of currently available forms.

Writing in the *18th Brumaire*, Marx considered that the peculiar character of social democracy was 'epitomised in the fact that democratic-republican institutions are demanded as a means, not of doing away with two extremes, capital and wage-labour, but of weakening their antagonism and transforming it into a harmony.' (2) This weakening of antagonism can be related to the social-democratic rhetoric of the period which attempted to propose a new social order based on the dissolution of class boundaries and the suppression of the concept of class struggle. (3) In its place, though the term was not explicitly used, was the idea of the 'middle class' as a 'third force' in society - an idea directly relayed by social-democratic tradition into the strategy of the 'third road' to political reconstruction. This strategy played a crucial part in the social hegemony of the time, a key mechanism whereby, in the face of the antagonism between the bourgeoisie and the working class, the third force was seen as the mediating pillar and the basic stabilising factor. This notion had wide currency, particularly in the latter part of the period, and is fully developed in Orwell's *The Lion and the Unicorn* and Priestley's *Out of the People*, as well as in Labour Party documents.

This new force, styled erroneously as a class, became the site for the replacement of antagonism by the notion of 'difference' (in skills, talent, merit etc.), the focal point for the circulation of individuals in a constant process of 'mobility' between the bourgeoisie and the working class. It can be argued that this tendency was very active in the period and left its traces in a range of discursive processes. The agents of this tendency - the professional, administrative and managerial strata, or the 'tertiary sector' - belonged to various different classes, but shared a very prominent part in the circulation of the complex ideological processes of social-democratic discourse which, in the form of political writings, social reportage, and fictions of a 'third road' type, helped to secure consent for a radical change in the nature of British society articulated in the <u>symbolic</u> potential of the Labour victory of 1945. In viewing the <u>period as</u> one of transformation (Gramsci's <u>transformism</u>) and of 'settlement', reference can be made to modes of analysis developed by Gramsci:

> It may be ruled out that immediate economic crises of themselves produce fundamental historical events; they can simply create the terrain more favourable to the dissemination of certain modes of thought, and certain ways of posing and resolving questions involving the entire subsequent development of national life. (4)

To view the period 1929-1945 therefore in the reductive terms of 'crisis politics' is to simplify a time in which the social authority of the dominant bloc was enlarged by means of a complex process in which it secured contradictions by a series of negotiations:

The dominant group is co-ordinated concretely with the
general interests of the subordinate groups, and the life
of the state is conceived as a continuous process of
formation and superseding of unstable equilibria -
equilibria in which the interests of the dominant
group prevail, but only up to a certain point, i.e. stopping
short of narrowly corporate interests.
(Gramsci, *Prison Notebooks*) (5)

The Case of Cronin's *The Citadel*

A.J. Cronin's *The Citadel* (1937) was third in the U.S. bestseller list for 1937 (161,108 copies sold) and second in the following year. It was, and is still, very unusual for a book to appear among the top ten bestsellers in successive years (*Rebecca* was another example in the period). There was no equivalent list compiled for British sales at that time, so it is difficult to place the work in any popularity scale, but during 1936-7 it was selling up to 10,000 copies a week (in hardback) and sold over 200,000 within a year of publication. Total sales are difficult to assess, but they are certainly well in excess of a million in the U.S. alone. Gollancz have kept it almost continuously in print - with thirty five impressions in hardback and at least nine paperback reprints. The novel had a great impact on the social and political life of the time (the film, made in 1939, brought its concerns to an even wider audience) and impressed many political observers - Bevan among them. A recent Radio Four programme (18.1.81) claimed that it helped create a climate for the National Health Service and contributed to the stamping out of the system of pernicious over-charging by some consultants. These 'effects' are impossible to assess and are forced to rely upon entirely impressionistic assumptions, but it was certainly one novel among many in this period which had characters set in a social and political context of conflict and crisis. How the conflict and crisis were formulated is one of the subjects of my inquiry. In many of these social melodramas the central character was often young and idealistic, yet fallible. In the particular instance of *The Citadel*, the hero is drawn back from indulgence and excess by the exemplary witness of his ex-schoolteacher wife, whose <u>ethical</u> presence is a critical level in the text.

Cronin was quite a prolific writer of what might be termed middlebrow 'social romance', but the only novel comparable in its sociopolitical concerns is the very powerful *The Stars Look Down* (1935), set in the Northumberland mining area and focussed upon an ambitious miner's rise to be an M.P. This could possibly indicate that there was something in the period which 'wrote Cronin', and more particularly, perhaps, which motivated this kind of 'social romance' in a particular direction, because it is not in any way characteristic of this mode of writing to be produced within a socio-political reference. Only Delderfield, really, of postwar writers has continued to work within this context and, even then, in very attenuated form.

To put it simplistically, for the moment, I shall be trying to discover the mechanisms which operated in the formation of a specific <u>repertoire</u> of political, intellectual, sociological and literary resources at a particular moment, a moment in which it seems as if the <u>oppositional</u> elements of popular culture were, uncharacteristically in some forms, on the surface of the texts and, however contained within a subscripted formulation, even challenge the central 'romance' by opening up margins of alternative possibility, particularly in the sphere of the political. <u>At that time</u>, this opening up of margins seems to be a defining element in fictions like those by Cronin, Priestley, Spring, Llewellyn etc. How political transformation is, ultimately, placed within these fictions cannot just be analysed from a position within literary culture, but for the moment a recurring image of the oppositional can, at least, be listed as a defining element, a staple, of a certain kind of fiction in the period. The situation of the 'dispossessed' became an appropriate subject for intermediate fictions, arguably for the first time on such a scale.

How the situation of the 'dispossessed' is constructed is the material of a larger inquiry, but it is interesting to note, in passing, how we tend to treat Cronin as a 'formula' or 'hack' writer, a fine storyteller, immensely popular among a certain readership (social melodrama and romance), whereas in the Soviet Union (and in Czechoslovakia) he enjoys a very different popularity, with a complete edition of his works produced with scholarly introduction and annotation. The reasons for this are very complex and to do with matters well beyond the scope of this paper - questions of cultural translation, the 'modernist hegemony' in Anglo-American valuation, perhaps a certain political 'sentimentality' etc.

In the period in question, the 'dispossessed', or, more importantly perhaps, their representatives in organised labour, deliberately chose to work through non-revolutionary methods in their opposition and resistance to capitalism. What constituted the dominant means of foregrounding one particular and, ultimately, exclusive version of political change and the eradication of alternative and contending discourses, is a question related to the role of popularisation as a particular mechanism of hegemonic power. During the interwar years historians have discovered a number of economic, social and political factors which tended to make the working class both more and less politically radical. In the period 1929 to 1945 circumstances which operated against the emergence of a revolutionary potential tended to prevail, and at a number of levels and in a range of activities it is possible to detect a process whereby a dominating perspective on working class experience is identified as part of a fairly broad, and relatively classless (or, at least, that is how it was mediated) radical rhetoric based upon working class exploitation and dispossession. This was appropriated at a level of, what can be perhaps described as, representative identification on behalf of the professions, intellectuals etc., who made an emotional subscription to a political struggle. (It should be mentioned here that over half of the Labour M.P.'s elected to the 1945 Parliament were Fabians - part of the 'nouvelle couche sociale' - and by far the largest element drawn from a single profession were lawyers). So my earlier comment about the representatives of organised labour deliberately choosing to work through non-revolutionary methods refers to a much more complex process of selection, and repression, of possible strategies - roads to change.

In trying to relate Cronin's thirties fiction to certain ideological practices of the period, the main concern will not be with 'radical' content as such, but with the specific mode of writing, its structuring of perceptions, and its rhetorical figurations. The period itself used 'brow' terms to define categories of fiction (to define, it should be said, for marketing purposes), and these categories were constructed in the ideologies and practices of particular institutions - the education system, and through the production, marketing, and distribution of books as 'literature', 'general fiction', or 'romance' in publishing, libraries, and book clubs. (6) Other questions which need attention are concerned with the 'interpellation' of readers in texts through the orderings of language found both in discourses and social practices, and not simply by a composite reader inferred from a single text. Initially, however, the ways in which the formal structurings of the text position, or build in, the reader must be analysed. Can these formal mechanisms, and the perceptions produced in the text, be related in any way to the dominant perceptions and reference systems of a particular stratum in the social formation?

Without wishing to talk in terms of a 'representative' man of the period, or trying to single out a particular disposition as typical or characteristic, the description made of Herbert Morrison by his biographers offers an interesting angle on the kind of writers and writing I am concerned with:

> Morrison was very much the spokesman of his own class. He represented the suburbs, where lived the clerk, the minor civil servant, the municipal employee, the technician, the laboratory assistant, the elementary school teacher, the commercial traveller, the small tradesman and shopkeeper and the office executive. Morrison realised their significance as a new force in politics, totally different from the middle class of the nineteenth century. In alliance, with the working class they could overturn the 'established' classes and create a 'well-ordered, well-run society in which neither accident of birth nor occupation determines the status of the individual, but only the efficiency of his contribution to the social whole'. (7)

Time and time again it is such an alliance which is the addressee of social democratic rhetoric in the period, and in both Orwell and Priestley's formulation of the people it is such groupings which they have in mind. How much this 'alliance' became both 'sender' and 'receiver' of social democratic messages, or was simply the target audience, is a matter of some debate, but certainly this stratum is identifiable in specific, individualised instances in a range of intermediate fictions of the time, as a kind of moral referent. The figure is either a professional person identifying with 'the underdogs of society' or an exceptional, socially mobile member of the working class, both experiencing the conditions of that class and representing it politically, almost always in 'liberal-heroic' terms and within an ethic of 'service', itself bourgeois.

Quite often the professional/working class representative figures converge in a single character - an 'alliance personality' as the new hero. This format is seen quite clearly in a writer like Cronin who, while working with the articulations of the 'new' subject of social inquiry in the thirties, functions within a preconstructed frame of social melodrama with a firmly drawn, and manichean, scale of personality. With the exception of the 'hero', who may slip positions in the scale, all the figures in the text occupy an 'essentialist' point on the scale - they are 'recast'. The representation of women, working class behaviour, the ruling class, and of certain forms of political practice is already 'known' - their spaces are already allocated (selected from currently existing discourses), the writing fills them in, naturalises them once more as part of the existing relations. This says nothing, of course, of the unassimilable elements, contradictory and ambiguous, those which do not fit. These will be the subject of specific analysis, with particular attention being paid to the structuring of antagonisms and the fear, and containment, of violence by exposing it, over and over again, to a single definition and representation. The reference to the 'pre-cast' is intended to locate those elements which

give the text its quality of 'unflagging narrative', and produce a
'relaxing, diverting novel', 'a gripping, if dated story' (phrases from
the Radio 4 programme). This cannot be resolved simply in terms of manipulation, or implantation, but must be seen as part of a long process -
literary-cultural and political - the problematic of bourgeois writing
and its parameters. This is, essentially, a battle over meanings within
the repertoire of available 'rhetorics.

In writing about the Industrial novels of the 1840's Williams says:

> Recognition of evil was balanced by fear of becoming involved.
> Sympathy was transformed, not into action, but into withdrawal.
> We can all observe the extent to which this structure of feeling
> has persisted, into both the literature and social thinking of
> our time. (8)

In the 1930's, however, 'withdrawal' was not the mode of sympathy used.
A sympathetic identification with the conditions of the working class
was made through a social-democratic perspective, or, to be precise, the
emotional expression of its radical rhetoric. In fiction, the transformation was produced within the melodramatic mode, with a resolution
in terms of the 'law of the heart'. It is this mode which contains the
potentially unassimilable (working class violence, for example) and
legitimises a preferred fictional model of action, at least analogous,
at the level of structure, to the social democratic model: integrationist.

Cronin carried out a good deal of private research into disease when
he was a G.P. in Wales in the early 1920's. As a result he was asked, in
1924, by the Ministry of Mines to tour the coalfields of Britain and make
a comprehensive study of the conditions that produce pulmonary diseases.
His later fictions obviously draw upon such 'investigative' experience,
as did those of a number of his contemporaries who also undertook official, or 'journalistic' investigations.

For all its exposure of conditions in the South Wales coalfields,
The Citadel, with its use of melodrama, sentiment and coincidence, is
projected ultimately within a structure of romance, although Cronin is
commonly seen as 'a popular, middle of the road, commonsense, realist
writer'. Actually only one half of the novel is situated within South
Wales - the more 'naturalistic' section, treating social problems and
linking poverty with disease which, though now commonplace, was at the
time part of an entirely new way of seeing health conditions. The text
is basically organised around 'a single, central and sentimental figuration' which gives it 'a simple and particularised coherence',* its emo-
tionally powerful and immediately communicable impact - its readability.
This is a condition of this kind of narrative, determined by its social
mode of reception: a setting for the dominantly available resource of
narrative fiction - 'the (seemingly) always-already-there' of realist
fiction. 'Seemingly', because its 'foregrounding' as a dominant mode
of writing is part of the history of the contestation of fictional resources. Its resolution of contradictions and its model of individualised
'victory' points also to its absences, its excluding limitations and sup-
pressions - especially in the way in which it collapses social stratification into terms of moral, or ethical, differentiation and variable
social obligation. Social relations are obscured and reduced - excess,
inequalities, and the structures of power and ownership are reproduced
in their manifest forms and/or in the terms of caricature and melodrama,

---

* Phrases used by Raymond Williams in 'The Welsh Industrial Novel',
Problems in Materialism and Culture, 1980, p. 227.

and not as indelible features of a sharply structured social system. To put it schematically, here Cronin, like many other writers of this kind of fiction, is representing the 'law of the heart' disguising itself as 'the law of the world'. (9) The perspective is, fundamentally, positivistic, written from a position deep inside liberal-radical ideology with its dependence on a 'well-ordered, well-run society' brought about by reformist mechanisms of change.

Social relations are presented in terms of a fictionally produced abstraction of their 'essence'; this essence (the immediate, transparent and subjectively rendered phenomena of the social formation) is represented in simplified and hyperbolic form, coherent and accessible - reproduced as, what may be termed, the text's 'knowledge', its representations of social reality. The rhetoric, sentiment, and mode of caricature of much Social Democratic polemic and practice is analogous in many ways, particularly in its frequent and repeated use of abstractions masked in political objectives - justice, decency, honesty, democracy, 'the people', etc.

What kind of text is *The Citadel*? By indicating earlier its romance characteristics, a partial definition of its mode was suggested - the dominant positioning of the reader seems to be through identification with one or two characters (Andrew and Chris Manson, together with a range of subsidiary variants - positive and negative - on their presentation). This, according to the English Group at Birmingham, places it inside a category of the 'lowbrow'. (10) However, it is also concerned with judgement and discrimination (in other words, the reader is positioned actively within the text in terms of issues and not just characters) which would situate it within the 'middlebrow' category of 'general fiction'. There is another factor which requires comment, and that is its publication by Gollancz, a 'progressive', in some ways even 'oppositional', publisher. Does this suggest that its potential audience may have included those who read it for its political content? Certainly there are instances of people claiming Cronin as a major influence in their political formation, but this kind of 'influence' is impossible to assess. All that is being suggested is that *The Citadel*, although it is conceived within a melodramatic mode, does have a relative openness - there is a contradictory element in its presentation of the disease/poverty condition which, if it doesn't constitute a critique of the melodramatic, at least allows for a differential reception of the text - its 'oppositional' possibilities are not entirely sealed. This is so because no single text determines its own decodings - the moment of production and reception is a vital factor. It may well be that social melodramas of this kind were readily mobilised for the eventual domination of a particular rhetoric and political perspective, but only as part of a specific network of converging discourses, a 'contestation of languages'. This is not to claim that in a situation where a revolutionary politics has gained ascendancy *The Citadel* would have been a seminal text, but that this particular kind of literary production is not, in itself, automatically conscriptable for domination, but is contradictory and ambivalent - is capable of other readings, other uses (compare the Russian example mentioned earlier); reception is a matter of history.

At this distance in time, it is hard to determine such questions, and it would certainly be an error to try and re-constitute a possible readership from the text itself. It is simply that the varied conditions of production (by, initially, a professional, middle-class male with considerable knowledge and first-hand experience of the subject matter of the texts - and with a first novel bestseller, *Hatter's Castle*, behind him), the 'crossbrow' ideological functions of the text, and its publication and distribution by the founder of the Left Book Club, seem to fulfil certain socio-cultural needs of the time which can be found actively

in the social mode of reception of other writings. *The Citadel* broke
every sales record in the nine years of Gollancz's operations as an
independent publisher. Cronin himself said:

> I have great joy over everything but the title. I don't
> like *The Citadel*; though it expresses the meaning of the
> book, it is too cold and, I think, suggests a war novel.
> I'll find a better one ... (11)

It is, in some ways, a 'war' novel, but how the war is conducted and
peace achieved (in political terms) makes it such an important text in
the period, particularly in the light of what was said earlier about
'dominant' and 'differential' appropriations of a text as a crucial part
of its reception. After the novel had received considerable publicity
(good reviews, adverse comment from the medical profession) Gollancz
launched a weekly campaign for the book in the *Observer*, which at least
indicates something about part of its target audience. One of the advertisements used a letter from Harrods: 'THE CITADEL HAS SET UP A RECORD
IN THIS LIBRARY, EXCEEDING BY 500 COPIES THE PURCHASE OF ANY ONE TITLE.'
In order to achieve its sales figures, *The Citadel* had to break through
what would have normally been thought of as its target audience - so
its reception was an extremely complex matter, much more so then, I
would speculate, than Cronin novels today which sell from within a much
simpler category. The *Observer*, Harrod's, Bevan, Labour Party researchers, '45,000 sold in 11 days' - this at least indicates an 'alliance'
readership, perhaps a condition of the reception of this kind of writing
in the period.

The experience and response resulting from the interrelation between
what is offered for reception and the socio-historical conditions under
which reception is realised is helpfully described by Naumann:

> Every individual reception of a work has always been preceded
> already by other receptions ... It is a question, however, of
> sociocultural capacities which the reader has acquired in the
> course of his life. In so doing, the social capacities the
> rules of commerce with literature, are subjectively 'broken'
> in the individual's appropriation, corresponding to his
> concrete socio-historical and individual situation. Here
> there are also marked out the special kinds of individual
> difference which help to condition the appropriation of
> literature, and of the work. (12)

In other words, although my analysis stresses the 'accommodative' features of Cronin's works with reference to their likely appropriations
at a particular socio-historical moment, it is not intended to argue that
the texts are unambiguous and relate only to an 'integrationist' perspective, but that their 'historico-functional' effect was negotiated primarily within that perspective: that is how they secure, or neutralise,
contradictions, by interpellating 'into its structure of discourse the
subjects of the popular classes' (13) - the experience of working-class
subordination and the possibilities of its transformation (because it is
a recurring item on the agenda foregrounded by the Depression, unemployment, social investigations etc.).

This is not to say, obviously, that in order to reach a wide, popular audience, intermediate fiction has always to construct its readership (potential) as subjects of its discourse in this way, but that
Cronin's fictions (and other Gollancz novels) construct a potentially
broad readership as 'subjects' not by extensive, and 'realistic', productions of working-class experience, but by the articulation of a

perspective generated from outside and above that experience but relating to it by a mechanism of identification and a developing social conscience. This is true even of David, the miner's son who becomes an M.P. and loses his seat in the 1931 election (in *The Stars Look Down*) because it is perspective which defines action for social change in terms of representative means, so the origin, or 'class position', of the subject is not the authenticating principle in the discourses. This puts the burden of cultural analysis of 'popularised' forms on the need always to relate the internal contradictions of a specific fictional text to the complex and contradictory form of the cultural/ideological/political field of its contemporary reception (the struggle over its subsequent receptions is another matter outside my scope, except to mention the ways in which Cronin, Priestley, Spring, Vera Brittain etc., are being appropriated by television as part of the means whereby existing relations are reproduced). In attempting to situate *The Citadel* and *The Stars Look Down* within a specific set of social and cultural relations, it is crucial to take full account of the positioning of subjects (e.g. 'the people') within ideological discourses which exist outside and are represented within the literary texts. In order to do this in the larger research project, analyses will be constructed around readings of the texts and with specific reference to the rhetoric and practice of social democracy in the period, and to, what has been called, 'the politics of containment' (WPCS 9). (14)

Andrew Manson, the central figure in *The Citadel*, is presented in many ways as a crusader and quest-figure, subject to trials of skill, alluring temptations, and moments of despair, on a journey in search of a grail constituted by moral integrity, social obligation, and scientific practice. Although Manson's achievement is represented in individualistic terms, this is considerably modified and adapted by reference to the professional integrity of three colleagues - Denny, Hope, and Stillman - dedicated to scientific medical practice determined by social obligation, and to the consistent spiritual investment of his wife, Chris, whose death is seen as symbolic and cautionary. The structural analogies with medieval romance are important as they mark the site of a pre-capitalist model of service (or stewardship) on behalf of the community, a combination of individual self-interest with the notion of a representative social function: in this context, the professional man distinguished by scientific knowledge and dedicated to the community, a secularisation of Christian ethics. In a comparable way, Labour politics were being transformed by the growth of a consensus around a Social democratic model of practice: efficiency, scientific planning, and gradualism. It is not being claimed that *The Citadel* reflects a changing political situation, or that it is an allegory of it, but that it is situated within and determined by various historical elements, included in which is the specific way in which the ideological practices of Social democracy signalled a shift in the positioning of 'the people' as subjects within the social formation - a positioning dependent very much upon the evacuation of 'class' from its discourses.

When Manson follows self-interest to the exclusion of principles, science and social duty, he is viewed in isolation from his wife, his vocation, and his real colleagues. The text, at these points, centres on a man dedicated to material gain, working within a specious medical fraternity, corrupt and indulgent, and serving a vulgar, luxury-orientated clientele. The casting of the clientele is significant - they are seen as parasitic, non-productive, immoral and wasteful. In other words, it advances a carefully selective image of the wealthy; missing is any reference to the owners of the means of production, financiers, or any

other bearers of real power in society. It is a token caricature of a
particular form of wealth and excess (focussed particularly on the
women, interestingly enough, which presents the abuses of wealth as a
moral category; the economy is oddly absent) - constructed mainly as an
emblem of intensive self-interest: 'They', the rich, the 'old gang'
seen as a disease which society must cure. Class relations are produced
in personalised terms. A style is foregrounded so that we perceive them
in stylised terms - real social relations, the structural conditions of
power and stratification, are occluded. Manson's personal and professional instability at this stage in the text is reinforced by his medical ineptitude - he co-operates in an operation which leads to a death.
When stable, he is actively associated with the saving of life. The
world of the impoverished working class confronts London society in the
personalised form of Mary's poverty and illness and her lack of access
to proper medical care, but it is a moral confrontation, constructed
around pity and negotiated through the representations of Manson as
mediator.

The moral scale of the narrative is simply structured, its fable
element seldom far from the surface - a structure of oppositions, manichean in a way, commonly seen and heard in the figurations of the vague
radical rhetoric of Social democracy - a simplifying, and containing,
discourse. Nowhere is there any reference to collective action or
direct action (with a single exception clearly marked as exceptional and
not exemplary - the blowing up of the sewers) or to class-related practices, but only to a group of ethically motivated individuals working for
'the people'. They are formulated in a way very close to the 'alliance'
spoken of by Morrison's biographers, the 'indeterminate stratum' of
Orwell's *Lion and the Unicorn*, and the new grouping referred to in
Priestley's *Out of the People*. The absence of politically motivated
class references, or of any commitment to concerted extra-parliamentary
activity (even more marked in *The Stars*, a more explicitly political
novel) characterised the policies and manifestoes of the Labour Party
throughout this period, particularly from 1937 onwards, when short-term
policies dominated conference agendas. The professional and administrative model derived from Fabian ideology, Parliamentary experience, and
TUC practices all shaped the Labour perspective, even if a militant
flavour was allowed to ornament and decorate its discourse. The War
however considerably altered the rhetoric of 'popular' discourse.

Is there any sense in which the modes of certain intermediate writings of this period could be interpreted as a symbolic defence of the
economic and political interests of the middle strata? - how do they
negotiate 'anxiety', for instance? What is the precise nature of this
mode of writing, and how is it generated? Is it peculiar to the middle
strata, or can it be seen as a mixture of modes derived from one, or
more, reference classes? Is it possible, following Laclau (1978), to
talk of style in terms of 'class belonging' - are cultural identifications to be considered as variables which enter into style and discourse?
Does the intermediate novel of the period represent a formulation which,
in its eclectic formation, marks an overlap of references and perspectives from adjacent classes? This refers back to an earlier point about
the constitution of readers as the subjects of discourses not as a
reflection of existing relations but as a projection of a potential subject - a newly forged 'alliance' based on identification and representation. This poses the question as to whether the middle strata of society
had a fixed social identity, or whether it developed an innovating cultural and political role in the period based upon the mediation and
diffusion of an attack upon the established order constructed around a

constitutional and reformist attitude. A vast and complex number of
discourses constituted this hegemonic mechanism for 'facing the future'
- they interpellated a 'social-democratic' image of 'the people' as the
subject of a new social order: a reconstructed and expanded middle
stratum. Can intermediate fictions be seen in any way as being constituted within and generating explanations of a distinctive social consciousness?

The main narrative tension in *The Citadel* between material self-
interest and an ideal of professional service is developed in a series
of contradictions and conflicts which, in themselves, can be seen as
familiar terms in the rhetoric, images, and figurations of the political
ideology of the middle strata of the time. That is to say, political
issues are often posed in abstract forms, and analysis often turned on
personal and abstract features of the social formation, and avoided
the use of class analysis. So, the main thematic motivation of *The
Citadel* is directed towards a struggle commonly experienced in the
middle strata, and close to the kind of scenario often articulated
within its political rhetoric. Its formal characteristics (mixture of
modes and levels of style) also need to be considered in terms of its
possible reference outside the text.

Is the combination of sentiment, melodrama, romance and 'social
realism' dominant in this period, and relatively insignificant at other
times?, and if so, does it coincide with the socio-political prominence
of the strata that these characteristics most closely represent? This
prominence was marked by an 'assimilative' mode of political practice
relatively insulated from, and insulating itself from, popular pressures
by consistently re-presenting these pressures through prescriptive figurations - a regional, pitiable and passive working class, a biographical
model for the styling of the representative hero, all direct action,
oppositional activity marked as anarchic, mob-like violence, and a middle
stratum form of identification through 'social conscience'. It has to
be remembered, also, that in this period the middle strata experienced
an improvement in their standard of living with the growth of new types
of housing aimed at a particular income/life style/occupational group,
a marked increase in consumer durables, new patterns of leisure and,
relatively speaking, full employment. This phase of prosperity, of
course, was accompanied by wholesale unemployment and economic stagna-
tion in the traditional industries - a combination which brought about
a vast increase in the scale of social reportage: a searching consideration of the condition of England, marked by a certain style and carried
out, for the most part, after the point when the depression had its worst
effects. The later war-time experience of evacuation also helped to
sharpen the 'social conscience' of this strata by direct encounters with
the conditions of deprivation.

Although *The Citadel* has an ideological format which places it inside the value-orientation of the middle strata (15) - the single-minded
rebelliousness of an individualistic nature against bureaucracy and
corruption, control of impulses, bold and simplified contrasts based on
a melodramatic appeal, and a certain restrained realism combined with
unromantic clarity - at the same time its focus on social conditions in
South Wales comes close to straightforward reportage at times. This
effect is mitigated, however, by the fact that social conditions are only
viewed in terms of Manson's relations to them, a relationship variously
shown as heroic, sentimental and melodramatic - part of the rhetoric of
the exceptional. There is also a sense of a pre-scripted, composite
image of the 'dispossessed'. Disease and inadequate sanitation are seen

from a narrow perspective, and not in a wider context of class relations
which would see the health issue as symptomatic of broader existing social
relations in this phase of capitalism. The concentration on bringing about
a change in the medical profession alone is itself part of a politically
reformist ideology.

The working classes are seen, selectively, from a middle stratum
perspective as objects of pity, and weak, diseased, and undernourished -
static and passive figures in a picture, as in a mode of 'photographic
realism' with its attention on the details of the foreground. It is a
mode which represents features which are only the manifest forms of the
existing social relations as the real relations. The working class is
seen as a series of discrete units - families, individuals, fathers,
mothers, children, miners in trouble etc. - perceived selectively that
is from a middle stratum stance which prioritises its values and organisa-
tional categories, intended to arouse in the readership contexts of response and appropriate referential and perceptual associations. This
technique forms part of the habitual mode of this discourse, a routine
process of the sedimentation of specific signifying codes in language
and figuration. The working-class is never seen as a class capable of
action and initiative on its own behalf, only in a 'clientelist' position. Manson relates to the class on the basis of his skill, qualifica-
tions, and social conscience. So, the 'social realism' is of a limited
dimension with a certain flatness and rigidity, presented at times with
the exaggerated gestures and attitudes of melodrama, a mode of writing
linked structurally with the tendency to caricature in the treatment of
the wealthy in the text. In addition to this, can be seen a strong level
of moral indignation, sentimentality in feeling, and a dedication to work
as the key element in social mobility - here a mobility based not on
self-interest or social aspiration, but social ideals. These would all
find a place within the middle strata's codes, strong on the question of
merit (Tawney is important here). The use of 'sentimental socialism',
together with a schematisation of figures, uniformity of types, and a
certain distortion in perspective is a feature of this mode of writing
designed to throw its central figure into relief as a person rebelling
against the requirement of performing the standardised functions of his
position (in the stratum) defined for him by others. This rebellion
(compare Denny and Manson's 'anarchic' action in blowing up the sewer)
takes the form of a moral campaign, founded on indignation, directed
against those who seem to perform their obligations less well, or towards
a social order (here presented in symptomatic form) which is judged to
have failed in its performance of its social function. The profile of
rebellion is individualist and ethical, de-politicised. As Fromm has
noted, 'Moral indignation has invariably been characteristic of the lower
middle classes from Luther's time to Hitler's', (16) and it is this which
forms the central emotional thrust in *The Citadel*, in a style both personalised and sentimental. It is precisely this style of indignation and
assertiveness which marks so much social reportage of the period -
'scientific' in its clarity, logical in argument, and morally indignant
in tone. Its combination of statistical data with personalised (often
sentimental) anecdotes brings it close in method and tone to many novels.
Reforms and rewards demanded were not phrased in personal terms but in
terms of justice, social equality, and democracy for all.

At the end of *The Citadel* a decisive shift has been marked in the
General Medical Council, based on a recognition of the worth of Hope,
Denny and Manson, bearers of the positive values of the middle strata.
The Citadel, fortress of the enemy (cf. Castle Perilous) has been be-
sieged and, this is vital, the cause of the attackers accommodated by

the incumbents and inserted into its future practices. Analogously, the assertive period of an ascendant social democratic ideology was acknowledged, accommodated, and internalised by the hegemonic class in the war and after. This was a process which would have been impossible without a substantial measure of support from the working class at this time. By pointing to the experience of the working class - but by representing it within their own categories of perception - members of the middle strata were able to resume leadership of that class in terms of a Parliamentary Socialism, ritually cleansed of its 1931 memory (a frequent reference in the fiction). They were able to claim a part in the shaping of popularised radicalism, particularly through the media of broadcasting (Priestley) and writing (Gollancz pamphlets etc.). The Citadel was penetrated, but not captured, nor its inhabitants overthrown; a vague consensus on the shape of a new social order was formed in a context of awareness about the failings of 'the old gang'. Displacement took the form of integration, not usurpation. The established stratification system was simultaneously reinforced and transformed, in its superstructural forms, in a way appropriate to the hegemonic level. The middle strata in this period, in their radical mode, articulated a political future with clear, and principled, reference to the deprivations of the working class, yet within a framework which belonged, ultimately, to the hegemonising class. It was an ideology which drew heavily for its images and narratives (literally and metaphorically) on the working class experience, but was conducted at the level of political practice on the terrain of the middle strata:

> All this is not to suggest that the popular radicalism of war-time Britain was, for the most part, a formed socialist ideology, let alone a revolutionary one. But, in its mixture of bitter memories and positive hopes, in its antagonism to a mean past, in its recoil from Conservative rule, in its impatience of a traditional class structure, in its hostility to the claims of property and privilege, in its determination not to be robbed again of the fruits of victory, in its expectations of social justice, it was a radicalism eager for major, even fundamental, changes in British society after the war. (17)

Popular fiction had an important function to discharge in the shaping of the memories of a 'mean past', but the critical problem for analysis is how it constituted that particular phenomenon as the subject of its discourses.

FOOTNOTES

1. S. Hall, 'Some Paradigms in Cultural Studies', *Annali - Anglicistica*, 1978, 3.

2. K. Marx, *The Eighteenth Brumaire of Louis Bonaparte* (1852), Penguin, 1973, p.176.

3. This section is very much indebted to Poulantzas in his *Classes in Contemporary Capitalism*, NLB, 1975.

4. A. Gramsci, *Prison Notebooks*, 1971, p.184.

5. *ibid.*, p.182.

6. These ideas have been developed in 'Thinking the Thirties' in *Practices of Literature and Politics*, Proceedings of the Essex Conference on the Sociology of Literature, July 1978, University of Essex, 1979.

7.   quoted in Paul Addison, *The Road to 1945: British Politics and the Second World War*, 1975, p.50.

8.   R. Williams, *Culture and Society*, 1958, p.119.

9.   cf. L. Althusser, *For Marx*, Penguin, 1969, p.133.

10. *ibid.*, (6) above.

11. Sheila Hodges, *Gollancz: The Story of a Publishing House, 1928-1978*, Gollancz, 1978, p.72.   All the material relating to the publication of *The Citadel* is drawn from this source.

12. M. Naumann, *New Literary History*, 8 (1), 1976, pp.107-126.

13. Hall, *ibid.*

14. 'The Politics of Containment - 1935-45', *Working Papers in Cultural Studies*, 9, Birmingham, 1976.

15. A useful article on this is V. Kavolis, 'Artistic Preferences of Urban Social Classes', *Pacific Sociological Review*, Vol.8, no.1, Spring 1965, pp.43-41.   (I have drawn upon it extensively in the foregoing discussion).

16. Erich Fromm, *Escape from Freedom*, 1941, p.96.

17. R. Miliband, *Parliamentary Socialism*, 1961, p.274.

THE BOUNDARIES OF HEGEMONY
Scriptwriting at Gainsborough
Studios during World War II

Sue Harper

I should indicate at the outset that I feel no need to apologize for the rather 'empiricist' tendency of this paper. It seems to me that much of the curiously literal-minded theoreticism of recent work in the sociology of literature and film has tended to ignore the complexity of artistic history (particularly of the recent past) and has imposed a false unity onto it. When I attempted to account for the vitality and continuity of certain quasi-aristocratic themes in popular art of the 1940's, I decided to use methods of investigation which may seem depressingly pedestrian to some; for example, putting advertisements in the 'trade' papers and then conducting interviews with workers in the publishing industry and at Gainsborough studios, (1) using advertising and promotion material produced by publishing houses and film companies, selecting directive replies and diary material from Mass-Observation, critically reviewing *Kinematograph Weekly*, *Daily Film Renter*, *The Author*, and even *Peg's Paper*. The marketing, selection of target audience, and precise audience response of popular texts seems to me to be of equal importance to a study of their level of discourse. Naturally, the latter is crucial, but stripped of attention to the production context, it can lead to a dangerous ahistorical formalism. A sociology of culture should, I suggest, be as much concerned with the how and the what as well as with the why. The general distaste for these 'nuts-and-bolts' of ideology displays an over-fastidious dislike of dirtying the hands; the purity of some recent types of theoretical investigation would blench at anything so prosaic as writers' union practice, or a study of their income tax returns. Such work may, however, give a comfortingly empirical underpinning to analyses of authorship theories in a specific period.

The set of relations preferred by a hegemonic class are rarely straightforwardly presented in popular art, whether in literature or film. That class's interests may often best be served in fiction by permitting another group or class fraction to substitute for it; by according a temporary dominance elsewhere, a hegemonic class may excise or fruitfully rehearse its own anxieties. I have described in detail elsewhere the function of the 'landed' theme in the popular historical novel of World War II - a period not noted for the efficacy of the aristocratic classes. (2) Of equal interest is the series of Gainsborough costume melodramas made from these novels. A group of screenwriters played a major role in shifting the landed protagonists from the ambiguous margins of the acceptable (the space they occupy in the novels) to the outer reaches of that forbidden, dangerous territory which they inhabit in the films. This group of writers, who had jointly developed concepts of the 'writerly' role, were instrumental in altering the audience provenance of the texts from the middle to the working class, as I hope to show.

A massive box office success was achieved by Gainsborough's cycle of costume melodramas, which were made with the same production star, and technical teams.(3) The weekend premier dates for these films are *The Man in Grey*, (July, 1943), *Fanny by Gaslight* (May, 1944), *Madonna of the Seven Moons*, (December, 1944), *The Wicked Lady* (December, 1945), *Caravan* (April, 1946) and *Jassy* (August, 1947). The films have a rich visual texture and evince a preoccupation with the sexual mores and lifestyle of the upper reaches of the landed classes. They all have a nineteenth century setting, apart from *The Wicked Lady* and *Madonna*, whose gypsy/peasant half is determinedly devoid of modern reference. Moreover all the films contain protagonists (often visually or diegetically linked with 'gypsyness') who actively seek sexual pleasure and whom the plot ritually excises by the end.

Gainsborough attempts to retain a continuity with a crucial and profitable strand in popular culture, and it was efficacious in predicting and exploiting public taste of the period. Both films and books were shamefacedly dismissed by their audiences as merely pandering to fantasy, but the patterns and codes of such 'escapism' is usually period- and class-specific, and the nature of the films' class appeal is predicated upon the type of 'audience creativity' they required. The almost unparallelled critical opprobium which these films attracted is an index of their distance from the concerns of 'polite' culture. *Caravan* is "not what is known as a critics' picture ... not for a moment compellingly realistic"; (4) *The Wicked Lady* was a "carefully compounded bromide, its lines aiming no higher than *Mabel's Weekly*". (5) Only those papers writing for a specifically working-class audience made positive critical responses. (6) Although humanist 'high-art' critics invoked the style of documentary realism, it is clear that the marked and enduring audience preference for Gainsborough's style of 'disguise' of class and sexual issues is of importance in any 'map' of taste of the period.

A particular set of production circumstances permitted screenwriters at Gainsborough to operate in a relatively unhindered way. J.A. Rank's acquisition of the studio in 1941 at first left the existing team unhampered. His philistinism - 'Who is Thomas Hardy?' (7) - permitted literati such as R.J. Minney to gain intellectual control at the studio until mid-1946, and enabled entrepreneurs such as Ted Black to exploit their instinct for popular taste. Although financial control rested with Rank, the range and complexity of whose empire rendered him all but invincible, the Ostrer brothers were permitted to run the studio in as tight a way as they wished. It is clear that the Ostrers and Minney parted company, intellectually speaking, with Rank over the question of the latter's definition of culture as basically educational. Minney suggested that a Shakespeare film which could only appeal to a minority audience should only cost £70,000: "the commodity must be what the public wants, and what the public is at present educated enough to like." (8) Rank was increasingly drawn into 'quality' films such as *Caesar and Cleopatra*, which as projects had critical kudos but which were financial disasters and necessitated a consolidation of his disparate interests.

All the above films except *Jassy* were made under studio conditions dominated by Black, the Ostrers and Minney; the appointment of Sydney Box in August 1946 led to a huge percentage increase in the cost of sets and locations, and probably to the demise of the studio at Shepherd's Bush in March 1949. (9) Management philosophy expressed itself in the area of careful pre-shooting costs and tight commodity control. Very stringent analysis of the shooting diary was in evidence on *The Wicked*

Lady: "it had to be kept up to the minute ... everything had to be kept absolutely ... we had to be able to explain what the delay was and whose fault it was. Inquests all the time." (10) Gainsborough producers attempted considerable control over the stars' behaviour, but did not interfere with artistic matters unless the budget was exceeded. (11) There was very little location work, and the rigorous six-week schedule necessitated night Art Direction. (12) Such conditions were deemed necessary by studio producers in order to ensure a certain excess profit. Ostrer noted "I want the whole amount budgeted for the film to appear on the screen in the production, and not to have a large percentage frittered away behind the scenes in extravagant and needless waste." (13) Also emphasised was the need for careful assessment of market size, advance breakdown of costs, and predictability of the product's visual style and profit. (14) The profitability of the costume cycle was considerably greater than the Gainsborough films in modern dress (15) since, besides being more popular, the former were cheaper to make due to tighter control. Producers explicitly placed no credence in bad reviews by critics, (16) since high costs could only be justified by mass appeal. Hence the studio's 'low-brow' orientation. Star appearances, elaborate advertising and negotiation of longer bookings, (17) were the means of capturing a large audience.

Industrial relations at Gainsborough were, of course, quiescent during the war and until late 1945. (18) Under the aegis of Charlie Wheeler, the shop steward of ACT at the studio, it became fairly militant by 1949. (19) However, all the sections had separate union meetings, and an overall studio union consciousness was difficult to establish. (20) Interestingly, the union structure was precisely analagous to the management's. None of the units were kept informed of the others' filming activities: 'it all came from high up, and we were the last in the line'. (21) This is Taylorism anglicized; skilled workers are proletarianized by being kept ignorant of the meaning and direction of the whole product. All interviewees on the technical side attested to the separateness of management and labour: "they were all so far removed from us"; "you'd get the occasional morning visit from Black or Ostrer, but then they'd disappear"; "all the heads stuck together. They used to eat together at lunchtime." (22)

It is crucial for our purposes to note that the scriptwriters were separated from the rest of the workforce and were in a privileged relationship with the studio management. As I hope to show, they were engaged in making a bid for intellectual power, and their interests were allied with the management's. Only they and the Heads of Departments saw the rushes with the producers; (23) comments and criticism were filtered down privately to the technical workers. (24) The intellectual chain of command meant that new script pages were constantly replacing old ones at very short notice. (25) This made an intellectual or critical engagement by the technical workforce impossible, and it deprived them of a sense of corporate responsibility. That was 'carried' by the scriptwriters. They attempted to circumvent production control by defining themselves as 'special' intellectual workers, and by altering the class orientation of the popular novels on which the films were based. The choice of the novels and the 'slanting' of the scripts can partly be accounted for by the dominance of R.J. Minney; but he shared a definition of authorship with the other Gainsborough writers, which is clarified by their joint work in the Screenwriters Association.

The novels which were chosen for adaptation were low-status, since they were written by and for women. (26) In these texts, ambiguous groups 'on the boundary' are selected, such as the aristocracy, gypsies, and women, and they are examined for signs of social pollution. They exhibit energy when poised thus. The high-born hero functions on the margin and generates creativity there; Lord Rohan in Lady E.F. Smith's *The Man in Grey* is a case in point. Only by ensuring a correct usage of the profits from 'rents' can the gentry hero survive in the written texts. (27) Any aristocratic energy is linked with that produced by gypsies, who symbolise exotic, eccentric, predominantly sexual energy of a group notoriously de-classed. Gypsy blood in the novels can be inclined to 'danger' and sexual excess, but these may be counterbalanced by second sight and 'special' knowledge. Sexually aggressive females topple into the 'polluted' category if they are tainted by gentry/gypsy colour, but unlike the other two groups, women are permitted to expiate their sexuality by recuperating it through marriage and 'true love'. I showed in *Red Letters 14* that it was the historical element in these gentry novels which appealed to a large war-time audience, and that this was largely composed of middle-class women who were in work. It does not seem possible, from Mass-Observation material at least, to establish what fraction of the middle-class they came from.

Clearly, the profitability of the Gainsborough films had to do with the existing reputation of the novels. The marked decline of the cycle was coterminous with Sydney Box's decision to eschew such texts, and the script problems with *The Bad Lord Byron* and *Christopher Columbus* were a contributory factor to the studio's final decline. Gainsborough's earlier screenwriting experience had been deeply and profitably embedded in popular forms, which other studios like Ealing and Cineguild had been unable to emulate. (28) The novels had all used an extremely complex series of 'framing' devices; but the scripts all begin without narrators *in medias res*. Although the film of *The Man in Grey* is structured as a meditation on a portrait, the flashback effect is concealed; *Caravan's* script begins with a reprise, but from half-way through the narrative. The first *Wicked Lady* script has two modern tramps interrupting Barbara's ghost, but this is removed from the final version of the film; (29) all that remains of 'ghostliness' is the camera movement and changed sound quality of her death. Gainsborough screenwriters plunge the audience, with few delayed gratifications, into 'unmediated' history; distancing techniques are replaced by ones of identification. The telescoping of time is irregularly signalled, such that the film's audience is encouraged to view everything as simultaneous; moreover there is less dialogue than in the novels. Information is carried instead by music, a language with easier access to the emotions. (30)

The foregrounding of class has a different emphasis in the scripts. Sir Ralph is accused by his fellows of 'betraying his own class', and the hero of *Fanny* suggests that 'a hundred years from now such class distinctions won't exist.' The novels balance the aristocracy against an undefined residuum, whereas the films compare aristocratic excess with 'professional' middle-class restraint, to the latter's advantage. Sir Francis in the novel is an amiable invalid - his wife says, "I never had any particular reason for hating him", (31) whereas the script converts him into a libertine of whom even whores remark "he's a beast - he's the worst of the lot!" (32) His comeuppance is signalled by the swamp to which he succumbs, and which the bourgeois hero successfully negotiates after appropriating the whip. (33) Rohan in *The Man in Grey* is converted from an honourable man declaring emotional severance from Hester (34) into a Byronic figure - 'I've yet to meet a woman I don't despise' - who beats Hester to death. (35) The script notes that 'the brutality of it [a dog fight] appeals to his sadistic sense.' The aristocratic quartet in *The Wicked Lady* propose a double divorce and 'swap', but the script does not permit them to flout convention.

On the whole, then, the scripts explicitly add to the novels such remarks as Rokesby's "I wonder what they [the gentry] ever did to deserve all this". Designed for a lower class audience than the novels, the scripts present the aristocracy as an unambiguous site of fascination, fear, and 'unspeakable' dark sexuality. Gypsies no longer present, as in the novels, an exotic eccentric wisdom, but a social threat. The *Caravan* script has them murder and rifle the body, whereas the book insists on their cultural purity; Pertwee converts the gypsy energy in *Madonna* into dirt and violence, (36) and has the virgin heroine raped by a gypsy instead of her husband. (37) Excessive female sexuality is similarly moved from the ambiguous margins into the 'danger' category by the scripts. They foreground the problems of female friendship, (38) and bitchy vituperation, (39) and structurally endorse Mason's gallows recommendation, "Never trust a woman". Hester is ritually excised because, as the script suggests, "in her black dress ... she does look very like a witch". The cinematic Barbara wants "a house - children - all the things I never thought would matter", as a restitution for wanting "a hundred mouths". The most significant alteration Arliss makes to *The Wicked Lady* is the revenge, by rape, of the returned Jackson. He is first glimpsed, mouthless, in a mirror and the sado-masochistic nature of their exchanges is absent from the book. (40) The scripts suggest that females are an unfathomable, almost pathological mystery. (41)

Gainsborough screen writers, then, exhibit different structures of feeling and class 'value' from the novels, and employ language stripped of literary resonance. They feature a 'proletarian' Byronic hero; the film Manderstoke and Jackson are clear 'borrowing' from Heathcliff. Moreover they accord more utterance to lower class characters. Belinda in the novel *Jassy* is a mute, to whom the film grants speech, and the Toby role in *The Man in Grey* is similarly transformed. Some attention to the production context and institutions of screenwriting may partially account for these phenomena.

R.J. Minney was largely instrumental in choosing the novels for dramatisation. (42) He defined popular fiction as melodrama, "with blood and thunder" (43) not without artistic merit but irrelevant to it; he believed in a structurally conservative Ur-text. (44) Plot simplification was necessary for audience pleasure, and he rejected the ideas of 'quality' critics. (45) "A full-blooded story such as may be found in the pages of the Bible" (46) could be held in common in written and cinematic fictions, but an efficacious adaptation had to remove power from the novelist.

Accordingly, Minney attempted to place more power with the script 'author' by suggesting that he should also direct. (47) This was explicitly upheld by Crabtree, (48) and more crucially by Arliss who both scripted and directed two of the films. (49) Rank is reported to have been sympathetic to such claims. (50) Although Maurice Ostrer had demanded a "cast-iron script" before shooting, (51) studio practice was to implement last-minute alterations according to screenwriters' interpretations of the rushes. (52) Gainsborough screenwriters had remarkably advantageous notice arrangments, (53) and novelists were never in evidence on set. (54) The studio staff were in agreement with the notion of scriptwriter-as-author, and deliberately avoided reading the novels: "we thought that it didn't do to get too involved like that, because you put all sorts of emotions into it, and the script would change a relationship, or chop things, and then you'd be upset." (55) The excision of the novelists permitted the scripts to be more directly tailored for a different class of consumption. It is of interest that the only script problems in our cycle were on the post-Box *Jassy*. Saloman's case for credit (comprising 47 letters) was submitted for arbitration to the Screenwriters Association in 1946, but Box's dismissal of him was upheld. (56)

The only extant authorship theory advanced by a Gainsborough scriptwriter, Margaret Kennedy, shows a marked advance on earlier professional definitions. (57) Kennedy's ideal project is a film of *The Eve of St. Agnes*; (58) she discourages the novelist from adapting his own text, as he will "break his heart" on realising "how anomalous his position is, and how small the chance that any fragment of his ideas will find its way to the screen". (59) The 'illiteracy' of the screen audience produces only three alternatives; to 'adapt a second-rate book towards which one has no conscience', (60) to become an 'author-cutter' with 'directional power', (61) or to develop the 'vacant and pensive' writing mood in the director. (62)

It is a familiar argument; that mass culture has lamentably replaced a high one of literary value, and that the artist either totally concedes, hack-like, or fights for total control. Either way the original novelist is excluded from the act of mediation. By 1951 these views were accepted by such critics as C.A. Lejeune. (63)

The scriptwriters at Gainsborough were highly specialised (64) and had sufficient initiative to found, in March 1937, the Screenwriters Association. (65) Kennedy, Pertwee, Gilliatt, Minney, Launder and Arliss were founding members, and continuity existed through until the mid-1940's, with Minney taking a major role. (66) The SWA, in a quasi-autonomous relationship to the Society of Authors, insisted that novelists sell texts for films outright. An unpublished letter from Launder ingenuously suggested that "The committee invariably elects to membership novelists of repute who have sold the film rights of their work", (67) (my underlining); but very vew novelists indeed were registered, apart from Priestley and Cronin. The Association fought for higher basic payments, for the creation of a jointly-owned 'story fund', (68) for the freedom of radio film-critics, (69) and for free collective bargaining for a loose affiliation of individuals. Two events suggest that its institutional definitions had become widely acceptable; its contraction as a 'voluntary' workforce for the M.o.I. (70) and the acceptance by the Inland Revenue of its terms of reference: "From what Mr. Williams and Mr. Minney have said, I understand that nearly all screenwriters can be said to exercise a profession, and if they take contracts from time to time, they do so incidentally in the cause of that profession, and not in the intention of obtaining a post and staying in it." (71)

Two disputes further clarify the SWA's definition of authorship as non-industrial and 'free'. As early as 1943 the ACT had claimed to be the negotiating body; (72) the SWA membership firmly rejected its claims, (73) and Launder noted that "screen-writers are neither reactionary conservatives nor reactionary unionists, but just simple, progressive, benevolent anarchists." (74) By 1947 the SWA felt empowered to act as a trade union, and Cripps reprimanded the ACT for its intransigence. (75) G.D.H. Cole added his support to the SWA's claims for autonomy: "I think the screenwriters must act with authors and other creative artists and must not let themselves be swallowed up." (76) So notions of writerly creativity and craftsmanship were indubitably linked to a loose guild structure and the institutional power of the SWA was able to defeat the powerful, Rank-backed 'Scenario Institute Ltd.' of del Guidice. Del Guidice suggested that Minney underestimated the audience, (77) and attempted to establish a rival institution more concerned with 'culture' and 'quality'; his and Rank's Institute would be a quasi-university, with 'an intellectual and artistic atmosphere' (78) to raise cultural standards. The SWA took particular offence at the notion that 'this is a private commercial venture although not really a speculative one'; (79) del Guidice's proposal to buy up film rights from books before publication (80) was rejected on the grounds of the power this would place in the hands of monopoly capital. The campaign launched by the SWA routed the Institute; even Balcon saw it would produce a 'corner' of story wealth. (81) Thus the SWA rejected monopolism and 'trade' arrangements; (82) it wished screen authors to be 'free' to negotiate a percentage rate for resale of their own work. (83)

Gainsborough screenwriters, then, had a highly developed degree of awareness of their own institutional, material and industrial constraints; they fought to place themselves in a different market relationship from the popular novelists. The latter had arrived, either by private research or individual instinct, at market dominance; Gainsborough screenwriters desired instead a loosely-strung, 'free', corporate authorship. Pettybourgeois in origin and outlook, they paid more explicit attention to questions of mass audience and artistic control than the novelists did. Because of their rejection of the mass-culture manufactory within which they worked, Gainsborough screenwriters were unable to reproduce the structures of social feeling of the novels. In the latter, ramshackle though they were in cultural mediation, women, gypsies, the aristocracy are dynamically poised in a sophisticated balance, and offer a pleasingly 'ambiguous' choice to the audience, whose class anxieties they may then defuse. In the scripts, on the other hand, these groups are impelled head-long into a dark chasm where only fear and excess reside. The audience is granted little creativity by the scripts, which arguably create, rather than defuse, class anxiety.

The vision of history offered by the scripts is frequently undercut or contradicted by other visual structures in the films such as costume or Art Direction. Clearly, the audience for these films could decode their complex and sometimes inconsistent messages, and could, indeed, proficiently 'read' the narrative inscribed into the costumes and the sets, as well as receive the verbal language of the script. (84) This latter was provided by a group of intellectuals anxious to separate themselves off as a kind of 'aristocracy of labour' from the rest of the workforce. *En route* to achieving this, they shifted the aristocracy and other marginal groups further away from an audience which was predominantly working-class, thus profoundly affecting the texts' ideological function.

If we analyse the composition of the audience for these films, we see that the mass audience of the 40's tended to be young, semi-skilled and urban, though clearly the exclusion of servicemen from wartime surveys has an unbalancing effect. (85) It is clear that working-class preference was not for realism; technical school girls refer much less frequently to 'realism' as a criterion than do other, higher, educational groups. (86) A very high proportion of cinema enthusiasts were women mainly from the semi-skilled areas of the working-class. (87) There was, predictably, an appreciable gender difference in film taste in the period. One of the Mass Observation directives for November 1943 was 'what films have you liked during the past year? Please list in order of liking'. The question was not a 'priority' one, and it was the last of six, and this must be taken into account; but it is notable that relatively speaking, far fewer men than women liked *The Man in Grey*, and for reasons of 'good taste', 'real history', and nostalgia for times of pleasant sexual inequality. (88) The women in this survey preferred costume melodrama for reasons of star identification and visual pleasure. (89) The class origins of the female audience are clearer in Mayer's survey. A hairdresser reconstructs herself after viewing, as 'the lovely heroine in a beautiful blue crinoline with a feather in her hair'. (90) Female masochism clearly found ample material in these films; a typist notes Mason's similarlity to Rhett Butler, remarking 'I simply revel in bold, bad men'. (91) (The boldness and 'badness' having been increased by the scriptwriters.)

Of paramount importance is the 'dream' sequence in Mayer's 1946 book. The women are asked to describe any dreams produced by the viewing of films, and they select from the costume melodramas resonant images which are potent cultural symbols: the mirror and the whip. A typist draws the 'seven moons' sign on the mirror without knowing what it means, but 'nothing further from the narrative'; (92) a clerk saw 'the terrifying look on James Mason's face as he beat Hester to death', (93) (another scriptwriting 'addition' to the novel). The dream-work of these respondants selects out symbols of self-identification and male dominance. What is seen in the mirror is not understood. What is unlike the self is predatory. Clearly the films tended to aid a kind of ritual expression and excision of female fears. The role played by the female scriptwriters in this process (as opposed to the males) can only be a question of surmise; but the films provided a 'model' for the body language of working-class schoolgirls, (94) and made them 'speechless with longing'. (95) There was a clear collusion between the scriptwriters and the studio publicists; the orientation of the scripts towards the female working-class audience is echoed in the publicity material for all these films. The press-book for *Madonna*, for example, attempts to define schizophrenia as a specifically female ailment, suggesting the heading 'SPLIT-MIND DISORDER GIVES IDEA FOR YEAR'S FINEST ROMANCE!' Managers were advised to trade on that great female characteristic, 'curiosity', and suggestions were made as to how the costumes in the film could be given working-class appeal.

I have attempted to show, in a lengthy and perhaps cumbersome way, some determinants on the role of a small group of screenwriters in the 1940's, and have suggested the means by which they catered to, and affected, mass taste by a particular type of cultural mediation. Much remains to be done; but it is precisely in the area of such difficult, contradictory and complex 'evidence' I suggest, that the usefulness of the notion of hegemony can be investigated - at least in the context of a sociology of culture.

FOOTNOTES

All places of publication are London

1. Some of these are published in a very curtailed form in the forthcoming *British Film Institute Dossier on Gainsborough*.

2. In 'History with Frills: the Historical Novel in World War II', in *Red Letters 14*.

3. See *Kineweekly*, 20/12/45, 19/12/46 and *Daily Film Renter*, 29/4/46 and 9/5/46.

4. *The News of the World*, 14/4/46.

5. *The Chronicle*, 19/11/45.

6. See the (undated) review of *The Wicked Lady* from *Reynold's News* in the BFI microfiche collection.

7. A. Wood, *Mr. Rank*, 1952, p.123.

8. R.J. Minney, *Talking of Film*, 1947, p.19.

9. *The Times*, 3/3/49. See Kineweekly 19/4/45 for a cost breakdown of *The Man in Grey* and *The Daily Herald* 2/3/48 for one of *The Bad Lord Byron*.

10. Interview with Mrs. Paddy Porter, continuity girl at Gainsborough, in forthcoming BFI Dossier.

11. Interview with Mr. Maurice Carter, Art Director at Gainsborough, *ibid*.

12. *ibid*.

13. *The Cinema*, 5/1/45. See also *Kineweekly*, 21/3/45. Minney, *op. cit.*, p. 77 concurs with Ostrer's costings.

14. *Kineweekly*, 19/4/45.

15. *ibid*. See also *Kineweekly*, 4/2/43 and 20/12/45..

16. Kineweekly, 19/4/45.

17. *ibid*.

18. *Today's Cinema*, 3/8/45, 14/8/45 and 21/8/45.

19. See interview with Mrs. Porter, *op. cit.*, and with Mr. Bill Slater, sound recordist and dubbing mixer, *op. cit.*

20. Interview with Mr. Denis Mason, boom operator, *op. cit.*

21. Interview with Mrs. Porter, *op. cit.*

22. Interviews with Mrs. Porter, Mr. Mason, Mr. Carter, *op. cit.*

23. Interviews with Mr. Salter and Mr. Mason.

24. Interview with Mr. Mason.

25. *ibid*.

26. *Life and Death of the Wicked Lady Skelton*, by Magdalen King-Hall, 1944, *Madonna of the Seven Moons*, by Marjorie Lawrence, 1931 (repr. 1945) and *Caravan* by Lady E.F. Smith, 1943. Also - *The Man in Grey* by Lady E.F. Smith, 1941, *Jassy* by Norah Lofts, 1944, *Fanny by Gaslight* by Michael Sadleir, 1940.

27. This is more fully argued in *Red Letters 14*.

28. See E. Britton, *Blanche Fury: the Book of the Film*, 1948, and W.P.J. Rodgers, *Bedelia, the Film Edition* (undated).

29. The end of the script has 'thundering hooves' as Barbara's ghost makes its escape.

30. Attention to the last fifteen minutes of *Madonna* will show five minutes of dialogue to ten of highly atmospheric music.

31. Lady E.F. Smith, *Caravan*, 1943, p.202.

32. The film *'Oriana'* also remarks, 'he changed the moment we became married - he became evil'.

33. See the architect in *The Wicked Lady*, the librarian in *The Man in Grey*, the dispossessed worker-aristocrat in *Jassy*. The writer in *Caravan* succeeds to 'gentrification' by marriage.

34. Lady E.F. Smith, *op. cit.*, p.245.

35. 'You'll die for it - in my own time and in my way'. This film was scripted by Leslie Arliss and Margaret Kennedy. Ronald Pertwee scripted *Caravan* and *Madonna*, Doreen Montgomery and Aimee Stuart wrote *Fanny*, and Campbell Christy did *Jassy*. *The Wicked Lady* was scripted by Arliss.

36. M. Lawrence, *The Madonna of the Seven Moons*, 1931, pp.14, 155.

37. *ibid.*, p.131 - 'at last his long-held patience gave way, and he took by force what should only be given in love'.

38. From *The Man in Grey* script in BFI library - 'never make no friends of women'. From the *Madonna* script - 'what have you done with my mother,'.

39. From the *Wicked Lady* script:
a) 'You two have shared so much'.
b) 'I'd rather look worn than dull.'
c) 'And this wedding dress. You might as well wear that while you're at it.'
'Wear that, I wouldn't be buried in it.'

40. From the *Wicked Lady* script:
a) 'I hate you.'
'But I am thrilled by you.'
b) 'I like to drive a hard bargain.'
'So do I.'
c) 'O, Jerry, just one more.'
'I've heard you say that before - under different circumstances!'
Jackson does die on the scaffold in the novel.

41. From *Madonna* script: "The woman's a mystery - she always was." From the *Wicked Lady* script: "I can't think what can have happened to her. She used to be so sweet."

42. See N. Lee, *Log of a Film Director*, 1949, pp.34-35, on *Madonna:* "The experts said there wasn't a film in it. The subject had been rejected so often that it was regarded as voodoo. Minney went quitely to work, wrote his own script, planned the production, costed it, launched it ..."

43. R.J. Minney, *Talking of Films*, 1947, p.4.

44. *ibid.*, p.35.

45. *ibid.*, p.43. Here he rejects documentary as unable to fulfil "the diversional and emotional needs of the audience."

46. *ibid.*, p.4.

47. *ibid.*, pp.70-71.

48. Crabtree directed *Caravan* and *Madonna*. In the *Caravan* material (in BFI Library) he suggests that "it is imperative for a director to be vitally interested in the story."

49. Arliss had been a scenario editor at Gainsborough. [Memo. 15/5/44 from Launder in the Screenwriters Association files at Society of Authors.] Arliss was co-opted to the Executive Committee to discuss credits in 1946, and he and Kennedy were on the Council of the SWA until 1954.

50. See N. Lee, *op. cit.*, p.133. He suggests that Rank permitted six 'author'/directors to operate; Launder, Gilliatt, Arliss, Coward, Ambler and Minney.

51. *Kineweekly*, 19/4/45.

52. Mason interview, Appendix I, p.vi.

53. Unpublished letter from Launder to Society of Authors, 11/11/46 (SOA files). Very highly paid screenwriters could be hired by the week.

54. Mason interview, *op. cit.* The only mention of a novelist's presence anywhere is in the publicity material for *Caravan*.

55. Salter interview, *op. cit.*

56. Unpublished letter from Somerset Maugham to Society of Authors, 29/1/47, and Executive Committee Minutes of the Society, 27/1/47 (SOA files).

57. Such as Ursula Bloom's *ABC of Authorship*, 1938, which is obsessed with presentation (pp.8, 11) and with using the lowest common denominator of discourses.

58. M. Kennedy, *The Mechanical Muse*, 1942, p.39.

59. *ibid.*, p.29.

60. *ibid.* See also p.41: "no script ... can convey ideas to a community which never reads."

61. *ibid.*, p.52.

62. *ibid.*, p.53. In this room the director will "cultivate that inner eye which <u>turns the thing seen into the imagined thing</u> " (my underlining).

63. In *The Observer*, 1/7/51, she notes that "T.E.B. Clarke is the 'author' of *The Lavender Hill Mob* in the way that many more distinguished authors are not, in the sense that he has taken as large a share in the final shaping of the product as the director himself."

64. For example, Val Guest as a 'gag' writer, or Pertwee as a 'period' adapter; he did *Magic Bow* and *The First Gentleman*, as well as *Madonna* and *Caravan*.

65. Lee, *op. cit.*, pp.131, 133.

66. The executive committee of 18/7/44 had Launder, Gilliatt, Minney and Arliss, and Minney was sent on the Association's behalf to conferences at Paris and Madrid.

67. Unpublished letter from Launder to the Society of Authors, 18/7/44 (SOA files).

68. Draft constitution, 11/3/37, resolution 14: "To provide facilities to encourage the register of stories and scenarios which members might consider to their advantage." (in SOA files).

69. Report of the General Meeting of the SWA, 18/7/44 (in SOA files).

70. Unpublished letter from Launder to Secretary of SOA, 5/1/42 (in SOA files): "It is our business to suggest or consider stories and ideas with the object of recommending to the Ministry suitable subjects for propaganda films. We believe the majority of writers will not look upon payment." Note that they produce <u>ideas</u>, not actual treatments.

71. Unpublished letter from Inalnd Revenue to Launder, 12/10/43 (in SOA files).

72. On the basis of a small body of documentary writers within the ACT Launder notes to the Secretary of SOA, in a letter dated 20/5/43: "it would seem to be ridiculous if a small group consisting of documentary writers were to be in such a position as to be able to put through an agreement affecting the conditions under which the writer works in film studios, without the consent of the great majority."

73. See account of a mass SWA meeting, 25/9/46, in SWA files.

74. Unpublished letter from Launder to Screenwriters Guild, June, 1947 (in SWA files).

75. Unpublished letter from Morgan to the Secretary of SOA, 12/10/47: "I hear that the ACT have been rapped over the knuckles by Cripps, and told to interest themselves a little more in production, and a little less in power politics."

76. Unpublished letter from G.D.H. Cole to Morgan, 8/11/47 (SOA files).

77. *Kineweekly*, 1/1/43. See also A. Wood, *op. cit.*, pp.134-7.

78. Unpublished letter from del Guidice to the Secretary of the SOA, 10/12/42, (in SOA files).

79. *ibid.*

80. Unpublished letter from del Guidice to Secretary of SOA, 14/12/42.

81. Rough notes made by Balcon for the private information of Kilham Roberts (of the Society of Authors), undated, but with other material pertaining to del Guidice in SOA files.

82. Undated account (probably 43) of official SWA attitude to the Scenario Institute - probably for press release.

83. Unpublished letter from Launder to Kilham Roberts, 15/4/43, (SOA files).

84. I have described this in 'Costume and Art Direction at Gainsborough - Contradictory Discourses' in the forthcoming BFI dossier on the studio.

85. J.P. Mayer, *British Cinemas and their Audiences*, 1948, pp.148, 252, 255, 257, 262, 271. See also K. Box, *The Cinema and the Public*, 1946, and K. Box, and L. Moss, *War-Time Survey: The Cinema Audience*, 1943.

86. B. Kesterton, *The Social and Emotional Effects of the Recreational Film on Adolescents of 13 and 14 Years of Age in West Bromwich Area*, University of Birmingham Ph.D. thesis, 1948, p.89.

87. See Mayer, *op. cit.*, p.254, and K. Box, and Moss and Box, *op. cit.*

88. See Mass-Observation Directive, November 1943, replies by Bartram, Metcalf and Fisher.

89. *ibid.* See replies by Collins, Flavin, Campion and Clift.

90. Mayer, *op. cit.*, p.22.

91. *ibid.*, p.73.

92. Mayer, *Sociology of Film*, 1946, pp.201-2.

93. *ibid.*, p.213. See also p.217, firewoman's dream.

94. W.D. Wall, and W.A. Simpson, "The Effects of Cinema Attendance on the Behaviour of Adolescents as seen by Contemporaries," *British Journal of Educational Psychology*, 1949.

95. Kesterton, *op. cit.*, p.99.

ORIENTALISM AND ITS PROBLEMS

Dennis Porter

My reading of Edward W. Said's important book, *Orientalism*, (1) has occurred in the context of an inquiry into travel literature and its modes of representation. I come to it preoccupied by such questions as the following: What are some of the principal forms that travel literature has taken? What techniques of reportage and representation does it employ? What happens when a writer encodes atomized features of an alien culture into the linguistic codes and conventional narrative forms of a culture of reference? Does a natural language itself set up subject/object relations that are also power relations? Are we so positioned by a given historical and geopolitical conjuncture that misrepresentation is a structural necessity or is there a place of truth?

From such a reading perspective, *Orientalism* is valuable for a number of reasons. Influenced both by Gramscian thought on hegemonic formations and by that Foucauldian discourse theory which is summed up in the concept of the episteme, Said's book delimits a field of inquiry in the West that it designates 'Orientalism' and defines as a relatively unified discourse that over the centuries has been virtually coterminous with Western consciousness of the East. Said makes it clear that he is concerned with the way in which the so-called Orient, from the Eastern Mediterranean to South East Asia, 'became known in the West as its great complementary opposite since antiquity'(58) . His focus is not therefore on a possible 'correspondance between Orientalism and the Orient, but with the internal consistency of Orientalism and its ideas about the Orient ...'(5) . Furthermore, Orientalism is variously defined as 'a Western style for dominating, restructuring, and having authority over the Orient'(3) , as a hegemonic Western discourse dependent on 'a distribution of geopolitical awareness into aesthetic, scholarly, historical, and philosophical texts'(120) . Said's book has then the character of a Nietzschean genealogy which delimits a given field of inquiry in order to expose the multiple mystified relations between knowledge and power, culture and politics.

In a discussion of the methodological problems raised by his study, Said notes that he is not interested in 'a coarse polemic' nor a detailed and atomistic 'series of analyses', neither with 'the general groups of ideas overriding the mass of material' nor 'the much more varied work produced by almost uncountable   individual writers'(8)   In spite of the fact that he will focus on 'the British, French and American experience of the Orient taken as a unit'(16) , it is his intention to take account of 'individuality' as well as of the 'general and hegemonic context'(9) . Yet the methodological problems raised by Said's work are formidable and they appear in a particularly crucial form almost from the beginning.

From his introduction on, Said vacillates over the opposition between truth and ideology. On the one hand, he reaches the conclusion that there is no distinction between pure and political knowledge. (2) He even claims that ' ... all cultures impose corrections upon raw reality, changing it from free-floating objects into units of knowledge'(67) . On the other hand, in a discussion of representation he seems to imply, if only negatively, that a form of truth is obtainable; he comments for example that ' ... what is commonly circulated is not truth but representations' (21) , that there is perhaps a 'real' and consequently knowable Orient. It is on account of hegemonic discourse, therefore, that 'Truth ... becomes a function of learned judgement, not of the material itself ...' (67) .

Whereas the second set of propositions implies the existence of a place of truth, of the possibility of emergence from hegemonic discourse into a beyond of true knowledge, the first set denies the idea of any knowledge pure of political positioning. The contradiction is never fully resolved in Said's book in part because he deals in such problematic concepts as 'raw reality' and 'the material itself' without reference to an epistemology that legitimates them. Moreover, the important consequence from the point of view of this paper is that if one attempts to discover whether alternatives to Orientalism are possible, whether a knowledge as opposed to an ideology of the Orient can exist, Said is of no help in spite of the acknowledgement that such alternatives are a pressing need. He writes for example, 'Perhaps the most important task of all would be to undertake studies in contemporary alternatives to Orientalism, to ask how one can study other cultures and peoples from a libertarian, or a nonrepressive and nonmanipulative perspective'(24) .

If the first set of propositions, concerning the lack of distinction between pure and political knowledge, is true, then Orientalism in one form or another is not only what we have but all we can ever have. (3) If, on the other hand, as Said sometimes implies, truth in representation may be achieved, how can it be justified on the basis of a radical discourse theory which presupposes the impossibility of stepping outside of a given discursive formation by an act of will or consciousness? That this fundamental contradiction goes unresolved in Said's book is, I believe, due to the incomparability of the thought of Said's two acknowledged *maîtres*, Foucault and Gramsci, of discourse theory and hegemonic theory. (4)

On the one hand, in spite of the systematic periodization in which Foucault engages in such early works as *Madness and Civilization* and *The Order of Things* - one remembers the tripartite schema of a pre-classical, a classical, and a modern age - the emergence of such discourses is historically grounded in relatively perfunctory ways. Such discourses are posited as synchronic structures or period problematics that are embodied concurrently in verbal, social, and material formations. But the whole question of process, of passage from one such problematic to the next, is left in abeyance. The concept of hegemony, on the other hand, derives precisely from Gramsci's effort to think the problem of the reproduction, by consent and not by force, of the existing power relations of bourgeois society as process. Because it is grounded in consciously interventionist thought, hegemony is able to posit such reproduction by consent as the result of ideological representation and of institutional manipulation within different social formations. Commenting on hegemony in *Marxism and Literature*, (5) Raymond Williams defined it as a form of practical consciousness that concerns not only 'the articulate upper levels of ideology' but also 'a whole body of practices and expectations, over the whole of our living: our senses and assignments of energy, our shaping perceptions of ourselves and our world'(110). In the context of this paper, however, the most important feature of hegemony is that it always implies historical process. In Williams' words again: 'It has continually to be renewed, recreated, defended, and altered, challenged by pressures not at all its own'(112) . Such a sense of hegemony as process in concrete historical conjunctures, as an evolving sphere of superstructural conflict in which power relations are continally reasserted, challenged, modified, is absent from Said's book.

The problem is further compounded because unlike Foucault, who posits not a continuous discourse over time but epistemological breaks between different periods, Said asserts the unified character of Western discourse on the Orient over some two millennia, a unity derived from a common and continuing experience of fascination with and threat from the East, of its irreducible otherness. He is thus led to claim a continuity of representation between the Greece of Alexander the Great and the United States of President Jimmy Carter, a claim that seems to make nonsense of history at the same time as it invokes it with reference to imperial power/knowledge. Accordingly, one important reason why Said apparently cannot suggest the form alternatives to Orientalism might take in the present is that his use of discourse theory prevents him from seeing any evidence of such alternatives in the past. In fact, because he does not reflect on the significance of hegemony as process, he ignores in both Western scholarly and creative writing all manifestations of counter-hegemonic thought. Because Said is understandably eager to confront Western hegemonic discourse head on, he ignores Raymond Williams' warning that the reality of cultural process must always include 'the efforts and contributions of those who are in one way or another outside or at the edge of specific hegemony'(113) . The consequence is serious. The failure to take account of such efforts and contributions not only opens Said to the charge of promoting Occidentalism, it also contributes to the perpetuation of that Orientalist thought he set out to demystify in the first place. Thus although Said claims that what interests him as a scholar is the detail and that he intends to be attentive to individual voices, virtually no counter-hegemonic voices are heard. Even when he praises an occasional scholar for a rare objectivity, he does not show how within the given dominant hegemonic formation such an alternative discourse was able to emerge.

If one is attentive to the crucial contradiction that *Orientalism* embodies and to its failure to reflect on hegemony as process, then it is possible to see at least three kinds of alternatives to orientalist discourse. First, the very heterogeneity of the corpus of texts among which Said discovers hegemonic unity raises the question of the specificity of the literary instance within the superstructure. Yet no consideration is given to the possibility that literary works as such have a capacity for internal ideological distanciation that is usually absent from political tracts or statesmen's memoirs. Second, Said does not seem to envisage the possibility that more directly counter-hegemonic writings or an alternative canon may exist within the Western tradition. Third, the feasibility of a textual dialogue between Western and non-Western cultures needs to be considered, a dialogue that would cause subject/object relations to alternate, so that we might read ourselves as the others of our others and replace the notion of a place of truth with that of a knowledge which is always relative and provisional. At this stage in my thinking about travel literature and the methodological questions raised by *Orientalism*, I have only attempted to reflect on the first of the alternatives mentioned, namely the possibility of ideological distanciation within works of the Western literary canon and I shall limit myself to that in what follows.

Foucauldian discourse theory does not raise the possibility of the relative autonomy of aesthetic production. Unlike Althusserian thought, it has nothing to say on the question of the specificity of the literary instance or on the overdetermination of literary artifacts. Both of these concepts have perhaps a distinctly old-fashioned sound for Essex conferees but I do not believe their explanatory power has been exhausted yet. In any case, in establishing the unity and continuity of Western discourse on the Orient, Said finds grist for his mill in a wide variety of written documents, from records of parliamentary debates and official reports to the memoirs of imperial pro-consuls, scholars' exhaustive tomes, travellers' tales, fiction and poetry. Yet although he is himself a literary scholar and critic, he adopts Foucault's strategy of making no qualitative distinctions between a variety of texts produced under a variety of historical conjunctures for a wide variety of audiences. (6) Such an approach has its usefulness and it is clearly important not to practice afresh that form of mystification which has traditionally distinguished among all written products a category of the literary and has then gone on to separate it from all other forms of textual production. If I use literary here, therefore, it is only to make a qualitative distinction between texts that are characterized by a self-interrogating density of verbal texture and those that offer no internal resistance to the ideologies they reproduce. I take the literary instance to signify all texts - traditionally literary, philosophical, historical, etc. - which are of sufficient complexity to throw ideological practices into relief and raise questions about their own fictionalizing processes. Such an approach will, I hope, show that there already exists within Orientalism itself alternative and only partially silenced counter-hegemonic voices that have expressed themselves differently at different historical moments.

The case is best made by means of specific examples and I have chosen for this brief demonstration two works from the hybrid products of travel literature, two works that were written almost nine hundred years apart, yet that from Said's point of view belong to a single Western tradition of discourse. The first is the thirteenth century *Travels* of Marco Polo, a work that antedates the period of European exploration and colonial expansion which began with the Renaissance and continued into the early decades of our own century. The second is T.E. Lawrence's *Seven Pillars of Wisdom*, a work that is usually read as an arch-imperialist text written at a time when Western power and influence were still at their height. Said refers to both works. He mentions Marco Polo's *Travels* only once in order to situate the work in that Western tradition which goes back to Herodotus and Alexander the Great, and which visited, conquered and subdivided the Orient, breaking it down into the Near East or Levant and the Far East. T.E. Lawrence and his story of the Arab revolt are briefly referred to on a number of occasions but there is no extended discussion of Lawrence's work. In the remainder of this talk I will focus on each of these works in turn.

Marco Polo's *Travels* is cited as one example among many of what Said refers to as 'a typical number of encapsulations; the journey, the history, the fable, the stereotype, the polemical confrontation. These are the lenses through which the Orient is experienced, and they shape the language, perception, and form of the encounter between East and West (59)'. Yet what does such a 'typical encapsulation' amount to in the case of Marco Polo? Is it even possible that such a complexly overdetermined work as this late medieval travel journal could constitute itself as a unified and homogeneous discourse? Produced by a member of the mid-thirteenth century Venetian merchant class in collaboration with a ghost writer, Rustichello of Pisa, who specialized in chivalric romances, and written not in Italian but in the language most commonly used for such romances, Old French, Marco Polo's *Travels* is a work striking for the heterogeneity of its authorship, materials, motifs, and point of view.

Apparently reconstructed from Marco Polo's travel notes, the work presents itself as the account of a marvellous journey but it has little of the unified aesthetic effect of *The Odyssey* or of a romance by Chrétien de Troyes. Its episodes are of far greater significance than its whole. Its focus is not inward but outward; it records not the experiences and trials of a hero in a world subject to magic transformations, but the sights and places, people and objects, that cross the traveller's path as he moves through geographical space. The epic topoi of councils of war and battle, and the evocation of court life and of the marvellous associated with romance are in the end less significant than the descriptions of topography, farming, towns, industry, customs and manners. In the words of the translator of the Penguin edition, 'a stock formula of knight errantry is introduced into the report of a trade mission'(117) . (7)

What is most surprising in a scholar of Said's sophistication is the swiftness with which he categorizes such a work without reference to its historical moment. Yet the historical conjuncture of thirteenth century Venice is such that the representation produced by one of its citizens of a journey through the Middle and Far East raises questions that must give pause. The journey itself was only possible at that time as a result, first, of the crusades which reestablished a foothold for European power on the Western perimeter of the Near East and, second, of the recently completed Mogul conquest of vast territories previously dominated by Moslem armies. The sea and land routes that had long been barred to European trade with the East were once again open. Further, the specific subject of the travels was himself a member of the merchant class of a commercial and trading republic; the object was a multiplicity of peoples and cultures scattered across Asia and the Near East, standing in a complex of politically hegemonic relationships to each other and subordinated above all to Mogul overlordship. In Marco Polo's telling the latter appears most spectacularly in the China of Kubilai Khan, that previously legendary land of Cathay in which the warrior culture of the Moguls dominated and was in part assimilated by the higher culture of medieval China itself.

There is no doubt that *The Travels* contain passages and judgements that echo the Western hegemonic discourse as defined by Said. Tropes that have Oriental treachery, idolatry, opulence, and cruelty as signifieds frequently recur. 'The Saracens of Tabriz', notes the authors, 'are wicked and treacherous. The law which their prophet Mohamed has given them lays down that any harm they may do to one who does not accept their law, and any proportion of his goods, is no sin at all'(57) Later on, the inhabitants of Belor are said to live 'very high up in the mountains. They are idolators and savages, living entirely by the chase and dressed in the skin of beasts. They are out and out bad'(80) . Yet it is important to realize that the judgments passed here are not simply those of any European on any 'Oriental'. They are those of a Christian for the religious enemy and of a merchant used to trading in luxury commodities for a community of hunters with none of the crafts and possessions he associates with higher civilizations.

But perhaps one of the most remarkable features of the work is the way in which a new sense of geographical space comes to emerge. Its representations of the vast territory extending from the Eastern shores of the Mediterranean into China and India suggest not an undifferentiated monolith but a diverse and fragmented object. It may be 'imaginative geography', it may use criteria for the establishment of truth that have ceased to be current in the West since the seventeenth century, it may mix notations from life with hearsay and legend, it nevertheless enlarges the West's sense of the scale and variety of the East. Taken as a whole *The Travels* suggest how under certain conditions newly observed phenomena may be incorporated into a given mode of literary production. A kind of *pensée sauvage* is involved that combines old literary forms with a new subject matter and a different set of class interests. The dominant chivalric and Christian ideology of aristocratic romance is largely submerged here beneath the concerns of a trading class. Marco Polo's preoccupation with aspects of the material life of the regions he passes through has something in common with the passion displayed in romance for the marvellous in the form of rare and precious commodities, from gold and silver to gems, jewelry, silk, and finely wrought objects in general. In Marco Polo's case, however, such a passion is supplemented by a far more down to earth interest in natural environment and natural resources, animal life, food production, manufacturing and commodity production, military power and weaponry, shelter and dress, not to speak of more abstract topics such as religious belief, political and social organization, and moral conduct. The fabulous and demonic East of the early medieval Christian tradition is in part demystified to the extent that the forces and raw materials of production are intermittently focussed on along with the relations of production. The romance tradition may have supplied the conventions that enabled the authors to represent the court of Kubilai Khan to some extent as if it were King Arthur's legendary court. Yet the systematic notations on the power of the Great Khan and the institutional mechanisms employed to maintain it amount to a kind of historical reportage that breaks through the forms of the controlling discourse. Included are descriptions of the highly rational organization, equipment, and vast size of the standing armies, the architecture of the fortified palaces, the system of vassalage, the raising of taxes as well as of armies, and the severity with which rebellion is put down.

At the same time in the image projected of the Kubilai Khan's court and empire, Oriental otherness is mediated by an idealizing tendency that assimilates it to a Western tradition of wise kingship whose legendary exempla were King Arthur and Charlemagne. Most striking is the representation of the Mogul Emperor's court as not only a place of order and tranquility, grandeur and splendor, but also of respect for civilized values, religious tolerance, and openness to commerce of all kinds with the outside world. When compared with the representation of Eastern peoples in such canonical epic works as the eleventh century Northern European *Chanson de Roland* or the twelfth century Spanish *Poema de mio Cid*, Marco Polo's *Travels* embody a new spirit of tolerance that is bound up with a more flexible because less consecrated literary genre and with the interests of a trading republic. In the epic tradition the heroic cult of the Christian warrior and his aristocratic code of honor is set off against the barbarism of the religious enemy, the Saracen. Marco Polo breaks out of the theocratic and militaristic mold of thought that informs medieval epic literature in order to discover for the West a non-Moslem East that is astonishing by its scale, diversity, wealth and particularity.

The Travels certainly involves a preliminary mapping, a fixing of settlements and tracing of routes, that may be regarded as a form of preliminary reconnoitring on behalf of those Western trading interests, missionaries and diplomatic envoys that would ultimately make possible the forms of domination associated in our time with colonial and neo-colonial control. In that sense Said is obviously right; knowledge is always power, whether or not it is actualized over geographical space or remains merely potential. But in the era before European ascendancy the assumption of European superiority is not automatic even where the form of literary representation involved is that of European subject to Eastern object, of observer to observed. In the late thirteenth century, at a time when the Mogul conquest was still comparatively recent, it was the European who was in awe of Eastern power and Eastern armies and not vice versa. And the attitude of respect was undoubtedly reinforced in Marco Polo's case because during his long years of residence in the East his status as merchant seems to have been conflated with that of a courtier at the court of the Great Khan.

As a result of such a conjuncture, the most characteristic passages of *The Travels* are those in which the authors summarize in a dozen lines or less the noteworthy features of a town or region that Marco Polo passed through. The description of Kerman is typical:

> Kerman is a kingdom on the edge of Persia. It used to be governed by an hereditary ruler; but, since the Tartars conquered it, the lordship no longer goes by inheritance, but the Tartar suzerain grants it as his own pleasure. In this kingdom originate the stones called turquoises; they are found in great abundance in the mountains, where they are dug out of the rocks. There are also veins producing steel and *ondianique* in great plenty. The inhabitants excel in the manufacture of all the equipment of a mounted warrior - bridles, saddles, spurs, swords, bows, quivers, and every sort of armour according to local usage. The gentle women and their daughters are adepts with the needle, embroidering silk of all colours with beasts and birds and many other figures. They embroider the curtains of the nobles and great men so well and so richly that they are a delight to the eye. And they are no less skilful at working counter-panes, cushions, and pillows.(62)

The passage is characteristic in a number of ways. Its straightforward and apparently ahistorical notations contain, in fact, a variety of references to a specific historical moment and mode of production. It refers directly to a geographical location and the political circumstance of Mogul overlordship that dated from roughly the mid-thirteenth century. It also focuses directly on the region's sources of wealth in precious stones and mineral deposits before describing the finished craft products in which it specialized. Kerman is considered noteworthy because it functioned both as a centre for the thirteenth century, Middle Eastern, small arms industry and as a place where fine silk embroidery was produced for the luxury trade by means of a cottage industry dependent on the labor of noble women. What Marco Polo records is the product. The work and the workers are almost invariably ignored except where, as here, it is deemed noteworthy because the workforce of embroiderers is composed of noble women. The process and means of production most often go unobserved.

Although the point is not made explicitly, it is clear that the significance of the craft products involved had become central to the economy of the whole Near and Far East during the period of Mogul domination. The maintenance and equipping of huge standing armies, whose superiority was founded on the mobility and fire-power of massed cavalry armed with crossbows, was crucial not only to the consolidation of Mogul power but also the production and circulation of wealth throughout the Mogul empire. At the same time a rich and powerful warrior aristocracy whose taste had been refined by contact with older civilizations provided an important stimulant to trade in luxury commodities throughout that empire and beyond. Thus in its own understated way this short passage - and the complete work is composed of hundreds of relatively similar passages - draws attention to the fact of conquest and political power, to the repressive apparatus that achieves and maintains it, to social relations, and to the economic base, including modes of production and exchange.

The important general point about travel literature, which *The Travels* confirms, is that travel is undertaken for a great variety of purposes and the specific purpose involved in a given case is always to a greater or lesser degree a determinant of what is noted or considered noteworthy. Consequently, the attention paid by a writer in a travel book is always ideological but rarely ideologically identical from work to work. A traveler always comes from somewhere - from a country, language community, class - and typically writes the record of his journey for a particular public in the land from which he came. In one sense, therefore, it is almost an advantage for a modern reader to have little information on Marco Polo the historical individual. In the absence of a biography it is possible to concentrate more easily on *The Travels* as a collective seeing. Insofar as one can refer to Marco Polo's eyes at all, they can the more easily be understood as the eyes of a subject constituted by the particular place he occupied in an historically given social formation. The seeing done in *The Travels* is the seeing of the merchant class of the Northern Italian manufacturing and commercial republic of Venice, a trading and port city so placed at the head of the Adriatic as to be within easy reach of Northern and Western Europe and open to the East across the Mediterranean. Finally, however, such seeing is always in the end mediated by the forms of literary representation available at a particular time and those in the case of *The Travels* were most prominently the romance, the journey, the chronicle, and the fable. At the same time the wealth of details of Marco Polo's book also call up a forgotten literature that has not survived except perhaps in libraries and museum archives, that is to say a literature of informal representation and clerkly record-keeping such as one might find in ambassadors' or merchants' letters, in the descriptions of business transactions and of possibilities for trading ventures.

The question raised by *The Travels* is then, can one ever speak of a unified Western discourse even at a specific historical moment let alone across centuries of historical change? At the very least shouldn't one speak of a variety of national and class discourses that give rise to all manner of overdetermined cultural products? In short, isn't discourse theory in its pure form subject to the charge of essentialism and of being unsusceptible to historical grounding? Don't Marco Polo's *Travels* suggest that if one is looking for alternatives to Orientalism, they are already here from the beginning in the contradictory accounts of the various Easts that are embodied in the variety of literary texts centered in a variety of class discourses and the literary genres through which they achieved canonical expression, from the aristocratic *chansons de gestes* of the eleventh century down to the chronicle cum romance of a Venetian merchant adventurer?

Equally as much as Marco Polo's thirteenth century work, T.E. Lawrence's *Seven Pillars of Wisdom* can only properly be read as a complexly determined cultural product of the early twentieth century. This modern work of close to seven hundred pages is characterized by a heterogeneity and fragmentariness comparable to its medieval predecessor. It suggests once again that the kind of 'typical encapsulations' to which Said refers are often, in fact, fields of ideological forces in a state of tension. The form of a journey that they typically take may begin with a departure and end with a return but such symbolic closure does not reduce the contradictory energies that traverse the work the reader reads. Lawrence's account of the Arab revolt and his part in it contains innumerable anecdotes, and events, descriptions of place and people, evocations of mood and attitude. His text is cross-hatched with historical, political, socio-economic, and psychological determinations that once again make the whole concept of Orientalism appear to be a counter-mystification.

The reasons why *The Seven Pillars of Wisdom* is resented not only by Arabs but by all those whose sensibilities have been heightened to racial doctrines by twentieth century history is obvious enough. Because it tells the story of the Arab nationalist revolt against the Ottoman Empire from the point of view of a British army officer, it suggests that the prime mover in the cause of Arab unity and its leading military strategist was an Englishman. It promotes the myth that a white European male in a position of leadership is an essential ingredient if colored peoples are to pursue a national goal and be an effective fighting force. In other words, *Seven Pillars*, like Marco Polo's *Travels*, lends itself to a reading that relates it directly to the tradition of hegemonic Western discourse which Said has dubbed Orientalism. And there are, in fact, a great many passages that would support such a reading. The opening chapters in particular may serve to remind us that before he was commissioned as a liaison officer to Arabia, Lawrence had some experience as an 'Arabist' and had worked for two years as an archaeologist in Syria and Mesopotamia. It is no accident, therefore, if the authoritative voice which sketches in the history of the Middle East up to the outbreak of the first World War and comments on the racial and cultural characteristics of the peoples involved is the voice of Orientalist discourse as described by Said. Such a tradition allows Lawrence to refer unequivocally to the 'Semitic consciousness' and to assert the existence of an essence possessed in common by all Semites. In Lawrence's lexicon, it should be noted that Semite is virtually synonymous with Arab although it also includes Jews. Typically, Lawrence's assertions take the form of a proper noun or third person pronoun linked by the usually plural copula 'are' to an adjective or adjectival phrase. Sentences such as the following are typical: 'Semites had no half-tones in their register of vision. They were a people of primary colours, or rather of black or white, who saw the world always in contour. They were a dogmatic people, despising doubt, our modern crown of thorns ... They were a limited, narrow-minded people, whose inert intellects lay fallow in incurious resignation'(36) . (8) At such moments Lawrence shows no critical awareness of that nineteenth century European discourse on race in general that is speaking through him, a discourse that transmitted the doctrine of national characteristics and fixed ethnic identities, of essences transmitted that were enabling or disabling for individual members of a given race. It is such a received wisdom that allows him to dismiss the Syrians as 'an ape-like people having much of the Japanese quickness but shallow'(45) .

Seven Pillars of Wisdom is then an extreme case, a work apparently written from a position of privilege and authority - the privilege of race, class, and gender - within the Western hegemonic world order. If such a work can be re-read, shown to be fissured with doubt and contradiction, it will confirm how under certain conditions Orientalist discourse far from being monolithic allows counter-hegemonic voices to be heard within it. If it is true that a given hegemonic order is reproduced in part through the mechanism of exposing succeeding generations to the literary canon, a reading that uncovers doubt and contradiction within a canonical work obviously raises the possibility of counter-hegemonic energies. In the case of *The Seven Pillars*, the reason why such a struggle can occur is that for a complex set of social and psychological causes, a particular background and training are brought into conflict with experience by a particular insertion into geopolitical events. And it is within the space of the text that a literary sensibility such as Lawrence's transcribes the set of oppositions involved. Thus although the reader is frequently treated to passages of received Western wisdom such as those quoted above, such passages alternate with others in which Lawrence allows his own consciousness of contradiction to surface. At the same time he also often becomes so absorbed by the aesthetic problems posed by representation and by the play of works on the page that new possibilities emerge unbidden from their combinations. As a result, Western ideological representation may be perceived by an appropriately positioned reader to be both asserted and put into question. In the few minutes remaining I will suggest how this occurs.

The most obvious quality of *The Seven Pillars of Wisdom*, like that of *The Travels*, is its generic heterogeneity. It combines the elements of a campaign diary, an autobiographical memoir, a travel book, a history, and a romance with those of a modern epic in prose whose central subject is men at war in all their horror and heroism. Yet it is this heterogeneity that accounts for the work's strength. Because it follows no single model but shifts often within a single chapter from an historical and political text to autobiography and epic, there arise textual dissonances that constitute a challenge to Western hegemonic thought at a time when the narrator was an officer in the major enforcing apparatus of such thought, the British army. This challenge occurs at a number of levels and is best explained as a dual overdetermination, that of an author as well as of a text.

To begin with, it is obvious that Lawrence himself was no political *ingénu*, no Beau Geste. The politics of the Arab revolt are, in fact, right up front in the work's Introduction and opening chapters. Lawrence makes it very clear that the Arab war against domination by the Ottoman Empire was treated by the Western allies and by Germany as an extension of the European war into the Middle East. The Anglo-French purpose was to defeat Germany's allies, the Turks, in order to maintain their influence over the area and to keep open their strategic links with the Far East through the Suez canal. To this end, as Lawrence shows, elements in the British government and military establishment saw the usefulness of making common cause with the Arabs in a campaign against Turkey. Inserted into such a military and geopolitical conjuncture by historical forces beyond his control, Lawrence asserts how from the beginning his loyalties were divided. Insofar as a war between imperialist powers was in this case also an anticolonialist struggle of liberation, the war itself was subject to a double determination that Lawrence was forced to live. As an officer in the British army, he was committed to pursuing the war aims and colonial policies of the government he served. As companion in arms of the Arabs, he believed himself morally committed to the cause of Arab national independence. Thus Lawrence's Introduction, which situates its writer in the post-war peace conference at Versailles, is also his epilogue: it tells of the betrayal of Arab hopes to which Lawrence himself was a reluctant party - 'the only thing remaining was to refuse rewards for being a successful trickster'(24) .

The complexity of the narrator's persona, his aspirations and self-doubt, his sense of estrangement from his own culture, the sympathy for and distance from the Arab culture he shared for roughly two years, are part of the story Lawrence tells. What he does not tell, at least not directly, is the contradictions he was forced to live at other levels.

Lawrence was constituted as a subject by a set of ideological formations and structures which are familiar and include an upper-middle-class family background, the Church of England, the public school, an Oxford college, a professorial mentor who was both an Arabist and a recruiter for the British intelligence service, a British archaelogical expedition to the Near East, and the British army itself. Thus Lawrence was first formed by a number of state ideological apparatuses, including finally that British archaelogical school which took the ancient Near East as its province and object of knowledge, and transferred, as a consequence of the first World War, to serve in the army that helped keep the Middle East open to European scholarly penetration and intellectual control. The continuity between the two state apparatuses confirms, of course, Said's ideas on power/knowledge. On the basis of Lawrence's biography it is possible to reconstruct further the series of interpellations to which he would have been subject in the ideologically saturated discourses and social structures of the late Victorian and Edwardian school, drawing rooms and college common rooms as well as in the canonical texts of history, thought, and literature that were the prescribed readings of all aspirants to functions within the higher cultural apparatus of the British imperial order of the time. Yet resistance to such constitution as imperial subject of an hegemonic world order is apparent both in the biographical data and in Lawrence's text itself.

Lawrence was himself sensitive to the contradiction already embodied in the notion of the 'amateur soldier'. To put on a uniform against one's will is to see oneself as a divided person, to reserve part of oneself from the commitment to soldiering and to establish a distance between one's role and one's self. In Lawrence's case the complexity of his situation was further heightened when he gave up British khaki for the costume of an alien culture. To wear the robes of a Bedouin Arab was to cease in part to be British even if it could not mean that he thereby became Arab. (9) Involved is a form of cultural transvestism that enhanced the ambiguities of an identity already subject to self-doubt.

The matter of Lawrence's illegitimacy or his homosexuality are not themselves at issue here. What is important, however, is a sensibility that for one reason or another was obviously deviant in relation to a Christian bourgeois mainstream that celebrated the virtues of patriarchy and of family. Unlike the campaign memoirs of generals from Caesar to Patton and Montgomery, therefore, *Seven Pillars of Wisdom* records movements of desire and aspiration along with military and political events; it is often deeply personal in its accents, managing among other things to suggest simultaneously the anguish and urgency of sex in the desert, where the only women available were the prostitutes of the rare settlements: 'In horror of such sordid commerce our youths began indifferently to slake one another's few needs in their own clean bodies - a cold convenience that, by comparison, seemed sexless and even pure. Later, some began to justify this sterile process, and swore that friends quivering together in the yielding sand with intimate hot limbs in supreme embrace, found there hidden in the darkness a sensual coefficient of the mental passion which was welding our souls and spirits in one flaming effort' (28). The passage manages to be both passionate and impersonal, projecting desire on to others but participating in it through a celebratory prose that down to such a tender phrase as 'our youths' or the word 'clean' links it to a familiar, if underground, British homoerotic tradition. Warrant for such deviancy was, of course, an important element in male public school and Oxbridge culture at the time. The idealization of Greek art and thought gave a spiritual justification to the cult of youthful male beauty and of love between males as a higher, chaster bond than that which could exist between men and women.

If such passages as the above show how socio-biographical overdetermination comes to be expressed in Lawrence's text, they also combine with a wide variety of other and similar passages to suggest the kind of overdetermined cultural object that is *Seven Pillars of Wisdom* taken as a whole. As was noted earlier, Lawrence's work has as its model not a single literary genre but several. And it is in large part because the author shifts in his text from genre to genre that the work's contradictions emerge. They are present as a radical stylistic heterogeneity, as a variety of contents, as shifting authorial distance and point of view. If, as Althusser claimed in two familiar essays, (10) literary works are neither knowledge nor ideology but are significant because they use ideology as their raw material and transform it by putting it on display, then *Seven Pillars of Wisdom* is able to achieve this largely because of the radical disjunction between elements. Whether or not one swallows one's Althusser whole, however, it is clear that Lawrence's work does not easily submit to a reading founded on the mystifications of organic form.

It is a war story and a travel journal and the tale of a moral and political coming of age. Passages that reproduce a generalized Orientalist discourse alternate with those that recall the intensity and tedium of war, the confusions of sexual desire and spiritual yearning, and scenes of thrilling natural beauty. The late romantic pursuit of intense sensation for its own sake conflicts with the Victorian code of chivalry and service to country that was mediated by the public schools. The modern epic material of battles and preparation for battle, of Bedouin camps by night, of councils of war and the clash of wills and purposes, strategy and tactics, is joined to the romance theme of personal quest, of self-testing and self-discovery under the most extreme conditions. Moreover, the romance theme is joined to the peculiarly modern motif of the divided self, of the split between the public and the private, between the man of action and the man of anguish who suspects all causes along with his own motivations.

Lawrence's eclectic text employs, then, the narrative techniques and devices and echoes and the themes and attitudes of a variety of genres of the Western literary tradition from as far back as the Homeric epic - he was later to translate *The Odyssey* - and chivalric romance down through the Victorian poets and writers up to such contemporaries as Kipling and Conrad. Along with the campaign literature of Caesar, Napoleon and others, one of the rare works he mentions reading by name is significantly enough the *Morte d'Arthur*. That Lawrence's work is a product of the literary instance, of the kind of textual self-interrogation which when read appropriately both reproduces and illuminates its ideological raw materials, is finally most obvious in certain passages of apparently realist reportage. A paragraph that describes Ashraf camel riders suggests the qualities of Lawrence's prose:

> They wore rusty-red tunics henna-dyed, under black cloaks, and carried swords. Each had a slave crouched behind him on the crupper to help him with rifle and dagger in the fight, and to watch his camel and cook for him on the road. The slaves, as befitted slaves of poor masters, were very little dressed. Their strong, black legs gripped the camels' woolly sides as in a vice, to lessen the shocks inevitable on their bony perches, while they had knotted up their rags of shirts into the plaited thong about their loins to save them from the fouling of the camels and their staling on the march. Semna water was medicinal, and our animals' dung flowed like green soup down their hocks that day.(157)

On the level of the signified this is very obviously the Eastern other of Western ideological representation. The color of the costumes signify oriental brilliance, the weapons warlike ferocity, the slaves despotic practices. In the play of difference and identity by means of which we report back on the alien to our culture of reference, such a passage insists on Near Eastern difference. Yet the very vividness of this group portrait and the precision of its detailing are designed to reverberate in a reader's mind and body, both stimulating a *frisson nouveau* and communicating a shock of recognition. On the one hand, the passage is striking for the peculiar libidinal investments located in the particularity of the images. On the other hand, if this is the East, it is an East that recalls the heroic age of Greek epic; it is a reminder of the classical European past. The Near East here appears in the guise of an ally not an enemy, admired for the strength of its primary colors and the wholeness of its energies. The desert Arab becomes in part an expression of the age-old nostalgia for the supposed lost wholeness of the primitive world, a modern noble savage, who is different not only from the half-Europeanized and decadent Turk but also from city Arabs. From this point of view, the scene is implicitly noteworthy because it appears against the unstated background of a contemporary European mutedness of tone, world-weariness and cynicism. Thus it is far from clear that in the implied contrast between Western civilization and Eastern barbarism - the traditional Orientalist trope - the good is on the European side. The hidden obverse of the Arabia of such a passage is after all European *fin-de-sièclisme* and world-weariness. It contrasts with other paragraphs that point to the duplicity of Western power politics and to Western industrial progress as the new Western barbarism.

Finally, perhaps the most significant feature of the passage is that it demonstrates how *Seven Pillars of Wisdom* is a self-conscious work of literature in a positive sense. One is made aware of the excess of signifier over signified. Because Lawrence is obviously preoccupied by the weight and shape of the paragraph on the page as an order of words, his attention is diverted from properly hegemonic questions. As a result, the passage illuminates the potential ideological irresponsibility of language wherever an eroticized phantasy is granted the freedom to indulge itself in a literary space. From the first line to the last, the passage displays its concern for phrasing and for energizing combinations of monosyllables and alliterative patterns, as well as for an arresting anal/oral simile. The foregrounding of words as signifiers releases forces that have a capacity for producing the unexpected.

The notion of new possibilities as inherent in previously untried combinations of words, as a Utopian potential emerging within the play of the poetic function of language, is perhaps best illustrated by a short sentence that comes soon after the passage just quoted: 'We got off our camels and stretched ourselves, sat down or walked before supper to the sea and bathed by hundreds, a splashing, screaming mob of fish-like naked men of all earth's colours'(159) . Such a sentence reminds us that we are in the presence of the literary instance because its significance is not in what it asserts, in any generalizing thought it expresses about East or West, but in a vision of a mingling where all previous categories break down. Further, its power is in the sharp impression of a scene which only exists as a newly invented verbal order but which nevertheless suggests a previously unrealized potential. And it is a potential for which there is no support in the dominant hegemonic discourse. The imagery of baptism and of a fresh emergence from the sea as a collectivity of races - 'fish-like naked men of all earth's colours' - amounts to a politically Utopian idea as well as a homoerotic phantasm. It is in any case an altogether unthinkable thought within the discourse of Orientalism as defined by Said.

In the light of all this the reason why Said is unable in the end to suggest alternatives to the hegemonic discourse of Orientalism is not difficult to explain. First, because he overlooks the potential contradiction between discourse theory and Gramscian hegemony, he fails to historicize adequately the texts he cites and summarizes, finding always the same triumphant discourse where several are frequently in conflict. Second, because he does not distinguish the literary instance from more transparently ideological textual forms he does not acknowledge the semi-autonomous and overdetermined character of aesthetic artifacts. Finally, he fails to show how literary texts may in their play establish distance from the ideologies they seem to be reproducing.

NOTES

1. (Vintage Books: New York, 1979.)

2. Said's comment on this point seems incontrovertible: 'No one has ever devised a method of detaching the scholar from the circumstances of life, from the fact of his involvement (conscious or unconscious) with a class, a set of beliefs, a social position, or from the mere activity of being a member of a society'(10).

3. Fredric Jameson has made the point in connection with historical writing: '... we need to take into account the possibility that our contact with the past will always pass through the imaginary and through its ideologies, will always in one way or another be mediated by codes and motifs of some deeper classification system or pensée sauvage, some properly political unconscious.' 'Marxism and Historicism', *New Literary History* (Autumn, 1979), p.45.

4. I am thinking particularly of the early Foucault through *The Order of Things*, the Foucault who seems to have been most influential for Said during the time he was writing *Orientalism*.

In this connection the problems raised by discourse theory have been touched on, among others, by Stuart Hall in 'Cultural Studies and the Centre: some problematics and problems' and by Chris Weedon, Andrew Tolson, Frank Mort in 'Theories of language and subjectivity'. The former writes: 'Foucault, following the lead of Lévi-Strauss, though in a different way, directs attention to the internal relations and regularities of any field of knowledge. He remains agnostic about their general determining conditions and about their "truth". He examines them largely from a "topographical" or genealogical vantage point ...'(p.57). Weedon, Tolson and Mort comment, 'However, the point of focus specified by discourse analysis - that is, the regularity of its organization and its field of effects - tends to militate against any examination of the interrelation between the emergence and continuity of a discourse and forms of resistance, struggle and contestation' (p.214). *Culture, Media, Language* (Hutchinson, London, 1980).

5. (Oxford University Press: Oxford, 1977.)

6. As a literary scholar himself, Said is, of course, aware of textual complexity and qualitative difference between the variety of works he touches on: 'One remembers that Lane's *Manners and Customs of the Modern Egyptians* is a classic of historical and anthropological observation because of its style, its enormously intelligent and brilliant details, not because of its simple reflection of racial superiority ...'(15).

7. *The Travels*, translated by Ronald Lathan (Penguin: Harmondsworth, 1958).

8. *The Seven Pillars of Wisdom* (Penguin: Harmondsworth, 1962.)

9. 'In my case, the efforts for these years to live in the dress of Arabs, Arabs, and to imitate their mental foundation, quitted me of my English self, and let me look at the West and its conventions with new eyes: they destroyed it all for me. At the same time I could not sincerely take on Arab skin: it was an affectation only'(30).

10. 'A letter on Art in Reply to André Daspre' and 'Cremonini, Painter of the Abstract', *Lenin and Philosophy and Other Essays* (Monthly Review Press: New York and London, 1971).

DIFFERENCE, DISCRIMINATION AND THE DISCOURSE OF COLONIALISM* (1)

Homi K. Bhabha

> To concern oneself with the founding concepts of the entire history of philosophy, to deconstitute them, is not to undertake the work of the philologist or of the classic historian of philosophy. Despite appearances, it is probably the most daring way of making the beginnings of a step outside of philosophy.
>
> (Jacques Derrida, "Structure, Sign and Play")

To describe the racist discourse of colonial power as constructed around a 'boundary dispute' is not merely to pun the political with the psychoanalytic. It is the object of my talk today to suggest that the construction of the colonial subject in discourse, and the exercise of colonial power through discourse, demands an articulation of forms of difference - racial and sexual. Such an articulation becomes crucial if it is held that the body is always simultaneously inscribed in both the economy of pleasure and desire and the economy of discourse, domination and power. I do not wish to conflate, unproblematically, two forms of the marking - and splitting - of the subject nor to globalise two forms of representation. I want to suggest, however, that there is a theoretical space and a political place for such an articulation - in the sense in which that word itself denies an 'original' identity or a 'singularity' to objects of difference, sexual or racial. If such a view is taken, as Feuchtwang (2) argues in a different context, it follows that the epithets racial or sexual come to be seen as modes of differentiation, realised as multiple, cross-cutting determinations, polymorphous and perverse, always demanding a specific and strategic calculation of their effects. Such is, I believe, the moment of colonial discourse. It is the most theoretically underdeveloped form of discourse, but crucial to the binding of a range of differences and discriminations that inform the discursive and political practices of racial and cultural hierarchisation.

Before turning to the construction of colonial discourse, I want to briefly discuss the process by which forms of racial/cultural/historical otherness have been marginalised in theoretical texts committed to the articulation of *différance*, *signifiance*, in order, it is claimed, to reveal the limits of Western metaphysical discourse. Despite the

---

* I would like to thank Dr Stephan Feuchtwang of The City University for providing the critical and companionable context in which this essay was written.

differences (and disputes) between grammatology and semiology both practices share an anti-epistemological position that impressively contests Western modes of representation predicated on an episteme of presence and identity. In facilitating the passage 'from work to text' and stressing the arbitrary, differential and systemic construction of social and cultural signs, these critical strategies unsettle the idealist quest for meanings that are, most often, intentionalist and nationalist. So much is not in question. What does need to be questioned, however, is the mode of representation of otherness, which depends crucially on how the 'West' is deployed within these discourses.

The anti-ethnocentric stance is a strategy which, in recognising the spectacle of otherness, conceals a paradox central to these anti-epistemological theories. For the critique of Western idealism or logocentrism requires that there is a constitutive discourse of lack imbricated in a philosophy of presence, which makes the differential or deconstructionist reading possible, 'between the lines'. As Mark Cousins (3) says, the desire for presence which characterises the Western episteme and its regimes of representation, "carries with it as the condition of its movement and of the regulation of its economy, a destiny of non-satisfaction". This could lead, as he goes on to say, "to an endless series of playful deconstructions which manifest a certain sameness in the name of difference". If such repetitiousness is to be avoided, then the strategic failure of logocentricism would have to be given a displacing and subversive role. This requires that the 'non-satisfaction' should be specified positively which is done by identifying an Anti-West. Paradoxically, then, cultural otherness functions as the moment of presence in a theory of *différance*. The 'destiny of non-satisfaction' is fulfilled in the recognition of otherness as a symbol (not sign) of the presence of *signifiance* or *différance*: otherness is the point of equivalence or identity in a circle in which what needs to be proved (the limits of logocentricity) is assumed (as a destiny or economy of lack/desire). What is denied is any knowledge of cultural otherness as a differential sign, implicated in specific historical and discursive conditions, requiring construction in different practices of reading. The place of otherness is fixed in the West as a subversion of Western metaphysics and is finally appropriated by the West as its limit-text, the Anti-West. This results in a disciplinary gaze upon difference that disavows the castrating and negating return of the look of the Other.

For instance, having decentred the sign, Barthes finds Japan immediately insightful and visible and extends the empire of empty signs universally. Japan can only be the Anti-West:

> Empire of Signs? Indeed, if we imply that the signs are empty and the ritual is a godless one. Just look at the study of signs (Mallarmé's dwelling place) ... out there, any view, be it urban or domestic or rural. And so that we may see how it is put together, let it be illustrated by the Shikdai corridor ... in this corridor, as in the ideal Japanese house, devoid or nearly so of furniture, there is no place which in any way designates property; no seat, no bed, no table provides a point from which the body may constitute itself as subject (or master) of a space. The very concept of centre is rejected (burning frustration for Western man everywhere provided with his armchair and his bed, the owner of a domestic position.(4)

Look next at Kristeva's remarkable *About Chinese Women*. (5) There is a dizzy moment in Chapter 5, when she encounters in another culture, the limits of logocentrism and phallocentricism. At this point she tries, in her own words, 'to do or write something of her own'. Thus in a 'writing' once more deferred ... in a China where appropriately 'nothing is finished, where everything is possible' she produces at the limits of her language and her culture, the static portraits of Chinese women fixed, observed, anatomised, atomised, entirely surveyed. What returns across the uncomprehending faces of the Chinese women is the resounding echo of her own discourse as well as a problem that bothers, borders on another question which she puts to Derrida in an interview in *Positions*: (6) What are the logocentric and ethnocentric limits of the sign and its correlates?

To the question of ethnocentricity Derrida turns explicitly only twice in a long and brilliant exposition of logocentrism. Once to say that 'translation' between languages and cultural systems is always a regulated transformation: and a second time to say, not surprisingly, that 'everyday language is not innocent or neutral. It is the language of Western metaphysics and it carries with it not only a considerable number of presuppositions of all types, but presuppositions inseparable from metaphysics'. (7)

What Derrida does is to fix the problem of ethnocentricity repeatedly at the limits of logocentricity, the unknown territory mapped neatly on to the familiar, as presuppositions inseparable from metaphysics, merely another limitation of metaphysics. Such a position cannot lead to the construction or exploration of other discursive sites from which to investigate the differential materiality and history of colonial culture. The interiority and immediacy of Voice as 'consciousness itself', central to logocentric discourse, is disturbed and dispersed by the imposition of a foreign tongue which differentiates the gentleman from the native, culture from civilization. The colonial discourse is always at least twice-inscribed and it is in that process of *différance* that denies 'originality', that the problem of the colonial subject must be thought.

To address the question of ethnocentricity in Derrida's terms, one could explore the exercise of colonial power in relation to the violent hierarchy between written and aural cultures. One might examine, in the context of a colonial society, those strategies of normalisation that play on the difference between an 'official' normative language of colonial administration and instruction and an unmarked, marginalised form - pidgin, creole, vernacular - which becomes the site of the native subject's cultural dependence and resistance, and as such a sign of surveillance and control.

Finally, where better to raise the question of the subject of racial and cultural difference than in Stephen Heath's masterly analysis of the chiaroscuro world of Welles' classic 'A Touch of Evil'. I refer to an area of its analysis which has generated the least comment, that is, Heath's attention to the structuration of the border Mexico/USA that circulates through the text affirming and exchanging some notion of 'limited being'. Heath's work departs from the traditional analysis of racial and cultural differences, which identify stereotype and image, and elaborate them in a moralistic or nationalistic discourse that affirms the origin and unity of national identity. Heath's attentiveness to the contradictory and diverse sites within the textual system, which construct national/cultural differences in their deployment of the semes of 'foreignness', 'mixedness', 'impurity', as transgressive and corrupting, is extremely relevant. His attention to the turnings of this much neglected subject, as sign (not symbol or stereotype) disseminated in the codes (as 'partition', 'exchange', 'naming', 'character', etc.), gives us a welcome sense of the circulation and proliferation of racial and cultural otherness. Despite the awareness of the multiple or cross-cutting determinations in the construction of modes of sexual and racial differentiation there is a sense in which Heath's analysis marginalises otherness. Although I shall argue that the problem of the border Mexico/USA is read too singularly, too exclusively under the sign of sexuality, it is not that I am not aware of the many proper and relevant reasons for that 'feminist' focus. The 'entertainment' operated by the realist Hollywood film of the '50's was always also a containment of the subject in a narrative economy of voyeurism and fetishism. Moreover, the displacement that organises any textual system, within which the display of difference circulates, demands that the play of 'nationalities' should participate in the sexual positioning, troubling the Law and desire. There is, nevertheless, a singularity and reductiveness in concluding that:

> Vargas is the position of desire, its admission and its
> prohibition. Not surprisingly he has two names: the name
> of desire is Mexican, Miguel ... that of the Law American
> - Mike ... The film uses the border, the play between
> American and Mexican ... at the same time it seeks to hold
> that play finally in the opposition of purity and mixture
> which in turn is a version of Law and desire. (8)

However liberatory it is from one position to see the logic of the text traced ceaselessly between the Ideal Father and the Phallic Mother, in another sense, in seeing only one possible articulation of the differential complex "race-sex" - it half colludes with the proffered images of marginality. For if the naming of Vargas is crucially mixed and split in the economy of desire, then there are other mixed economies which make naming and positioning equally problematic 'across the border'. For to identify the 'play' on the border as purity and mixture and to see it as an allegory of Law and desire reduces the articulation of racial and sexual difference to what is dangerously close to becoming a circle rather than a spiral of *différance*. On that basis, it is not possible to construct the polymorphous and perverse collusion between racism and sexism as a mixed economy - for instance, the discourses of American cultural colonialism and Mexican dependency, the fear/desire of miscegenation, the American border as cultural signifier of a pioneering, male 'American' spirit always under threat from races and cultures beyond the border. If the death of the Father is the interruption on which the narrative is initiated, it is through that death that miscegenation is both possible and deferred; if, again, it is the purpose of the narrative to restore Susan as 'good object', it also becomes its project to deliver Vargas from his racial 'mixedness'. It is all there in Heath's splendid scrutiny of the text, revealed as he brushes against its grain. What is missing is the taking up of these positions as also the <u>object</u> (<u>ives</u>) of his analysis.

The difference of other cultures is other than the excess of signification, the *différance* of the trace or the trajectory of desire. These are theoretical strategies that may be necessary to combat 'ethnocentricism' but they cannot, of themselves, unreconstructed, represent that otherness. There can be no inevitable sliding from the semiotic or deconstructionist activity to the unproblematic reading of other cultural and discursive systems. There is in such readings a will to power and knowledge that, in failing to specify the limits of their own field of enunciation and effectivity, proceed to individualise otherness as the discovery of their own assumptions.

What is meant by colonial discourse as an apparatus of power will emerge more fully as the paper develops a critique of specific, historical texts. At this stage, however, I shall provide what I take to be

the minimum conditions and specifications of such a discourse. It is
an apparatus that turns on the recognition and disavowal of racial/cul-
tural/historical differences. Its predominant strategic function is
the creation of a space for a 'subject peoples' through the production
of knowledges in terms of which surveillance is exercised and a complex
form of pleasure/unpleasure is incited. It seeks authorisation for its
strategies by the production of knowledges of coloniser and colonised
which are stereotypical but antithetically evaluated. The objective of
colonial discourse is to construe the colonised as a population of de-
generate types on the basis of racial origin, in order to justify conquest and to establish systems of administration and instruction. Despite the play of power within colonial discourse and the shifting positionalities of its subjects (e.g. effects of class, gender, ideology,
different social formations, varied systems of colonisation etc.), I am
referring to a form of governmentality that in marking out a 'subject
nation', appropriates, directs and dominates its various spheres of
activity. Therefore, despite the 'play' in the colonial system which
is crucial to its exercise of power, I do not consider the practices and
discourses of revolutionary struggle, as the under/other side of 'colonial discourse'. They may be historically co-present with it and intervene in it, but can never be 'read off' merely on the basis of their
opposition to it. Anti-colonialist discourse requires an alternative
set of questions, techniques and strategies in order to construct it.

Through this paper I shall move through forms of colonial discourse
or descriptions of it, written from the late 19th century to date. I
have referred to specific historical texts in order to construct three
theoretical problems which I consider crucial. In Temple's work the
circulation of power as knowledge; in Said's the fixation/fetishisation
of stereotypical knowledge as power; and in Fanon's the circulation of
power and knowledge in a binding of desire and pleasure.

The social Darwinist problematic of Charles Temple's *The Native
Races and Their Rulers* (9) (1918), enacts the tension between 'the free
and continual circulation' that natural selection requires and the
effects of colonial power which claims to assist natural selection by
controlling racial degeneracy but, through that intervention, must necessarily impede free circulation. The colonial system then requires some
justification other than mere material necessity; and if justification
is understood as both vindication and correction, then we can see in this
text a crucial adjustment in the exercise of colonial power. In the face
of an ambitious native 'nationalist' bourgeois, Temple's text marks the
shift in the form of colonial government, from a juridical sovereign exercise of power as punitive and restrictive - as harbinger of death - to
a disciplinary form of power.

Disciplinary power is exercised through indirection on the basis of
a knowledge of the subject-races as 'abnormal'. They are not merely de-
generate and primitive but, Temple claims, they also require the 'abnorma-
lity' of imperialist intervention to hasten the process of natural selection. If 'normalisation' can imply even the faint possibility of an absorption or incorporation of the subject-races then, like mass-rule at
home, this must be resisted in the colonies. The natives are therefore
'individualised', through the racist testimony of 'science' and colonia-
list administrative wisdom, as having such divergent ethical and mental
outlooks that integration or independence is deemed impossible. Thus
marginalised and individualised, the colonial subject as bearer of racial
typologies and racist stereotypes is re-introduced to the circulation of
power as a 'productive capacity' within that form of colonial government
called Indirect Rule.

The co-option of traditional elites into the colonial administration is then seen to be a way of harnessing the ambitious life-instinct of the natives. This sets up the native subject as a site of productive-power, both subservient and always potentially seditious. What is increased is the visibility of the subject as an object of surveillance, tabulation, ennumeration and, indeed, paranoia and fantasy. When the upward spiral of natural selection encounters differences of race, class and gender as potentially contradictory and insurrectionary forces, whose mobility may fracture the closed circuit of natural selection, social Darwinism invokes what Temple calls 'the decrees of all-seeing Providence'. This agency of social control appeals in desperation to God instead of Nature to fix the colonised at that point in the social order from which colonial power will, in Foucault's specification, be able simultaneously to increase the subjected forces and to improve the force and efficacy of that which subjects them.

Colonial power produces the colonised as a fixed reality which is at once an 'other' and yet entirely knowable and visible. It resembles a form of narrative in which the productivity and circulation of subjects and signs are bound in a reformed and recognisable totality. It employs a system of representation, a regime of truth, that is structurally similar to Realism. And it is in order to intervene within that system of representation that Edward Said proposes a semiotic of 'Orientalist' power, which is revealing of, and relevant to, colonial discourse.

> Philosophically, then, the kind of language, thought, and vision that I have been calling orientalism very generally is a form of radical realism; anyone employing orientalism, which is the habit for dealing with questions, objects, qualities and regions deemed Oriental, will designate, name, point to, fix what he is talking or thinking about with a word or phrase, which then is considered either to have acquired, or more simply to be, reality ..... The tense they employ is the timeless eternal; they convey an impression of repetition and strength ..... For all these functions it is frequently enough to use the simple copula *is*. (10)

But the syllogism, as Kristeva once said, is that form of Western Rationalism that reduces heterogeneity to two-part order, so the *copula*, then, is the point at which this binding preserves the boundaries of sense for an entire tradition of philosophical thinking. Of this, too, Said is aware when he hints continually at a polarity or division at the very centre of Orientalism. (11) It is, on the one hand, a topic of learning, discovery, practice; on the other, it is the site of dreams, images, fantasies, myths, obsessions and requirements. It is a static system of 'synchronic essentialism', a knowledge of 'signifiers of stability' such as the lexicographic and the encyclopaedic. However, this site is continually under threat from diachronic forms of history and narrative, signs of instability. And, finally, this line of thinking is given a shape analogical to the dream-work, when Said refers explicitly to a distinction between 'an unconscious positivity' which he terms *latent* Orientalism, and the stated knowledges and views about the Orient which he calls *manifest* Orientalism.

Where the originality of this account loses its inventiveness, and for me its usefulness, is with Said's refusal to engage with the alterity and ambivalence in the articulation of these two economies which threaten to split the very object of Orientalist discourse as a knowledge and the subject positioned therein. He contains this threat by introducing a binarism within the argument which, in initially setting up an opposition between these two discursive scenes, finally allows them to be correlated as a congruent system of representation that is unified through a political-ideological <u>intention</u> which, in his words, enables Europe to advance securely and <u>unmetaphorically</u> upon the Orient.

This seems to be a rather unremarkable resolution to a remarkably insightful problem. It is compounded by a psychologistic reduction when, in describing Orientalism through the nineteenth century, Said identifies the <u>content</u> of Orientalism as the unconscious repository of fantasy, imaginative writings and essential ideas; and the <u>form</u> of manifest Orientalism as the historically and discursively determined, diachronic aspect.

To develop a point I made a moment ago, the division/correlation structure of manifest and latent Orientalism leads to the effectivity of the concept of discourse being undermined by what I will call the polarities of intentionality. This is a problem fundamental to Said's use of the terms <u>power</u> and <u>discourse</u>. The productivity of Foucault's concept of power/knowledge is its refusal of an epistemology which opposes form/content, ideology/science, essence/appearance. 'Pouvoir/Savoir' places subjects in a relation of power and recognition that is not part of a symmetrical or dialectical relation - self/other, Master/Slave - which can then be subverted by being inverted. Subjects are always disproportionately placed in opposition or domination through the symbolic decentering of multiple power-relations which play the role of support as well as target or adversary. It becomes difficult, then, to conceive of the <u>historical</u> enunciations of colonial discourse without them being either functionally overdetermined or strategically elaborated or displaced by the <u>unconscious</u> scene of latent Orientalism. Equally, it is difficult to conceive of the process of subjectification as a placing <u>within</u> Orientalist or Colonial discourse for the dominated subject without the dominant being strategically placed within it too. There is always, in Said, the suggestion that colonial power and discourse is possessed entirely by the coloniser which is a historical and theoretical simplification. The terms in which Said's Orientalism are unified - which is, the intentionality and unidirectionality of colonial power - also unifies the subject of colonial enunciation.

This is a result of Said's inadequate attention to representation as a concept that articulates the historical and fantasy (as the scene of desire) in the production of the 'political' effects of discourse. He rightly rejects a notion of Orientalism as the misrepresentation of an Oriental essence. However, having introduced the concept of 'discourse' he does not face up to the problems it makes for the instrumentalist notion of power/knowledge that he seems to require. This problem is summed up by his ready acceptance of the view that,

> Representations are formations, or as Roland Barthes has said of all the operations of language, they are deformations. (13)

This brings me to my second point. It is, that the closure and coherence attributed to the unconscious pole of colonial discourse and the unproblematised notion of the subject, restricts the effectivity of both power and knowledge. It is not possible to see how power functions productively as incitement and interdiction. Nor would it be possible, without the attribution of ambivalence to relations of power/knowledge to calculate the traumatic impact of the return of the oppressed - those terrifying stereotypes of savagery, cannibalism, lust and anarchy which are the signal points of identification and alienation, scenes of fear and desire, in colonial texts. It is precisely this function of the stereotype as phobia and fetish that, according to Fanon, threatens the closure of the racial/epidermal schema for the colonial subject and opens the royal road to colonial fantasy.

Despite Said's limitations, or perhaps because of them, there is a forgotten, underdeveloped passage which, in cutting across the body of the text, articulates the question of power and desire that I now want to take up. It is this:

> Altogether an internally structured archive is built up from the literature that belongs to these experiences. Out of this comes a restricted number of typical encapsulations: the journey, the history, the fable, the stereotype, the polemical confrontation. These are the lenses through which the Orient is experienced, and they shape the language, perception, and form of the encounter between East and West. What gives the immense number of encounters some unity, however, is the vacillation I was speaking about earlier. Something patently foreign and distant acquires, for one reason or another, a status more rather than less familiar. One tends to stop judging things either as completely novel or as completely well-known; a new median category emerges, a category that allows one to see new things, things seen for the first time, as versions of a previously known thing. In essence such a category is not so much a way of receiving new information as it is a method of controlling what seems to be a threat to some established view of things. ...... The threat is muted, familiar values impose themselves, and in the end the mind reduces the pressure upon it by accommodating things to itself as either 'original' or 'repetitious'. ...... The Orient at large, therefore, vacillates between the West's contempt for what is familiar and its shivers of delight in - or fear of - novelty. (14)

What is this other scene of colonial discourse played out around the "median category"? What is this theory of encapsulation or fixation which moves between the recognition of cultural and racial difference and its disavowal, by affixing the unfamiliar to something established, in a form that is repetitious and vacillates between delight and fear? Is it not analogous to the Freudian fable of fetishism (and disavowal) that circulates within the discourse of colonial power, requiring the articulation of modes of differentiation - sexual and racial - as well as different modes of discourse - psychoanalytic and historical?

The strategic articulation of 'coordinates of knowledge' - racial and sexual - and their inscription in the play of colonial power as modes of differentiation, defense, fixation, hierarchisation, is a way of specifying colonial discourse which would be illuminated by reference to Foucault's post-structuralist concept of the *dispositif* or apparatus. In displacing his earlier search for discursive regularity as *episteme*, Foucault stresses that the relations of knowledge and power within the apparatus are always a strategic response to <u>an urgent need</u> at a given historical moment - much as I suggested at the outset, that the force of colonial discourse as a theoretical and political intervention was the need, in our contemporary moment, to contest singularities of difference and to articulate modes of differentiation. Foucault writes:

> .... the apparatus is essentially of a strategic nature, which means assuming that it is a matter of a certain manipulation of relations of forces, either developing them in a particular direction, blocking them, stabilising them, utilising them etc. The apparatus is thus always inscribed in a play of power, but it is also always linked to certain coordinates of knowledge which issue from it but, to an equal degree, condition it. This is what the apparatus consists in: strategies of relations of forces supporting and supported by, types of knowledge. (15)

In this spirit I argue for the reading of the stereotype in terms of fetishism. The myth of historical origination - racial purity, cultural priority - produced in relation to the colonial stereotype functions to 'normalise' the multiple beliefs and split subjects that constitute colonial discourse as a consequence of its process of disavowal. The scene of fetishism functions similarly as, at once, a reactivation of the material of original fantasy - the anxiety of castration and sexual difference - as well as a normalisation of that difference and disturbance in terms of the fetish object as the substitute for the mother's penis. Within the apparatus of colonial power, the discourses of sexuality and race relate in a process of functional overdetermination, "because each effect ... enters into resonance or contradiction with the others and thereby calls for a readjustment or a re-working of the heterogeneous elements that surface at various points". (16)

There is both a structural and functional justification for reading the racial stereotype of colonial discourse in terms of fetishism. (17) My re-reading of Said establishes the structural link. Fetishism, as the disavowal of difference, is that repetitious scene around the problem of secondary castration. The recognition of sexual difference - as the pre-condition for the circulation of the chain of absence and presence in the realm of the Symbolic - is disavowed by the fixation on an object that masks that difference and restores an original presence. The functional link between the fixation of the fetish and the stereotype (or the stereotype as fetish) is even more relevant. For fetishism is always a 'play' or vacillation between the archaic affirmation of wholeness/similarity - in Freud's terms: 'All men have penises'; in ours 'All men have the same skin/race/culture'; and the anxiety associated with lack and difference' - again, for Freud 'Some do not have penises'; for us 'Some do not have the same skin/race/culture'. Within discourse, the fetish represents the simultaneous play between metaphor as substitution (masking absence and difference) and metonymy (which contiguously registers the perceived lack). The fetish or stereotype gives access to an 'identity' which is predicated as much on mastery and pleasure as it is on anxiety and defence, for it is a form of multiple and contradictory belief in its recognition of difference and disavowal of it. This conflict of pleasure/unpleasure, mastery/defence, knowledge/disavowal, absence/presence, has a fundamental significance for colonial discourse. For the scene of fetishism is also the scene of the reactivation and repetition of primal fantasy - the subject's desire for a pure origin that is always threatened by its division, for the subject must be gendered to be engendered, to be spoken. The stereotype, then, as the primary point of subjectification in colonial discourse, for both coloniser and colonised, is the scene of a similar fantasy and defence - the desire for an originality which is again threatened by the differences of race, colour and culture.

My contention is splendidly caught in Fanon's title *Black Skin White Masks* where the disavowal of difference turns the colonial subject into a misfit - a grotesque mimicry or 'doubling' that threatens to split the soul and whole, undifferentiated skin of the ego. The stereotype is not a simplification because it is a false representation of a given reality. It is a simplification because it is an arrested, fixated form of representation that, in denying the play of difference (that the negation through the Other permits), constitutes a problem for the representation of the subject in significations of psychic and social relations.

When Fanon talks of the positioning of the subject in the stereotyped discourse of colonialism, he gives further credence to my point. The legends, stories, histories and anecdotes of a colonial culture offer the subject a primordial Either/Or. (18) Either he is fixed in a consciousness of the body as a solely negating activity Or as a new kind of man, a new genus. What is denied the colonial subject, both as coloniser and colonised, is that form of negation which gives access to the recognition of difference in the Symbolic. It is that possibility of difference and circulation which would liberate the signifier of skin/culture from the signifieds of racial typology, the analytics of blood, ideologies of racial and cultural dominance or degeneration. "Wherever he goes" Fanon despairs, "the negro remains a negro" - his race becomes the ineradicable sign of negative difference in colonial discourses. For the stereotype impedes the circulation and articulation of the signifier of 'race' as anything other than its fixity as racism. We always already know that blacks are licentious, Asiatics duplicitous ...

There are two 'primal scenes' in Fanon's *Black Skin White Masks*: two myths of the origin of the marking of the subject within the racist practices and discourses of a colonial culture. On one occasion a white girl fixes Fanon in look and word as she turns to identify with her mother. It is a scene which echoes endlessly through his essay *The Fact of Blackness*: "Look, a Negro ... Mamma, see the Negro! I'm frightened. Frightened." "What else could it be for me", Fanon concludes, "but an amputation, an excision, a haemorrhage that spattered my whole body with black blood." (19) Equally, he stresses the primal moment when the child encounters racial and cultural stereotype in children's fictions, where white heroes and black demons are proffered as points of ideological and psychical identification. Such dramas are enacted every day in colonial societies, says Fanon, employing a theatrical metaphor - the scene - which emphasises the visible - the seen. I want to play upon both these senses which refer at once to the site of fantasy and desire and to the sight of subjectification and power.

The drama underlying these dramatic 'everyday' colonial scenes is not difficult to discern. In each of them the subject turns around the pivot of the 'stereotype' to return to a point of total identification. The girl's gaze returns to her mother in the recognition and disavowal of the Negroid type; the black child turns away from himself, his race, in his total identification with the positivity of whiteness which is at once colour and no colour. In the act of disavowal and fixation the colonial subject is returned to the narcissism of the Imaginary and its identification of an ideal-ego that is white and whole. For what these primal scenes illustrate is that looking/hearing/reading as sites of subjectification in colonial discourse, are evidence of the importance of the visual and auditory imaginary for the histories of societies. (20).

It is in this context that I want to briefly allude to the problematic of seeing/being seen. I suggest that in order to conceive of the colonial subject as the effect of power that is productive - disciplinary and 'pleasurable' - one has to see the surveillance of colonial power as functioning in relation to the regime of the scopic drive. That is, the drive that represents the pleasure in 'seeing', which has the look as its object of desire; is related both to the myth of origins, the primal scene, and the problematic of fetishism; and locates the surveyed object within the 'imaginary' relation. Like voyeurism, surveillance must depend for its effectivity on "the active consent which is its real or mythical correlate (but always real as myth) and establishes in the scopic space the illusion of the object relation". (21) The ambivalence of this form of 'consent' in objectification - real as mythical - is the ambivalence on which the stereotype turns and illustrates that crucial bind of pleasure and power that Foucault asserts but, in my view, fails to explain.

My anatomy of colonial discourse remains incomplete until I locate the stereotype, as an arrested, fetishistic mode of representation within its field of identification, which I have identified in my description of Fanon's primal scenes, as the Lacanian schema of the Imaginary. The Imaginary, (22) as you probably know, is the transformation that takes place in the subject at the formative mirror phase, when it assumes a discrete image which allows it to postulate a series of equivalences, samenesses, identities, between the objects of the surrounding world. However, this positioning is itself problematic, for the subject finds or recognises itself through an image which is simultaneously alienating and hence potentially confrontational. This is the basis of the close relation between the two forms of identification complicit with the Imaginary - narcissism and aggressivity. It is precisely these two forms of 'identification' that constitute the dominant strategy of colonial power exercised in relation to the stereotype which, as a form of multiple and contradictory belief, gives knowledge of difference and simultaneously disavows or masks it. Like the mirror-phase 'the fullness' of the stereotype - its image as identity - is always threatened by 'lack'.

The construction of colonial discourse is then a complex articulation of the tropes of fetishism - metaphor and metonymy - and the forms of narcissistic and aggressive identification available to the Imaginary. Stereotypical racial discourse is then a four-term strategy. There is a tie-up between the metaphoric or masking function of the fetish and the narcissistic object-choice and an opposing alliance between the metonymic figuring of lack and the aggressive phase of the Imaginary. One has then a repertoire of conflictual positions that constitute the subject in colonial discourse. The taking up of any one position, within a specific discursive form, in a particular historical conjuncture, is then always problematic - the site of both fixity and fantasy. It provides a colonial 'identity' that is played out - like all fantasies of originality and origination - in the face and space of the disruption and threat from the heterogeneity of other positions. As a form of splitting and multiple belief, the 'stereotype' requires, for its successful signification, a continual and repetitive chain of other stereotypes. This is the process by which the metaphoric 'masking' is inscribed on a lack which must then be concealed, that gives the stereotype both its fixity and its phantasmatic quality - the same old stories of the Negro's animality, the Coolie's inscrutability or the stupidity of the Irish which must be told (compulsively) again and afresh, and is differently gratifying and terrifying each time.

In any specific colonial discourse the metaphoric/narcissistic and the metonymic/aggressive positions will function simultaneously, but always strategically poised in relation to each other; similar to the moment of alienation which stands as a threat to Imaginary plenitude, and 'multiple belief' which threatens fetishistic disavowal. Caught in the Imaginary as they are, these shifting positionalities will never seriously threaten the dominant power relations, for they exist to exercise them pleasurably and productively. They will always pose the problem of difference as that between the pre-constituted, 'natural' poles of Black and White with all its historical and ideological ramifications. The know-ledge of the construction of that 'opposition' will be denied the colonial subject. He is constructed within an apparatus of power which contains, in both senses of the word, an 'other' knowledge - a knowledge that is arrested and fetishised and circulates through colonial discourse as that limited form of otherness, that fixed form of difference, that I have called the stereotype. Fanon poignantly describes the effects of this process for a colonised culture:

> ... a continued agony rather than a total disappearance of the pre-existing culture. The culture once living and open to the future, becomes closed, fixed in the colonial status, caught in the yolk of oppression. Both present and mummified, it testifies against its members .... The cultural mummification leads to a mummification of individual thinking .... As though it were possible for a man to evolve otherwise than within the framework of a culture that recognises him and that he decides to assume. (23)

My four-term strategy of the stereotype tries tentatively to provide a structure and a process for the 'subject' of colonial discourse. I now want to take up the problem of discrimination as the political effect of such a discourse and relate it to the question of 'race' and 'skin'. To that end it is important to remember that the multiple belief that accompanies fetishism does not only have disavowal value; it also has 'knowledge value' and it is this that I shall now pursue. In calculating this knowledge value it is crucial to try and understand what Fanon means when he says that:

> There is a quest for the Negro, the Negro is a demand, one cannot get along without him, he is needed, but only if he is made palatable in a certain way. Unfortunately the Negro knocks down the system and breaks the treaties. (24)

What this demand is, and how the native or negro is made 'palatable' requires that we acknowledge some significant differences between the general theory of fetishism and its specific uses for an understanding of racist discourse. First, the fetish of colonial discourse - what Fanon calls the epidermal schema - is not, like the sexual fetish, a secret. Skin, as the key signifier of cultural and racial difference in the stereotype, is the most visible of fetishes, recognised as 'common knowledge' in a range of cultural, political, historical discourses, and plays a public part in the racial drama that is enacted every day in colonial societies. Secondly, it may be said that the sexual fetish is closely linked to the 'good object'; it is the prop that makes the whole object desirable and lovable, facilitates sexual relations and can even promote a form of happiness. The stereotype can also be seen as that particular 'fixated' form of the colonial subject which facilitates colonial relations, and sets up a discursive form of racial and cultural opposition in terms of which colonial power is exercised. If it is claimed that the colonised are most often objects of hate, then we can reply with Freud that

> affection and hostility in the treatment of the fetish - which run parallel with the disavowal and acknowledgement

of castration - are mixed in unequal proportions in
different cases, so that the one or the other is more
clearly recognisable. (25)

What this statement recognises is the wide range of the stereotype, from the loyal servant to Satan, from the loved to the hated; a shifting of subject positions in the circulation of colonial power which I tried to account for through the motility of the metaphoric/narcissistic and metonymic/aggressive system of colonial discourse. What remains to be examined, however, is the construction of the signifier of 'skin/race' in those regimes of visibility and discursivity - fetishistic, scopic, imaginary - within which I have located the stereotypes. It is only on that basis that we can construct its 'knowledge - value' which will, I hope, enable us to see the place of fantasy in the exercise of colonial power.

My argument relies upon a particular reading of the problematic of representation which, Fanon suggests, is specific to the colonial situation. He writes:

the originality of the colonial context is that the economic
substructure is also a superstructure ... you are rich because you are white, you are white because you are rich.
This is why Marxist analysis should always be slightly
stretched every time we have to do with the colonial problem. (26)

Fanon could either be seen to be adhering to a simple reflectionist or determinist notion of cultural/social signification or, more interestingly, he could be read as taking an 'anti-repressionist' position (attacking the notion that ideology as miscognition, or misrepresentation, is the repression of the real). For our purposes I tend towards the latter reading which then provides a 'visibility' to the exercise of power; gives force to the argument that skin, as a signifier of discrimination, must be produced or processed as visible. As Abbot says, in a very different context,

whereas repression banishes its object into the unconscious,
forgets and attempts to forget the forgetting, discrimination
must constantly invite its representations into consciousness, re-inforcing the crucial recognition of difference
which they embody and revitalising them for the perception
on which its effectivity depends. .... It must sustain itself on the presence of the very difference which is also
its object. (27)

What 'authorises' discrimination, Abbot continues, is the occlusion of the preconstruction or working-up of difference:

this repression of production entails that the recognition
of difference is procured in an innocence, as a 'nature';
recognition is contrived as primary cognition, spontaneous
effect of the 'evidence of the visible'. (28)

This is precisely the kind of recognition, as spontaneous and visible, that is attributed to the stereotype. The difference of the object of discrimination is at once visible and natural - colour as the cultural/political sign of inferiority or degeneracy, skin as its natural 'identity'. However, Abbot's account stops at the point of 'identification' and strangely colludes with the success of discriminatory practices by suggesting that their representations require the repression of the working-up of difference; to argue otherwise, according to him, would be to put the subject in an impossible position, an impossible awareness, since it would run into consciousness the heterogeneity of the subject as a place of articulation. (29)

Despite his awareness of the crucial recognition of difference for discrimination and its problematisation of repression, Abbot is trapped in his unitary place of articulation. He comes close to suggesting that it is possible, however momentarily and illusorily, for the perpetrator of the discriminatory discourse to be in a position that is unmarked by the discourse to the extent to which the object of discrimination is deemed natural and visible. What Abbot neglects is the facilitating role of contradiction and heterogeneity in the construction of authoritarian practices and their strategic, discursive fixations.

Although the 'authority' of colonial discourse depends crucially on its location in narcissism and the Imaginary, my concept of stereotype-as-suture is a recognition of the ambivalence of that authority and those orders of identification. The role of fetishistic identification, in the construction of discriminatory knowledges that depend on the 'presence of difference', is to provide a process of splitting and multiple/contradictory belief at the point of enunciation and subjectification. It is this crucial splitting of the ego which is represented in Fanon's description of the construction of the colonial subject as effect of stereotypical discourse: the subject primordially fixed and yet triply split between the incongruent knowledges of body, race, ancestors. Assailed by the stereotype,

> The corporeal schema crumbled, its place taken by a racial epidermal scheme ... It was no longer a question of being aware of my body in the third person but a triple person ... I was not given one, but two, three places. (30)

This process is best understood in terms of the articulation of multiple-belief that Freud proposes in the essay on Fetishism. It is a non-repressive form of knowledge that allows for the possibility of simultaneously embracing two contradictory beliefs, one official and one secret, one archaic and one progressive, one that allows the myth of origins, the other that articulates difference and division. Its knowledge 'value' lies in its orientation as a defence towards external reality, and provides, in Metz's words,

> the lasting matrix, the effective prototype of all those splittings of belief which man will henceforth be capable of in the most varied domains, of all the infinitely complex unconscious and occasionally conscious interactions which he will allow himself between believing and not-believing .... (31)

It is through this notion of splitting and multiple belief that, I believe, it becomes easier to see the bind of knowledge and fantasy, power and pleasure, that informs the particular regime of visibility deployed in colonial discourse. The visibility of the racial/colonial other is at once a point of identity 'Look at a Negro' and at the same time a problem for the attempted closure within discourse. For the recognition of difference as 'imaginary' points of identity and origin - such as Black and White - is disturbed by the representation of splitting in the discourse. What I called the play between the metaphoric - narcissistic and metonymic - aggressive moments in colonial discourse - that four-part strategy of the stereotype - crucially recognises the prefiguring of desire as a potentially conflictual, disturbing force in all those regimes of 'originality' that I have brought together. In the objectification of the scopic drive there is always the threatened return of the look; in the identification of the Imaginary relation there is always the alienating other (or mirror) which crucially returns its image to the subject; and in that form of substitution and fixation that is fetishism there is always the trace of loss, absence. To put it succinctly, the recognition and disavowal of 'difference' is always disturbed by the question of its re-presentation or construction. The stereotype is in fact an 'impossible' object. For that very reason, the exertions of the 'official knowledges' of colonialism - pseudo-scientific, typological, legal-administrative, eugenicist - are imbricated at the point of their production of meaning and power with the fantasy that dramatises the impossible desire for a pure, undifferentiated origin. Not itself the object of desire but its setting; not an ascription of prior identities but their production in the syntax of the scenario of racist discourse; colonial fantasy plays a crucial part in those everyday scenes of subjectification in a colonial society which Fanon refers to repeatedly. Like fantasies of the origins of sexuality, the productions of 'colonial desire' mark the discourse as

> a favoured spot for the most primitive defensive reactions such as turning against oneself, into an opposite, projection, negation ... (32)

The problem of origin as the problematic of racist, stereotypical knowledge is a complex one and what I have said about its construction will come clear in this illustration from Fanon. Stereotyping is not the setting up of a false image which becomes the scapegoat of discriminatory practices. It is a much more ambivalent text of projection and introjection, metaphoric and metonymic strategies, displacement, overdetermination, guilt, aggressivity; the masking and splitting of 'official' and fantasmatic knowledges to construct the positionalities and oppositionalities of racist discourse:

> My body was given back to me sprawled out, distorted, recoloured, clad in mourning in that white winter day. The Negro is an animal, the Negro is bad, the Negro is mean, the Negro is ugly; look, a nigger, it's cold, the nigger is shivering, the nigger is shivering because he is cold, the little boy is trembling because he is afraid of the nigger, the nigger is shivering with cold, that cold that goes through your bones, the handsome little boy is trembling because he thinks that the nigger is quivering with rage, the little white boy throws himself into his mother's arms: Mama, the nigger's going to eat me up. (33)

It is the scenario of colonial fantasy which, in staging the ambivalence of desire, articulates the demand for the Negro which the negro disrupts. For the stereotype is at once a substitute and a shadow. By acceding to the wildest fantasies (in the popular sense) of the coloniser, the stereotyped other reveals something of the 'fantasy' (as desire, defense) of that position of mastery. For if 'skin' in racist discourse is the visibility of darkness, and a prime signifier of the body and its social and cultural correlates, then we are bound to remember what Karl Abraham (34) says in his seminal work on the scopic drive. The pleasure-value of darkness is a withdrawal in order to know nothing of the external world. Its symbolic meaning, however, is thoroughly ambivalent. Darkness signifies at once both birth and death; it is in all cases a desire to return to the fullness of the mother, a desire for an unbroken and undifferentiated line of vision and origin.

But surely there is another scene of colonial discourse in which the native or negro meets the demand of colonial discourse; where the subverting 'split' is recuperable within a strategy of social and political control. It is recognisably true that the chain of stereotypical signification is curiously mixed and split, polymorphous and perverse, an articulation of multiple belief. The black is both savage (cannibal) and yet the most obedient and dignified of servants (the bearer of food); he is the embodiment of rampant sexuality and yet innocent as a child; he is mystical, primitive, simple-minded and yet the most worldly and accomplished liar, and manipulator of social forces. In each case what is being dramatised is a separation - <u>between</u> races, cultures, histories, <u>within</u> histories - a separation between <u>before</u> and <u>after</u> that repeats obsessively the mythical moment of disjunction. Despite the structural similarities with the play of need and desire in primal fantasies, the colonial fantasy does not try to cover up that moment of separation. It is more ambivalent. On the one hand, it proposes a teleology - under certain conditions of colonial domination and control the native is progressively reformable. On the other, however, it effectively displays the 'separation', makes it more visible. It is the visibility of this separation which, in denying the colonised the capacities of self-government, independence, western modes of civility, lends authority to the official version and mission of colonial power. Colonial fantasy is the continual dramatisation of emergence - of difference, freedom - as the beginning of a history which is repetitively denied. Such a denial is the clearly voiced demand of colonial discourse as the legitimisation of a form of rule that is facilitated by the racist fetish. In concluding, I would like to develop a little further my working definition of colonial discourse given at the start of this paper.

Racist stereotypical discourse, in its colonial moment, inscribes a form of governmentality that is informed by a productive splitting in its constitution of knowledge and exercise of power. Some of its practices recognise the differences of race, culture, history as elaborated by stereotypical knowledges, racial theories, administrative colonial experience, and on that basis institutionalise a range of political and cultural ideologies that are prejudicial, discriminatory, vestigial, archaic, 'mythical' and, crucially, are recognised as being so. By 'knowing' the native population in these terms, discriminatory and authoritarian forms of political control are considered appropriate. The colonised population is then deemed to be both the cause and effect of the system, imprisoned in the circle of interpretation. What is visible is the <u>necessity</u> of such rule which is justified by those moralistic and normative <u>ideologies</u> of amelioration recognised as the Civilising Mission or the White Man's Burden. However, there co-exists within the same apparatus of colonial power, modern systems and sciences of government, progressive 'Western' forms of social and economic organisation which provide the manifest justification for the project of colonialism - an argument which, in part, impressed Karl Marx. It is on the site of this co-existence that strategies of hierarchisation and marginalisation are employed in the management of colonial societies. And if my deduction from Fanon about the peculiar visibility of colonial power is acceptable to you, then I would extend that to say that it is a form of governmentality in which the 'ideological' space functions in more openly collaborative ways with political and economic exigencies. The barracks stand by the church which stands by the schoolroom; the cantonment stands hard by the 'civil lines'. Such visibility of the institutions and apparatuses of power is possible because the exercise of colonial power makes their <u>relationship</u> obscure, produces them as fetishes, spectacles of a 'natural'/racial pre-eminence. Only the seat of government is always elsewhere - alien and separate by that distance upon which surveillance depends for its strategies of objectification, normalisation and discipline.

The last word belongs to Fanon:

.... this behaviour [of the coloniser] betrays a determination to objectify, to confine, to imprison, to harden. Phrases such as 'I know them', 'that's the way they are', show this maximum objectification successfully achieved.
... There is on the one hand a culture in which qualities of dynamism, of growth, of depth can be recognised. As against this, [in colonial cultures] we find characteristics, curiosities, things, never a structure. (35)

FOOTNOTES

1. There are two major problems with this account which emphasise the tentative and introductory nature of the essay. First, despite the subject's problematic accession to sexual difference which is crucial to my argument, the body in this text is adamic. Realising that the question of woman's relation to castration and access to the symbolic requires a very specific form of attention and articulation, I chose to be cautious till I had worked out its implications for colonial discourse. Secondly, the representation of class difference in the construction of the colonial subject is not specified adequately. Wanting to avoid any form of class determinism 'in the last instance' it becomes difficult, if crucial, to calculate its effectivity. I hope to face both these issues more fully in the book that I am working on at present: *Power and Spectacle: Colonial discourse and the English Novel* to be published by Methuen.

2. S. Feuchtwang, 'Socialist, Feminist and Anti-racist Struggles' in m/f, No.4, 1980, p.41.

3. Mark Cousins, 'The Logic of Deconstruction', in *The Oxford Literary Review*, Vol.3, No.2, 1978, p.76.

4. R. Barthes, *L'Empire des Signes* (Editions Skira, 1970), pp.148-50.

5. J. Kristeva, *About Chinese Women* (Marion Boyars, 1977), pp.157-9.

6. J. Derrida, 'Semiology and Grammatology' in *Positions* (Chicago 1981).

7. *Ibid.*, p.19.

8. S. Heath, 'Touch of Evil', Pt.II in *Screen*, Vol.16, No.2, 1975, p.93.

9. Charles Temple, 'The Native Races and their Rulers' excerpted in P.D. Curtin,*Imperialism* (Walker & Co., 1971), pp.93-105.

10. E. Said, *Orientalism* (Routledge,1978), p.72.

11. *Ibid.*, p.206.

13. E. Said, *op.cit.* p.273.

14. *Ibid.*, pp.58-59.

15. M. Foucault, 'The Confession of the Flesh' in *Power/Knowledge* (Harvester,1980), p.196.

16. *Ibid.*, p.195.

17. See S. Freud, Fetishism (1927) in *On Sexuality* V.7 (Pelican Freud Library,1981), p.345 ff; for fetishism and 'the imaginary signifier' see C. Metz 'The Imaginary Signifier', Ch.5 in *Psychoanalysis and Cinema* (Macmillan 1982). See also Steve Neale, 'The Same Old Story: Sterotypes and Differences' in *Screen Education*, No.32/33.

18. F. Fanon, 'The Fact of Blackness' in *Black Skin White Masks* (Paladin,1970), see pp.78-82.

19. Fanon,*ibid.*, p.69.

20. C. Metz, *op.cit.*, pp.59-60.

21. *Ibid.*, pp.62-63.

22. For the best account of Lacan's concept of the Imaginary see J. Rose, 'The Imaginary' in *The Talking Cure* ed. C. MacCabe (Macmillan, 1981).

23. F. Fanon, 'Racism and Culture' in *Toward the African Revolution* (Pelican, 1970), p.44.

24. F. Fanon, *Black Skin White Masks*, p.114.

25. S. Freud, *op.cit.*, p.357.

26. F. Fanon, *The Wretched of the Earth* (Penguin, 1969).

27. P. Abbot, 'On Authority', *Screen*, Vol.20, No.2, Summer 1979, pp. 15-16.

28. *Ibid.*, p.16.

29. *Ibid.*, p.16.

30. F. Fanon, *Black Skin White Masks*, p.79.

31. C. Metz, *op.cit.*, p.70.

32. J. Laplanche and J.B. Pontalis, 'Phantasy (or Fantasy)' in *The Language of Psychoanalysis* (Hogarth, 1980), p.318.

33. Fanon, *Black Skin White Masks*, p.80.

34. See K. Abraham, 'Transformations of Scopophilia', *Selected Papers* (Hogarth, 1978).

35. Fanon, 'Racism and Culture', *op.cit.*, p.44.

THE NEW ART HISTORY

Margaret Iversen

One of my more extravagant fantasies is to be a modern Pandora, to open the vault where the art of the past is stored and to release all the energy of the objects inside. When I find a book or an article which inspires interest in an area once closed to me, I am grateful for this and for its methodological inventiveness which might be just the key I need. My complaint is that such books are so few and far between and I blame this dearth on the methodological procedures informing mainstream art history. The first half of this paper, 'The Problem', is a critique of those procedures; the second half 'The Solution', reviews some promising developments in the field and proposes some guidelines for an alternative study of art.

The Problem

The task of the best writing in art history has always been that of re-animating the art of the past. During the 19th century this was done by means of the category of development. The ambitious world-historical schemes of German *Kunstgeschichte* were formulated in order to make the past intelligible and accessible, as well as to situate, to underwrite, or to criticize the contemporary situation. The positivist reaction to these schemes retreated to a quasi-causal explanation of the art of restricted periods or of individual artists. This served to correct many factual errors of attribution and dating, but failed to offer an alternative solution to the problem of relating the past to the present. This historically 'authentic' empiricism, which in its Marxist variant finds causal links with the mode of production, relies on the older model to avoid antiquarianism which, as Fredric Jameson says, "'solves' the problem of the relationship between present and past by the simple gesture of abolishing the present as such ...". (1) Contemporary art historians' recourse to the 19th century notion of history as a logical unfolding is motivated by the recognition that some procedure is necessary in order to make the past intelligible and relevant to us. And so one finds sub-Hegelian speculations like the following one from Edward Lucie-Smith's book, *Movements in Art Since 1945*.

> Art, it seems to me, has been making steady progress in one direction at least: it tends to concern itself less and less with the tangible object, and is merely the agent which sets in motion a series of physiological and psychological changes within the spectator. (2)

Yet this attempt at recovering the past is doomed in advance because, as I want to argue, we have lost the urgency which once attached to the notion of historical development. We need new strategies.

Another 'solution' to the problem of our relation to the art of the past is simply to assume a universal category of aesthetic value. Quite apart from the dubiousness of the assumption, the strategy necessitates abstracting some bare formal quality from the particular thematic or iconographic value of works of art. The notion of universal aesthetic value makes all artistic achievement not just similar, as with the developmental model, but the same.

These traditional strategies are by now impediments to a truly vital study of art. Another impediment is our anachronistic conception of what counts as art. The explosion of art forms today should open the way for a study of a wider variety of visual artefacts from all ages. Yet old hierarchies persist. The oldest of these, going back to Pliny and Vitruvius, are hierarchies based on materials and technique. Works of art fashioned from more precious material are more highly valued. The degree of technical difficulty mastered in a work is also an ancient criterion of value. The dominant notion of Fine Art today is basically a 17th century Italian invention. A hierarchy of the arts was then established on the basis of subject matter. Religious or mythical narratives which require the insight of a poet or philosopher were most highly esteemed, while landscape and still-life were left to Dutch and Flemish artists working in Rome. This hierarchy of genres was confirmed by Lebrun and the French Academy, reiterated by Reynolds, (3) first President of the Royal Academy, and later by Ruskin. Ruskin's hierarchy was 1) Sacred subjects, 2) Acts or meditations of Great Men, 3) Passions and events of ordinary life, so-called genre painting. (4) There is room for movement between these categories, thus Landseer, although a painter of animals, is a 'man of mind' and so has 'greatness of style'. Contemporary art history adheres to this hierarchy in so far as craft, design, items of popular culture, fashion do not have sufficient 'mind' to sustain much serious study.

There were already signs of stress on the traditional hierarchy of the arts at the close of the 19th century. The Viennese art historian, Alois Riegl, made pleas for the inclusion of ornament as one of the Fine Arts. (5) Inevitably, he does so by elaborating a theory of the history of ornament. The assumption is that if ornament has a continuous history, then it is a proper Fine Art. Fine Arts are those that participate in the evolution of western culture. The artefacts of non-European culture do not participate, and so are worthy of archaeological or anthropological interest only. "There is no art in the whole of Africa, Asia, or America", quoth Ruskin. Euro-centrism survives in art history to its diminishment.

Of course, some periods of western art were also once considered to be beyond the pale. Riegl, again, wrote his *Spätrömische Kunstindustrie* (6) to show that late Roman art was not the fortuitous result of barbarian invasion, but a necessary stage in the internal development of art leading to our modern conception of space and, on that account, deserves to be aesthetically valued and seriously studied.

On the whole, contemporary art historians no longer construct such bold world-historical schemes, although many a general introduction to art history is couched in terms of a walk out of the caves of Altamira, through the corporeal reality of the Renaissance, to stare into the blinding light of abstraction. Most, however, are inclined to settle on a limited branch or on an individual artist, and chart that restricted development. The point is that development is still the context in which art is understood. While it is true that works of art have to be inserted into some context in order to be made intelligible, it is not clear that development is the only or the best sort of context.

It seems to me that art historians are still bowed under the authority of 19th century paradigms and, as a result, the discipline is in grave danger of becoming sterile. This is so because the historical procedure, having lost its metaphysical underpinning, either builds castles in the air or mechanically orders information. History is no longer the all-embracing category of knowledge that it used to be. We no longer see an over-all pattern or directedness in history. The notion of progress, especially, has lost currency for a generation which has seen scientific 'progress' flip-flop over into the possibility of self-inflicted extinction. Gombrich's *Art and Illusion* (7) is in this respect a famous last stand. We are much more likely to regard past cultures as dynamic systems, fields of forces if you like, full of conflicting interests, constituted by different economic, political and social organizations and operating with very different systems of value. We are conscious that quite different uses can be made of visual images which might serve magical, ritual, devotional, political or economic ends. Our subject should not be art at all, but visual artefacts, their production and function within different social systems. As I said, this expansion should follow on the very heterogeneous nature of moden art. One clear symptom of art historians' reluctance to accept the radically altered conception of modern art is the gulf between academic art history and art criticism. The two functions hardly overlap. Voicing a similar lament, James Ackerman speaks of 'dry history and wet criticism' as the double penalty paid for this division of labour. (8)

The Solution

There is a desperate need for a discipline which studies the life of visual signs within society. I have arrived at an alternative method for this discipline by abstracting general procedures from a few texts which seem to me particularly inventive and successful. I have supplemented these with some practical historical work of my own. The method that emerges from this study involves an historical semiotics of the visual sign, psychoanalysis and politics. It includes both an account of the context of production and a consideration of the discourses which construct a work of art's initial reception and subsequent recuperations. Two of the texts which I have found particularly useful were written, not by academic art historians, but by scholars who have come to visual art from literature. This is not surprising since literary studies have proved far more receptive to contemporary theoretical debates than art history.

One such book is the recently published study of 18th century French art by Norman Bryson called *Word and Image*. (9) Bryson abandons the old 'saga' of stylistic development from French Baroque, through rococo excesses, to the reaction of neo-classicism and replaces this with an analysis based on the period's volatile relation to the visual sign. Paintings of the period seem to be either extremely 'discursive', a kind of imagery colonized by the word, or 'figural', resisting literariness. This broad schema is supported by detailed readings of paintings which contrive to re-animate as intractable an artist as Greuze. According to Bryson, we find these paintings peculiar and maddening partly because of their extreme discursiveness. The figures must be legible as stereotypes of different ages and conditions within the family so that they may be brought together in a moment of extremity which abolishes difference in a common emotion. Greuze's paintings are also odd because, as Bryson says, they are the sites of simultaneous representations of incompatibles. The girl in *The Broken Pitcher*, for example, bears the marks both of a child with chubby hands and large head and of a woman with full lips and tumescent breasts: she is a virgin who has been sexually initiated. *La Mère Bien-aimée* (Fig.1) is even more difficult to swallow and was so for Greuze's contemporary, Diderot. Here sexual pleasure and parenting are superimposed. Bryson concludes:

> Greuze cannot resist his dangerous fusions, and it begins to emerge that for him the image is the place where happinesses that reality keeps separating may be returned to blissful unity. (10)

It is appropriate to raise the question of the place of unconscious or repressed desire in the formation of these images. It would also be appropriate to pursue questions about the ideology of the family and of salon-going Parisians' attraction to these rural domestic dramas.

Bryson's colleague at King's College Cambridge, John Barrell, has written an equally inventive study of the representation of the rural poor in 18th and early 19th century English landscape painting. *The Dark Side of the Landscape* (11) is a good example of a text which seeks out what Jameson has called the 'political unconscious' of art. (12) The term is exact since Barrell understands the paintings he treats as wish-fulfillments on the part of painters and patrons. They present, as he says, 'a mythical unity' which 'attempts to pass itself off as an image of the actual unity of the English countryside innocent of division'. Yet close reading "discovers evidence of the very conflict it seems to deny". (13) Although throughout this period labourers in agriculture must be represented as honest and hard-working, in 1755 it was still possible for Gainsborough to represent interrupted labour as in *Landscape with a Woodcutter Courting a Milkmaid* (Fig.2) which includes a ploughman at work in the background. While the painting immediately suggests that work and play are both parts of English rural life, it functions to conceal the division between producer and consumer. In other words, the articulation of a difference between times for work and play both expresses and conceals the social difference between those who work and those who play. The polite viewer could identify with the foreground figures who "hover between a courtly and a rustic identity", (14) a clear case of what Freud called condensation in dreamwork. This is how Barrell characterizes Gainsborough's landscapes:

> all these pictures, then, confirm the boasted equality of
> Merry England and deny it too. They proclaim the liberal
> ideology of a rich, happy, harmonious land, in which all
> men work together and all consume the fruits of that common
> industry; while they portray the repressive actuality, that
> the sweets of life are reserved for the rich, the sweat for
> the poor; and their success is to conceal this contradiction,
> by the careful handling of iconography and structure. (15)

The ideological function of images is enforced and carried forward by the discourses which immediate and subsequent generations produce, sometimes spectacularly reversing a work's original intervention. Michelangelo's *David* is a striking case in point. It is a commonplace of art historical discourse that the *David* distills the heroic and democratic ideals of the Florentine Republic: "in the vigorous forms and the proud visage is recognizable the heroic conception of man as a free creature and as Master of Fate". (16) But the circumstances of its original intervention give pause for thought. In October 1494, the tide of public opinion was turning against the Medici. Michelangelo, living with his patron Piero as he had with Lorenzo before him, fled Florence. He returned in 1501 when the political situation had stabilized under the new Republic, but he received no commissions until a change in the constitution made the *Gonfaloniere* a life-term appointment on the model of the *Doge* of Venice. The first life-*Gonfaloniere* was Pietro Soderini, an admirer of Michelangelo. Just twelve days after his installment, Michelangelo was awarded the commission for the *David*. Shortly before its completion a meeting was called to decide where to position the 'Giant'. Michelangelo himself was not present but it would appear that his view was put by the Herald of the *Signoria* who spoke first:

I have turned over in my mind those suggestions which my
judgement could afford me. You have two places where the
statue may be set up: the first, where the Judith stands;
the second, in the middle of the courtyard where (Donatello's)
David is. The first might be selected because the Judith is
an omen of evil, and no fit object where it stands, as we
have the cross and lily for emblems; besides, it is not proper
that the woman should kill the male; and, above all, this
statue was erected under an evil star, as you have gone continually from bad to worse since then. Even Pisa has been
lost. The *David* of the courtyard is an imperfect statue because the leg thrust backward is poor; and so I should advise
you to put the Giant in one of these places, but I give preference myself to that of the *Judith*. (17)

Most of the committee members voted for the Loggia de' Lanzi adjacent to the *Palazzo*, but the statue was eventually installed in the more
honorific site in front of the seat of government on the spot where
Judith had stood. The *Judith* had originally been in the garden of the
Medici Palace, but when they were expelled, it was removed and placed
in the *Piazza* as a symbol of Republican victory.

The installation of Michelangelo's *David* must have been a politically risky business. We read in Lucca Landucci's Diary that

on the 14th of May 1504, the marble Giant was taken from the
Opera. It came out at 24 o'clock, and they broke the wall
above the gateway enough to let it pass. That night some
stones were thrown at the colossus to harm it. Watch had to
be kept at night; and it made way very slowly ... (18)

Klein and Zerner, the editors of the collection of documents from which
I have quoted, remark, "the act of vandalism mentioned by Landucci may
have been promoted by political considerations because Donatello's
Judith, which was to be dethroned, was particularly dear to the radical
Republicans of the old school". (19) The facts certainly point in this
direction, but so important is the continuing ideological value of *David*,
one reads in Frederick Hartt's book of Michelangelo's sculpture, "a band
of mischievous youths, perhaps supporters of the exiled Medici, stoned
the statue". (20)

It is the job of the art historian both to decipher the work itself
as an intervention and to assess the discourses which it prompts. One
of the most palpable disjunctions between intervention and reception was
suffered by Manet's *Olympia* first shown in the Salon of 1865 (Fig.3).
Champfleury wrote in a letter to Baudelaire, "like a man who falls in
the snow, Manet has made a hole in public opinion". (21) This is an
apt simile, for all the conflicting responses seem wide of the mark.
Some reviled the model as dirty and vulgar. Zola defended the painting
by brushing aside its subject matter and by drawing attention to stylistic features. Manet is the kind of painter for whom "subject matter is
a pretext for painting", he said. Valéry was later to write of the
'ritual animality' of *Olympia*, 'that monster of banal sensuality' and
pointed to the ribbon isolating 'her empty head from her essential being'
(22) In the recent debate conducted in *Screen* magazine, Tim Clark sym-
pathises with the confusion of the Salon critics and castigates the
painting for its failure to signify in 1865. The figure refuses to
occupy a place in the available taxonomy of woman or in the class structure. (23) Peter Wollen responds that it is not a question of failing
to signify, but the representation of real contradictions, and assimilates the picture to the structure of a fetish. (24)

I take exception to all these responses because they don't explain why I find it such a positive, even feminist, image. *Olympia*, and other paintings of women by Manet, work against the comfortable relation of viewer and viewed enshrined in the tradition of western art. This is the thesis advanced by Rosalind Krauss, who attends to an earlier work by Manet called *Nymph Surprised* (Fig.4). (25) The title, given by Manet himself, suggests that the theme of the painting is not just a bather, but one surprised by an intruder. The picture is related to the theme of Susanna and the Elders, in particular to Rembrandt's version in the Hague and to an engraving after Rubens. Manet reworks the theme in two ways. First, the figure no longer inhabits the landscape, but seems like a brightly illuminated model set against a studio backdrop; secondly, the voyeurs internal to the scene have been eliminated. Rembrandt's painting elicits our sympathy; we empathize with Suzanna's plight and so distance ourselves from the voyeurs in the bushes. In the case of Manet's painting, however, as soon as we see the thematic allusion, we must recognize ourselves as the voyeuristic Elders. As Krauss suggests:

> Manet no longer invites sympathetic involvement in the emotional world of the picture; he creates a scene which makes one realize one's own disjunction from the work of art, as look begins to fuse with violation. (26)

Manet's intention was to deny easy access to the contemplation of a naked woman. The consciousness which it opens up makes

any comfortable viewing position impossible.

I think this is what disconcerted the critics and crowds at the salon where *Olympia* was exhibited. It was supposed to turn the act of looking back on itself; instead everyone looked elsewhere. As with the *Nymph Surprised*, Manet relies on our simultaneous awareness of a similar image, in this case Titian's *Venus of Urbino*, and invites us to compare it with his point by point denial of the traditional regime of looking. To this end, he has propped the figure up high so that she looks down at us instead of coyly up. He has stiffened the figure and made its outlines sharp and clear. He lets her hair disappear into the screen behind. Almost as a joke, he replaces the Venus's sleeping puppy with a hissing black cat. Finally, the Renaissance space is abruptly brought forward. The classic icon of the nude is recalled only in order to be criticised. It is a consciousness raising picture.

One further Manet painting may help my argument. *La Servante de Bocks* (Fig.5) is composed of a serving maid dispensing beer to men who face the other way. The men gaze at the distant figure, a fantasy woman on the stage. Like the prisoners in Plato's Cave they mistake the impoverished reflection for the real. But the construction of Manet's painting has inverted this order for us.

I want to offer one further, and very different, example in order to illustrate how this model can be turned to the analysis of mass media images such as advertisements. My example is an ad for Clairol hair colour. (27) Its New York setting suggests big business and sophistication, while the woman's clothes suggest a 'masculine', even aggressive, female. The camera angle is about level with her knee. From these clues we gather that this ad plays on middle class women's career aspirations. But it also latches on to the unconscious mechanism of this desire. The jubilant kicking leg is graphically balanced by the slogan "I found it". What she has found is thus associated with the phallic leg. This is underscored by the name of the product 'Happiness' (penis), and by the photographs of the containers at the bottom of the page which present a cinematic series of an erection. The ad exploits the woman's movement first by identifying it with careerism, then by accentuating woman's sense of lack within Patriarchy, and finally by implying that the product will make her feel whole.

Summary

My proposal for the study of visual artefacts in terms of intervention, reception and subsequent recuperations has several points to recommend it. 1) Because it focuses on very specific kinds of intervention, the method allows for close reading of individual works of art. It therefore avoids *a priori* and global notions of style and class which can blunt sensitivity to the nuances of particular instances. This is the great weakness of Nicos Hadjinicolaou's approach in *Art History and Class Struggle*.(28) 2) My method necessitates detailed historical research in order to gauge the political and artistic circumstances of an intervention. 3) Its attention to subsequent discourses reveals those sedimented layers which impinge on our perception. These discourses are themselves interventions as, indeed, is my own. 4) Its sense of art as a kind of discourse resists identifying the meaning of the work with surrounding critical responses. 5) Finally, it brings to the foreground the political dimension of the visual sign. To use an analogy, it turns Saussure's famous one-sided chess game into a contest between oppressor and oppressed. There are determinate sets of social conditions, given artistic practices, genres, stylistic and thematic paradigms, but many possible moves within these constraints. Each move, each very singular intervention, has to be thought dialectically and strategically. It is this sense of contestation, of struggle, which unites the past with our present.

Notes

1. Fredric Jameson, "Marxism and Historicism", *New Literary History*, XI, 1 (Autumn, 1979), p.45.

2. Edward Lucie-Smith, *Movements in Art Since 1945* (London: Thames and Hudson, 1969), p.22.

3. Sir Joshua Reynolds, *Discourses*, especially Discourse III.

4. John Ruskin, *Modern Painters*, Vol.III, Chap.3.

5. Alois Riegl, *Historische Grammatik der bildenden Künste*, eds. Karl M. Swoboda and Otto Pacht (Graz-Köln: Herman Bohlaus Nachf., 1966).

6. Alois Riegl, *Die Spätromische Kunstindustrie* (Wien: Der Österr. Staatsdruckerei, 1927).

7. Sir Ernst Gombrich, *Art and Illusion: a study in the psychology of representation*, Bollingen Series XXX.5 (Princeton University Press, 1960).

8. James S. Ackerman, "Art History and Problems of Criticism", *Dedalus* (1960), p.253.

9. Norman Bryson, *Word and Image: French Baroque Painting of the Ancien Régime* (Cambridge University Press, 1981).

10. *Ibid.*, p.137.

11. John Barrell, *The Dark Side of the Landscape: the rural poor in English Painting 1730-1840* (Cambridge University Press, 1980).

12. Fredric Jameson, *The Political Unconscious: narrative as a socially symbolic act* (London: Methuen, 1981).

13. Barrell, p.5.

14. *Ibid.*, p.51.

15. *Ibid.*, p.52.

16. Charles de Tolnay, *The Youth of Michelangelo* (Princeton University Press, 1943), p.98.

17. Robert Klein and Henri Zerner, *Italian Art 1500-1600*, Sources and Documents (Englewood Cliffs: Prentice Hall, 1966), p.41.

18. *Ibid.*, p.44.

19. *Ibid.*, p.39.

20. Frederick Hartt, *Michelangelo: the complete sculpture* (London: Thames and Hudson, 1969), p.106.

21. Letter of May 1865 cited in Theodore Reff, *Manet: Olympia* (London: Allen Lane, 1976), p.16.

22. For documentation of these and other critical responses see Reff, cited above, and George Heard Hamilton, *Manet and his Critics* (New York: W.W. Norton and Co., 1969).

23. Timothy J. Clark, "Preliminaries to a Possible Treatment of 'Olympia' in 1865", *Screen*, 21, 1 (Spring, 1980), pp.18-42.

24. Peter Wollen, "Manet: Modernism and Avant-Garde", *Screen*, 21, 2 (Summer, 1980), pp.15-26.

25. Rosalind Krauss, "Manet's Nymph Surprised", *Burlington Magazine*, CIX (1969), pp.622-627.

26. *Ibid.*, p.624.

27. The photograph is taken from Judith Williamson, *Decoding Advertisements* (London: Marion Boyars, 1978) p.37. The interpretation is my own.

28. Nicos Hadjinicolaou, *Art History and Class Struggle*, trans. Louise Asmal (London: Pluto Press, 1978). For a critical commentary see Alan Wallach, "In Search of a Marxist Theory of Art History", *Block*, 4, (1981), pp.15-17.

ANNUS MIRABILIS: SYNCHRONY AND DIACHRONY

John Frow

'1642', '1789', '1848', '1936': past Essex conferences have taken as their organizing principle the *annus mirabilis*, a point of historical intensity defined politically (as revolutionary conjuncture) and implying a convergence of economic and ideological modes of production in the production of political revolution. Synchronic organization presupposes at least that these instances form a totality, that they are causally, and with whatever complexity, interrelated; but the form of this causality, and its implications for a 'sociology of literature', have remained an open problem. The year 1936, for example, offers no obvious temporal correlations. Politically it was marked by the beginning of the Spanish Civil War, the election of the Popular Front government in France, and by the German occupation of the Rhineland; but in terms of literary production it was a largely unremarkable year. If one were to select the most 'significant' cultural events of that year (that is, events that we can retrospectively see to have had consequences, to have marked the closure, the deflection, or the initiation of particular historical series), one might perhaps choose the publication of Keynes' *General Theory of Employment, Interest and Money*; Allen Lane's founding of Penguin Books; or the release of *Modern Times* and *Gone with the Wind*.

This is to say that the principle of the synchronic cross-section lays bare quite disparate temporal series, whilst assuming their simultaneity at some level. Unless the principle is purely mechanical it works as an *histoire totale*, supposing 'that one and the same form of historicity operates upon economic structures, social institutions and customs, the inertia of mental attitudes, technological practice, political behaviour, and subjects them all to the same type of transformation'. (1) But this totality is also interstitial, a point (or a dispersed set of points) of passage from one state of affairs to another, and as such it is teleologically defined. The order of the *annus mirabilis* - the selection of the systems to which we will ascribe significance (publishing, for example, because of the consequences of the paperback revolution), and their particular temporal density and direction - is constructed from the relative closure of a larger narrative, in which the possible is replaced by the necessary, the contingent becomes systematic.

This necessity is of course no more than that of our later knowledge; and a retrospective teleology and a retrospective totalization are thus mutually implicated. Both aspects depend upon what Jameson calls 'the logical fallacy ... of anachronistically designating a term of one system as the "precursor" of a term in a system that does not yet exist'. (2) To put this more positively, both are forms of writing, with no claim to access to the immediacy and unpredictability of an open system. Synchrony and diachrony, in other words, are categories of knowledge, not of being. Their status is methodological rather than ontological; they refer not to entities but to perspectives on phenomena. (3) The theoretical consequences of this are then either that synchrony is taken to be the form of logical, systemic description and diachrony a principle of random, accidental variation, a representation of the actual and concrete in relation to an ideal order; or that diachrony is subordinated to synchrony: both are taken to be forms of logical ordering, and both are therefore in a sense 'synchronic'.

This formulation will be familiar from Althusser's rejection of the concepts of synchrony and diachrony as forms of existence of historical time which imply on the one hand a conception of time as homogeneous, continuous, self-contemporaneous, and on the other the mere contingency of historical change. (4) Synchrony and diachrony are rather, Althusser argues, to be defined as 'the concept of the two forms of existence of the object of knowledge, and hence as two forms existing purely inside knowledge. Synchrony represents the organizational structure of the concepts in the thought-totality or system (or, as Marx puts it, "synthesis"), diachrony the movement of succession of the concepts in the ordered discourse of the proof'. (5). But the effect of this reformulation is to displace the theoretical problem to a different level, where the question of the determination of 'the organizational structure of the concepts' and of their 'movement of succession - in the ordered discourse of the proof' is silently passed over. Despite Althusser's recognition that knowledge is produced within a determinate 'mode of production of knowledges' defined by a network of material and economic, social, and ideological relations, and that the state of the (ideological) raw material that knowledge works is a part of the conditions of production of knowledge and therefore sets its possible limits,(6) knowledge is consistently withdrawn from its social determinations. The model used is implicitly that of an indeterminate structure (a series of contiguous systems unstructured by relations of dominance and subordination) rather than the effectively dialectical model of overdetermined structure. The further problem that follows from this definition is not that 'history' is evacuated from the theorization of the mode of production (this empiricist charge misses the force of the definition of history as a discursive construct and attempts simply to re-establish history as a non-discursive presence within discourse), but rather that it begs the question of how to define diachrony as a system: the problem becomes acute with Balibar's attempt to formulate a structuralist account of transitional modes of production.

The debate around the concept of transition has become the *locus classicus* within marxism of the problem of diachrony, and it is also the weak link in the theorization of the conceptual unity of a mode of production. The first stage of the debate was conducted in the 1940's and 1950's, largely in the pages of *Science and Society*, and it concentrated on the transition between the feudal and the capitalist modes of production. (7) What was at stake was the periodization of capitalism in England: the orthodox version, apparently supported by both Marx and Engels, was that a capitalist mode of production was established and 'dominant' in England by the sixteenth century; Hill and Dobb, by contrast, argued that the Civil War involved, not the maintenance of an evolved capitalism against a monarchist/feudal counter-revolution but rather the moment of class struggle (between an alliance of merchant bourgeoisie, freehold farmers and small tenants on the one hand, and feudal landowners on the other) which was to put capitalism and a capitalist state structure in place. It is significant, however, that both sides in the debate have difficulty thinking with a model which directly derives social classes from economic categories. Thus Dobb wrote, in an essay of 1941: 'How could the seventeenth century struggle be treated as a bourgeois-democratic revolution when it came a century and a half before the rise of capitalist production? Whence a bourgeoisie to carry through the revolution, if the capitalist mode of production was not yet in being at all? Moreover, what was the prevailing mode of production in Stuart England, anyhow?' (8) It was clearly not feudal; but it also could not be merchant capitalism, which was fully developed only at a later period; the petty mode of production was still not extricated from feudal relations of production; and the concept of 'absolutism' is a purely superstructural label. Subsequently, in *Studies in the Development of Capitalism* (1946), Dobb attempted a more precise periodization. The decline of feudalism is located in the fourteenth to fifteenth centuries; and the rise of capitalism in the early seventeenth century. He is thus led to characterize some two hundred years of English history as 'neither feudal nor yet capitalist', (9) that is, as 'transitional'.

Part of the importance of this 'missing' mode of production was of course that it implicitly posed the question of the 'missing' mode of production in Stalinist Russia: neither capitalist nor communist. The *Science and Society* debate was 'resolved' by appeal to the historical record; but the recourse to historical description failed precisely to theorize the concept of transition. What does become clear, especially with the extension of the discussion to other social formations, is the plurality of possible passages to a capitalist mode of production. Perry Anderson takes up this point in *Lineages of the Absolutist State*. Arguing against the universalization of 'feudalism' as a purely economic structure defined independently of its specific juridical, political and ideological superstructures, he notes that it is only in capitalism that the economy becomes a self-contained order because of the fact that 'the means whereby the surplus is pumped out of the direct producer is "purely" economic in form: the wage contract'. By contrast, 'all other previous modes of exploitation operate through extra-economic sanctions - kin, customary, religious, legal or political. It is therefore on principle always impossible to read them off from economic relations as such. The 'superstructures' of kinship, religion, law or the state necessarily enter into the constitutive structure of the mode of production in pre-capitalist social formations'. (10) It then becomes evident 'that the complex imbrication of economic exploitation with extra-economic institutions and ideologies creates a much wider gamut of possible modes of production prior to capitalism than could be deduced from the relatively simple and massive generality of the capitalist mode of production itself ...' (11) - perhaps even (although Anderson doesn't take this step) as many modes of production as there were social formations. And this possibility might in turn make us doubtful as to the 'massive generality' of capitalism, and suggest a similar collapsing of the capitalist mode of production into a 'family' of capitalist social formations.

The difficulties in theorizing the concept of transition become more pointed in the 'structuralist' methodology of Balibar and Bettelheim. Reiterating Marx's 'obvious' comment that the transition from one mode of production to another can never be an irrational hiatus since production never stops, Balibar remarks that transition therefore 'cannot be a moment of destructuration, however brief. It is itself a movement subject to a structure which has to be discovered'. Forms of transition 'are therefore themselves modes of production', but they are qualitatively different from self-reproducing modes of production. (12) The concept of diachrony will be reserved for 'the time of the transition from one mode of production to another', although strictly speaking what is at issue is a theory 'of the diachrony', since 'all theory is synchronic insofar as it expounds a systematic set of conceptual determinations'. (13) The concept of diachrony thus refers ambivalently to real time and to a specific form of its conceptualization; and to this ambivalence corresponds a splitting of the concept of mode of production into one form which is 'eternal', synchronic, and governed by a structural causality; and another form which is temporal, diachronic, and governed by a teleological causality. (14)

For Bettelheim this duality is to be located not in the object but in the epistemological consequences of marxist methodology. *Capital* is the study of a theoretical system, not an empirical object. There will therefore be a gap between the concept of a mode of production and any actual economic system, and this gap is characterized by 'residues' and 'impurities' which are not, however, specific to transitional modes (unless we consider all economies to be transitional). (15) It is a question then of two distinct theoretical levels in the description of transition: the level of the constitution of a mode of production, describing an actual historical passage; and the level of the ideal passage from one mode of production to another. At this second level of abstraction the 'succession in the realm of ideas may be different from the real transition from one economic system to another'; accordingly, 'while we can conceive of abstract laws of passage from one mode of production to another, we cannot state that any law of linear succession is historically necessary', and 'the very complexity of the social structures rules out any unilinear development'. (16) In order to account for this complexity we need a theory of the structure of the conjuncture, understood as a theory of the real, complex totality of levels, the 'historical' as opposed to the 'ideal' - and the representation of this 'concrete' proceeds 'by reconstituting in concepts the organic totality of a socio-economic formation'. (17)

'Structuralist' marxism thus tends either to an axiomatic dissolution of 'irrational' content into the conceptual system, or else to a recognition of facticity as a determinant of form and so to the loss of systematic autonomy in a descriptive methodology lacking in theoretical power. Even as it seeks to overcome it, it reconfirms the empiricist opposition between the abstract and the concrete.

A more recent attempt to resolve this 'transformation problem' is the nominalism of Hindess and Hirst: that is, the move to a less gross level of analytic generality, taking the form of an insistence that the structure of a social formation cannot be derived from the concept of a determinate mode of production, and that the presence of a mode of production is not sufficient to secure its own conditions of existence (these have a relative independence and are determined by the specific conditions of the class struggle). (18) Thus 'it is no longer possible to represent either the reproduction or the transformation of a mode of production as the realization of an inner principle of identity (in the case of eternal production) or of contradiction (in the case of transformation). On the contrary, both the production and the transformation of a mode of production must be analyzed in terms of a determinate material causality, as the definite effects of specific real relations.' The necessity not to internalize the economic, political and ideological conditions of existence of a mode of production within the concept of its structure places the theoretical emphasis on the 'transitional conjuncture' in which the transformation or non-transformation of a mode of production is only a possible outcome of the class struggle. (19) There can therefore be no general theory of transition, only specific conjunctural theories, (20) and this gives rise to the paradox that, whereas a mode of production can be analyzed not empirically but only at the level of its concept, the spaces between modes of production are subject to no general theory, only to conjunctural analysis.

This anomaly is overcome in the later work of Hindess and Hirst by a strong form of nominalism, in particular an attack on 'the idea that necessary effectivities postulated in a general concept of the capitalist mode of production can be, directly or indirectly, 'mapped' on to capitalist social formations ... It follows from this rejection that there can be no necessary and general periodization of capitalist social formations at the level of a concept of capitalist mode of production.' (21) There is no 'massive generality' of capitalism: the concept of mode of production cannot be applied to historical analysis because it depends upon the epistemological model of the 'appropriation' or 'assimilation' of the concrete by the abstract. To deny this form of knowledge is to deny 'the objects or entities constituted by it: that is, self-conditioning social totalities whose determinations and effects could be apprehended in abstraction as generalities'. (22) There can be no knowledge relation mediating ontologically heterogeneous realms.

But what remains problematic here is, again, the retention of the very categories that are being rejected. The 'history' to which the concept of mode of production is seen not to be pertinent is equated with the extra-discursive real; but if, as is argued in *Pre-capitalist Modes of Production*, a historical social formation is an object of and within discourse, then the 'application' (an intratextual relation of general to specific concepts, or of levels of formalization) would seem to be perfectly valid. That is, it would seem to be possible to retain the relation of 'appropriation' as a relation, not between the 'conceptual' and the 'real' but between different levels of conceptual generality, different logical levels, and to dispense with the 'concrete' as a category of extradiscursive presence.

The central problem in theorizing transition is that the concepts of synchrony and diachrony refer both to modes of temporal organization and to modes of logical organization. In current usage 'synchrony' means both the 'same time' of a cross-section of disparate series (that is, the time of the relations or articulations within a polychronic system) and also the 'timelessness' of an order of concepts. Diachrony means both 'real time', and that which is non-systemic or which represents a rupture with a system.

Temporal and logical modes of organization will coincide completely only within the framework of a theological or metaphysical world order. Assuming their non-coincidence, and assuming that for any theorization to be possible the synchronic dimension, at least, must be conceived as a logical (discursive) ordering, then we can reach a simple schematization of two possible alternative models:

a)

	synchrony	diachrony
time	-	+
logic	+	-

This model generates the non-theorizability of diachrony, as resistance to the non-time of the concept. In the second model, both synchrony and diachrony are taken to be systemic (both are 'synchronic'):

b)

	synchrony	diachrony
time	-	+
logic	+	-

Here time is completely spatialized: as a category of discourse it becomes a descriptive component of a system, and as such is amenable to theorization. In principle this second model should make it possible to break down the oppositions (real time/logic, non-systemic/systemic) on which it is itself constructed. I'll return to this question later. For the moment it should be noted that the conceptualization of synchrony as real time is in both cases rejected, on the assumption that the synchronic order is always an *a posteriori* construct, built from a knowledge of the later development of different series. The time-slice can't be inherently significant and its developments are only retrospectively examples of necessity.

These two models correspond roughly to the two main groups of strategies employed at previous Essex conferences for dealing with the principle of the synchronic cross-section. The first group I shall call 'historical' sociology, and I mean by this the attempt to reconstruct the conceptual and chronological specificity of discrete historical series and the relation of the literary system to other systems and practices. The philosophical problematic is that of mediation, and I distinguish, rather arbitrarily, four forms of mediation.

The first and most traditional works from literary texts to agents and classes, and to their positioning within a structure of hegemony. Thus John Oakley writes that 'the sociology of literature is centrally concerned with the derivation of structures in the text from relations of production'; and 'in so far as ideology, an enclave within the text, is a transformation of productive relations, literature can (at least accumulatively) point to the groups with whose productive relations its ideology 'fits' - in spite of substitutions and colourings'. (23) Similarly, Ian Birchall reads Pascal's texts as a direct expression of his class position: 'If we read him, we should do so in order to encounter a lucid spokesperson for the enemy, and not to pretend that he is somehow on our side.' (24)

The second form of mediation involves an analysis of the displacement or overdetermination of one code or realm onto/by another. The first of two main modes of displacement of the political is through representations of sexuality. Writing on Tennyson's *The Princess* Terry Eagleton argues that 'the dominant semiotic code' - that of sexuality - 'does indeed, in its turn, encode other ideological motifs, one of which I have already adumbrated - the question of a certain transitional crisis in the nature of state power, occasioned most directly by the sharpening of the class struggle in the 1840's, by the stage of development of the productive forces, and by the minatory spectre of the events in France. As what we might risk calling a 'psychoanalysis of the bourgeois state', the text subtly imbricates the questions of the production of sexuality and the production of political power - the reshaping of the symbolic order and the qualified recasting of the structures of bourgeois dominance'. (25) Sandra Findley and Elaine Ho y, writing on seventeenth century women's autobiography, note the political implications of the restriction of women's writing to the sphere of the 'private', (26) and Christine Berg and Philippa Berry, writing on female prophets in the seventeenth century, characterize the period as that of 'a near revolution in literary perceptions of the relation between sexuality and language, as well as ... of a temporary social and sexual revolution'. (27) A variant of this mode - for example in Francis Barker's paper on the diversion of desire and the emergence of the bourgeois cogito in the 'implicitly censored narration' of Pepys' *Diary*, (28) or in Stan Smith's discussion of the 'crisis of the subject' in the 1930's (29) - concerns the historical status and the historical modification of the category of the subject.

The second major mode of metaphorical displacement is onto language. Here the analytic practices range from David Aers and Gunther Kress's reading-off of Milton's 'themes' and 'underlying vision' from the syntactic organization of language in the prose works, (30) to the University of East Anglia English Studies Group's mapping of the representational strategies which, in the British historical conjuncture of 1789, 'produced a homogeneous set of discourses which systematically elided certain features of the French Revolution and foregrounded others', (31) and to Graham Pechey's extraction, from a discussion of mutations in the ontological status of discourse in the Romantic period, of the radically different political implications of the constitutive and writerly function of language in Blake, and of Wordsworth's logocentrism. (32)

The third form of mediation is developed through a conception of literary discourse as sublimation - that is, as a complex form of expressivity. For Jean Rohou, using categories reminiscent of the subject/object dialectic in Adorno, literature is the metaphorical resolution of an historical contradiction between desire and social constraint. (33) Within the framework of Renée Balibar's neo-Bernsteinian reductionism 'literary works are essentially sublimations of the conflicts lived out in the practice of language'. (34) Jameson's account, in *The Political Unconscious*, of the operation of mediation as 'the invention of an analytic terminology or code which can be applied equally to two or more structurally distinct objects or sectors of being', (35) and his analysis of, for example, Conrad's 'style' in terms of the concepts of rationalization and reification, (36) is the most forceful recent example both of the strengths and of the real weaknesses of this ultimately expressive concept of mediation.

In a paper on Russian Formalism given at the first of the Essex conferences Ray Selden wrote that 'in Shklovsky's hands history dissolves into mere contingency and becomes re-internalized in the synchrony of the system. The solution of the problem required a theoretical perspective which would permit (1) the articulation of the literary and the extra-literary systems, and (2) the overcoming of the contradiction between the synchronic and the diachronic.' (37) It is the articulation at least of discursive practices that constitutes the fourth form of mediation, and most strikingly in Raymond Williams' 'Forms of English Fiction in 1848'. From an initial, teleologically marked distinction between dominant, residual, and emergent institutions and practices (38) Williams proceeds to a description of the different levels of literary production in 1848. He distinguishes four levels: first, a dominant (or predominant) level which is not that of 'bourgeois realism' but rather of the forms of 'historical romance' and the 'consciously exotic', and which are in fact 'residual'; (39) second, fiction whose thematic structure is specifically 'bourgeois' and which is largely made up of family magazine serial fiction and of religious and moral tracts; (40) third, fictional forms corresponding to a subordinate and a repressed culture: working class fiction on the one hand, pornography and scandal on the other; (41) and finally, fiction which we can now, in retrospect, see to have been mainstream: that of the Brontes, Mrs Gaskell, Thackeray and Dickens. In contrast to the first model of mediation, which derives textual structures from relations of production (or vice-versa), Williams' argument is that there can be no direct classification of formal strategies in accordance with a pre-given grid of class positions: rather, 'within the complex class interlock, opposition and the experience of subordination were being expressed at different levels which do not cohere'. (42)

These, very schematically, are the predominant models of synchronic totalization through which the Essex project is put to work. One or other of these models is at least implicit in most papers, and a model of 'historical' sociology is also implicit in the overall organization of the conferences: that is, in the juxtaposition of analyses of disparate literary and non-literary fields of discourse. What seems to me problematic in all of them is the dependence upon categories of systematization (period, hegemony or ideology, genre, text) which are posited as real and given to knowledge, yet which are clearly retrospective constructs. The problem, in other words, is the postulation of a time which is self-identical and which is separate from the time of construction of these categories. (43) This problem is confronted in a second group of strategies, more limited in number, which I shall call 'political' sociology. Here a recognition of the necessarily anachronistic construction of descriptive categories leads to a politicization of texts through their insertion into the time of <u>reading</u>: rather than being fitted into a past conjunctural system the <u>text</u> is set at least partly in opposition to it.

To some extent of course this group of strategies overlaps with the first. Let me give three examples. The first is John Coombes' reading of the 'political aesthetics' of the *18th Brumaire*. Through an analysis of the logic of the figures of mask, theatre and representation Coombes traces the process by which the rhetorical distinction between illusion and reality turns back on itself and is eventually 'forced into a condition of complexity approaching virtual unreadability, the project of the work emerging as the revelation of the questionability of its own narration'. (44) As in Jeffrey Mehlman's reading of the text, (45) the problem of linguistic representation is linked to the explanatory failure of the concept of political representation; but 'to say, in this connection, that the text "reflects" the situation external to it is an evident and gross oversimplification - unless of course the term "reflection" is taken in a more than usually complex sense to indicate a conceptualization of the text's determinants which, by drawing attention obliquely through its very "literariness" to their questionability, constitutes an active intervention in their continuing history'. (46)

The second example is Fredric Jameson's reading of *Paradise Lost*, a reading which proceeds from a double caution. The first is that Jameson is as much concerned with the continuing ideological power and potential political force of religion (for example, its complex role in the Iranian revolution) as with the particular displacements it operates in seventeenth century England. (47) The second is an argument that any expressive or allegorical reading of *Paradise Lost* in terms of pre-given historical generalizations about the failure of revolution, etc., can merely substitute for and pre-empt the findings of a concrete reading. Here again, the (construction of the) formal structure of the text is seen to be in contradiction with its thematic content, and Jameson concludes that 'the poem ... illustrates and documents, not a proposition about human nature, not a type of philosophical or theological content, but rather the operation of ideological closure: in this way, a poem in which as we have said the political is repressed nonetheless ends up by producing a political reading of itself'. (48)

The third example is a paper by Jerry Palmer, 'Between Macchiavelli and Marx: 1789 and the Discourses of State and Power', delivered at the *1789* conference but not published in the conference proceedings. Palmer takes '1789' not as a 'real' historical site but as the pretext for a catachronistic projection of the jacobinist moment of leninism, and as itself in turn retrospectively projecting, appropriating, and constrained by a macchiavellian model of state power, one which continues to haunt the Communist tradition. As in the *18th Brumaire*, history is conceived not as a point of presence but as a slippage, an oscillation between the repetition of a past and the anticipation of a future.

I should stress that both groups of strategies posit a structure 'defined in the future anterior, by the future results of present phenomena'; (49) both depend upon a form of narrative closure. The second group, however, is less dependent upon a monolithic concept of totality. It is therefore in principle better equipped to reject the application of a uniform temporality to different series, and to construct a non-linear concept of diachrony. Its 'history' will be textual: a process of writing with a political function in the present. The dangers here will be that of positing (as Hindess and Hirst do in a notorious passage of *Pre-capitalist Modes of Production*) (50) the 'present conjuncture' from which the past is constructed as a pure presence; and that of using the complexity of relations between disparate series as an excuse for dispensing with questions of causality.

In the rest of this paper I want to make a few tentative suggestions towards rethinking the specificity of the diachronic status of the literary system. The first is that it is crucial to differentiate the temporalities of the economic, political, and ideological levels of a social formation. If we assign to the economic level the temporality (or the theoretical problematic) of the transition between modes of production; to the political level that of the revolutionary conjuncture; and to the ideological level that of the dialectic between system (or régime of signification) and the 'break' with its regularities, it will become possible to avoid the homologizing metaphors of a 'transitional mode of literary production' or of literary 'crisis' or 'revolution'. The rhythms of discontinuity will be specific to each instance, but will also be historically differentiated.

The model I am proposing is basically a Russian Formalist model of the intertextual dynamic of literary history. (51) What is at issue here is in fact a dual temporality: on the one hand the continuous time of the linear self-reproduction of the system, and on the other the discontinuous time or times of acts of new production. The latter will form the basis for the initiation of the time of new systems, but these acts are also inscribed negatively within the time of the systems from which they deviate. They thus have no fixed temporality: as a determinate negation the new text functions as a kind of anti-time, but its ideological appropriation will generate the positivity of a new order. Nor can we properly think in terms of a single time of new production: the productive or reproductive activity of the text will have a different valency through its multiple inscription into new systems; the times of its appropriations will determine its multiple textuality.

This is not a description of a closed or 'internal' process, since the time of literary history will be that of the progressive sedimentation of a chain of synchronic interactions with other structures (for example, the discursive structures which are textually worked). Nor is it a universal model. If each period produces its own particular time,

(52) then literary history will be a bundle of such times rather than a sequence passing through a homogeneous frame. It is thus specific to the form of historicity of a literary mode of production.

In seeking to qualify an initially univocal model aesthetic production Jauss has distinguished between (1) a preformative and norm-giving stage, (2) a motivating and norm-forming stage, and (3) a transformative and norm-breaking stage. (53) The first of these would correspond to oral and folk literatures, and would belong to what Lotman calls the 'aesthetic of identity': that is, an aesthetic which functions through a positive and constructive use of stereotypes, and through the confirmation of expectations; through a repetition of sameness on the basis of the difference of sameness; and through improvization on the basis of strict rules. The third stage would comprise written literature of the capitalist period and would belong to Lotman's 'aesthetic of opposition', which is based on a concept of originality; on the breaking or absence of expectations; and on deconstruction rather than construction - on complication rather than simplification. (54)

Insofar as these can be seen as historical (but not necessarily linear) categories, we can posit that Jauss's second, motivating and norm-forming stage (covering, roughly, written literature of the precapitalist period) will contain elements of both aesthetics: both a respect for the structure of the canon, and a transformation of the canon that goes beyond a simple improvization. This is of course a gross generalization, but it will be sufficient to indicate the necessary historical relativity of any model of literary history. The crucial point here is that these forms of historicity are not inherent in texts. The time of new production is not originary, and it is not continuous. It is constructed *nachträglich* in the process of reading, as a hypothetical relation to a system, or rather as a relation both to the system of production and to systems of reception. This situated construction of the time of the text obliterates the 'firstness of the "prior" event, placing in question the possibility of an event that could be isolated in its self-contained moment of occurrence'. (55)

We will thus be led to adopt a position of methodological indeterminacy (what used once to be called a dialectical methodology) in which structure is located neither in the past nor in the present but only in the relationship between the two. This relationality will itself then be taken as the object of analysis, producing not 'readings' but a conceptualization of the ideological and rhetorical strategies by which 'reading' is produced as a social practice, and of the semiotic and institutional constraints on reading: especially its determinate production(s) within the educational apparatus. The concept of diachrony can now be more precisely defined. It does indeed correspond to real time, but this time is that of our relation to the past: the time of a relation between two systems, and thus also a discursive or logical time. Within a system, diachrony can be thought as an informational rupture: that is, as a set of metacommunications about anterior states of the system; (56) this set is itself constructed within the metadiscourse of reading, which is in turn constrained by a semiotic regime of signification which sets institutional limits to and valorizations of reading (but these can, under certain conditions, be resisted or refused or transformed).

What this conception makes possible is a challenge to the givenness of the category of History, and to that objectivism used by many marxists as an epistemological safety-rail. I'll extend it too to challenge the loose misapplication of the concept of materialism which is used to close off the revolutionary potential of a semiotic conception of history and discourse. Let me make it clear that I intend by this neither a denial of the applicability of the concept of the 'material' to its proper domain, nor a denial of the relations of power, determination and constraint which the concept of materialism gestures at without theorizing. My challenge refers only to the displacement of questions of social structure onto a metaphysical problematic. The theoretical problem has consequences, which are not merely terminological, for much recent marxist work on the superstructures (cf. *Language and Materialism, The Material Word*); the difficulties can perhaps be exemplified in Williams' celebration of the 'materiality' of 'notations' as being somehow equivalent to a marxist theory of language; (57) or in both Eagleton's and Jameson's nostalgia for the supposed 'materiality' of the 'referent', and their use of the concept of History as, in Derrida's words, 'a final repression of difference'. (58)

It seems to me, by contrast, that a semiotic understanding of history and of the social formation opens up precisely the opportunity that marxist literary theory needs: not to produce new readings of texts, or a new analytic methodology, but to be able to extend its practices to other forms of discourse and to the 'extra-literary' realm itself. The increasing sophistication of literary theory - our awareness of the rhetorical and constitutive status of discourse, of the mutual implication of meaning and desire, of the production of power relations within language - is threatened with aridity so long as it is restricted to 'literary' texts. The chance and the challenge that marxists have is to extend this knowledge to those other discourses in which the 'real' is constructed - the discourses of law, of psychology, of science, of history and economics, and to everyday practices of language. This is not a question of deducing relations of power from apparently extra-discursive instances, but of constructing these instances as themselves structures of signification, and of understanding the play of power and truth within discourse.

****

Here, more or less, is where the presentation of the present paper (but it was another paper, of which this is not the presence) ended. But even conference papers, like all forms of writing, have a multiple temporality and a multiple textuality. So I'll impose a different form of closure by talking briefly of how it was opened out, how it failed to conclude its argument.

Three questions among many. The first concerned the strategic value of my critique of the application of the concept of materialism. I could answer this on theoretical grounds; but it may well be that in political terms the critique could be perceived as directed against marxism itself (which was not my intention), or as a scholastic attack on a useful shorthand concept. My feeling remains that good political practice requires, in the long run, adequate theoretical concepts.

The second question concerned the attempt to elaborate a systemic conception of diachrony. The suggestion was made that it might be possible to use precisely Saussure's 'bad' concept of diachrony, as the contingent and non-theorizable, to formulate a concept of the instance of alterity, of the unthinkable, as that which breaks with the imaginary closure of any system and with the imperialism of discursive categorization. I leave this as an open question.

The third concerned the status of the concept of time in my diagram: specifically, if every series (politics, literature ...) within a social formation has its own specific time, what connection can there be between series? I see two possible answers to this: one, which I reject, would be to suppose the homogeneity at some level of the time of a social formation: that is, to equate synchrony with real time. The other would be to define synchrony as a logical category, a category of representation, which covers two logical levels: that of the construction of time as relations of tense and causality, and that of the construction of specific temporalities of production of these 'internal' relations. The possibility of the interlock and overlap of series would be given only insofar as any series can function as a metadiscourse, theoretically or practically incorporating representations of other series, and so also the disparate times of those series. These representations would of course be 'different' from the 'real' series; and the resolution of the question of sameness and difference can only be made from the point and the time of our theoretical situation: which in its turn is historically specific, a historical fiction to be constructed elsewhere.

NOTES

1. Michel Foucault, *The Archaeology of Knowledge*, trans. A.M. Sheridan Smith (London: Tavistock, 1972), p.10.

2. Fredric Jameson, *The Political Unconscious* (London: Methuen, 1981), p.139.

3. Oswald Ducrot and Tzvetan Todorov, *Encyclopaedic Dictionary of the Sciences of Language*, trans. Catherine Porter (Baltimore: Johns Hopkins University Press, 1979), p.179.

4. Louis Althusser and Etienne Balibar, *Reading Capital*, trans. Ben Brewster (London: NLB, 1970), pp.96, 106-108.

5. *Ibid.*, pp.67-68.

6. *Ibid.*, pp.42.43.

7. Cf. Rodney Hilton (ed.), *The Transition from Feudalism to Capitalism* (London: NLB, 1976).

8. Quoted in Keith Tribe, *Genealogies of Capitalism* (London: Macmillan, 1981), pp.12-13.

9. Maurice Dobb, *Studies in the Development of Capitalism*, second edition (London: Routledge and Kegan Paul, 1963), p.19; cf. Paul Sweezy, "A Critique", *The Transition from Feudalism to Capitalism*, p.49.

10. Perry Anderson, *Lineages of the Absolutist State* (London: NLB, 1974), p.403.

11. *Ibid.*, p.404.

12. Etienne Balibar, *Reading Capital*, pp.273-274.

13. *Ibid.*, pp.297-298.

14. Cf. Barry Hindess and Paul Hirst, *Pre-capitalist Modes of Production* (London: Routledge and Kegan Paul, 1975), p.274.

15. Charles Bettelheim, *The Transition to Socialist Economy*, trans. Brian Pearce (London: Harvester, 1975), p.15.

16. *Ibid.*, p.20.

17. *Ibid.*, pp.149-150.

18. Hindess and Hirst, *Pre-capitalist Modes of Production*, p.15.

19. *Ibid.*, p.278.

20. *Ibid.*, p.279.

21. Anthony Cutler, Barry Hindess, Paul Hirst and Athar Hussain, *Marx's 'Capital' and Capitalism Today*, Vol.I (London: Routledge and Kegan Paul, 1977), p.106.

22. Barry Hindess and Paul Hirst, *Mode of Production and Social Formation* (London: Macmillan, 1977), p.2.

23. John Oakley, "The Boundaries of Hegemony: Pater", *Literature, Society and the Sociology of Literature: Proceedings of the Conference held at the University of Essex, July 1976*, ed. Francis Barker *et al.* (University of Essex, 1977), p.18.

24. Ian Birchall, "The Appropriation of Pascal", *1642: Literature and Power in the Seventeenth Century: Proceedings of the Essex Conference on The Sociology of Literature, July 1980*, ed. Francis Barker *et al.* (University of Essex, 1981), p.111.

25. Terry Eagleton, "Tennyson: Politics and Sexuality in 'The Princess' and 'In Memoriam'", *1848: The Sociology of Literature: Proceedings of the Essex Conference on the Sociology of Literature, July 1977*, ed. Francis Barker *et al.* (University of Essex, 1978), p.98.

26. Sandra Findley and Elaine Hobby, "Seventeenth Century Women's Autobiography", *1642*, p.34; cf. also Marxist-Feminist Literature Collective, "Women's Writing: 'Jane Eyre', 'Shirley', "Villette', 'Aurora Leigh', *1848*, pp.185-206.

27. Christine Berg and Philippa Berry, "Spiritual Whoredom: an Essay on Female Prophets in the Seventeenth Century", *1642*, p.38.

28. Francis Barker, "The Tremulous Private Body", *1642*, p.8.

29. Stan Smith, "Scars and Emblems: 1936 and the Crisis of the Subject", *1936: The Sociology of Literature, Volume II - Practices of Literature and Politics: Proceedings of the Essex Conference on the Socioloty of Literature, July 1978*, ed. Francis Barker *et al.* (University of Essex, 1979), pp.344-379.

30. David Aers and Gunther Kress, "Historical Process, Individual and Communities in Milton's Early Prose", *1642*, p.285.

31. U.E.A. English Studies Group, "Strategies for Representing Revolution", *1789: Reading Writing Revolution: Proceedings of the Essex Conference on the Sociology of Literature, July 1981*, ed. Francis Barker *et al.* (University of Essex, 1982), p.82.

32. Graham Pechey, "1789 and After: Mutations of 'Romantic' Discourse'", *1789*, pp.81-100.

33. Jean Rohou, "The Articulation of Social, Ideological and Literary Practices in France: The Historical Moment of 1641-1643", *1642*, p.140.

34. Renée Balibar, "An Example of Literary Work in France: George Sand's 'La Mare au Diable'/'The Devil's Pool' of 1846", *1848*, p.42.

35. Fredric Jameson, *The Political Unconcscious*, p.225.

36. *Ibid.*, p.226.

37. Ray Selden, "Russian Formalism and Marxism: An Unconcluded Dialogue", *Literature, Society and the Sociology of Literature*, p.99.

38. Raymond Williams, "Forms of English Fiction in 1848", *1848*, p.277.

39. *Ibid.*, p.278.

40. *Ibid.*, p.279.

41. *Ibid.*, p.280.

42. *Ibid.*, p.281.

43. Clearly there are many exceptions to this: for example the reflections on the theoretical construction of "the thirties" in English Studies Group, Centre for Contemporary Cultural Studies, "Thinking the Thirties", *1936, Vol.II*, pp.1-20.

44. John Coombes, "The Political Aesthetics of 'The 18th Brumaire of Louis Bonaparte'", *1848*, p.18.

45. Jeffrey Mehlman, *Revolution and Repetition: Marx/Huge/Balzac* (Berkeley: University of California Press, 1977).

46. Coombes, "The Political Aesthetics of 'The 18th Brumaire of Louis Bonaparte'", *1848*, p.19.

47. Fredric Jameson, "Religion and Ideology", *1642*, p.320.

48. *Ibid.*, pp.335-336.

49. Hindess and Hirst, *Pre-capitalist Modes of Production*, p.277.

50. *Ibid.*, pp.212-213.

51. In what follows I draw on concepts elaborated in my "System and Norm in Literary Evolution: For a Marxist Literary History", *Clio* 10:2, 1981, pp.155-181

52. Cf. Karl Marx, *Capital I* (New York: International Publishers, 1967), p.18: "Every historical period has laws of its own".

53. H.R. Jauss, "Racines und Goethes *Iphigenie*", *Neue Hefte für Philosophie* 4 (1973), p.45.

54. Jurij Lotman, *The Structure of the Artistic Text*, trans. Ronald Vroon (Ann Arbor: Michigan Slavic Contributions No.7, 1977), pp.289.292.

55. Andrew Parker,"'Taking Sides' (On History): Derrida Re-Marx", *Diacritics* Vol.II, September 1981, p.70.

56. Cf. Anthony Wilden, *System and Structure* (London: Tavistock, 1972), p.354.

57. Raymond Williams, *Marxism and Literature* (London: Oxford University Press, 1977), p.170.

58. Jacques Derrida, *Marges de la philosophie* (Paris: Ed. de Minuit, 1972), p.12.

BAKHTIN, MARXISM, AND POST-STRUCTURALISM

Graham Pechey

It may help to situate the project of this paper if I say that it sets out to elaborate the implications of something I wrote three years ago. Some of you may have read a review of Medvedev's *The Formal Method of Literary Scholarship* in which I suggested that the 'other side' of this 'downright contestation' of Russian Formalism was a 'symptomatic reading' of its texts - 'an obverse of polemic determining from within the very positions from which the polemic is conducted'. (1) The fact that I would now want to delete the 'perhaps' with which (incidentally) that statement was qualified and argue the point at length is no mere accident of autobiography: it is rather a necessity of *autocritique* forced upon me by the direction in which the debate around literary theory has shifted since then. Substitute 'deconstructive' for 'symptomatic' and the issue clarifies at once; in a moment when deconstruction appears to have a monopoly of radicalism and novelty in the theorization of discourse we need to turn from applause for the style of Bakhtinian polemic or the paraphrase of Bakhtinian themes to the deconstructive and indeed self-deconstructive activity which is the determining obverse of both. In other words, what needs now to be presented as exemplary is not the gestures of negating or positing but the textual *process* which conditions and exceeds these gestures. Bakhtinian theory is sometimes referred to as 'post-formalism', as if it were a question of merely being chronologically the later of two related but 'full' positions. It would be truer to characterize it as a post-structuralism coinciding with the displacement that brought about structuralism itself: a paradox from the standpoint of literal dating which usefully points to a changed meaning of the prefix, inasmuch as 'post-' now signifies not contingent succession but the status of the already-posterior which Bakhtinian theory shares with all other discourses whatever. Formed in the transformation of other texts, Bakhtinism is subject to an endless post-dating and an anticipation equally endless.

Now of course it is not only a deconstructive reading of Formalism that we read in Bakhtin; the other crucially formative encounter - with Saussurean linguistics - could also be held up as a model of such a reading. In that encounter, conducted under the signature of Voloshinov, the concept of the sign and the concept of ideology are so brought together that they transform each other, the sign taking on the historicity and ideology the materiality that would make them into concepts of historical materialism. (2) To argue this case we would need to show that the replacement of the sign by the concept of the <u>utterance</u> - the real unit of social sign-production which necessarily escapes analysis into the neutral virtualities of the system of language - is in no sense a logocentric move. Appearances notwithstanding, it is the condition of a quite radical challenging of the famous Saussurean dichotomies, and in the first place of the bifurcation into *langue* and *parole*. The theory of the utterance reverses Saussure's priorities without becoming a theory of *parole*, in the manner of a stylistics. We would need to show that the Bakhtinian theory is distinct not only from stylistics, which stands to linguistics in a relation of mere parasitism and complementarity, but also from the seemingly cognate projects of Benveniste and Mukařovský, which seek to replace Saussure's bifurcation with new bifurcations. (3) An instructive parallel might be found in Gramsci's dialogue with Croce: 'politics' is rescued from arbitrariness and irrationality to which it is condemned in Croce's text in much the same way as the domain of the utterance is rescued from Saussure's; in both cases Marxist positions are elaborated in the deconstruction of a non-Marxist antagonist. (4) I mention these possible heads of another argument only in order to broaden the basis for discussion; the Bakhtinian reading of Formalism will be my sole concern in the rest of this paper.

I had better begin by outlining in broad terms the direction my argument will take. For this purpose I will draw on certain Bakhtinian expressions in a provisional way, recognizing their inadequacy in themselves. They are these:

'discourse in life':'discourse in art'
'discourse in the novel':'discourse in poetry'

The spacing is meant to indicate a developing particularization which is only a convenience of argument; it is not meant to legislate for any genetic order in the development (so-called) of the theory. In the reversal of these two hierarchized oppositions and the transformation or redefinition of the newly-privileged (left-hand) term, we have the two moments of formation of Bakhtinian theory. Bakhtin looks as it were from discourse in general towards 'artistic' discourse and then, within what Formalism calls 'verbal art' itself, he looks from novelistic towards poetic discourse 'in the narrow sense'. (5) In each case he breaks with Formalist theorizing at just those points where the latter had not broken with (or had only incoherently questioned) traditionalist presuppositions. The first of these views from outside pulls poetics back in the direction of rhetoric; the second ensures that this general theory of discourse in relation to power is no classicizing throwback but rather a theory of the non-canonical and decentring forces within ideology which was unprecedented in its time and is still not superseded. 'The novel' is Bakhtin's name for these forces in so far as they manifest themselves in the forms of writing. I hope to show that his answer to the Formalist notion of the literary is an abstracting (hypostasizing) removal from communication - the notion of the 'self-valuable' word - is not a new pragmatics of communication shorn of its prescriptive character, but a wholly new space where this theoretical see-saw no longer functions. This space is arrived at not in any external attack on the Formalist texts; it is the result of occupying these texts, getting inside them and inviting them to have the courage of their metaphors.

Our demonstration of all this requires that we take a lengthy detour, the first stage of which is an understanding of the deconstruction of the concept of form which Russian Formalism had already carried out. In an early move this concept is nominally retained on the basis of a preliminary reversal: outside becomes inside, and 'form' is undoubtedly redefined in a way that breaks with the idealism of the age-old form-content couple. On this (traditional) view form and content are the terms of a correlation within the work; neither can be invoked without also invoking this internal correlation. Formalism decisively detaches 'form' from this correlation by insisting that the work is all form: form is 'the whole entity'; (6) content is non- or pre-aesthetic and can only enter the work by becoming a formal element along with the rest. Now to say that the content of the work is its form (as Shklovsky does in some contexts) is only to confirm the ancient dualism in a murder of definition which is anything but deconstructive. Formalism sidesteps this dead-end by setting up, in effect, two *external* correlations:

Form in general:absence of form
A particular form:other forms

In the first of these new correlations 'poetic language' stands over against an aformal (aesthetically neutral) 'practical language' in a distinction which cuts across the old generic distinction of 'poetry' and 'prose' and has all the appearance of being absolute. The 'literariness' which Formalism takes as its object is founded in this negative external correlation which for all its provocation has to bear the blame for the weakness of much early-Formalist writing. What then takes its place is our second - differential rather than negative - external correlation, whereby the work cannot be understood apart from the historical succession and interaction of forms. Literary history proceeds not by the expression of new contents but by a dynamic of the replacement of old forms whose literariness has been exhausted. This firm articulation of textuality upon the movement of intertextual relations is the great strength of the Formalist case; we are not surprised to find both Bakhtinism and structuralism carrying it forward.

If we turn now to the two other key concepts of Formalism - the device and the function - we can see that their elaboration was compelled by the need to move beyond the traditional terms and abolish the inside-outside couple for good and all. The 'device' is plainly a quasi-technological riposte to the quasi-theological 'symbol' or 'image' of Symbolist discourse. Potebnya's theory of poetry as 'thinking in images' sets up a criterion at once too narrow and too broad: 'practical language' (the Formalists argued) also employed images while poetry doesn't need images to be poetic. Far from using different methods to the same communicative end of 'clarifying the unknown by means of the known', (7) the two modes use the same methods to secure different ends. The Formalist notion of the peculiar signifying orientation of the 'poetic' is derived by antithesis from the Symbolist notion of familiarizing: 'forms' are 'made difficult' in order that 'objects' may be 'made strange'. Now the texts of Formalism are notoriously confusing on this issue of defamiliarization: what is it that the textual devices defamiliarize? Signifier, signified, or referent? And if either signifier or signified, what is in question: first-order (linguistic) or second-order (semiotic) signs? or both? Defamiliarization is also sometimes a device in its own right and sometimes the principle of all devices *per se*. Still, what we can say about this new concept of the device is that it effectively revives the old rhetorical concept of the figure - a far wider category than the image, which is ordinarily limited to lexical and punctual devices. The device extends the working of the figure further still, taking in all the levels of language and structuring: parallelism, for example - almost all the devices discussed by the Formalists are variants of this originally purely syntactic figure - works on the phonic level to produce rhyme, assonance, alliteration; on the semantic level to produce metaphor; and on the level of narrative plotting to produce 'tautological' repetitions of events. At the same time there is a narrowing as compared with the figure: the device has nothing to do with communication; it is self-referring and asks to be 'seen'. Its defamiliarizing work effects a 'semantic shift' (8) which paradoxically effaces its own semantic nature, at once exploiting and cancelling meaning, dissolving intelligibility into 'perceptibility'. A palpable advance upon the concept of 'form', the device is nonetheless a somewhat problematic occupant of the conceptual field of Formalism. Born in what I've called the negative external correlation, it has a tendency to revert to the internal correlation even as it is pushed forward towards the 'strong' or differential correlation of later Formalist theorizing. It collapses

into reversion to the extent that it is coupled (as it often is) with
'materials', thereby reproducing under another name the form-content
dichotomy. It is then pushed forward to the extent that Formalism begins
to negotiate the historical dimension of the literary - that is to say,
as defamiliarization migrates to the diachronic plane, becoming for
Shklovsky in particular the motor of literary history. In Shklovsky's
discourse the device survives unmodified by this migration and (a related
point) the extra-literary relations of the literary have no place in what
is an unregenerately isolationist argument, let alone the question of
what determines the path taken by the lateral deviation of forms at any
given juncture. The device could be said to be both condition and result
of the elision of these questions, which only become frameable when the
device is superseded by the function.

This supersession takes place in the later texts of Tynyanov: substituting for the early conception of the work as a 'sum of devices' the
notion of a 'dynamic integration' of hierarchically-ordered elements, he
also sketches for Formalism a cultural theory in which the principle of
the irreducible relationality of elements is no less firmly followed.
For Tynyanov 'formal elements' have no substantive existence; they are
functions within systems: products of a twofold interrelation, with like
elements in other systems and with unlike elements in their own. (9)
The work as a system of 'constructive' functions can only be understood
in relation to the system of 'literary' functions which makes up the
current literary order, and this in turn must be referred to the system
of 'verbal' functions which makes up the culture as a whole. Literary
historiography is concerned with the closest cultural series to the
literary system - with 'social conventions' mediated by language, their
common denominator. An element originating in one of these series -
what Bakhtin will later call an *ideologeme* - becomes a constructive
function in the work and simultaneously a literary function beyond it,
in a complex overdetermination. In short, Tynyanov thinks the whole
relationship of the literary to the extra-literary in intertextual terms,
as a relation of 'like to like'. (10) The concept of the device - including the allied concept of 'motivation' and its antithesis the device
'laid bare' and unmotivated - could not, and did not, survive this move.
(11) Tynyanov in 1924 had said that devices studied without reference
to the evolution of forms were 'in danger of being studied outside their
functions'; (12) in 1927 the device is dropped altogether. Late Formalism, then, is the result of a steady distancing from the negative correlation and a correspondingly steady elaboration of the differential
alternative. The function enables the transition to what is in effect
a third correlation and the last reach of Formalist theory: that of
systems. This step is taken in the Jakobson-Tynyanov theses of 1928,
and with it the structuralist project is launched. (13) Or is it? If
the theses are of interest to us here as indicating the route that
Bakhtinism did not take out of and away from Formalism, they are equally
interesting for their critique of the Saussurean paradigm. On the one
hand we could say that Bakhtinism catches Formalism on its way to structuralism, diverting it in a Marxist direction; on the other hand we
could say that the nascent structuralism of the theses is also an incho-
ate post-structuralism which Bakhtin emulates and completes as much as
contests. Both propositions are true, as a brief look at the theses
will show.

In what sense is Jakobson-Tynyanov a structuralist text? According
to Benveniste, structuralism constitutes its object as 'a system whose
parts are all united in a relationship of solidarity and dependence' and,
while asserting the 'predominance of the system over the elements', also
defines the 'structure' of the system 'through the relationships among

the elements'. (14) Clearly Jakobson-Tynyanov is a structuralist text insofar as it uses just such a concept of system to oppose an atomism of the literary 'fact'; the analogy with Saussure and the linguistic 'fact' is plain enough. However, Jakobson-Tynyanov is post-structuralist - at odds with the later Western-European projects descending from Saussure - insofar as it proposes a quite different conception of the systemic. The Saussurean system is closed in the strict sense that its components are also its determinants and that it itself determines nothing else; any one such system exists only to codify random diachronic events by exploiting them in new synchronic relationships. By contrast, the late-Formalist system is intended precisely to theorize both the internal dynamic of distinct cultural orders and the dynamic of their correlation, their mutation in widely diverging temporalities. Moreover, it is open, at once determined and determining, in both the synchronic and the diachronic dimensions. We should note that Jakobson-Tynyanov invades Saussure's own scientific heartland: in arguing that the concept of system could be used to theorize not only synchronic regularity but also diachronic productivity, this text speaks consistently of 'literature' and 'language'. It is of discourse in general that the theses speak when they insist that all difference is historical and all history differential, a movement of structuring. So far, so good; it is when the closing theses broach the issue of what determines the particular path of 'evolution' and resolve it by appeal to the (global) 'system of systems' that the compatibility with historical materialism breaks down. These intersystemic relations are so formulated as to elide the model of dominance-subordination and of contradiction which is held to characterize relations within the textual and intertextual moments of the literary system itself. As we move from the work through genre to the literary 'series' and on to the wider reaches of the social formation, so the emphasis on the 'deforming' dominant weakens and is replaced by a contiguity of systems from which all hint of struggle and hegemony has been expelled. Bakhtinian theory is what we have when this inconsistency is overcome: the principle of intertextual contradiction is applied truly universally, instead of being forsaken half-way. The 'series' identified by Tynyanov as being in closest correlation with the literary - 'social conventions' - reappears in Bakhtinism as 'behavioural ideology', and their common implication in the verbal is re-asserted. Theorizing this region of ideology at least as fully as its literary neighbour, Bakhtin then reverses Formalist procedure by viewing the latter from the vantage-point of the former. We should recall that the Bakhtinian intervention in this field was made in the context of contemporaneous attempts to synthesize Formalism and Marxism (as it were) sponsorially and organizationally: Jakobson-Tynyanov was published in *Novyi Lef* precisely with this aim in mind. The Marxism of Bakhtin's intervention diverges sharply from any strategy which confirms the two positions in their self-presence and exteriority to each other, inasmuch as it is elaborated in a realization of the critical potential of a Formalism on the verge of the structuralist mutation. The best illustration of this is *Marxism and the Philosophy of Language*, published the year after Jakobson-Tynyanov. In this text the Jakobson-Tynyanov position on synchrony and diachrony is taken up and rethought as the contest and complicity of the two great lineages of linguistic enquiry - on the one hand the Humboldtian and on the other the Cartesian, incarnated in the twentieth century by (respectively) Vossler and Saussure. In the one tendency an objectivism is predicated upon the regularity of language, while in the other the productivity of language entails a subjectivism, a privileging of individual stylistic 'creation'. (15) Voloshinov produces his materialist alternative to both not by an external attack on either but by occupying the space of their mutual limitation. In this space he is able to think what he calls 'the objective social regulatedness of ideological creativity', thereby breaking a long historical deadlock which Jakobson-Tynyanov had made visible.

The question now arises: How exactly does Bakhtinism bring about this radical interruption and diversion of Formalist concepts? I would like to suggest that the answer lies in a reading which attends to the textuality of the Formalist texts, in turning upon *them* their own abiding preoccupation with the textual, uncovering the metaphoricity in their conceptuality. We have seen that 'device' (sometimes rendered as 'technique') is 'technological', a coinage deriving from the anti-Symbolist polemic. 'Function', for all its appearance of being at home unproblematically in late-Formalist discourse, is a logico-mathematical borrowing in which the will to overcome the problems of the device generates further difficulties. More important than either, though, is the tropology of power and hierarchy with which both co-exist and which borrows its terms from the class struggle: 'struggle' itself, along with 'revolt', 'conflict', 'destruction' - these terms recur throughout. Even the 'dominant', though less vivid, belongs in this field. A passage from Shklovsky may be taken as representative:

> Each new school of literature is a revolution - something like the emergence of a new class. But that, of course, is only an analogy. The defeated line is not annihilated, it does not cease to exist. It only topples from the crest, drops below, for a time lying fallow, and may rise again as an ever-present pretender to the throne. Moreover, in practice, things are complicated by the fact that the new hegemony is usually not a pure instance of a restoration of earlier form, but one involving the presence of features from other junior schools, even features (but now in a subordinate role) inherited from its predecessor on the throne. (16)

'Only an analogy': Skhlovsky's modest disclaimer is disarming. It is as if the *Eighteenth Brumaire* had been turned inside-out, with the textuality of revolution inverted into the (permanent) revolution of textuality - a revolution which takes place in the hermetically-sealed palace of verbal art. (17) Late Formalism lives off the productivity of this trope - it unites the otherwise disparate texts of Shklovsky and Tynyanov - and is 'unthinkable' without it. What is then striking is that this 'social' tropology only operates where literary diachrony is at issue; it is glaringly absent when the social itself is being negotiated. Tynyanov's text of 1927, where precisely this move to the extra-literary is made, is as notable for this absence as it is for the absence of the 'device' and its associates. The rhetoric of Formalism then shifts from the metaphoric to the metonymic pole, repressing the (implicit) similarity of the social by an explicit stress on its contiguity. Now the interest in thus uncovering the 'unconscious' of Formalist theory increases when we recall that this rhetoric (in the sense of the play of tropes) is in the business of consciously revolutionizing the relationship between poetics and the discipline of rhetoric itself. Eikhenbaum had spoken of 'the necessity of reviving rhetoric alongside poetics'; (18) it would be truer to say that Formalism revives rhetoric within poetics: rhetoric achieves its occupation of the aesthetic at the cost of its wider jurisdiction within discourse in general. It is then not surprising that, in engaging the historical dynamic of the literary, Formalism calls into being a sublimated version of the articulations of discourse and power - a displaced shadow-show of power relations. The wider social or ideological dimension emerges as an inert antitype of the lively politics of discourse played out on the inside of the literary; the battle of forms fades into a ballet of functions. For Formalism, it seems, the great intertextual drama was unplayable without the 'self-valuable word' as protagonist; to accord the same role to the word of ideology was to undermine the specificity of 'verbal art'. Bakhtin, no less interested in 'specifying', does just that, re-establishing poetics within rhetoric and theorizing the literary sign and the ideological sign together.

The Bakhtinian transformation may now be precisely described. We might say that Bakhtinism proceeds by literalizing and applying Formalism's metaphors of the 'social' to the social 'itself'. A better formulation would be this: Bakhtin substitutively reverses Formalist procedure by using 'literary' categories in the conceptualization of the social and the ideological. This chiastic move is manifested in Voloshinov's discussion of the 'genres' of 'behavioural ideology': as early as 1926 we find him insisting that 'the potentialities of artistic form' are 'already embedded' (19) in the latter. The title of this early Bakhtinian text - 'Discourse in Life and Discourse in Art' - already hints at the reversal and at the need for an equal and reciprocal theorization of both domains. This text is remarkable for a passage in which the twin errors of Formalism and psychologism are analysed; both (we are told)

> attempt to discover the whole in the part, that is, they take the structure of a part, abstractly divorced from the whole, and claim it as the structure of the whole. (20)

Voloshinov goes on:

> Those methods that ignore the social essence of art and attempt to find its nature and distinguishing features only in the organization of the work artefact are in actuality obliged to project the social interrelationship of creator and contemplator into various aspects of the material and into various devices for structuring the material. In exactly the same way, psychological aesthetics projects the same social relations into the individual psyche of the perceiver. This projection distorts the integrity of these interrelationships and gives a false picture of both the material and the psyche. (21)

What appears here as a conclusion about Formalism could be read as a starting-point in it: a reversal of this 'projection' of social relations into the work would bring about their reinstatement in their proper locus; a synecdochic mystification only needs to be exploded for the whole to shift from the inside to the outside of the part. In a close parallel with Marx's deconstruction of the commodity, Bakhtin rescues the 'work artefact' from its fetishization by compelling the technical categories of Formalism into the rhetorical categories which they at once mimic and distort. The hierarchical relations located by Formalism within the work are rethought as the (no less hierarchical) immanently social relations in which any utterance is inscribed. In all utterances 'relations among people stand revealed, relations merely reflected and fixed in verbal material'; the specificity of the artistic utterances resides not in its digression from this immanent sociality but precisely in its intensification: 'a poetic work is a powerful condenser of unarticulated social evaluations - each word is saturated with them'. (22) A poetics adequate to the understanding of this sociality would need to be (or be a branch of) the 'sociology of discourse' sketched out in Voloshinov's text. There is no mere coincidence in the fact that in this prolegomenal text many of the oldest terms of rhetoric make their appearance, and that its keynote is the (re-)assimilation of the literary to the more 'public' ideological discourses, notably the juridical and political. The historical significance of this move cannot be too strongly underlined. In the Romantic mutation the condition of the specificity of 'art' had been its assimilation to 'everyday' ideology conceived as a private domain - an area of freedom for the subject outside institutions, of unconditioned privacy in which the writ of the more public discourses does not run - and the very notion of the 'aesthetic' took shape in the conceptual space thus hollowed out. Now to contest the expressivism or mimeticism raised on this basis (as Formalism consistently does) is to leave the aesthetic itself undeconstructed. The term 'aesthetic' in Bakhtinian discourse has been redefined out of all recognition, inasmuch as it realizes the 'potentialities' of an everyday-ideological domain which is always already structured like the juridico-political, always already written. Formalism had only gone as far as to bracket-out the authorial 'psyche' as a cause of the work; Bakhtinism takes the more radical step of theorizing this 'cause' as an effect of the same (discursive) order as the work itself. The upshot is a thoroughgoing deconstruction of the aesthetic in which its formal possibilities are read back into ideological domains whose bifurcation into private and public had given birth to it in the first place.

So much for the first of our 'two moments of formation of Bakhtinian theory'; the second moment makes good a great and potentially disabling absence in the first as it is (in more than one sense) classically represented in the text of 1926. This is the lack of any reference either to the unofficial 'lower' strata of 'discourse in life' or to their counterpart in 'discourse in art': namely, the novel. The project of 1926 was at bottom a neo-rhetorical and indeed even classicizing project which would have left Bakhtinism roughly where 'speech-act theory' is fixed today. (We recall that Bakhtin was trained as a classicist.) The difference and the relationship between the two moments may be measured in the distance between this early essay and one of 1934-35 which appeared in English translation in 1981 under the title 'Discourse in the Novel'; doubtless the crucial nexus here was the path-breaking work on Dostoevsky which intervened: no neo-rhetoric could survive unmodified an engagement of that depth with the peculiar productivity of novelistic discourse. (23) As with the first moment, my procedure will be to isolate the Formalist concept(s) in the transformation of which the Bakhtinian position is produced. What did Formalism make of the novel? Formalism theorizes the prose genres only after, and then by analogy with, those of poetry. Two strategies are adopted: fiction is held to reproduce in its repetitive sequences the linguistic devices (such as rhyme) of the same order in poetry; or the language of fiction is itself investigated for its quasi-poetic textuality. In both cases fiction is admitted to the canon of 'verbal art' only insofar as these effects are more or less foregrounded, deflected from the referential. Only the second strategy will concern us here. The rubric under which Formalism develops it is that of *skaz* - that form of prose writing which (allegedly) displays in its style an 'orientation' towards 'oral speech'. Bakhtin takes his cue from this problem of the (idiosyncratic) narrator in fiction, not only reformulating it in itself but also elaborating out of it those great themes of dialogue and carnival which transgress all disciplinary boundaries.

Skaz is a preoccupation of early Formalism and of Eikhenbaum in particular. (24) However, in this instance Bakhtin has the advantage of a prior critique within Formalism, or at least on its periphery. Viktor Vinogradov's reformulation of the problem is the decisive enabling condition of Bakhtin's move. (25) Let us take Eikhenbaum first. *Skaz* for him 'departs in principle from the written language and makes the narrator as such into a real figure', thereby freeing the prose genres from the joint domination of 'plot' and of 'a culture geared to writing and printing'. (26) Happily the mixed mode of realist fiction was now undergoing a process of fission into its constituent forms and of these forms those that were oriented towards 'voice' were pushing an already devitalized novel genre into obsolescence. Eikhenbaum concludes: 'our relationship to the word has become more concrete, more sensitive, more physiological'. (27) In other words, Formalism sees in *skaz* the pure presence of speaking uncontaminated by writing and anterior to all institution. The problem of other speech in the authorial context is mooted only to be dropped, forgotten in the rush to embrace the fullness of orality. Vinogradov's assault on Eikhenbaum is directed at the latter's polarization of speech and writing and at the myth of the unity and purity of speaking. *Skaz* is redefined as a form of (prose) writing which is oriented not towards the undifferentiated phonicity of 'oral speech' but towards a particular oral genre - the 'narrative monologue' - which is distinguished (among other things) by 'having as its goal the forms of the written language'. (28) It is 'an artistic construction taken to the second power', (29) an orientation towards a spoken form which is itself always already oriented towards the forms of writing. Beyond this, it displays 'whimsical forms of a multilingual mixture' and 'a conscious blending of various linguistic spheres'. (30) The *skaz* which mimics this genre assumes and exploits the existence of distinct linguistic practices within one and the same national language; it could not arise otherwise. Predicated upon this multilinguality, indefinable apart from it - no mere linguistic markers can fix a phenomenon so variable socially and historically - *skaz* is also the great operator of multilingualism in the whole field of prose writing. Formalism had tended to privilege the short story over the novel as the special locus of *skaz* effects; in Vinogradov's text *skaz* is the means by which non-canonical discourses subvert the 'conservative dogmas' of prose in general and 'create anew the whole world'. The dialogue of characters can (and does) accommodate such discourses, but with nothing like the effect that is generated by their permeation of the narrative itself. The effect of 'free verbal play' is possible only when other speech is not subordinated to plot or characterization but is itself rather the context of dialogue: a context without a placing pretext or 'motivation' in the Formalist sense. Such, then, is *skaz*: a context of narration not only without pretext but also refusing the status of a pretext for other texts; unmotivated and unmotivating, non-unified and non-unifying, it 'usually absorbs' the speech of characters or at least 'struggles with it'. (31)

Bakhtin's response to this powerful deconstruction of Formalist phonocentrism is to take it further still in the same direction. Vingogradov's sweeping generalization of the work of *skaz* becomes in Bakhtin that ubiquitous phenomenon of prose writing which he calls the 'double-voiced' or 'dialogical' word, and of which *skaz* proper is only one of the types: parody, stylization, and polemic share with it the dialogism which arises when two or more speech-acts of equal semantic weighting come together in a dynamic and internal relation. (32) Novelistic 'polyphony' is what we have when this play of voices is the textual dominant and when the finalizing forces of plot and of authorial authority are more or less subordinated. Single-voiced discourse is exemplified in the direct voice of the author with its claim on referential transparency and in the speech of characters which has been reduced to a mere theme or 'object' of authorial intentions, a manipulated transparency ignorant of its own service of those intentions. Now it is in Vinogradov's formulation of this (so to speak) priority-finality of the authoritative single voice that we can locate the point of departure for Bakhtin's most productive - his most decisively deconstructive -

move. The passage in which this formulation appears is worth quoting at length:
> In those epochs when the forms of written, literary, artistic speech experience a revolution, it is *skaz* which helps language to break with the past. Indeed *skaz* is psychologically limited only when it is attached to the image of a person or his designated representative, that is, to a verbal label. Then to some extent the illusion of an everyday situation is also created, even if object accessories of the illusion are not indicated. The amplitude of lexical oscillations grows narrow. The stylistic motion leads a secluded life within the narrow confines of a linguistic consciousness that is dominated by the social mode of life that is to be presented. Meanwhile *skaz*, proceeding from the author's 'I', is free. The writer's 'I' is not a name but a pronoun. Consequently, one can conceal under it whatever one wants to. It is able to conceal forms of speech appropriated from constructions of various bookish genres and from *skaz*-dialectal elements. An integral psychology is a superfluous burden for the writer. The writer's broad right to transform has always been acknowledged. In the literary masquerade the writer can freely change stylistic masks within a single artistic work. To be able to do this he needs only a large and heterogeneous linguistic workshop. Such an artist, a reformer of the literary language, transforms his work into a motley garment, woven from variations of different written *skaz* forms, from declamatory-oratorical speech, and even from the introduction of verse or forms close to it. It is natural that the element of *skaz* becomes the main reservoir from which new aspects of literary speech are drawn. The conservatism of the written literary language is overcome by infusing into it living, varied dialectal elements and their individual, artificial imitations through the means of *skaz*, the transmissive instance between the artistic element of oral creation and the stable tradition of the literary stylistic canon. (33)

There can be no doubt that in this distinction between a *skaz* bound to 'the image of a person' and a 'free' *skaz* of the authorial 'pronoun' we have an early state of Bakhtin's much broader distinction between the singleness of 'objectivized' social-typical discourse and the doubleness of those manifold discourse types which institute the priority of other speech. But this is not all that this extraordinary passage can be made to yield: the textuality of this celebration of textuality needs to be brought out if we are to see what Bakhtin made of it. Consider the fields of metaphor on which it draws: how it 'reminds' mainstream Formalism of two of the tropologies it seems curiously to have 'forgotten' in its theorization of *skaz*. 'Workshop' and 'reservoir' connote the technological and adumbrate an aesthetic of 'production' just as 'device' does within early Formalism. 'Revolution', 'break with the past', 'transform', 'conservatism' apply implicitly political metaphors to cultural practice. Outrunning these tropologies, through - exerting irresistible pressure upon them - is a third, exemplified in 'literary masquerade', 'stylistic masks', and 'motley garment': a tropology, in short, of carnival. The anonymous (pronominal) writing subject is an analogue of the reveller who is (as Kristeva puts it) 'neither nothingness nor anybody'. (34) The *skaz* text conceived as endlessly mutable 'garment' revives the very etymology of 'text' itself. (We are not far here from Peirce's thesis of the primacy of the pronominal over all nomination whatever.) In 'free' *skaz* the textual garment is not secondary to a given identity; it is itself the production of identities.

To take stock of the yield of Vinogradov's text, we need to look first back to Eikhenbaum and then forward to Bakhtin. In bracketing-out the authorial subject, reducing it to nothingness - refusing to think the problem of the authorial position by expelling the subject so prematurely and undialectically - Formalism frees the category of the subject for the mischief it so plainly makes when *skaz* is discussed. The radical and multiple otherness of other speech is cancelled in the oneness of so-called 'oral speech', the quasi-physical substance of a secular Word in which the play of even the most outrageous *skaz* is subject to closure. Vinogradov not only seizes on this repressed problem of the author but also finds himself thinking it as an anti-type of the sacerdotal: the metaphor of the carnivalesque spectator-participant counters Eikhenbaum's virtual priesthood of the spoken word with the ambivalence of writing. Bakhtin for his part isolates this metaphor of the author-as-anonym from its competitors in Vinogradov's text (artisan and revolutionary) as the one most capable of escaping altogether the logic of presence and absence, the 'one' and the 'nought'. This irreducible double of the author as verbal reveller is then - and it is this move that is decisive - applied to the other participants in the textual transaction. Read back into everyday ideology, the metaphor of the verbal reveller produces the new theoretical object of carnival signification. Speaker, spoken-about, and spoken-to are themselves quite openly texts or signifiers - 'masks' with no claim (as Bakhtin himself puts it) to 'an authentic incontestable face'. (35) Author, hero, and reader have the same status in that equally new theoretical object: the polyphonic novel. Both are of course also firmly historical phenomena, and Bakhtin's mature work is given over to an exploration of the historical relationship between them. Carnival doesn't abolish the immanently social and hierarchical relations in which the ideological sign is inscribed; only the terms of these relations are none of them out of play as signified in a transcendence. Carnival is the permanent possibility within everyday ideology of inverting hierarchies, dissolving their absolutism in relativity. It is what we have when the social relations in which the sign is constituted are flagrantly intertextual, its terms (participants) interchangeable anonyms. Now it is worth recalling that the text of 1926 - the text of our first 'moment' - had described these relations as 'relations among people, relations merely reflected and fixed in verbal material'. Carnival and polyphony are clearly unthinkable under this definition of the sign (work, utterance): however helpful it had been in pushing beyond Formalism, this description could not survive the passage to the second 'moment'; its supersession is the index of the self-deconstruction forced upon Bakhtin as the limits of his neo-rhetorical project are revealed. The 'people' of which it speaks appear to transcend 'relations' which in turn transcend a (dispensable) 'verbal material'. Carnival undermines such transcendences in Bakhtinian theory with the same summary justice that it exercises on their counterparts in history.

This brings us, finally, to the new perspective in which Bakhtinism places poetic discourse by viewing it from 'outside' - from its 'own' historical outside, to be precise: the other because and in spite of which it exists at all. What is this other? In engaging this issue Bakhtin speaks not of carnival and polyphony but (respectively) of 'the novel' and 'heteroglossia', their less exceptional correlatives. These are broader categories: where carnival discourse is anti-official, heteroglossia is the multiplicity of unofficial linguistic practices in general; likewise the novel with its dialogism is the general case of which polyphony is the most uncompromising realization. It is in their orientations towards this heteroglot intertext that poetic and novelistic discourse most sharply diverge. The novel is that order of discourse which is open to and echoes - by exploiting - the rich multilingualism of 'social heteroglossia', whereas poetic discourse classically behaves as if it were not surrounded by the latter in all its writings and rewritings, and its only dealings were immediately with its object. Historically, poetry is bound up with the politically and culturally centralizing forces within ideology, while the novel participates in those decentralizing forces against which any unitary language has always and everywhere to posit itself. Both poetry 'in the narrow sense' and the system of linguistic norms are predicated upon a tacit exclusion of these forces. This is not to say that the verse genres are inherently hostile to dialogism or that monologism doesn't have its way in the prose genres; on the contrary. There are no monological texts properly speaking - only monological readings. The very disciplines of discourse themselves ensure these readings, complicit as they are with the whole centralizing and unifying project as it has unfolded historically. More than anything else it is the separation of poetics and rhetoric, with their strictly segregated fields of competence, that has guaranteed the invisibility of dialogism in the forms of writing, first dichotomizing 'prose' and 'verse' and then (when the prose genres come to be canonized) theorizing prose with the categories devised for the canon of poetic writing. We have seen the Formalists taking rhetoric up into poetics on the latter's terms only to fail what Bakhtin calls the 'acid test' (36) posed by novelistic discourse. (On this score Shklovsky is at one with Leavis!) (37) We have seen Bakhtin in his first 'moment' taking poetics up into rhetoric largely on rhetoric's terms only to move on to a new terrain altogether, beyond both. It is a terrain which our contemporary theorists of discourse have yet to occupy.

FOOTNOTES

1. G. Pechey, 'Formalism and Marxism', *The Oxford Literary Review* 4:2 (1980). This article was written in the summer of 1979.

2. V.N. Voloshinov, *Marxism and the Philosophy of Language* (New York and London, 1973); see especially Part I.

3. See E. Benveniste, 'The Levels of Linguistic Analysis' in *Problems in General Linguistics* (Miami, 1971), pp. 101-112; and J. Mukařovský, *On Poetic Lnaguage* (Lisse, 1976), pp. 50-59. Benveniste proposes the two 'universes' of 'language' and 'discourse'; Mukařovský speaks in similar vein of the 'spheres' of 'semantic statics' and 'semantic dynamics'.

4. The case of Bakhtinism might cause Perry Anderson to modify his claim that a 'constant concourse with contemporary thought-systems outside historical materialism' is 'a specific and defining novelty of Western Marxism as such'. See his *Considerations on Western Marxism* (London, 1976), pp. 56-58.

5. By 'poetry in the narrow sense' Bakhtin means the discourse of the 'straightforward' canonical genres (epic, lyric, tragedy). There is no correlation here with the 'verse' genres as opposed to 'prose' in the purely technical-compositional distinction: *Don Juan* and *Eugene Onegin* are instances of novelistic discourse on Bakhtin's terms. The phrase is used throughout 'Discourse in the Novel' and elsewhere in *The Dialogic Imagination* (Austin and London, 1981).

6. B. Eikhenbaum, 'The Theory of the Formal Method' in L. Matejka and K. Pomorska (eds), *Readings in Russian Poetics* (Cambridge, Mass., 1971), p. 12.

7. V. Shklovsky, 'Art as Technique' in L.T. Lemon and M.J. Reis (eds), *Russian Formalist Criticism* (Nebraska, 1965), p. 6.

8. *Ibid*, p. 21. Lemon and Reis use the phrase 'unique semantic modification'. 'Semantic shift' is used in the translation quoted by D.W. Fokkema in 'Continuity and Change in Russian Formalism, Czech Structuralism, and Soviet Semiotics', *PTL* 1 (1976), p. 159.

9. The Tynyanov text I draw on here is his 'On Literary Evolution' of 1927. Translations may be found in Matejka and Pomorska, *op cit*, pp. 66-78 and E. and T. Burns (eds), *Sociology of Literature and Drama* (Harmondsworth, 1973), pp. 179-190.

10. J. Frow, 'System and History: A Critique of Russian Formalism', *The Oxford Literary Review* 4:2 (1980), p. 62.

11. Tynyanov historicizes the concept of 'motivation' in the text of 1927, citing as an example 'nature descriptions in old novels': whereas we might read such descriptions as mere motivation for 'transitions or retardation' (a characteristically Shklovskian move), 'in a different literary system' they might be the 'dominant element' with the 'story' providing the motivation for **them**. It is worth noting that Tynyanov continues to use the concept of the 'device' in another text of 1927. See 'The Fundamentals of Cinema' in R. Taylor (ed), *The Poetics of Cinema* (Oxford, 1982), where the devices of film are held to enjoy an independence of 'naturalistic "motivation in general"'. Evidently Tynyanov saw no danger in using the concept in a synchronic account of contemporary cultural production.

12. J. Tynyanov, 'The Literary Fact'; quoted in L.M. O'Toole and A. Shukman (eds), *Formalist Theory* (Oxford, 1977), p. 38.

13. R. Jakobson and J. Tynyanov, 'Problems of Research in Literature and Language', O'Toole and Shukman, *op cit*, pp. 49-51. This is the only full English translation available. Translations of eight of the nine theses may be found in Matejka and Pomorska, *op cit*, pp. 79-81 and *New Left Review* 37 (1966), pp. 58-61. There is no translation of the (anonymous) introduction with which it was accompanied on first publication in *Novyi Lef* and in which the Formalist project is praised for its rigorous scientificity. See J. Garson, 'Literary History: Russian Formalist Views 1916-1928', *Journal of the History of Ideas* 31:3 (1970).

14. Benveniste, *op cit*, p. 83.

15. See Voloshinov, *op cit*, pp. 45-63. There is a clear parallel here with Derrida's critique of the competing explanatory schemes of structuralism and phenomenology: see the useful summary in C. Norris, *Deconstruction: Theory and Practice* (London and New York, 1982), pp. 50-55. The early Bakhtin appears to have been an adherent of the *idealistische Neuphilologie* of the second (Vosslerite) tendency and to have broken with it between 1924 and 1926. My source here is 'The Roots of Russian Semiotics of Art' by L. Matejka in R.W. Bailey *et al* (eds), *The Sign: Semiotics around the World* (Ann Arbor, 1978), pp. 146-172. Parts of the early paper cited by Matejka were (oddly) published for the first time in Moscow 50 years later under the title 'Towards the Aesthetics of the Word': see the translation in *Dispositio* 4:11-12 (1979).

16. This passage appeared first in *Rozanov* (1921) and then again in *Theory of Prose* (1925). The translation used here is from a longer passage quoted in Matejka and Pomorska, *op cit*, p. 32.

17. Nobody seems to have noticed that Shklovsky's famous thesis of the 'legacy' in literary history passing 'not from father to son but from 'uncle to nephew' (enunciated in the same text) reproduces another motif from the *Eighteenth Brumaire*.

18. Matejka and Pomorska, *op cit*, p. 34. Bakhtin notes this statement with approval in a footnote to the 'Discourse in the Novel': see Bakhtin, *op cit*, p. 267.

19. V.N. Voloshinov, 'Discourse in Life and Discourse in Art', published as an Appendix to his *Freudianism: A Marxist Critique* (New York, 1976), p. 98.

20. *Ibid*, p. 97.

21. *Ibid*, p. 97.

22. *Ibid*, pp. 109 and 107.

23. There is no translation of the 1929 version of Bakhtin's monograph on Dostoevsky; my statement is made on the basis of a reading of the revised and expanded edition of 1963.

24. The first and best-known of Eikhenbaum's articles on *skaz* is of course 'How Gogol's "Overcoat" is made' in R.A. Maguire (ed), *Gogol from the Twentieth Century* (Princeton, 1974), pp. 267-291. The positions of this article are assumed in what follows, even though it is not directly quoted.

25. See V. Vinogradov, 'The Problem of *skaz* in Stylistics', *Russian Literature Tri-Quarterly* 12 (1975), pp. 237-250. This text dates from 1926. Bakhtin seldom lets go by an opportunity of praising the 'brilliance' of Vinogradov's work on the stylistics of prose.

26. B. Eikhenbaum, 'Leskov and Contemporary Prose', *Russian Literature Trip-Quarterly* 11 (1975), p. 214.

27. *Ibid*, p. 223.

28. Vinogradov, *op cit*, p. 242.

29. *Ibid*, p. 240.

30. *Ibid*, p. 244.

31. *Ibid*, p. 248.

32. See the extract from the Dostoevsky book reproduced as 'Discourse Typology in Prose' in Matejka and Pomorska, *op cit*, pp. 176-196. In this study of discourse types Bakhtin explicitly contests Eikhenbaum's definition of *skaz* proper: *skaz* is characterized in the first place by an 'orientation towards another speech-act'; its 'oral' character is adventitious, a mere consequence of this primary orientation. 'Orientation towards oral speech' - Eikhenbaum's conception - is adequate only in the case of the (single-voiced) phenomenon of a narrative discourse delegated to a 'literary' narrator whose speech is 'enlivened' by 'oral intonations'. This is nothing more than compositional convenience and has nothing to do with the special productivity of *skaz*; it is a disguise covering an authorial identity rather than a guise constructing one; not an interorientation of two signifiers but a signifier portending a signified. Bakhtin cites Turgenev as an example.

33. Vinogradov, *op cit*, pp. 248-249.

34. J. Kristeva, *Desire in Language* (London, 1980), p. 74.

35. Bakhtin, *op cit*, p. 273. Bakhtin goes on to speak of *skaz*, stylization, and parody as 'various forms of verbal masquerade': see p. 275.

36. *Ibid*, p. 261.

37. I have in mind Leavis's notion of the novel as 'dramatic poem'.

CAPITALISING HISTORY:

NOTES ON *THE POLITICAL UNCONSCIOUS*

Samuel Weber

In a book first published in 1955, *The Liberal Tradition in America*, Louis Hartz advanced a thesis which, if it has been largely bypassed by intellectual historians today, (1) could nonetheless be of considerable interest to English-speaking literary critics seeking to understand the situation of their discipline. Hartz argued that American liberalism, which he considered as the dominant paradigm of political thought, and action, in the United States, could best be understood in terms of the European history from which, at a certain point, it detached itself. As a result of thus being separated from the conflictual dynamics of European history, American liberalism, Hartz affirmed, lost the sense of its own historical and social relativity and came to hypostasise itself as an absolute, a tendency that was reinforced both by the universalist and naturalist character of liberalist categories and values (which Hartz identified with the thought of Locke), and by the real absence of a strong, prebourgeois ('feudal') social tradition in the New World. Thus, the Lockean axiom of the natural liberty of individuals, 'born free', which in its European context was endowed with a very non-natural, polemical-strategical significance as an ideological attack upon feudal values, appeared, in the new, American setting, to be rather a statement of universal fact. To use the familiar terms of contemporary speech-act theory, the Lockean paradigm thus lost its performative connotations when it emigrated to America, where it imposed its authority all the more effectively by presenting itself as an essentially constative act. For Hartz, the result was a national history and culture blinded from its birth, as it were, to its own conditions of possibility and dominated by a liberalism that was as absolute and autocratic as its European model had been critical and dynamic.

The process of separation, which Hartz later designated as one of 'fragmentation', (2) thus entailed two, correlative, but not unambiguous gestures. The first was that of <u>universalisation</u>. It was not that the Lockean tenet of naturally free individuals claimed universal validity, for that was true of the European paradigm no less than the American. Rather, the implicit but decisive context in which those claims operated was transformed drastically due to the absence of the historical antagonists against which Lockean thought developed its articulations. In short, without Robert Filmer, as the spokesman for a feudally-oriented, aristocratic society, the status of Locke's thought was altered: it became <u>static</u> precisely for want of the other. Instead of advancing its claims to universal validity within a social and political sphere that was anything but homogeneous, it could present them as being coextensive with that sphere itself (which, in a certain sense, they were, since the emigration American colonials did not reinstate the force of the European feudal past, but only that of its burgeoning bourgeois present). The Lockean paradigm thus was able to institutionalise itself as what Hartz calls an 'absolutist' or 'compulsive' liberalism that dominated - and still dominates - the American intellectual tradition.

The second gesture implied in this process, a correlative of the first, entails the status of conflict, ethically, epistemologically, politically. By thus universalising itself, American liberalism no longer accepted the necessity of historical and social conflict as had been the case, inevitably, for its European version. As Hartz puts it, it lost 'that sense of relativity, that spark of philosophy, which European liberalism acquired through an internal experience of social diversity and social conflict.' (3) This does not, of course, mean that American liberalism denied conflict entirely - which would have been a rather remarkable feat - but rather, that it redefined the place and the nature of conflict, precisely by placing it within a 'natural' context, which, qua natural, could not itself be considered as subject to conflict or to (legitimate) controversy. Thus, the most aggressive competition among private individuals and groups could be encouraged, whereas any challenge to the 'natural' hierarchy subordinating public to private was not. Conflict was accepted only as a technical instrument in order to achieve ends which were held to be above (legitimate) conflict.

Whatever the merits of Hartz's arguments as an explanation of American political culture - and my feeling is that they deserve more serious discussion than they have received - they undoubtedly cast considerable light on the more recent transformation undergone by certain French thinkers as they have been imported into the United States (and, perhaps more generally, into the English-language universe of discourse (4)). If authors such as Derrida, Foucault and, to a lesser extent, Lacan, have been granted admission into the American Academy, the price they have had to pay has generally entailed the universalisation and individualisation of their work, which has thereby been purged of its conflictual and strategic elements and presented instead as a self-standing methodology.

Such a transformation is both ironic and revealing. It is ironic, because one of the most powerful impulses in the development of what in the English-speaking world has become known as 'structuralism' and, more recently, 'post-structuralism', was precisely the profound suspicion of -isms, beginning with Lévi-Strauss' critique of the concept of 'totemism', in which he saw the symptomatic effort of Eurocentric anthropology to project its own values and categories, in order to reduce and to appropriate alien, non-Western cultural phenomena. Such a suspicion of universal values did, it is true, coexist for a while with the aspiration of establishing a new system of science with a claim to universal validity, but such aspirations were rather rapidly abandoned. Thus, while the term 'structuralism' is, of course, not a translator's invention, that of 'post-structuralism', it seems, is, and in any case serves to obscure the antisystematic impulse at work in the thought of the writers thus designated. Indeed, labels such as 'deconstruction' and 'discourse analysis' serve to arrest the movement of the texts to which they refer by implying that behind those writings there is a stable and static core that can be accepted or rejected as such.

What is revealing about this process of universalisation is the institutional context in which it takes place. For the universalisation of 'post-structuralist' thinkers conforms to the intellectual ethos of the institution that monopolises almost entirely their American importation: the University. The University universalises, individualises, and in the process excludes conflict as far as possible. Or rather, it delegitimises conflict, in the name of pluralism. Pluralism allows for a multiplicity of coexisting, even competing interpretations, opinions or approaches; what it does not allow is for the space in which these interpretations are held to take place to be itself considered conflictual. Its borders are given, and its structure, bipolar. Interpretations are right or wrong, better or worse, strong or weak, true or false, but the

category of opposition, used to prescribe such alternatives, is itself
held to be beyond dispute, and indeed is used to define conflict. The
latter, in short, is held to be one theme among others, rather than an
aspect of the process of thematisation (or objectification) itself.
'Scholarship' and 'research' may investigate conflict, but they do not -
or must not - as such partake of it. The function of 'pluralism' is precisely to deny the necessity of conflict, in the name of peacefully
coexisting diversity.

It may seem dubious to assert that the American university is actively
engaged in the maintenance and reproduction of this 'universalist' ethos,
when it is more or less common knowledge that the temper of Anglo-
American thought, as opposed to that of the European continent, has been
resolutely 'nominalist' for many centuries. But, just as Hartz's use of
Locke suggests, nominalism does not exclude universalism, although it certainly endows it with a different form from that determined by a more
'realist' philosophy. As a recent example, I shall cite Stanley Fish's
book, *Is There a Text in this Class?* At first glance, the position articulated there would seem to be resolutely anti-universalist. Since texts
have no intrinsic meaning, but instead are constructed ever-anew by whatever particular interpretive assumptions 'happen to be in force', (5) the
significance of texts can and does change all the time. There would seem
to be, then, little place for universally valid statements. But if this
holds for interpretive statements, it would seem not to be the case for
the meta-critical assertions that constitute Fish's own critical position.
In a manner that is curiously reminiscent of Sartre, Fish reiterates that
text and reader are <u>always in a situation,</u> <u>always engaged in</u> an institutionally determined <u>activity,</u> etc. The theory thus implied by the
'always-in' assertions must claim universal validity.

Fish's theory of institutional authority thus displays many of the
same general tendencies Hartz discerns at work in American Liberalism
(although Fish himself might well demur at such a classification), namely:
universalisation, individualisation and the containment (or delegitimation)
of conflict. This will doubtless seem a curious assertion to make concerning a critic who has obviously enjoyed and exploited the polemical
aspects of the profession more than most, and moreover, one whose entire
emphasis is placed upon the non-individual, communal or communitarian
aspects of the interpretive process. But the paradox is dissipated when
one realises that the concept of the collective, or the community of
interpreters invoked by Fish is ultimately nothing but a generalised,
indeed a universalised form of the individualist monad: autonomous, self-
contained and internally unified, not merely despite but because of the
diversity it contains. And if there can be no doubt that Fish's own, often
highly polemical practice points up the importance of conflict, of the
agonistic aspect of interpretation, his <u>theory</u> of the authority of interpretive communities functions not to explain such conflict, but to explain
it away. And it explains it away simply by asserting that it is <u>contained</u>
by - i.e. <u>within</u> - whatever monad (set of assumptions, interpretive institution, etc.) the critic is said to be situated. If conflict is a part of
interpretation, and the latter is always situated <u>within</u> an institution,
then institutions themselves cannot be subject to the conflict it contains.
The institution thus emerges as the condition of possibility of controversy, and hence, as its arbiter, but not as an instance that is itself
constituted by and in response to such conflict.

Thus, if Fish criticises the extensive universalism of traditional
theorists, such as John Searle, the 'once and for all' of universally
valid rules, it is only to replace it with the no less universal, individualist temporality of 'one-at-a-time': <u>first</u> this one, <u>then</u> the next,
etc. This is why Fish cannot tolerate <u>ambiguity,</u> the coexistence of

diverging or incompatible elements at one and the same time, splitting the 'one-and-the-same' into conflictual disunion. For the temporal structure of 'one-and-the-same', the identity of the instant, is the building block with which Fish constructs his theory of a linear succession of discrete, self-contained moments, be it that of the reading-process or that of the relation of institutions to each other and to themselves.

If, then, the efficacy of critical judgements will depend upon whatever 'interpretive assumptions happen to be in force', Fish's entire theoretical effort is directed to making us forget that force does not just happen, that assumptions are never simply in force (as one is never simply in a single place), but rather that they must always be enforced, and that this, in turn, implies precisely that relation to, and resistance of, the other - that the individualistically conceived 'community', interpretive or otherwise, will not acknowledge. (5a) Which is also why, although Fish may have finally stopped 'worrying' about interpretation, the real causes of that worry still remain to be addressed. (6)

Those causes, as both Fish's book and the reception of French 'poststructuralism' indicate - albeit by default - entail precisely the question of conflict and of its status: as an epistemological category, as a factor in cultural activity, and more generally as a force in social and political processes. If the American liberal mind has defined itself by the ethical exclusion or rather, by the containment of conflict as an historical process, such liberalism is being increasingly challenged today, even while it reacts with ever-more transparent intensity, and often, intolerance. In short, the emigration of contemporary French theory to the United States (and to the English-speaking world, in general), far from merely reinforcing the liberal delegitimatisation of conflict, is also undermining it. And in so doing, this importation calls into question not merely the hitherto prevailing lines of demarcation, but also the manner in which those lines have traditionally been drawn. It is no accident that 'margins', 'borders', 'framing', 'exclusions' and Moebius-strips have come to designate, and to disrupt, the convenient opposition of 'inside-versus-outside', which, as Hartz's entire analysis implies, dominates the liberal containment of conflict. It is also significant to recall that for the most part those French thinkers whose work has been most influential, have themselves been situated on the margins of the French University System. For it has been the particular, although historically conditioned, genius of French society, deriving directly from its bourgeois revolutionary tradition, to have been able to reconcile institutionalisation and change by establishing a series of elite institutions, thus allowing intellectual labour to develop in a climate that is relatively free from what Bourdieu and Passeron have rightly described as the 'reproductive' constraints inherent in all educational systems. The Collège de France, Ecole Normale Supérieure, Ecole Pratique des Hautes Etudes, CNRS, Paris-VII - these are the organisms that have enabled what Hartz aptly calls 'philosophy' to survive in France. 'Philosophy', in his sense, designates not simply a 'discipline' but rather a mode of thought that remains imbued with 'that sense of relativity ... acquired through an internal experience of social diversity and social conflict.' (6a) I emphasise 'internal experience' because it is precisely this which the positive disciplines, at least insofar as they are subject to the traditional strategy of legitimation prevalent within the educational establishment, must exclude. They must exclude, or at least reduce the purport of their own inner disunity and internal conflictuality, and above all, of the inevitably conflictual process by which, through exclusion and subordination, disciplines define their borders and constitute their fields. And they must deny such exclusivity in the name of an ideal of knowledge, science and of truth that deems these to be intrinsically conflict-free, self-identical and hence, reproducible as such, and transmissible to students. Ultimately, such an ideal both reflects and supports the self-image of a society that imposes its authority precisely by denying the legitimacy of its structural conflicts, and hence, of its relation to alterity. For the admission of the constitutive importance of such relations would amount to a disavowal of the categories of universality, individualism and consensus that form the foundation of American Liberalism, and of the institutions that perpetuate it.

This, then, explains the challenge of the recent import of certain French thinkers into an American academic scene alternately fascinated, and frightened, by the possible consequences of this incursion. For the tendency most visible today goes in the direction of a relegitimisation of conflict within the ethics of intellectual activity, and this in turn cannot but affect, more or less profoundly, institutions that define such activity in terms such as 'scholarship' and 'research', words which already suggest the substantial self-identity of the 'objects' they presuppose. Instead of the serene, detached character of such 'scholarship', based in turn upon a conception of cognition as an essentially constative process - whether construed as 'discovery', 'experimentation' or as 'construction' - intellectual activity has come increasingly to define itself as a 'performative' language-game, although the notion of 'performance' has often been equated with 'productive', rather than understood as a form of play. Nevertheless, the notion of 'strategy' as it is applied to theoretical argumentation has begun to cease to be merely a synonym for 'instrumental', as it still is in the writings of John Searle, for instance, (8) and to recover its etymological connotation, with a reference to conflicting forces.

If the outcome, or even direction of these transformations are difficult to predict, it nevertheless seems highly probable that the re-evaluation of the necessity and the legitimacy of conflict that is currently under way will impose a renewed concern and confrontation with Marxism. For the latter is a theory not only of the necessity of conflict as an <u>object</u> of study, but also as the medium in which thought itself operates. To the extent, therefore, that the liberal paradigm of consensus and conciliation is increasingly challenged, Marxism is bound to emerge as one of the most significant alternative models. If the Hartzian analysis of the liberal image of historical development as a kind of entelechy - as the unfolding of possibilities already contained, as it were, in germ, in the individual (or collectively individual) subject - then it is clear that the Marxist version of Hegelian dialectics, with its emphasis upon struggle and conflict as the motor of all becoming, provides in one sense an extreme counter-image. And yet, as is usually the case with contraries, the Marxian model is often legitimised in terms of the same liberal categories it is attacking: the universality of cognition, of 'science', objective necessity, an individualist conception of subjectivity.

It is precisely this aspect of Marxism, in conjunction with the political and ideological position of the Communist Party in post-war France - with its claim to be the sole legitimate heir of the revolutionary tradition - that explains the critical, often hostile relations of most structuralist and 'post-structuralist' thinkers towards Marxism. What is not immediately evident to most Americans, having grown up with the Red Scare, MacCarthyism and a virulent tradition of anti-socialist and anti-communist persecution, is the extent to which Communism and Marxism could, within the capitalist society of post-war France, nevertheless have exercised an influence, especially upon the intelligentsia that would have let it appear increasingly more as a <u>part</u> of the social establishment rather than as a challenge to it. Yet, if Marxism was criticised by Lévi-Strauss, Foucault, and implicitly, at least, by Lacan and Derrida, it was not because - as did American liberalism - it insisted upon the inevitability and legitimacy of conflict, but rather because it claimed to resolve it, once and for all.

In the United States, by contrast, the nature in which Marxism has been systematically, and often hysterically, excluded from the pale of respectability, has allowed it to become identified with the process of exclusion itself, particularly inasmuch as the latter has generally been denied to have taken place at all. If Liberalism can be described as that form of exclusion which, wherever possible, denies its own exclusivity; which denies that exclusions are an inseparable concomitant of every possible inclusion; or which accepts exclusions only in order to exclude it (the traditional definition of individual freedom, limited only by that of other individuals) - then Marxism is the name of what Liberalism most seeks to exclude, the inevitability of exclusion itself. As a theory of class-conflict, Marxism does not ask whether, but rather which exclusions are necessary. To this, American Liberalism has traditionally responded: Marxism itself.

If this response has been uniquely effective, it is, Hartz argues, for the same reasons that Liberalism has been able to install itself as a static and total world-view: the absence of a feudal past. Without Filmer to define and to demarcate the polemical thrust of Locke, the message of Marx lost its meaning. (9) The liberal notion of the natural liberty of the individual, 'born free', expands to cover the entire horizon, leaving little room for socialist (collective) alternatives.

It is in this traditionally small space, but with a momentum drawn in large part from the 'post-structuralist' incursion into the liberal enclosure, that Fredric Jamesons's *The Political Unconscious* seeks to drive a wedge. It is a powerful, almost heroic attempt alternately to entice and to intimidate, to cajole and to browbeat its readers, presumably most or all members in good standing of the English-speaking 'interpretive community', whose principal home-base is doubtless American university departments of literature. And the way in which it goes about defining its task indicates that *The Political Unconscious* strives to appeal to the widest number of these colleagues in the broadest possible way: its goal is 'to restructure the problematics of ideology, of the unconscious and of desire, of representation, of history, and of cultural production'.(10) Nothing less, it seems, is required if 'the traditional dialectical code' of Marxism is to be adequately 'defended' in the particular arena where Marxist criticism must operate, that of 'the intellectual marketplace today'. [*10*] Marxism may want to replace commodity-relations, but in the meanwhile it must know how to sell itself on the market it hopes, some day, to abolish. Nor is this marketplace to be conceived of too simplistically, as constituting merely the external context of Marxist criticism. 'Interpretation,' Jameson declares, 'is not an isolated act, but takes place within a Homeric battlefield, on which a host of intepretive options are either openly or implicitly in conflict.' [*13*, my italics]. However, this acknowledgement of interpretation as an activity that is not merely collective, but also agonistic, remains itself 'an isolated act' within *The Political Unconscious*, and the grounds for this are already foreshadowed by the word I have placed in italics: 'within'. Jameson's use of the word here is all the more striking, since one would normally have expected the word 'on', battles being usually fought on, rather than within, battlefields. But this shift responds to an imperative that dominates the theoretical arguments developed by *The Political Unconscious*, one which strangely recalls the position of Fish. Briefly stated, what the two books have in common, despite their obvious differences, is the priority they assign, axiomatically as it were, to the 'in'. For Jameson no less than for Fish, the interpretive process and everything it entails, takes place within a space that is already delimited, and which therefore allows us, in principle, to comprehend the events that it is held to contain.

To be sure, the consequences that the two critics draw from this common conception are different. For Fish, the fact that the interpreter is always in a 'situation' points to the role of the institution, of the interpretive community as the ultimate and decisive authority, that defines the situation one is always in. The questions that this conclusion leaves unanswered are obvious enough. Above all, as Jameson's statement, and Fish's practice suggest, there is the question of conflictual, agonistic interpretations and their adjudication or evaluation: do such conflicts indicate conflicting 'institutions' (or 'sets of interpretive assumptions'), i.e. a certain exteriority, or do they occur 'within' an essentially unified institution? Can the alternative even be posed without recognising that the relation between interpretation and institution cannot be the one-way street that Fish's affirmations tend to imply: you interpret as you do because you are already in an institution, already indebted to a set (i.e. single, unified) of assumptions, etc. In short, a theory of interpretive conflict is required, and precisely this, Fish's 'principled account of change' [367] does not, and probably - given its own axiomatics, its parti pris for the Inside and for the Insiders - cannot offer.

If Fish, then, seeks to avoid the problems of historical and social conflict by reducing them to a discrete succession of self-contained, monadic moments (first this, then that, etc.), Jameson's strategy is to try to sell Marxism as the most powerful Insider of them all (albeit one that has been largely ignored and neglected until now):

> The priority of a Marxian interpretive framework ... is here conceived as that 'untranscendable horizon' that subsumes such apparently antagonistic or incommensurable critical operations, assigning them an undoubted sectoral validity within itself, and thus at once canceling and preserving them. [10, my italics]

Again, the pitch here recalls Fish's peroration at the end of *Is There a Text in this Class?* - 'We have everything that we always had - texts, standards, norms, criteria of judgment, critical histories, and so on ... it is just that we do all those things within a set of institutional assumptions that can themselves become objects of dispute.' [367] The last phrase, of course, points to the essential problem that Fish's position denies, rather than addresses. And it is this problem that Jameson seeks to resolve, in a sense by presenting 'Marxism' as the operator that both reverses the question of Fish's title, and also transforms it, substituting for its question-mark, a resounding exclamation-point: 'There Is a Class in this Text!' Jameson assures us, and 'Marxism' alone can tell us what it is, since only Marxism contains it. We will still have everything we have always had, everything that we have been taught and that we teach others, everything that gives us our daily bread and our (dwindling) privileges; for everything is 'at once cancelled and preserved', 'apparently antagonistic or incommensurable critical operations' are put in their proper places; that is, we are put in our proper places, places that are 'assigned' to us as our property in exchange - for there is always a price, to be sure - for our accepting the authority of Marxism.

The deal is tempting, no doubt. And all the more so, since it is cushioned in a most attractive, self-critical, gift-wrapping:

> The ideological critique [of Marxism] does not depend on some dogmatic or 'positive' conception of [itself] as a system.

Rather, it is simply the place of an imperative to totalise, an imperative, Jameson adds, that can also be directed at Marxism itself, in its various forms, in order to reveal 'their own local ideological limits or strategies of containment' [53]. As ideological criticism, then, Marxism is 'simply' the place of the imperative to totalise, nothing more, nothing less. But is that place so simple to find, especially if its name can often be distorted or disguised by forms of Marxism which themselves must be subjected to 'the imperative to totalise'? If Marxism can transcend such deficiencies, if it can be criticised in its own name, it is only because its own 'place' is coextensive with another space which bears another name, that of History. Writ large. And it is with this gesture, capitalising History, that Jameson takes up the challenge of 'post-structuralist' thought which, as is clear throughout *The Political Unconscious*, is both the most immediate adversary and the (more or less) silent partner.

The 'post-structuralist' challenge to History, as I have already suggested, entails its persistent suspicion of the teleological perspective of totalisation in which historical 'development' has traditionally been conceived. This suspicion goes back at least to Nietzsche who, in *The Genealogy of Morals* for instance, argued that the 'assigning' of 'purposes' as the 'meaning' of a phenomenon is nothing but a mode of interpretation that seeks to impose itself by masking its particular, partisan character in the guise of the thing itself. A process which is not merely 'performative', but agonistically and violently so, dislodging the previously dominant interpretive scheme in order to take its place. Such a process can present itself as the mere 'constatation' of a teleological, or entelechical movement of its object, of which it is the simple porte-parole. History, then, whether as ethnocentrism (Lévi-Strauss), phallogocentrism (Derrida), the genetic/developmental stages of object-development (Lacan), or as a strategy of power operating by the exclusion of discontinuity (Foucault), has been subjected to a reexamination that has tended both to question the qualities of self-identity, universality and objective necessity hitherto attributed to it, and to redefine that attribution itself as part of a strategy that seeks to impose itself precisely by denying its own strategic, partisan character.

It is evident that such a move bears certain resemblances to the conception of thought as ideology developed by Marxism. The difference, of course, is that whereas Marxism retains the oppositions of 'science' and 'ideology', of true and false consciousness, as well as the notion of historical objectivity as their indispensable and constitutive dividing-line, most of the thinkers mentioned either explicitly or implicitly include all of these categories in the agonistic process itself.

Jameson's response to this challenge is to perform precisely the gesture that he seeks to exclude, by attributing it to 'ideology': that of attempting to 'contain' the adversary. This 'strategy of containment' - which the ideology-critique of Marxism, Jameson asserts, seeks to expose through its 'imperative to totalize' (but is not such an imperative itself already the mirror-image of what it seeks to contain?) - consists of two gestures: acknowledgement and incorporation.

Acknowledgement:

The Political Unconscious accordingly turns on the dynamics of the act of interpretation and presupposes, as its organizational fiction, that we never really confront a text immediately, in all its freshness as a thing-in-itself. Rather, texts come before us as the always-already-read; we apprehend them through sedimented layers of previous interpretations, or - if the text is brand-new - through the sedimented reading habits and categories developed by those inherited interpretive traditions [...

Hence,] our object of study is less the text itself than the
interpretations through which we attempt to confront and to
appropriate it. [*9-10*, my italics]

After this, one might have expected a study of the procedures, mechanisms
and approaches of interpretation in terms of their strategic, agonistic
operation on 'the academic marketplace'. But such a discussion, presumably, would not simply 'cancel and preserve' all competing critical positions, it would not simply assign them their proper place - it would displace them in a space that could no longer be safely contained by the 'discipline' of literary studies, as we know it today. The analysis of the
literary text, not as a self-identical object, but as an element in a
highly conflictual, ambivalent power-struggle, would have consequences for
the organisation and practice of the discipline of literary studies, as it
is institutionally established, of which not the least disruptive would be
the redefinition of its 'borders', its relation to other disciplines and
above all, to other modes of thought, whether these have been disciplined
already or not. What would ultimately be raised is the issue of the
existing definition and delimitation of knowledge, as well as the conditions of its practice: in short, the discipline and the university.

But the acknowledgement of the dependency of texts upon their interpretation remains just that: an isolated act without any further consequences. (10a) Perhaps this is because the informing intention is not to
disrupt 'the academic marketplace today', but rather to stake out the
claims of Marxism 'within' it. In any case, the terms in which the relation of texts to interpretation, and hence, to the 'Homeric battlefield'
within which the latter is said to take place, already announces what is
to come: if texts are only given to us 'through' sedimented layers of previous interpretations, 'through' sedimented reading habits, then they still
remain what they are, in and of themselves, even after passing through
those layers of sedimentation. The text may be mediated by its interpretations, but its meaning is not structurally constituted by these readings;
rather, it is contained in the text, just as the text itself is contained
within the space of History.

Here, then, is the meaning of History for *The Political Unconscious*:
it is the name of that space which contains and comprehends everything else,
including, first and foremost, the 'text'. Hence, Jameson's insistence on
the fact that History and text are inseparable, but also non-identical:

> History is not a text, not a narrative, master or otherwise,
> but ... an absent cause [which] is inaccessible to us except
> in textual form ... Our approach to it and to the Real
> necessarily passes through its prior textualization, its
> narrativization in the political unconscious. [*35*, author's
> italics]

The text, then, is something that we - necessarily - must pass through, on
our way somewhere else, to something as 'prior' to the text as the latter
is prior to our 'approach to it': History, as 'absent cause'.

Viewed from a formal perspective - which is not necessarily the same
as a formalist one - Jameson's defence of Marxism is caught in a double
bind: it criticises its competitors as being ideological in the sense of
practising 'strategies of containment', that is, of drawing lines and
practising exclusions that ultimately reflect the particularities - the
partiality and partisanship - of special interests seeking to present themselves as the whole. But at the same time its own claim to offer an alternative to such ideological containment is itself based on a strategy of
containment, only upon one which seeks to identify itself with a whole
more comprehensively than that of its rivals.

If there is a difference, then, between 'Marxism' and 'ideology', it cannot be determined purely at the level of form, since both seek to contain and to comprehend their competitors in the name of a certain objectivity. The difference, rather, must reside in the kind of objectivity appealed to. Which is why, towards the end of the long, introductory theoretical chapter, Jameson finally, after telling us what History is not - a text, a narrative - attempts to tell us what it is:

> History is therefore the experience of Necessity, and it is this alone which can forestall its thematization or reification as a mere object of representation or as one master code among many others. Necessity is not in that sense a type of content, but rather the inexorable form of events; it is therefore a narrative category ... a retextualization of History ... [*102*, author's emphasis]

If the Marxist comprehension of History is distinct from ideological strategies of containment, it is not, strangely enough, because of the contents of that History, but because of its form. Marxism, it turns out, is form after all, or rather, a certain kind of form. Not that of narrative as such, but that of a particular type of narrative, that which tells us 'why what happened ... had to happen the way it did' [*101*]. Necessity, then, he experience of which defines History, is that form of narrative which is ultimately, and in principle, self-identical; the story it tells, could not be told otherwise, could not be changed, altered or modified, without being falsified and losing its necessity. If History is thus the 'absent cause', Necessity is the equally 'absent story', the Idea (in the Kantian sense) of a Story, of a Text, of a Narration that could not be told otherwise than it is - and hence, which 'is' not, which is absent, functioning only as a kind of regulative idea. But this idea is no mere fiction since through its putative absence it can be invoked to produce or to justify very real effects and practices: for instance, the legitimacy of judging actual, mundane narratives in terms of a text that is identical-to-itself, but whose identity is never immediately present-as-such. As an 'absent cause', such identity - whether it is called 'History', 'Literature', 'Work', 'Author' or whatever - always requires an intermediary, a critical spokesman in order to be heard. It cannot speak for itself, but must be spoken for. And yet, it must also provide the basis for distinguishing between true and false spokesmen, for is this not the essence, and justification, of the critical project and its practices?

And yet, if this is so, then the most dramatic of Jameson's attempts to provide a positive definition of History - 'History is what hurts ... what refuses desire and sets inexorable limits to individual as well as collective praxis' [*102*] - raises the question: hurts whom? The readers of *The Political Unconscious*? Its author? The brokers in the academic marketplace? Its customers? But what if all of these were searching precisely for some instance that might set 'inexorable limits' to their 'praxis', which, for want of authorised limits, was in the process of losing its sense of self-legitimacy? What, in short, if critics desired to be 'hurt' in this way, as a lesser evil, rather than to court the risks of being left beside themselves, 'beside the point', by desires they no longer controlled? Would 'History', Jameson's History, still simply 'hurt', or simply 'refuse desire'? The desire, for instance, to capitalise (on) History?

It seems likely, on the contrary, that a good many of those whose existence is tied to the academic marketplace would be neither hurt nor frustrated by a History which can be described as follows:

> This is indeed the ultimate sense in which History as ground and untranscendable horizon needs no particular theoretical

justification: we may be sure that its alienating necessities
will not forget us, however much we might prefer to ignore
them. [*102*]

Not to be forgotten, even by 'alienating necessities', may yet be preferable to the current uncertainties traversing the profession in regard to its social status and its institutional future. To hear that 'History as ground and untranscendable horizon needs no particular theoretical justification' is doubtless music to the ears of many scholars and critics for whom recent theoretical discussion has rendered the ground upon which the discipline has been based less than solid, and its horizons anything but clear or 'untranscendable'.

Like Fish's 'institution' or 'interpretive community', then, Jameson's History recommends itself as the best means of Saving the Text (and those who live by it):

> It is in detecting the traces of that uninterrupted narrative,
> in restoring to the surface of the text the repressed and buried
> reality of this fundamental history, that the doctrine of a
> political unconscious finds its function and its necessity. [*20*]

And, we might add, it is here that it also 'finds' much of its appeal; like Fish, Jameson could assure his readers (if he so chose), that the Marxism of *The Political Unconscious* will not be an engine of expropriation, but of appropriation: that it will help them in their efforts to appropriate the text, to enrich themselves by enriching the texts, that we will 'have everything that we always had', only more, better and safer than before. It is no accident that Jameson recommends Marxism in terms of its superior 'semantic richness', which in turn is directly related to its conception of History. The methodology outlined in *The Political Unconscious* capitalises directly upon this notion of History:

> Such semantic enrichment and enlargement of the inert givens
> and materials of a particular text must take place within
> three concentric frameworks, which mark a widening out of the sense
> of the social ground of a text ... [*75*]

These three 'frameworks' - the 'symbolic' or 'political' (in the narrower sense of events); the 'social', and the 'historical' - can be described as 'concentric' only because their centre is identified with the 'inert givens and materials of a particular text' - a text, in short, whose particularity coincides with its inertia, the fact that it is, once and for all, in its proper place within History, that is within a story waiting to be told, once and for all, in the one and only way. Like the movement of Capital itself, this story is never finished, but its end is always in sight. It is, Jameson suggests, a 'single, great collective story' with 'a single, fundamental theme ... the collective struggle to wrest a realm of Freedom from a realm of Necessity.' This great struggle produces 'vital episodes in a single, vast unfinished plot.' [*19-20*]. It is this plot, then, that *The Political Unconscious* suggests it is the critic's business to discover. It is a plot that promises to keep critics in business indefinitely - on the condition that its unity, singularity and self-identity are not themselves seen as an effect of interpretation, of narration, of 'textualization', but rather as their centre and frame, their ground and horizon.

But this plot, with its lure of limitless enrichment, contrasts strangely with the story it tells, and *The Political Unconscious* constantly returns to it like a criminal to the scene of the crime. The reader is thus led to reflect upon the tension that pervades *The Political Unconscious*, between the 'struggle' that is said to constitute the ultimate subject-matter of texts and of their interpretations, on the one hand,

and on the other, an essentially 'constative' or 'contemplative' conception of the process of interpretation itself. For notwithstanding the early remark about its agonistic, conflictual character, interpretation is described as a more or less faithfull reconstruction, reproduction or resuscitation of the 'buried reality' - or treasures - of the text. Conflict is thus confined to the thematic element of literature, leaving its hermeneutical discovery to pursue its mission of 'semantic enrichment' without any of the trials and tribulations associated with primitive accumulation as described by Marx.

The reason for this, of course, is that the problems faced by *The Political Unconscious* are determined not by the needs of primitive accumulation, but by the crisis of over-accumulation. Translated into the particular area of literary criticism, this is manifest in the fact that the problems of the discipline arise not from a scarcity of interpretive productivity, but from its excess. The problem is not so much how to interpret, but how to valorise interpretation, at a time when it is in danger of asphixiation from its uncontrolled proliferation.
And it is here, in its response to this problem, that *The Political Unconscious* is most revealing, of its own strategies and of the 'battlefield' within which they are designed to operate.

What is at stake, is the relation between individual and collective. For 'individualism' is one of the book's most explicit targets. 'One of the most urgent tasks for Marxist theory today,' remarks Jameson, towards the end of the book, 'is [to construct] a whole new logic of collective dynamics, with categories that escape the taint of some mere application of terms drawn from individual experience.' [*294*]. It is from this standpoint that Jameson interprets the structuralist and post-structuralist critique of subjectivity; however, he does not seem to realise that the rapprochement could work the other way as well: that the problem of 'individualism' might well be reinterpreted in terms of the aporias of constitutive subjectivity, a move that has been attempted by Derrida, Lacan, Foucault, but also, before them (albeit in a more Hegelian vein), by Adorno and Horkheimer. In this perspective, what could be more individualist than the notion of History as a 'single, vast unfinished plot' ready to appropriate everything - all otherness - as a part of itself? What could be more individualist than the notion of Historical Necessity as a story that cannot be told otherwise (and yet which, necessarily, always is)?

What Hartz describes as the compulsive, absolutist and profoundly illiberal core of American Liberalism, with its pretension to be the Whole, finds its exemplary manifestation in *The Political Unconscious* when Jameson describes the fissure of unity implied by the Marxian conception of History, and by the collective self-fulfilment which defines it teleologically:

> The unity of the body must once again prefigure the renewed organic identity of associative or collective life. ... Only the community, indeed, can dramatize that self-sufficient intelligible unity [or 'structure'] of which the individual body, like the individual 'subject', is a decentered 'effect', and to which the individual organism, caught in the ceaseless chain of the generations and the species, cannot ... lay claim. [*74*]

Despite the massive explicit emphasis on History, time, struggle and narration, there can never be any question but that the synchronic perspective has the first, and last, word. To determine History as totalisation, as a single, self-same narrative, as a process of unification and of integration - ultimately, in short, as a movement of identity and of presentation - is to assume a point of view from which the whole can be comprehended, a position, therefore, that must be essentially detached from and outside of what it seeks to contemplate. And such a position, in turn, is only conceivable if that which it identifies is already, intrinsically and spontaneously, self-identical: that is, if its defining limits are held to be the product of that which they contain, a product of the interior they protect but do not constitute (for otherwise, the process of delimitation itself would intrude and disrupt every possible determination of an object, thus excluding any possibility of a position being simply exterior to that which it posits ...).

It is here, then, that the category - although not necessarily the object - of individuality becomes a strategic necessity. To construe the collective or community in terms of a 'self-sufficient, intelligible unity' is merely to universalise the individual, held to be the source and the goal of its being. Every such gesture rewrites the Declaration of Independence, as the independence of the self from the other, of identity from alterity, of sameness from difference. And the ambivalence inherent in all such hypostases of individualism becomes particularly evident and illuminating when Jameson takes us to the place in Marx's writings where this notion of a utopian, collective unity is foreshadowed. It is in the figure of the Oriental despot, described by Marx in the *Grundrisse* as the incarnation of a social unity that totally subordinated the differences of its constitutive members. It is here, Jameson asserts, that 'the problem of the symbolic enactment of collective unity' is inscribed in the Marxian corpus, 'by Marx himself' [296]. What is of interest here, is not merely the fact that the model of collective unity seems situated at such a distance from the liberal individualism that dominates our political and social thinking, but rather, that despite this apparent distance - or perhaps because of it - it seems so close to us.

But just what is it that 'Marx himself' writes? Given Jameson's notion of Necessity as the Story of What Could Not Have Happened Otherwise, the response is particularly remarkable. For textually, there are <u>at least three</u> different versions in play here. First, there is the text of Marx 'himself', who, in German, remarks that the '*Gesamteinheit*' - the collective unity - 'is realized in the [Oriental] despot as the Father of many communities' ('... *der Gesamteinheit - die im Despoten realisiert ist als dem Vater der vielen Gemeinwesen*'). (11) Then, second, there is the English translation used by Jameson, in which the term 'despot' is rendered as '<u>the form</u> of the despot' ('... a unity realized in the form of the despot'). And finally, there is a third version, that which occurs in Jameson's commentary, placed in quotation marks although it does not correspond exactly to either of the other two texts. For Jameson <u>alters</u> the other versions once again, this time to read: 'the "body" of the despot' [295].

Where, now one is tempted to ask, is the 'absent cause' that can justify these alterations, and establish their 'necessity'? Where, except in a powerful <u>desire</u> to see History and Necessity as the <u>body</u> of the father, the body, that is, of a patriarch who is father of all but son of no one, and hence whose body, unlike that of 'the individual organism', is precisely <u>not</u> 'caught in the ceaseless chain of the generations and the species' [74], but is the Immortal Body of the Father.

Is it not this desire, to escape that 'ceaseless chain', which determines at once the rejection of a certain *enchainement* characteristic of the 'metonymic' impulse of 'post-structuralism', and the effort to replace it by a body which would be single, sane and whole?

Needless to say, this is not - despite the connotations of the book's title - the body that psychoanalysis teaches us to expect, unless we identify psychoanalysis with the ego-psychology of the autonomous subject so dear to American liberal culture. If Freud insists that the ego is

emphatically 'a bodily ego', (12) this body has little to do with the
patriarchal body of the Oriental Despot. The latter only becomes meaningful, for Freud, in the perspective of the parricide of *Totem and Taboo*,
as the unattainable and ambivalent fantasy that only ceases to be destructive, precisely, by becoming part of a symbolic chain. In this symbolisation the body is that which it has always been, 'a place from which
both external and internal perceptions may spring. It is <u>seen</u> like any
other object, but to the <u>touch</u> it yields two kinds of sensations, one of
which may be equivalent to an internal perception.' (13) If the body,
in *The Political Unconscious*, but not only there, to be sure, is thus
introduced as a <u>prefiguration</u> of communal identity and unity, it is to
help us forget that the body we <u>feel</u>, and <u>touch</u> - as distinct from that
which we <u>see</u>, expose or present - is neither whole nor unified, but a surface or <u>limit</u> in which external and internal perceptions are confounded
and never entirely differentiated. The body is thus, as undifferentiated
surface, the <u>matrix</u> of an ego whose perceptual-projective identity never
fully escapes its ambivalent origins, but rather develops in function of
them.

The notion of such a 'body-ego', although first articulated by someone working in the sphere of what is commonly known as 'individual psychology', is, therefore, considerably less 'individualistic' in its
categories than are the 'Durkheimian or Lukácscean vocabulary of collective consciousness' to which Jameson resorts, in the putative absence of
that non-individualist, 'whole new logic of collective dynamics' he anticipates and demands. But quite apart from the fact that such a 'logic' is
unlikely ever to arrive if we content ourselves with simply waiting for
it, while continuing to use terms derived from the very individualism we
hope, one day, to supplant - the very notion that such a mode of thought
would be 'wholly new' belongs to the same individualist thinking that
construes sameness and otherness in terms of simple, and mutually exclusive, opposition (albeit 'dialectical').

Rather than waiting for the New, we would probably do better to re-
examine the Old, under the suspicion that this theory - if we can ever
conceive of its possibility - is probably at work already, not as such or
full-born, but in bits and pieces. To recognise it, however, we may well
have to adopt a perspective quite different from that expressed by *The
Political Unconscious* - mindful, of course, of the fact that different is
not the same as unrelated. Indeed, the following formulation of Jameson's
perspective indicates precisely how such a differential relation, of New
to Old, may be conceived:

> This perspective may be reformulated in terms of the tradi-
> tional dialectical code as the study of *Darstellung*: that
> untranslatable designation in which the current problems of
> representation productively intersect with the quite dif-
> ferent ones of presentation, or of the essentially narrative
> and rhetorical movement of language and writing through time. [*13*]

Indeed, the dialectical notion of *Darstellung*, combining both the movement of representation, and that of presentation, adequately names the
hermeneutical perspective of *The Political Unconscious*, for which time is
in fact a medium 'through' which language 'moves', and which construes
the act of interpretation as an act of reconstruction, or rather, resuscitation:

> Only Marxism can give us an adequate account of the essential
> <u>mystery</u> of the cultural past, which, like Tiresias drinking
> the blood, is momentarily returned to life and warmth and
> allowed once more to speak, and to deliver its long-forgotten
> message in surroundings entirely alien to it. [*19*]

But if the interpreter here, in the light of Marxism, recovers some of the sacral power of the priestly function out of which interpretation originally developed, this is also entirely compatible with a more serene, more bureaucratic and technocratic depiction of the interpretive activity, for instance, as it is said to characterise that third and widest of Jameson's three concentric frameworks of interpretation, the Historical:

> Within this final horizon the individual text or cultural artifact ... is here restructured as a field of force in which the dynamics of sign systems of several distinct modes of production can be registered and apprehended. [*98*]

The interpreter here 'restructures' with the aim of registering and apprehending words whose connotations can hardly be overheard. The purpose of such restructuring is precisely to render the force-fields, the struggle and conflicts of History, appropriable by a contemplative, detached spectator, the traditional subject of scientific observation. History is thus to be made safe for cognition. Conflict is objectified, but the process of objectification itself is held to be outside the melee.

How different the picture of interpretation that emerges in *The Interpretation of Dreams* where, it is true, the 'dialectical code' in which the notion of *Darstellung* is at home, is replaced by something more difficult to name, if not with the word used by Freud himself: *Entstellung*, displacement, disfiguration, dislocation. The interpretive process that it determines, however, provides a striking contrast to the academic serenity described in *The Political Unconscious*. 'It should not be forgotten,' Freud writes,

> that the work of interpretation must struggle against the very psychic forces to which we owe the distortion of the dream [*welche die Entstellung des Traumes verschulden*]. It thus becomes a question of the relation of forces whether one's intellectual interest, capacity to overcome one's self, [*Selbstüberwindung*], psychological knowledge and skill in dream-interpretation enable one to master internal resistances. (14)

Interpretation, for Freud, does not reconstruct and resuscitate so that we may register and apprehend - it partakes of, and in, a process of conflict that no totalisation can ever comprehend. Which is why its effect is not simply the primitive or teleological accumulation of wealth, not the 'semantic enrichment' of the phenomena it interprets, but their impoverishment as well. Or rather, a transformation in which enrichment and impoverishment become very difficult, perhaps impossible, to distinguish. This is why, when Freud chooses a word to articulate the relation of *Entstellung* to 'the forces' from which it proceeds, it is derived from 'debt', *Schuld* (*verschulden*). The hermeneutics of *Entstellung* thus inscribe themselves in a tradition which can be retraced to *The Genealogy of Morals*, in which both history and interpretation are conceived as forms of a debt that is impossible to repay. By contrast, Freud - here and elsewhere - adds the implication that the debt in question cannot be construed as a static and stable obligation, but rather as an ambivalent and unresolvable tension. If the psychic conflict that structures the subject of desire precludes any enduring resolution, any kind of totalisation, the process of interpretation cannot simply renounce such aspirations either. For every interpretation must necessarily seek to arrest and to dominate the conflictual process of symbolisation it seeks to comprehend. In the text just cited, the ambivalence can on the one hand be retraced to the exigency of *Selbstüberwindung* - a term which means practically the opposite of its translation in the Standard Edition, which reads: 'self-discipline', since what is both required, and stated, is the overcoming-of-self, i.e. of the ego - and on the other, to the fact that such 'overcoming', the 'mastering of internal resistances', still inevitably entails mastery, control, discipline, and hence, as such, appeals to the very ego that it seeks to 'overcome'.

It is only in the recognition of such ambivalence, and in the articulation of its social and institutional consequences, that the notion of 'history' - but also that of 'text' - may be brought into play, in a game whose rules are neither those of the 'academic marketplace today', nor of the Liberal Tradition in America. For, as opposed to that tradition, to its compulsion to universalise, to individualise, and to delegitimise conflict, the players of this game will not have to ignore the fact that the rules themselves are at stake. And perhaps, that, for once, will allow us to care about something else than just winning.

FOOTNOTES

1. For reasons clearly foreseen by Hartz himself, and which liken the position of his work to that of Freud, whom he obviously knew well, although referring seldom to him. Concerning the reception of his theories, Hartz predicted that 'the liberal society [= Hartzian] analyst is destined in two ways to be a less pleasing scholar than the Progressive: he finds national weaknesses and he can offer no absolute assurance on the basis of the past that they will be remedied. He tends to criticize and then shrug his shoulders, which is no way to become popular, especially in an age like our own.' Louis Hartz, *The Liberal Tradition in America*, New York, 1955, p.32. For a latter-day confirmation of Hartz's prediction, see: Dorothy Ross, 'The Liberal Tradition Revisited and the Republican Tradition Addressed', in: John Higham and Paul J. Conklin, eds., *New Directions in American Intellectual History*, Baltimore and London, 1979, pp.116-130. Ross, who seeks to demonstrate the superiority of Pocock's vision of American history, in which 'the central issue' is 'the survival of the virtuous republic', over that of Hartz, whose arguments she simplifies to the point of caricature, arrives at the end of her article at a 'paradox' that precisely the work of Hartz could do much to explain: 'The real paradox of Progressive thought is that historicism, with its desire to secure values within history, ended in an ahistorical social science that had adopted the objective voice and strove to be value-free.' (p.128). The reading of Jameson in this article may, in this light, be considered as a Hartzian attempt to explain such a 'real paradox of Progressive thought'.

This is perhaps as good a place as any to express my gratitude to Neil Hertz, for calling the work of Hartz to my attention. Needless to say, but say it I shall, he deserves none of the blame for the use to which his hint has been put. From Hertz to Hartz ...

2. This term was introduced in a second book, *The Founding of New Societies* (New York, 1964), which Hartz published together with a number of collaborators, and in which he undertook to generalise, by the comparative study of a number of emigrant societies (the United States, Latin America, South Africa, Canada and Australia), the process of fragmentation.

3. *The Liberal Tradition* ..., p.14.

4. It would be tempting to try to explain the differences in the reception of current French theory in the different English-speaking countries precisely by referring to the comparative analyses developed in *The Founding of New Societies*.

5. Stanley Fish, *Is There a Text in this Class?*, Cambridge and London, 1980, p.vii. I shall discuss this book elsewhere in greater detail.

6. When Fish, at the conclusion of his book, claims that he has provided 'a principled account of change' (p.367) he states, by antiphrasis, the problem. For his theory of institutional determination is just as unable to account for change as the theories of the autonomy of literature it sets out to criticise, but whose basic category - that of monadic (individualist) self-identity - Fish preserves, displacing it simply from the 'work' to the 'institution'. From the perspective of the insider, change is never entirely explicable (which does not imply that the outsider is any better off).

6a. *The Liberal Tradition* ..., p.14 (my italics).

7. It is interesting to note that in those areas of intellectual activity where social power is directly determined by the production of knowledge, the understanding of the latter is far less 'constative' and far more 'performative', even ludic and agonistic; in the Humanities and Social Sciences, by contrast, where the pressures of social justification cannot be answered by direct reference to economic and technological power that results from research (and that determines it as well), a constative notion of 'truth' and associated ethical 'values' plays a far more conspicuous rôle.

8. See Samuel Weber, 'It', *Glyph* 4, Baltimore, 1978, 9 ff.

9. 'Socialism is largely an ideological phenomenon, arising out of the principles of class and the revolutionary liberal revolt against them which the old European order inspired. It is not accidental that America which has uniquely lacked a feudal tradition has uniquely lacked also a socialist tradition. The hidden origin of socialist thought everywhere in the West is to be found in the feudal ethos. The *ancien régime* inspires Rousseau; both inspire Marx.' *The Liberal Tradition* ..., p.6.

10. Fredric Jameson, *The Political Unconscious*, Ithaca, 1980, p.13. Further references to this book are given in square parentheses, in italics, in the body of the text.

10a. In *Inhibition, Symptom and Anxiety*, Freud describes 'isolating' as one of the 'techniques' that the ego can substitute for repression, to attain similar results. Instead of the objectionable idea being simply excluded from consciousness, 'its associative connections are suppressed or interrupted.' Freud emphasises that such a tendency is to be found in normal thought as well, where 'concentration provides a pretext' - or an occasion - 'to keep away not only what is irrelevant or unimportant, but, above all, what is unsuitable because it is contradictory.' Contradiction, here, excludes dialectical synthesis. (S. Freud, *Inhibition, Symptom and Anxiety*, Norton Library Edition, New York, 1959, pp.46-47). I have discussed the more general implications of 'isolating' in my *Legend of Freud*, University of Minnesota Press, Minneapolis, 1982, Part I.

11. Karl Marx, *Grundrisse*, Berlin, 1953, p.377.

12. Sigmund Freud, *The Ego and the Id*, The Norton Library, New York, 1980, p.16.

13. *Ibid.*, p.15.

14. Sigmund Freud, *The Interpretation of Dreams*, Avon Books, New York, 1965, p.563.